THE FATHERS
OF THE CHURCH

A NEW TRANSLATION

VOLUME 10

THE FATHERS OF THE CHURCH

A NEW TRANSLATION

Founded by
LUDWIG SCHOPP

EDITORIAL BOARD

Roy Joseph Deferrari
The Catholic University of America
Editorial Director

Rudolph Arbesmann, O.S.A.
Fordham University

Bernard M. Peebles
The Catholic University of America

Stephan Kuttner
The Catholic University of America

Robert P. Russell, O.S.A.
Villanova College

Martin R. P. McGuire
The Catholic University of America

Anselm Strittmatter, O.S.B.
St. Anselm's Priory

Wilfrid Parsons, S.J.
Georgetown University

James Edward Tobin
Queens College

Gerald G. Walsh, S.J.
Fordham University

TERTULLIAN

APOLOGETICAL WORKS
AND
MINUCIUS FELIX
OCTAVIUS

Translated by
RUDOLPH ARBESMANN, O.S.A.
SISTER EMILY JOSEPH DALY, C.S.J.
EDWIN A. QUAIN, S.J.

The Catholic University of America Press
Washington, D. C.

NIHIL OBSTAT:

JOHN M. A. FEARNS, S.T.D.
Censor Librorum

IMPRIMATUR:

✠ FRANCIS CARDINAL SPELLMAN
Archbishop of New York

September 25, 1950

The Nihil obstat and Imprimatur are official declarations that a book or pamphlet is free of doctrinal or moral error. No inplication is contained therein that those who have granted the Nihil obstat and Imprimatur agree with the contents, opinions or statements expressed.

ISBN-13: 978-0-8132-1555-6 (pbk)

Copyright 1950, by
THE CATHOLIC UNIVERSITY OF AMERICA, INC.
All rights reserved

Second Printing 1962
Reprinted 1985
First paperback reprint 2008

CONTENTS

GENERAL INTRODUCTION vii

TERTULLIAN

APOLOGY
Introduction 3
Text 7

THE TESTIMONY OF THE SOUL
Introduction 129
Text 131

TO SCAPULA
Introduction 147
Text 151

ON THE SOUL
Introduction 165
Text 179

MINUCIUS FELIX

OCTAVIUS
Introduction 313
Text 321

INDEX 403

INTRODUCTION

TERTULLIAN, or Quintus Septimius Florens Tertullianus, to give him his full name, was born about the middle of the second century at Carthage, where his father was a centurion of the proconsular cohort. Carthage, after her restoration by Julius Caesar, had not only recovered her former position as a center of commerce but had also become a seat of learning. Thus, Tertullian's father was in a position to provide his son with an excellent education in rhetoric, literature, and law. Tertullian's education, however, was not limited to these fields. His works furnish ample proof that he possessed a good knowledge of history, archaeology, medicine, and the greater part of the important systems of Graeco-Roman philosophy. He also wrote with equal facility in Latin and Greek. After having finished his studies, he must have spent some time at Rome. In one of his works,[1] he expressly mentions a personal experience he had in the Roman capital. Moreover, according to Eusebius of Caesarea, the fourth-century Church historian,[2] Tertullian distinguished himself at Rome by his outstanding qualities as a jurist. It is even possible that he wrote some books in the field of jurisprudence. In the Digests, a collection of extracts from the opinions of earlier jurists compiled by order of the Emperor Justinian, there appear some quotations from the writings of a jurist Tertullian (the titles are: *Quaestionum libri VIII; De castrensi peculio liber singularis*). The question of whether this otherwise unknown jurist is identical with the ecclesiastical writer of the same name has given rise to scholarly controversies. However this may be, Tertullian's

---
[1] *On the Dress of Women* 1.7.
[2] *Ecclesiastical History* 2.2.4.

writings which have come down to us leave no doubt that he had a solid juridical training.

His family was pagan and he himself confesses that he followed pagan customs and drank deep of the cup of worldly pleasures until, as a mature man, he became a Christian at Rome. In his writings he does not give a clear explanation of the reasons for his conversion. It seems, however, that he was moved to embrace the Christian faith by observing the perseverance of the Christians in the persecutions and the heroic courage of the martyrs. No early Christian writer has so emphasized the fact that the Church owed her triumph to sufferings: 'Crucify, torture, condemn, grind us to dust . . . whenever we are mowed down by you, our number increases; the blood of Christians is the seed.'[3]

After his return to Africa he soon began to play an important part in the Carthaginian Church, using his pen in defense of the faith which he had embraced. According to St. Jerome,[4] he also became a priest. A born fighter, Tértullian always had his eye upon an opponent whom he was eager to conquer: the pagan religion, the pagan governors, the Gnostics, and, finally, the Christian Church itself. His harsh and intolerant character, which kept him in a state of nervous irritation, led him, about A.D. 205 to the Montanists, a sect characterized by its emphasis on spontaneous ecstatic enthusiasm, eccentric asceticism, and various millenarian beliefs. So outstanding was his position in the African branch of this sect that its adherents were called Tertullianists. He lived in Carthage until death put an end to his stormy career some time after A. D. 220.

As a writer, Tertullian surpasses in originality all Latin Christians before St. Augustine. His works exhibit a profound knowledge of the past and its literature, and a great familiarity

---

[3] *Apology* 50.12f.
[4] *De viris illustribus* 53.

with the problems of his day. St. Jerome, unquestionably a critic above suspicion, exclaims in one of his letters:[5] 'Can anyone be more learned, more acute of mind than Tertullian? His *Apology* and his books *Against the Gentiles* contain all the wisdom of the world.' Vincent of Lerin[6] states that Tertullian was to the Latins what Origen was to the Greeks and goes so far in his praise as to say: 'Who was more learned that this man? Who more competent in things divine and human? With his amazing mental capacity he embraced the entire range of philosophy, all the different philosophical schools, their founders, followers, and systems as well as history and science under their multiple forms.' As to his personality, his qualities are not all praiseworthy. He is an aggressive, disputatious, headstrong, and uncompromising individual who is inclined to push his principles to the extreme, letting his logic run into paradox or driving home his points with remorseless wit and sarcasm. Moderation and appreciation of the opponent's point of view were alien to his fiery nature and irascible character.

That Tertullian possessed a speculative gift cannot be questioned, but his rhetorical and dialectical talents were far greater; this may explain the lack of systematic composition in his work. His attitude toward philosophy cannot be reduced to a formula since it is antithetical. Harsh and intolerant refusal alternates with appreciation. Both can be understood if we take into consideration that it was always from different aspects that he gave his opinion on this subject. According to him, the philosophers had gone astray in the knowledge of God and in matters concerning man's moral life; to him Christianity meant the whole truth, far surpassing any school of

---
5 *Epistulae* 70.5.
6 *Commonitorium* 18 [24] (ed. G. Rauschen, Florilegium Patristicum 5.42).

philosophy. As a result, he vehemently fought all doctrines at variance with the Christian faith, especially since he considered philosophy the mother of the Gnostic heresy. He contrasts the philosopher with the Christian, 'the disciple of Hellas' with 'the disciple of Heaven,' calling the former 'the friend,' the latter 'the foe of error.'[7] To him the philosophers are the 'patriarchs of the heretics,'[8] and philosophy is the work of demons.[9] On the other hand, Tertullian was much too highly educated a man not to see the usefulness of many philosophical doctrines. His own opinion concerning the natural reason in man, as a result of which even the pagan philosophers were able to recognize the truth to a certain degree, must have led him to have at least some regard for philosophy which he had rejected for polemical purposes. As a matter of fact, in his *The Testimony of the Soul,* Tertullian recognizes the elements of truth contained in philosophy, and their importance for giving support to the Christian truth.

Tertullian's language and style are a true expression of his passionate soul. Like Tacitus, he is supreme in the mastery of the Latin language. He is brief and concise. His sentences are terse; there is not a superfluous word, and yet each word is full of meaning, contains a world of thought and opens a boundless horizon to the imagination of the thinking reader. Often a whole series of thoughts is left out and suggested only by a particle. Because of this pregnancy of expression, Eusebius of Caesarea did not find it easy to translate passages from Tertullian's work into Greek. Tertullian must have been a difficult author for his own contemporaries, even more difficult than Tacitus for the Roman readers of his time. Because

---

7 *Apology* 46.18.
8 *On the Soul* 3.1.
9 *Prescription against Heretics* 7.

of his liking for the unusual, his boldness of expression, and his fondness for epigrammatic brevity which often leads him into obscurity, he is the most difficult among the Latin writers of Christian antiquity. He is also the most individual among them, despising all tradition. Owing to the fact that he had to express new and Christian ideas in an old and pagan idiom, he was compelled to coin a great number of new words, or radically to change the meaning of old ones. His innovations strongly influenced posterity; he became 'the real creator of the Latin of the Church.'[10]

In the East, Tertullian was read scarcely at all; only Eusebius quotes him. Even in the West he seems to have soon fallen into oblivion, probably because of his difficult and obscure style and his apostasy to Montanism.[11] As a result the text tradition is poor; a number of his works were lost entirely; the manuscripts of others perished after they had been used for the earliest printed editions; still others are preserved in a single ninth-century manuscript of the Biblio-

---

10 A. Harnack, *Geschichte der altchristlichen Literatur* I (Leipzig 1893) 667; cf. E. Norden, *Die antike Kunstprosa* (4th repr., Leipzig-Berlin 1923) 606ff.; P. de Labriolle, *History and Literature of Christianity from Tertullian to Boethius*, tr. by H. Wilson (New York 1925) 100ff.
11 At first sight it may seem strange that Tertullian, a man of rare intelligence, fell into the snares set by the wild speculations of Montanism. However, he had long lived in a state of mind which may be described as Montanist. He felt himself attracted by the great moral austerity of the Montanists and their view on ecstatic prophecy, which insisted on the necessity of progressive revelation. The 'new prophecy' as the Montanists themselves termed their movement, attempted not only to reinstate prophecy in the prominent place it had held in the life of the the early Christian communities, but also to surpass the two previous stages of divine revelation: the first stage, or 'infancy,' being represented by the Law and the Prophets; the second, or 'youth,' by the Gospel. In Montanus, the founder of the sect, and his associates, Prisca (or Priscilla) and Maximilla, the Montanists contended, revelation had reached the stage of full maturity, the Paraclete manifesting Himself to the world. The Montanist (or Tertullianist) group at Carthage was never very numerous; St. Augustine led the last adherents of the sect back to the Church.

thèque Nationale of Paris (*Cod. Paris.* 1622; also called *Codex Agobardinus* after Agobardus, a bishop of Lyons in the first half of the ninth century); only in the case of the *Apologeticum* is the situation better. It was the Humanists who raised Tertullian again to that honorable position he enjoyed in the days of St. Cyprian who, when he said to his servant, 'Give me my master,' meant Tertullian from whose writings he read daily.[12]

The works of Tertullian are usually classified as apologetical, dogmatico-polemical, and moral or disciplinary writings. It is as an Apologist that Tertullian appears in the works translated in this volume. A concise characterization of the work and achievements of the Christian Apologists seems, therefore, to be in order.

Among the rapidly increasing number of Christian converts of the second and third centuries, there were many highly cultured men. Some of them became the first Christian publicists who used the apparatus of contemporary learning to defend the Christians against the charges brought against them and to demonstrate that Christianity was the only true religion. These writers are called Apologists (from the Greek word *apologίa,* the defense), since their main purpose was the scientific vindication of the Christian religion. Although their writings had little or no effect on the official attitude of the Roman state of their period, they nevertheless deeply influenced historical development. Theirs was the first attempt at creating a Christian philosophy of life and they were fighters for man's highest earthly good: freedom of conscience upon which no state authority could infringe.[13]

There were plenty of motives urging literary efforts on be-

---
12 St. Jerome, *De vir. ill.* 53.
13 Cf., for instance Tertullian, *To Scapula* 2: 'It is the law of mankind and the natural right of each individual to worship what he thinks proper.'

half of the new religion. Jewish rabbis, pagan priests, wandering Cynic philosophers fought Christianity. Pagan rhetoric and philosophy made scientific attacks, striving to destroy Christianity by arguments addressed to the intellect. The rhetor Fronto of Cirta,[14] the witty but superficial Lucian of Samosata, the Platonist Celsus, the Neo-Platonists Porphyry and Julian the Apostate are only the most important names in a long list of pagan polemical writers. The emperors lent their ears to the numerous accusations and ordered the new religion suppressed. The contrast between the Christian and the traditional Roman attitude toward religion made it necessary to vindicate the Christian point of view.

Among the peoples of antiquity, religion was not a purely private concern but largely a matter of state, and the Roman state was especially wedded to the established religion. Every phase of social and national life was deeply rooted in polytheism, with the government demanding reverence for the national gods. This attitude made toleration of monotheistic religions almost impossible.

The Jews belonged to this class, but the Roman government generally showed itself tolerant toward them because their religion was based upon an ancient national tradition which the Romans respected. They were, therefore, excused from participation in pagan ceremonies, and it was for this reason that Tertullian called Judaism an 'authorized religion.'[15]

Conditions were entirely different, however, where the Christians were concerned. Their religion was neither ancient nor national; further, it aimed at universal expansion, its adherents admittedly striving to displace all other religions. Considering the close and seemingly indissoluble union which

---

14 Cf. Minucius Felix, *Octavius* Ch. 9, n. 7.
15 *Apology* 21.1.

had always existed between religion and the state in Roman public life, the authorities began to see in all this a threat to the very existence of the state itself. There seemed good reason for such fears when the Christians, though justly from their point of view, refused to offer divine worship to the Emperor.[16] Moreover, the Christians refused to participate in the loose revelries of their pagan fellow citizens, and did not illuminate their houses or decorate them with wreaths while public festivities were going on. Several rigorous Christian writers, such as Tertullian and Origen, even objected to military service. True, in all other things the Christians approved of the state as an institution and they meticulously fulfilled their civic duties as Christ and the Apostles had taught them to do. They even prayed for the Emperor and the Empire in their 'divine' services. However, their attitude toward paganism was enough to bring them under suspicion of being 'public enemies' or 'enemies of the Roman Emperor.'

Serious as this situation was, it became worse because of the wild and harmful notions which began to be circulated concerning them. Traces of these notions can be found as early as the beginning of the second century in the works of such Roman authors as Tacitus and Suetonius. It seemed to the Romans a form of atheism and the sum total of all wickedness that the Christians should hold themselves aloof from the pagan ceremonies and devote themselves exclusively to their pure belief in one God, without idols. Their ceremonies in celebrating the Holy Eucharist were distorted by gruesome rumors, as though they were akin to cannibalism. The *agápe*, a Christian community meal, was slanderously interpreted as an occasion for Oedipean intercourse. Another story had it that the pagan gods were angry at the Christians and for that

---

16 Cf. Tertullian, *To Scapula* Ch. 2, n. 2.

reason the latter were held responsible for all such public disasters as pestilence, floods, famine, invasions by the barbarians, and the like. This last accusation was especially dangerous because it came to be widely circulated and survived longer than any of the others—actually into the fifth century.

Because of these slanders, popular fury showed itself in a number of bloody outbreaks against the Christians, especially during the second century. Now and then it happened that the governor of a province took action against them, because of some private denunciation, or the urging of the mob, or simply on his own initiative. Later, from the middle of the third century, persecutions were ordered by the emperors themselves in general edicts. It was during this later period that the decisive contest between the Roman state and the Christian Church was fought out.

By defending the Christians from the accusations mentioned above and by demonstrating that the Christian religion was the only true one, the Apologists sought to obtain for Christianity tolerance under the civil laws. We should not be surprised that, at first, their writings show relatively little of positive Christian doctrine. They were content simply to present the fundamental notions of Monotheism, Divine Providence, Reward and Punishment after death, and Resurrection, without going into the Sacred Mysteries. They did not wish to discourage the prospective convert with a theological treatise, but were anxious to obtain a hearing for their faith and, therefore, just traced a brief sketch of it in broad outline. In the course of time, however, more and more space was given to a positive exposition of the Christian faith.

Greek philosophy was not accepted unqualifiedly by the Christian Apologists. Some of them openly and bitterly rejected it while others showed reserve and practiced eclectic methods. All of them, Greek as well as Latin, were motivated by the same principle, namely, to turn away from Greek philosophy and turn toward Christianity. They reasoned that philosophy was based on human reflection and was full of errors, while Christianity was based on divine Revelation and contained the whole truth. From this they concluded that the new element which Christianity had added made it the only true and reliable philosophy. Thus the Apology became a description of Christianity, setting forth, in a method analogous to that of the Platonic Socrates, the elements of truth and the moral ideals contained in the Christian point of view, and demonstrating the pagan errors. However, in doing so, the Apologists had of necessity to make use of the intellectual tools which Greek philosophy had forged, and since they came as converts from the Gentile world, they brought with them inevitably their former modes of thinking. Indeed, men like St. Justin Martyr and Clement of Alexandria never considered the wisdom of ancient Greece an accursed thing, but believed that it contained a kind of illumination from the Divine Logos adored by Christians in Jesus Christ. As Clement put it: Philosophy 'was a schoolmaster to bring the Hellenic mind, as the law the Hebrews, to Christ.'[17]

The Christian Apologies, composed according to the rules of Greek rhetoric and showing all the earmarks of popular philosophy, took the form either of an oration or of a dialogue. Of course, apologetical orations had been delivered since the earliest days of Christianity. St. Paul's discourse on the Areopagus at Athens,[18] for instance, is unquestionably a vivid Apology of Christianity. In this discourse, St. Paul starts from the spiritualized concept of God in Greek philosophy,

---

17 *Stromata* 1.5.28.
18 Acts 17.22ff. presents only an excerpt of this important and comprehensive discourse.

and then develops the fundamental ideas of the Christian philosophy of life. However, unlike St. Paul's discourse, the Apologies, which now appeared in oration form, were never actually delivered to an audience. They were rather open letters addressed to the emperors or Roman magistrates. Tertullian's *Apology,* for instance, is addressed to the provincial governors in general, his *To Scapula* to an individual governor. We do not know, of course, whether or not these Apologies were really brought to the notice of the addressees. They certainly reached the public at whom they were principally aimed. Thus we also find Apologies addressed directly to the people. As examples we may mention the numerous *Discourses to the Greeks,* or Tertullian's *To the Pagans (Ad nationes).* Finally, though some Apologies of this literary type were addressed, at least primarily, to private individuals, for instance, the three books of Theophilus of Antioch to Autolycus and the *Epistle to Diognetus,* nevertheless, they were intended for a wider circulation. As to the literary form of the dialogue, the Christian Apologists accepted from the ancients this literary genre which lends itself so well to philosophical controversy and employed it for their own purposes. Thus it is to be expected that both the structure and style of the Christian apologetical dialogue are determined by the tradition of it predecessor. As examples we may mention St. Justin's *Dialogue with Trypho,* and the first of the Christian dialogues in Latin, Minucius Felix's *Octavius.*

A closing remark may serve to complete the picture. If we except such highly gifted men as Clement of Alexandria and Origen, the Greek Apologists up to about the middle of the third century can hardly be called above average. The situation is different with the Latin Apologists. Not that their training had been superior, but in their writings we find a power which is missing in their Greek counterparts. The

Greek Apologists were perhaps more learned. However, controversies involving man's entire philosophy of life are not decided by erudition alone. Endowed with an instinct for the practical side of life, the Romans knew better than the idealistic Greeks how such a fight should be conducted. The old martial spirit was still alive in those late Romans to whom this struggle was a matter of life and death. In comparing the Greek and Latin Apologists in regard to their attitude to the state, we find the statements of the Greeks somewhat more loyal. The tuba of the Romans sounds differently: they bluntly deny the Roman state's right to existence. To Minucius Felix all Roman history is a succession of crimes; Rome's greatness had been built on the ruins of the world; it is not the proverbial piety of the Romans which gave them their imperial sway, but their unscrupulous interference which unfortunately did not receive its just punishment. With what biting ridicule does the same author treat the national gods! The Romans then preferred offensive warfare to defensive measures; in their hands the Apology became a *Kampfliteratur,* an instrument with which they fought intellectual combats in the arena of literature.

There are five works of Tertullian which can be classified as apologetical writings. The reader will find in the present volume his *Apology (Apologeticum), The Testimony of the Soul (De testimonio animae),* and *To Scapula (Ad Scapulam).* The other two are *To the Pagans (Ad nationes),* an Apology addressed to the pagan people, in which he refutes the accusations against the Christians, and criticizes pagan morals and beliefs; and his *Against the Jews (Adversus Judaeos),* a demonstration of the truth of Christianity from the prophecies. The main topics of the first three treatises mentioned above are: Monotheism, the Christian idea of Creation, the moral superiority of the Christians as opposed to the immorality of the pagans, and the political and social behavior of the Christians. We have thought it opportune to offer still another treatise of Tertullian, his *On the Soul* (*De anima*), an attempt at a Christian psychology.

RUDOLPH ARBESMANN, O.S.A.

SELECT BIBLIOGRAPHY

A. d'Alès, *La Théologie de Tertullien* (Paris 1905).
O. Bardenhewer, *Geschichte der altkirchlichen Literatur* II (2nd ed. Freiburg i. B. 1914) 377-442.
G. Esser, *Die Seelenlehre Tertullians* (Paderborn 1893).
E. J. Goodspeed, *A History of Early Christian Literature* (Chicago 1942) 210-226.
Ch. Guignebert, *Tertullien. Etude sur ses sentiments à l'égard de l'empire et de la société civile* (Paris 1901).
P. Guilloux, 'L'Evolution religieuse de Tertullien,' *Revue d'histoire ecclésiastique* 19 (1923) 5-24; 141-156.
H. Hoppe, *Syntax und Stil des Tertullian* (Leipzig 1903); *Beiträge zur Sprache und Kritik Tertullians* (Lund 1932).
P. de Labriolle, *La Crise montaniste* (Paris 1913) 291-456.
———, *History and Literature of Christianity from Tertullian to Boethius*, tr. by H. Wilson (New York 1925) 50-105.
E. Löfstedt, *Zur Sprache Tertullians* (Lund 1920).
J. Lortz, *Tertullian als Apologet* (2 vols. Münster 1927-28).
H. Meyer, *Geschichte der abendländischen Weltanschauung* II (Würzburg 1947) 33f.
P. Monceaux, *Histoire littéraire de l'Afrique chrétienne* I (Paris 1901) 177-462.
E. Norden, *Die antike Kunstprosa* (4th repr., Leipzig-Berlin 1923) 606-615.
R. E. Roberts, *The Theology of Tertullian* (London 1924).
M. Schanz, C. Hosius, and G. Krüger, *Geschichte der römischen Literatur, Handbuch der Altertumswissenschaft* VIII 3 (3rd ed. Munich 1922) 272-333.
C. de L. Shortt, *The Influence of Philosophy on the Mind of Tertullian* (London 1933).

TERTULLIAN
APOLOGY

Translated
by
SISTER EMILY JOSEPH DALY, C.S.J., Ph.D.
College of Saint Rose
Albany, New York

INTRODUCTION

AMONG THE WRITINGS of Tertullian, the *Apology* holds a pre-eminent position both by reason of its brilliant rhetorical style and of the compelling force of its argument. The esteem in which this work was held in ancient times is evident from the fact that it was translated into Greek, an honor which fell to the lot of only few other writings of the first centuries of the Christian era.[1]

From internal evidence it can be determined that the *Apology* was written toward the close of A.D. 197.[2] Hence, its composition fell early in the period of Tertullian's conversion from heathenism, before his ideas became tainted with the heresy of Montanus.

Although modeled on the Greek Apologies, Tertullian's defense adopts a style and tone conditioned by the circumstances under which it was written. In an attempt to open eyes blinded by prejudice to the true situation regarding the Christians, Tertullian addresses an 'open letter' to the officials of the Roman Empire. An obscure incident mentioned in the opening sentence, which was typical of the injustice perpetrated by those presiding to administer justice, may have been the immediate spark which ignited the fuse of this fiery outburst. With the precision and irresistible logic of a shrewd lawyer, the eloquence and rhetorical skill of a highly educated Roman, and the passion, abandon, and intensity which were native to this African genius, Tertullian defended his fellow Christians, pointing out the moral integrity of their way of

---

1 Cf. P. de Labriolle, *History and Literature of Christianity from Tertullian to Boethius,* tr. by H. Wilson (New York 1925) 71.
2 Cf. O. Bardenhewer, *Geschichte der altkirchlichen Literatur* II (2nd ed., Freiburg i. B. 1914) 397.

life and hurling back at their accusers in vigorous, virulent language charges of the most heinous crimes.

The appearance of the *Apology* marked the beginning of a new and revitalized period of Latin literature. Tertullian introduces those unique features of style which are to characterize all his later works; as Norden says, he combines the majestic peace of Tacitus with the turbulent passion and the pamphlet-like tone of Juvenal, as well as with the affected obscurity of Persius.[3] The Roman officials, upon reading this impassioned challenge, may well have awakened to a realization that not all who clung with such exasperating perseverance to the Christian faith were to be sneered at as lowly illiterates.[4]

Not only in style, but also in content, the *Apology* foreshadowed Tertullian's subsequent writings. It contained in embryo the main ideas which were later to be developed at length in individual treatises. The denunciation of Roman amusements in the *De spectaculis,* the arguments for liberty of conscience in *Ad Scapulam,* the main thesis of *De testimonio animae,* the legal arguments whereby the ground is cut from under the feet of the heretical Scriptural commentators in the *De praescriptione haereticorum* — all are adumbrated in the *Apology.* The work is significant, too, as a commentary on manners and morals in the Roman society of the second century. As a plea for social justice, it has an appeal for all men of all times everywhere.

The present translation is based on the critical text of H. Hoppe, in the *Corpus Scriptorum Ecclesiasticorum Latinorum* 69 (Vienna 1939).

---

3 Cf. E. Norden, *Die antike Kunstprosa* (4th repr., Leipzig-Berlin 1923) 606.
4 Cf. Labriolle, *op. cit.* 69.

INTRODUCTION

AMONG THE WRITINGS of Tertullian, the *Apology* holds a pre-eminent position both by reason of its brilliant rhetorical style and of the compelling force of its argument. The esteem in which this work was held in ancient times is evident from the fact that it was translated into Greek, an honor which fell to the lot of only few other writings of the first centuries of the Christian era.[1]

From internal evidence it can be determined that the *Apology* was written toward the close of A.D. 197.[2] Hence, its composition fell early in the period of Tertullian's conversion from heathenism, before his ideas became tainted with the heresy of Montanus.

Although modeled on the Greek Apologies, Tertullian's defense adopts a style and tone conditioned by the circumstances under which it was written. In an attempt to open eyes blinded by prejudice to the true situation regarding the Christians, Tertullian addresses an 'open letter' to the officials of the Roman Empire. An obscure incident mentioned in the opening sentence, which was typical of the injustice perpetrated by those presiding to administer justice, may have been the immediate spark which ignited the fuse of this fiery outburst. With the precision and irresistible logic of a shrewd lawyer, the eloquence and rhetorical skill of a highly educated Roman, and the passion, abandon, and intensity which were native to this African genius, Tertullian defended his fellow Christians, pointing out the moral integrity of their way of

---

[1] Cf. P. de Labriolle, *History and Literature of Christianity from Tertullian to Boethius*, tr. by H. Wilson (New York 1925) 71.
[2] Cf. O. Bardenhewer, *Geschichte der altkirchlichen Literatur* II (2nd ed., Freiburg i. B. 1914) 397.

life and hurling back at their accusers in vigorous, virulent language charges of the most heinous crimes.

The appearance of the *Apology* marked the beginning of a new and revitalized period of Latin literature. Tertullian introduces those unique features of style which are to characterize all his later works; as Norden says, he combines the majestic peace of Tacitus with the turbulent passion and the pamphlet-like tone of Juvenal, as well as with the affected obscurity of Persius.[3] The Roman officials, upon reading this impassioned challenge, may well have awakened to a realization that not all who clung with such exasperating perseverance to the Christian faith were to be sneered at as lowly illiterates.[4]

Not only in style, but also in content, the *Apology* foreshadowed Tertullian's subsequent writings. It contained in embryo the main ideas which were later to be developed at length in individual treatises. The denunciation of Roman amusements in the *De spectaculis,* the arguments for liberty of conscience in *Ad Scapulam,* the main thesis of *De testimonio animae,* the legal arguments whereby the ground is cut from under the feet of the heretical Scriptural commentators in the *De praescriptione haereticorum* — all are adumbrated in the *Apology.* The work is significant, too, as a commentary on manners and morals in the Roman society of the second century. As a plea for social justice, it has an appeal for all men of all times everywhere.

The present translation is based on the critical text of H. Hoppe, in the *Corpus Scriptorum Ecclesiasticorum Latinorum* 69 (Vienna 1939).

---

3 Cf. E. Norden, *Die antike Kunstprosa* (4th repr., Leipzig-Berlin 1923) 606.
4 Cf. Labriolle, *op. cit.* 69.

INTRODUCTION

SELECT BIBLIOGRAPHY

Texts

 H. Hoppe, *Corpus Scriptorum Ecclesiasticorum Latinorum* 69 (Vienna 1939).
 J. Martin, *Quinti Septimii Florentis Tertulliani Apologeticum* (Florilegium Patristicum Fasc. 6 Bonn 1933).

Translations:

 T. Glover, *Tertullian: Apology* (Loeb Classical Library, New York 1931).
 K. A. H. Kellner and G. Esser, *Tertullians ausgewählte Schriften* II, Bibl. d. Kirchenväter 24 (Kempten and Munich 1915) 33ff.
 J. P. Waltzing, *Apologétique. Texte établi et traduit avec la collaboration de A. Severyns*, Paris 1929.

APOLOGY

Chapter 1

MAGISTRATES of the Roman Empire, seated as you are before the eyes of all, in almost the highest position in the state to pronounce judgment: if you are not allowed to conduct an open and public examination and inquiry as to what the real truth is with regard to the Christians; if, in this case alone your authority fears or blushes to conduct a public investigation with the diligence demanded by justice; if, in fine—as happened lately in the private courts[1]—hatred of this group[2] has been aroused to the extent that it actually blocks their defense, then let the truth reach your ears by the private and quiet avenue of literature.

(2) Truth makes no appeal on her own behalf, because she does not wonder at her present condition. She knows that she plays the role of an alien on earth, that among strangers she readily discovers enemies, but she has her origin, abode, hope, recompense, and honor in heaven. Meanwhile, there is one thing for which she strives: that she be not condemned without a hearing. (3) As for the laws, supreme in their own realm, what have they to lose if she be given a hearing? Or shall their power be glorified the more for *this,* that they condemn her without a hearing? But, if they condemn her without a hearing, they will incur the stigma of acting unjustly; in addition, they will deserve the suspicion of realizing to some extent their injustice, in that they refuse to hear a case

---
1 The incident to which he refers is obscure.
2 Christians.

on which they would be unable to pass adverse judgment once it was heard.

(4) This, then, is the first grievance we lodge against you, the injustice of the hatred you have for the name of Christian. The motive which appears to excuse this injustice is precisely that which both aggravates and convicts it; namely, ignorance. For, what is more unjust than that men should hate what they do not know, even though the matter itself deserves hatred? Only when one knows whether a thing deserves hatred does it deserve it. (5) But, when there is no knowledge of what is deserved, how is the justice of hatred defensible? Justice must be proved not by the fact of a thing's existence, but by knowledge of it. When men hate because they are in ignorance of the nature of the object of their hatred, what is to prevent that object from being such that they ought not to hate it? Thus we counterbalance each attitude by its opposite: men remain in ignorance as long as they hate, and they hate unjustly as long as they remain in ignorance.

(6) The proof of their ignorance, which condemns while it excuses their injustice, is this: In the case of all who formerly indulged in hatred [of Christianity] because of their ignorance of the nature of what they hated, their hatred comes to an end as soon as their ignorance ceases. From this group come the Christians, as a result, assuredly, of their personal experience. They begin now to hate what once they were and to profess what once they hated; and the Christians are really as numerous as you allege us to be. (7) Men cry that the city is filled with Christians; they are in the country, in the villages, on the islands; men and women, of every age, of every state and rank of life, are transferring to this group, and this they lament as if it were some personal injury.

In spite of this fact, men's minds are not directed to the consideration of some underlying good. (8) They cannot guess more accurately; they do not choose to investigate more closely. Here only does the curiosity of mankind lack its keenness. They delight in their ignorance, while others rejoice in their knowledge. How much more fault would Anacharsis[3] have found with those who, though lacking in insight, pass judgment on those who have it than he did in the case of those unskilled in music judging musicians! (9) They prefer to remain ignorant because they are already filled with hatred. Consequently, they form a preconceived idea with regard to that of which they are ignorant. Yet, if they knew it, they could not hate it; because, if no ground for their hatred be found, it would certainly be best to cease their unjust hatred. On the other hand, if it is justly deserved, then their hatred, far from losing anything, even by the authority of justice itself, actually gains more reason for its continuance.

(10) 'But,' says one, 'a thing is not considered good simply because it wins many converts: How great a number of men are given thorough training for evil! How many go astray into ways of perversity!' Who denies that? Yet, if a thing is really evil, not even those whom it attracts dare to defend it as good. All evil is drenched with fear or shame by nature. (11) For example, evil-doers are anxious to remain in hiding. They shun the light. They tremble when caught; they deny when accused. Even under torture they do not easily or always confess. When condemned beyond all hope, they lament. They tell of the attacks upon themselves of an evil spirit;[4] their moral weaknesses they impute to fate or to the stars. What they recognize as evil they do not want to acknowledge as their own. (12) In what respect is the Christian like this? No one of them is ashamed, no one has any regrets, except that he was

---
3 Cf. Plutarch, *Solon* 5; Diogenes Laertius (1.8.103).
4 Cf. Tertullian, *Ad nationes* 1.1, where *malae mentis* is generally interpreted as the evil spirit.

not a Christian earlier. If a charge is brought against him, he glories in it. If he is accused, he offers no defense. When questioned, he confesses of his own accord. For the word of condemnation he gives thanks.⁵ (13) What kind of evil is this that has none of the natural signs of evil—fear, shame, subterfuge, repentance, lament? What crime is this for which the accused rejoices, when the accusation is the object of his prayer and the condemnation his joy? *You* cannot call this madness, you who stand convicted of knowing nothing about it.

Chapter 2

(1) If, then, it is decided that we are the most wicked of men, why do you treat us so differently from those who are on a par with us, that is, from all other criminals? The same treatment ought to be meted out for the same crime. (2) When others are charged with the same crimes as we, they use their own lips and the hired eloquence of others to prove their innocence. There is full liberty given to answer the charge and to cross-question, since it is unlawful for men to be condemned without defense or without a hearing. (3) Christians alone are permitted to say nothing that would clear their name, vindicate the truth, and aid the judge to come to a fair decision. One thing only is what they wait for; this is the only thing necessary to arouse public hatred: the confession of the name of Christian, not an investigation of the charge. (4) Yet, suppose you are trying any other criminal. If he confesses to the crime of murder, sacrilege, incest, or treason—to particularize the indictments hurled against us—you are not satisfied

---

5 Thus St. Cyprian, when condemned to death, exclaimed: *'Deo gratias!'* Cf. *Acta proconsularia S. Cypriani* 4 (*CSEL* 3.3. cxiii).

to pass sentence immediately; you weigh the attendant circumstances, the character of the deed, the number of times it was committed, the time, the place, the witnesses, and the partners-in-crime. (5) In our case there is nothing of this sort. No matter what false charge is made against us, we must be made to confess it; for example, how many murdered babies one has devoured, how many deeds of incest one has committed under cover of darkness, what cooks and what dogs were on hand. Oh, what glory for that governor who should have discovered someone who had already consumed a hundred infants!

(6) On the other hand, we find that it has been forbidden to search us out. For when Pliny the Younger[1] was in charge of his province and had condemned certain Christians and had driven others from their established position, he was so disturbed because of the numbers involved that he consulted Trajan, emperor at the time, as to what he should do thereafter. He explained that, except for their obstinate refusal to offer sacrifice, he had learned nothing else about their religious rites except that they met before daybreak to sing to Christ and to God and to bind themselves by oath to a way of life which forbade murder, adultery, dishonesty, treachery, and all other crimes. (7) Trajan wrote back that men of this kind should not be sought out, but, when brought to court, they should be punished.

(8) Oh, how unavoidably ambiguous was that decision! He says that they should not be sought—as though they were innocent; then prescribes that they should be punished—as though they were guilty! He spares them, yet vents his anger upon them; he pretends to close his eyes, yet directs attention toward them! Judgment, why do you thus ensnare yourself?

---

1 This famous letter of Pliny and Trajan's answer are found in Pliny's *Epistles* 10.96, 97.

If you condemn them, why not also search for them? If you do not search for them, why not also acquit them? Throughout the provinces troops of soldiers are assigned to track down robbers. Against traitors and public enemies each individual constitutes a soldier: the search is extended even to comrades and accomplices. (9) Only the Christian may not be sought out—but he may be brought to court. As though a search were intended to bring about something else than his appearance in court! So, you condemn a man when he is brought into court, although no one wanted him to be sought out. He has earned punishment, I suppose, not on the ground that he is guilty, but because he was discovered for whom no search had to be made.

(10) Then, too, when you deal with us in this matter, you do not follow the procedure prescribed for judging criminals. To others who deny their guilt you apply torture to force them to confess; to Christians alone, to force them to deny. Yet, if it were something evil, we would certainly go on denying it, and you would try to force us, by torture, to confess. For you would not think that an investigation of our crimes was unnecessary on the ground that you were sure they were committed because of the mere confession of the name. Why, to this very day, after the confession of a murderer, you, who know what murder is, nevertheless extract by torture the details of the crime from him who has confessed it. (11) Much more perverse is your treatment when you take it for granted from the confession of the name that our crimes have been committed and then, by torture, compel us to add a confession. You intend that by one and the same act we deny both our name and the crimes which you had taken for granted were committed merely from the confession of the name.

(12) It is not your wish, I suppose, that we, whom you believe the most utterly worthless of creatures, should perish.

You are in the habit of saying to a murderer: 'Deny it!' If one accused of sacrilege persists in confessing his guilt, you bid him be tortured [till he denies it]. If you do not act thus toward the guilty, then you indicate that you consider us absolutely innocent; you do not wish us, being absolutely innocent, to persist in a confession of that which you realize you must condemn, not out of justice, but of necessity. (13) A man proclaims: 'I am a Christian.'[2] He says what he is; you want to hear what he is not. You, who preside as judges to extract the truth, in our case alone take pains to hear a lie. 'I am,' says one, 'what you ask if I am. Why do you torture me into lying? I confess, and you torture me! What would you do if I were to deny?' Certainly, when others deny, you do not readily believe them; if we deny, you immediately believe us!

(14) Let this perversity of yours lead you to suspect that there is some secret underlying power which uses you as tools against the form and nature of exercising justice, and, in fact, against the very laws themselves.[3] Unless I am mistaken, the laws demand that evil-doers be brought to light, not concealed; they prescribe that confessed criminals be condemned, not acquitted. This is what senatorial decrees and imperial rescripts clearly set down. This empire, of which you are the ministers, is a government controlled by free citizens, not by tyrants. (15) Under tyrants, torture was employed in place of punishment; under you, it is restricted to examination only. Keep your law in so far as torture is necessary to effect a confession, and then, if it is forestalled by confession, torture will

---

2 Cf. the Acts of the Christian martyrs from the little town of Scilli in proconsular Africa (R. Knopf, *Ausgewählte Märtyrerakten*, 3rd ed. by G. Krüger [Tübingen, 1929] n. 6). Urged by the proconsul Vigellius Saturninus to deny their faith, the answer of each was: 'I am a Christian.'
3 St. Justin Martyr (*Apology* I 5;12;14) also attributes to the demons the motive which underlies men's perversity in conducting the trials of Christians.

be unnecessary; sentence is then required. The guilty must be freed by, not freed from, paying the punishment which is his due.

(16) Finally, no one makes an effort to acquit *him*.[4] He cannot even entertain a desire for this; that is why no one is forced into a denial. In the case of the Christian, you regard him as guilty of every crime, the enemy of the gods, rulers, laws, morals, and all nature. Yet you force him into a denial that you may acquit him, although you could not possibly acquit him unless he were to deny. (17) You are making a sham of the laws; you want him to deny that he is guilty, so that you may *make* him guiltless—and this, really, against his will! Now, you say, he is no longer responsible for his past. Whence comes this perversity of yours, that you should fail to realize that a voluntary confession is more to be trusted than a forced denial? Or [should you not fear] that one who has been forced into a denial may have made his denial without good faith, and, being acquitted, may immediately after the trial laugh at your malevolence and become once again a Christian?

(18) Since, then, you treat us differently from other criminals in every respect, having in mind one object only, that we may be cut off from that name—for we are cut off only if we do what non-Christians do[5]—you can understand that there is no crime at all in our case; it is a question merely of a name. This name a certain power of a rival agency[6] persecutes, making this its first and foremost aim, that men may be unwilling to obtain certain knowledge about that of which they are certain they have no knowledge. (19) Hence it is that they believe stories about us which are not proved and

---

4 I.e., a confessed criminal.
5 I.e., deny the faith.
6 Satan and his rebel angels.

they do not want any investigation, lest it be proved that the stories which they prefer to have believed are not true. It follows that the name, an object of enmity to that rival agency, is condemned by its mere admission because of crimes presumed, not proved. Therefore, if we confess, we are tortured; if we persevere, we are punished; if we deny, we are acquitted, because it is an attack on a name.

(20) Finally, why do you read from your indictment that so-and-so is a Christian?[7] Why not also that he is a murderer, if the Christian is a murderer? Why not adulterer, also, or whatever else you believe us to be? In our regard alone is it a cause of shame and annoyance to report us with the specification of our crimes? If the term 'Christian' involves in itself no element of guilt, it is extremely ridiculous that the charge is one of name only.

Chapter 3

(1) What should one say of the fact that many shut their eyes and force themselves to such hatred of the name that, even when they speak favorably of someone, they insert some hateful remark about this name? 'Caius Seius is a good man, except that he is a Christian.' Similarly, someone else says: 'I am surprised that Lucius Titius, otherwise a man of sense, has suddenly become a Christian!' No one stops to think whether Caius is good and Lucius sensible because he is a Christian, or is a Christian because he is sensible and good! (2) Men praise what they know and find fault with what they do not know. They contaminate their knowledge with their ignorance, although it would be more correct to

---

[7] According to court procedure, the name of the accused and his charge were read aloud from the record. The mere word, Christian, constituted the charge in many cases.

form a preconceived idea with regard to what is unknown from what is known than to condemn beforehand what is known because of what is unknown.

(3) Others censure those whom they knew in the past, before they acquired this name, as vagrant, good-for-nothing scoundrels, and they censure them in the very act of praising them. In the blindness of their hatred they stumble into favorable criticism. 'That woman! How dissolute and frivolous she was! And that young man, how much more prodigal and debauched he used to be! They have become Christians.' Thus, the name which was responsible for their reformation is set down as a charge against them. (4) Some, even, at the expense of their own advantage, bargain with their hatred, satisfied to suffer a personal loss, provided that their home be freed from the object of their hatred. A wife who has become chaste is cast out by her husband now that he is relieved of his jealous suspicions of her. A son, now docile, is disowned by a father who was patient with him in the past. A servant, now trustworthy, is banished from the sight of a master who was formerly indulgent. To the degree that one is reformed under the influence of the name he gives offense. The Christians' goodness is outweighed by the hatred borne them.

(5) Well, then, if it is simply the name that is hated, what guilt can attach to names? What fault can be found with words except that something in the word sounds rough or unlucky or abusive or immodest? The term 'Christian,' on the other hand, as far as its etymology goes, is derived from 'unction.' Even when you mispronounce it 'Chrestian'[1]—for your

---

[1] A vulgar confusion existed as to *Chrestós* and *Christós;* hence, the populace described Christians by the name of *Chrestiani* (*Chrestianoi*.) Cf. Tacitus, *Annales* 15.44; Suetonius, *Claudius* 25; Lactantius, *Institutiones divinae* 4.7.5.

knowledge of the word itself is uncertain—it is made up of 'sweetness' or 'kindness.' Hence, in harmless men even a harmless name is hated.

(6) But, I suppose, the religion is hated in the name of its founder. Is it anything new that some way of life gives to its followers the name of its teacher? Are not philosophers called Platonists, Epicureans, Pythagoreans after their founders? Are not the Stoics and Academics so called from the places of their meetings and assemblies? In the same way, are not doctors named after Erasistratus, grammarians after Aristarchus, and even cooks after Apicius? (7) No one takes offense at the profession of a name which has been handed down by a teacher together with his teaching. Of course, if anyone will prove that a school is bad and its founder likewise bad, he will prove also that the name is bad and deserves hatred because of the worthless character of the school and its founder. Consequently, before hating a name, it is fitting to examine first the character of the school with reference to its founder or the character of the founder with reference to his school. (8) But, in this case, investigation and knowledge of both are neglected. The name is seized upon; the name is subjected to punishment; although this religion and its founder are unknown, a word alone condemns them in advance because of the name they bear, not because they are convicted of anything.

Chapter 4

(1) Now that I have set down these remarks as a preface, as it were, to stigmatize the injustice of the public hatred against us, I shall take the stand to defend our innocence. Not only shall I refute the charges which are brought against us, but I shall even hurl them back upon those who make them, so that men may thereby know that among the Christians

those crimes do not exist which they are not unaware exist among themselves; and that, at the same time, they may blush when, as utter reprobates, they accuse—I do not say the most righteous of men—but, as they themselves would have it, their equals.¹ (2) We shall reply to each charge individually: to those which we are said to commit in secret, and to those which we are found to be committing before the eyes of all—charges on the basis of which we are held to be criminals, deceivers, reprobates, and objects of ridicule.

(3) Inasmuch as truth, which is on our side, answers all charges, in the last resort the authority of the law is hurled against it in such a way that either there is nothing to be said by way of retracting after the law has been appealed to, or, to your regret, the necessity of obedience takes precedence with you to regard for the truth.² Therefore, I shall first discuss with you the question of the law, inasmuch as you are its protectors. (4) In the first place, then, when you harshly lay down the law and say: 'Your existence is illegal!' and when you make this charge without any further investigation —which would certainly be more humane—you make profession of violence and of an unjust, tyrannical domination, if you are saying that Christianity is illegal simply because that is your will, not because it really ought to be illegal. (5) On the other hand, if you want a thing to be illegal because it ought to be, unquestionably that ought to be illegal which is evil. And, assuredly, from this very fact it is a foregone conclusion that what is good is legal. If I find that something is good which a law of yours has forbidden, is the law not powerless to keep me, in view of that previous conclusion, from doing that which, if it were evil, the law with full right would

---

1 I.e., men infected with the same vices they have.
2 Cf. Terence, *Andria* 68.

forbid? If a law of yours has erred, it is, I presume, because it was conceived by man; it certainly did not fall from heaven.

(6) Is it any wonder to you that a man may have erred in making a law or that he recovered his senses and rejected it? Why, consider even the laws of Lycurgus himself, revised by the Spartans: did they not inflict such sorrow upon their author that he condemned himself to solitary starvation?[3] (7) And what about yourselves? As your research daily throws more light upon the darkness of former days, do you not cut and hew all that old, overgrown forest of laws with the new axes of imperial rescripts and edicts? (8) Consider the Papian laws which oblige men to beget children at an earlier age than the Julian laws oblige people to contract marriage. Were they not, in spite of the weight of authority due to their old age, just a short time ago annulled by Severus, the most conservative of emperors, on the ground that they were utterly devoid of sense? (9) Again, the law used to be that those found guilty of bankruptcy might be cut in pieces by their creditors. Yet, by common consent, this cruel stipulation was later abrogated, and capital punishment was exchanged for a mark of disgrace. Proscription of a man's goods was intended to bring the blood to his cheeks rather than to shed it.

(10) How many of your laws lie hidden which still need to be reformed—laws which are not recommended by length of years or the high position of him who framed them, but solely by their profession of justice! On this ground, when they are recognized as being unjust, they deserve to be condemned, even when they themselves condemn. (11) How is it that we call them unjust? As a matter of fact, if it is merely a name they are punishing, they are actually stupid. On the other hand, if it is a question of actions, why do they depend

---
3 Cf. Plutarch, *Lycurgus* 29.

solely on the name in punishing actions, whereas in the case of others these deeds are punished when it has been proved that they were committed, and not merely because of a name? I am, they say, an adulterer. Why do they not question me? I am guilty of child murder. Why do they not wring a confession from me? I commit some crime against the gods, against the Caesars. Why am I not given a hearing, since I have an answer which will clear my name? (12) There is no law which forbids an investigation of the crime it prohibits, because a judge does not punish justly unless he knows that some illegal act has been committed, nor does a citizen faithfully observe a law if he is ignorant of what kind of crime the law punishes. (13) No law has to render an account of its own justice solely to itself, but to those from whom it expects observance. Besides, a law is under suspicion if it refuses to submit to examination, whereas it is worthless if it demands obedience without examination.

Chapter 5

(1) Let us consider to some extent the origin of laws of this sort. There was an ancient decree that no god should be consecrated by a victorious general without the approval of the Senate. M. Aemilius is well aware of this law in connection with his god, Alburnus.[1] It likewise carries weight for our cause, that among you divinity depends on human judgment. Unless a god please man, he simply will not be a god; man will have to be well-disposed toward the god! (2) So Tiberius, in whose reign the name of Christian entered the world, hearing from Palestine in Syria information which had revealed

---

[1] One of three references which Tertullian makes to this incident; cf. *Adversus Marcionem* 1.18; *Ad nat.* 1.10. Scholars may speculate, but they were unable to find further data which will relieve the obscurity of the phrase.

the truth of Christ's divinity, brought the matter before the Senate, with previous indication of his own approval. The Senators, on the ground that they had not verified the facts, rejected it. Caesar maintained his opinion and threatened dire measures against those who brought accusations against the Christians.[2] (3) Consult your histories: you will find in them that Nero was the first to rage with the imperial sword against this religion which was just at that particular time coming to life at Rome.[3] We actually glory that such a person took the lead in condemning us. For, whoever knows him can understand that nothing save some magnificent good was ever condemned by Nero. (4) Domitian, too, somewhat of a Nero in cruelty, made some attempts. But—being also, to a certain degree, human—he soon put a halt to what he had initiated and even recalled those whom he had exiled. Such have always been our persecutors, unjust, wicked, depraved men whom you yourselves are accustomed to condemn, while you have regularly recalled those whom they have condemned.

(5) But, of so many emperors from that time down to our own day who were wise in matters divine and human, show me one who persecuted the Christians! (6) On the contrary, we can point out our protector, if you will examine the letters of the most venerable emperor, Marcus Aurelius. In these letters he attests that the great drought in Germany was re-

---

2 In Ch. 21,24 of his *Apology*, Tertullian concludes his sketch of Christ's Passion and Resurrection by saying: 'All these facts about Christ were reported to Tiberius, the reigning emperor, by Pilate.' A letter of this kind is found in the apocryphal Acts of Peter and Paul (*Acta apostolorum apocrypha*, ed. Lipsius et Bonnet, I [Lipsiae, 1891] 118ff.). The apocryphal story which Tertullian seems to have known in connection with this letter, and which he mentions in Ch. 5, is lost (cf. E. Hennecke, *Neutestamentliche Apokryphen* [Tübingen and Leipzig, 1904] 75). The mass of apocryphal literature dealing with Pilate and his attitude toward the Christians, has, of course, no historical foundation.
3 Cf. Tacitus, *Ann.* 15.44.

lieved by rain which fell in answer to the prayers of the Christians who happened to be in his army.[4] Although he did not openly revoke the edict of persecution from these men, yet in another way he openly counteracted its effect, by threatening their persecutors with a sentence which was actually more horrible.[5] (7) What sort of laws, then, are those which are set in operation against us only by emperors who are wicked and devoid of justice, base and impious, deceptive and mentally deranged? These are the laws which Trajan nullified in part by forbidding that a search be made for Christians, laws which no Hadrian—eager investigator though he was of all that attracted his inquisitive mind, no Vespasian —conqueror though he was of the Jews, no Pius, no Verus ever enforced! (8) Assuredly, the worst of men would be more readily adjudged worthy of utter extermination by the best of emperors as being their natural enemies than by men of their own kind!

Chapter 6

(1) Now, I should like the most scrupulous guardians and avengers of the laws and institutions of our forefathers to answer with regard to their loyalty, their respect, and their obedience toward the decrees of their ancestors: whether they have been faithful to all of them; whether they have in no respect deviated from any of them, or caused any necessary and appropriate matters of discipline to be forgotten. (2) What has become of those laws which restrained extravagance and bribery? which forbade the spending of more than a hundred asses on a supper, or the serving of more than one hen—and

---

4 Cf. *infra,* Tert. *Ad Scapulam* 4 n. 11.
5 The accuser was to be burned alive.

that an unfattened one?¹ which removed a patrician from the Senate because he had ten pounds of silver, on the serious pretext of too lofty ambition?² which destroyed theaters just as soon as they were erected, as tending to corrupt morals?³ which did not permit the marks of dignity and noble lineage⁴ to be usurped rashly or with impunity? (3) I observe that suppers now have to be called 'centenarian' because of the 100,000 sesterces expended on them. Silver from the mines is even being converted into dishes—not for the use of Senators, which would be a mere trifle—but rather for freedmen or those whip-crackers⁵ whose backs are even yet breaking the whips. I see, too, that a single theater is not sufficient, or one without an awning. For, lest winter weather cast a chill upon their impure pleasures, the Spartans were the first to conceive the idea of a mantle for the games. I see, too, that there is no difference left between honorable matrons and prostitutes, as far as their dress is concerned.⁶

(4) As a matter of fact, as regards women, those customs of our ancestors which protected their modesty and sobriety have fallen into disregard. Why, no woman was acquainted with any gold except that on the one finger which her spouse had pledged to himself with the engagement ring. Women abstained so completely from wine that one who had unlocked the cupboard of the wine cellar was forced by her own family

---

1 Aulus Gellius, *Noctes Atticae* 2.24, names some of these sumptuary laws; cf., also, Macrobius, *Saturnalia* 3.17.
2 Cf. Valerius Maximus (2.9.4).
3 Cf. Tert., *De spectaculis* 10; Augustine, *De civitale Dei* 1.31.
4 *Viz.*, the gold rings, the senators' *latus clavus*, the knights' *angustus clavus*, and the *lunati calcei*.
5 Tertullian's *flagra rumpentes* (whip-crackers) is equivalent to the comic expression *flagritriba*, i.e., one who wears out the whip by being flogged. Cf. Plautus, *Pseudolus* 1.2.5.
6 The heavy cloaks of the Spartans were designed primarily for protection against winter weather. As to feminine garb, cf. Tert., *De cultu feminarum* 12.

to die of starvation. In fact, under Romulus, a woman who had merely touched wine was put to death with impunity by her husband Metennius. (5) That is the reason, too, why women had to offer a kiss to their relatives, that they might judge their breath. (6) What has become of that conjugal happiness so fostered by high moral living that for nearly six hundred years after Rome was founded no home sued for a divorce? Look at women now. Every limb is weighed down with gold; because of wine, no kiss is freely given. Yes, and now it is a divorce which is prayed for, as though that were the natural issue of marriage!

(7) Even the decrees which your fathers had prudently passed respecting your very gods, you, their most dutiful sons, have abolished. The consuls, with full approval of the Senate, drove Father Bacchus and his mysteries not only from Rome but from all Italy.[7] (8) During the consulship of Piso and Gabinius,[8] men who were by no means Christians, it was forbidden to have Serapis, Isis, and Harpocrates[9] with his dog-headed Anubis admitted into the Capitoline temple; that is, they were expelled from the solemn assembly of the gods. Their shrines were overthrown and they were banished. Thus did the consuls check the evils of these base and hateful superstitions. These gods *you* have restored, conferring upon them the utmost dignity.[10]

(9) Where is your religious feeling? Where is that reverence which you owe your ancestors? By your dress, your food, your manner of living, your attitude of mind, in fine, by your very speech, you have renounced your forefathers. You are

---

7 Cf. Livy (39.8ff.). The Senate passed the decree concerning the Bacchanals in 186 B.C.
8 58 B.C.
9 Harpocrates was the Egyptian god of silence.
10 Cassius Dio (47.15) relates that in 43 B.C. a new temple was erected for these banished gods.

forever praising bygone days, but in a far different manner do you live your everyday life. From this it is clear that, in departing from the laudable customs of your ancestors, you retain and preserve those which you should not, while those which you should have preserved, you have not. (10) Consider the traditions of your fathers which you appear to be keeping most faithfully, wherein, principally, you have deemed Christians guilty of transgression (I refer to your devotedness in worshipping the gods, a matter in which men of old most grievously erred). Though you have re-erected altars to Serapis, become by now a Roman, though you offer your licentious orgies to Bacchus, now a naturalized Italian, I will show in its proper place[11] that these traditions are being despised, neglected, and destroyed by you in contradiction to the precedent set by your ancestors. (11) I will now reply to that infamous charge about our clandestine crimes, that I may clear my path for those which are more manifest.

Chapter 7

(1) We are spoken of as utter reprobates and are accused of having sworn to murder babies and to eat them and of committing adulterous acts after the repast. Dogs, you say, the pimps of darkness, overturn candles and procure license for our impious lusts.[1] (2) We are always spoken of in this way, yet you take no pains to bring into the light the charges which for so long a time have been made against us. Now, either bring them into the light, if you believe them, or stop believing them, inasmuch as you have not brought them to light! Because of your hypocrisy, the objection is made against you

---

11 Cf. *infra*, Chs. 13-15.

---

1 Concerning these accusations, cf. *infra*, Minucius Felix, *Octavius* 9.5-7 and *infra*, Ch. 8 n. 2.

that the evil does not exist which you yourselves dare not bring to light. Far different is the duty you enjoin upon the executioner against the Christians, not to make them state what they do, but to make them deny what they are.

(3) The origin of this religion, as we have already said, dates from the time of Tiberius. Truth and hatred came into existence simultaneously.[2] As soon as the former appeared, the latter began its enmity. It has as many foes as there are outsiders, particularly among Jews because of their jealousy, among soldiers because of their blackmailing, and even among the very members of our own household because of corrupt human nature. (4) Day by day we are besieged; day by day we are betrayed; oftentimes, in the very midst of our meetings and gatherings, we are surprised by an assault. (5) Who has ever come upon a baby wailing, as the accusation has it? Who has ever kept for the judge's inspection the jaws of Cyclopes and Sirens, bloodstained as he had found them? Who has ever found any traces of impurity upon [Christian] wives? Who has discovered such crimes, yet concealed them or been bribed to keep them secret when dragging these men off to court? If we always keep under cover, whence the betrayal of our crimes?

(6) Rather, who could have been the traitors? Certainly not the accused themselves, since the obligation of pledged silence is binding upon all mysteries by their very nature. The mysteries of Samothrace and of Eleusis are shrouded in silence; how much more such rites as these which, if they were made public, would provoke at once the hatred of all mankind—while God's wrath is reserved for the future? (7) If, then, Christians themselves are not the betrayers, it follows that outsiders are. Whence do outsiders get their knowledge,

---

[2] Cf. Terence, *Andria* 68: *'veritas odium parit'* (truth brings forth hate.).

since even holy initiation rites always ban the uninitiated and are wary of witnesses? Unless you mean that the wicked are less afraid.

(8) The nature of rumor is well known to all. It was your own poet who said: 'Rumor, an evil surpassing all evils in speed.'[3] Why call rumor an evil? Because it flies? Because it testifies? Or because it generally lies? Even when it has a modicum of truth in it, rumor is not free from some taint of falsehood; it detracts from, adds to, or deviates from the truth. (9) What of the fact that it exists only on this condition, that it may not continue in existence unless it lies, and its life endures only so long as there is no proof? Of course, when proof comes, rumor ceases to exist; having, as it were, fulfilled its office of reporting the news, it passes it on as a fact. From then on the story is considered a fact, and called a fact. (10) For example, no one says: 'They say that such a thing has happened at Rome,' or: 'The story is that so-and-so was assigned to a province,' but: 'So-and-so was assigned to a province,' and: 'Such a thing happened at Rome.'

(11) Rumor, a word designating uncertainty, has no place where there is certainty. But does anyone except the unthinking believe rumor? One who is wise surely does not heed uncertainty. Everyone can reflect that however great the zeal with which the tale has been spread, however strong the assertion with which it was fabricated, it necessarily started at some time or other from one source. (12) Thence it creeps gradually along the grapevine of tongues and ears, and a defect in the tiny seedling so overshadows the other details of the rumor that no one reflects whether the first mouth sowed the seed of falsehood, as often happens, from a spirit of envy or a suspicious thought or from the pleasure some derive from lying—a pleasure not new-born, but inborn.

---

3 Virgil, *Aeneid* 4.174.

(13) It is well that time brings all things to light, as even your own proverbs and sayings testify, in accordance with the design of nature which has so ordained things that nothing remains a secret for long, even though rumor has not spread it abroad. (14) Rightly, then, is rumor alone for so long a time aware of the crimes of Christians; this is the witness you bring forth against us. What it has sometime or other spread abroad and over such an interval of time hardened into a matter of opinion, it has not yet been able to prove, so that I call upon the steadfastness of nature itself against those who assume that such accusations are credible.

Chapter 8

(1) Look! we set up a reward for these crimes: they promise eternal life. For the time being, believe it! On this point I have a question to ask: If you believed it, would you consider the acquisition of eternal life worth attaining with such a [troubled] conscience? (2) Come, bury your sword in this baby, enemy though he is of no one, guilty of no crime, everybody's son; or, if that is the other fellow's job, stand here beside this [bit of] humanity, dying before he has lived; wait for the young soul to take flight; receive his fresh blood; saturate your bread in it; partake freely! (3) Meanwhile, as you recline at table, note the place where your mother is, and your sister; note it carefully, so that, when the dogs cause darkness to fall, you may make no mistake—for you will be guilty of a crime unless you commit incest!

(4) Initiated and sealed in such mysteries as these, you live forever! I wish you would tell me if eternity is worth such a price; if it isn't, these crimes should not be believed. Even if you believed them, I tell you you would not want to commit

them. Even if you wanted to, I tell you you couldn't. How is it, then, that others can commit them, if you cannot? Why cannot you, if others can? (5) We, I suppose, have a different nature, being Cynopennae or Sciapodes;[1] we have a different arrangement of teeth, different muscles for incestuous lust! You who believe these crimes about any other man can commit them, too; you are a man yourself, just as a Christian is. If you cannot do these things, you ought not to believe them of Christians. For a Christian, too, is a man even as you are.

(6) 'But, without realizing it, they are deceived and imposed upon.' They were unaware that anything of the sort was asserted of Christians—and that they should examine and investigate the matter with all vigilance. (7) Yet, I suppose, it is customary for those who wish to be initiated to approach first the father of the sacred rites to arrange what must be prepared. Then he says, 'Now, you need a baby, still tender, one who does not know what death means, and one who will smile under your knife. You need bread, too, with which to gather up his juicy blood; besides that, candlesticks, lamps, some dogs, and bits of meat which will draw them on to overturn the lamps.'[2] Most important of all, you must come with your mother and sister.' (8) But, what if the latter are unwilling to come, or you do not have any? What about the Christians who are without relatives? A man cannot really be a Christian, I suppose, unless he is someone's brother or son. (9) Now, what if all those preparations are made with-

---

1 Fabulous creatures, believed to live in India and Lybia respectively; the Cynopennae being dog-headed, the Sciapodes possessing huge feet that served them as umbrellas. Cf. Pliny, *Naturalis historia* 7.2.23; Tert., *Ad nat.* 1.8.
2 The dogs were said to be tied to the lamps which would be upset and extinguished when the dogs jumped for meat tossed to them. Cf. *infra*, Min. Fel., *Oct.* 9.6f.

out the foreknowledge of those concerned? At any rate, after once experiencing it, they know of it and support and condone the procedure. 'They are afraid of being punished if they make it known.' Well, how can they deserve to be defended, since they would prefer to die outright rather than live with such crimes upon their conscience? Come now, granted that they are afraid, why do they persevere? The logical conclusion is that you no longer would want to be that which you would not have been at all, had you known ahead of time what it was.

Chapter 9

(1) To refute these points at greater length, I will point out that you yourselves commit these very crimes—sometimes openly, sometimes secretly—and that, perhaps, is the reason why you have believed them also of us. (2) In Africa, babies used to be sacrificed publicly to Saturn[1] even down to the proconsulate of Tiberius. He impaled the priests themselves on the very trees overshadowing their temple. The crosses were votive offerings to expiate their crimes. As witness of this there is the army of my own country,[2] which performed this task for this very proconsul. (3) Even now this holy crime is continued in secret. Christians are not alone in despising you; no crime is wiped out forever, or else some god is changing his ways. (4) Since Saturn did not spare his own sons, surely he did not insist on sparing the children of others, who, for example, were offered to him by their very own parents. They gladly

---

1 Cf. *infra*, Min. Fel., *Oct.* 30.3 n.1.
2 The meaning of the passage is obscure. Is the Tiberius who is mentioned not the emperor but a recent governor by that name? The *Codex Fuldensis* alone reads *patris nostri* for *patriae nostrae*, which is possible since Jerome (*De viris illustribus* 53) states that Tertullian's father was a centurion.

complied and they fondled their babies so that they would not be crying when they were sacrificed. Yet, there is considerable difference between murder and parricide!

(5) Among the Gauls, an older person was sacrificed to Mercury.[3] I leave to their theaters the stories of the Taurians. Look at conditions in that city of the pious race of Aeneas, a city renowned for its religious worship! There is a certain Jupiter[4] whom they bathe in human blood during the games held in his honor. 'But it is the blood of a beast-fighter,' you say. That, I suppose, is something of less value than the blood of a man! Or is it not worse because it is the blood of a bad man? At any rate, it is blood shed in murder. Oh, what a Christian Jupiter! He is his father's only son as far as cruelty goes![5]

(6) But, with regard to infanticide, since it makes no difference whether it is committed for a religious purpose or according to one's own choosing—although there is a difference between murder and parricide—I will turn to the people. How many, do you suppose, of those here present who stand panting for the blood of Christians—how many, even, of you magistrates who are so righteous and so rigorous against us—want me to touch their consciences for putting their own offspring to death? (7) If there is some distinction in kind between one act of murder and another, it is certainly more cruel to kill by drowning or by exposure to cold, hunger, and the dogs; for an older person would prefer to die by the sword. (8) But, with us, murder is forbidden once for all. We are not permitted to destroy even the fetus in the womb, as long as

---
3 Cf. Min. Fel., *Oct.* 6.1 n.9; 30.4; Aug., *De civ. Dei* 7.19; Suet., *Claud.* 25.
4 I.e., Jupiter Latiaris. Cf. Min. Fel., *Oct.* 23.6 n.17; 30.4 n.6.
5 Jupiter is ironically called a Christian, since he rejoices in human sacrifice as they are said to do. Jupiter was the only son whom his father Saturn failed to devour as a baby.

blood is still being drawn to form a human being.⁶ To prevent the birth of a child is a quicker way to murder. It makes no difference whether one destroys a soul already born or interferes with its coming to birth. It is a human being and one who is to be a man, for the whole fruit is already present in the seed.

(9) As for bloody food and such tragic dishes, read—I think it is related by Herodotus,⁷ but I am not sure—how, among some tribes, blood was taken from the arms and tasted by both parties in forming a treaty. Something was tasted, too, under Catiline.⁸ And they say that it was a custom among certain tribes of Scythians for every deceased member to be eaten by his relatives.⁹ (10) But I am going too far afield. Today, right here among you, to mark the devotees of Bellona, a thigh is slashed, the blood is taken in the hand and given them for their benefit.¹⁰ Again, consider those who with greedy thirst, at a show in the arena, take the fresh blood of wicked criminals as it runs down from their throats and carry it off to heal their epilepsy.¹¹ What about them? (11) And what about those who make a meal on the flesh of wild beasts taken from the arena, who prefer the meat of boar or stag? That boar has licked the blood off him whom he has spattered with blood in the struggle. The stag has rolled in the blood of a gladiator. The very bellies of the bears, still stuffed with undigested human flesh, are the object of their search. Thence

---

6 Regarding the sin of abortion, cf. Min. Fel., *Oct.* 30.2.
7 Herodotus (4.70) gives this account of the Scythians.
8 Sallust, *Catilina* 22.
9 Cf. Herodotus 4.26 (cf. 4.106; Pliny, *Nat. hist.* 7.2.9); Tertullian, *Adv. Marcionem* 1.1; St. Jerome, *Adv. Jovinianum* 2.7.
10 The text is very uncertain. Concerning the fanatic priests of the Asiatic goddess Bellona, cf. Min. Fel., *Oct.* 22.9 n.10; 30.5.
11 Regarding this superstitious belief in the power of human blood to cure epilepsy, cf. Pliny, *Nat. hist.* 28.1.2; Celsus, *De medicina* 3.23.7; Min. Fel., *Oct.* 30.5 n.9.

does man belch forth flesh that was nourished with human flesh. (12) You who eat these animals, how far removed are you from the banquets of the Christians?

And do those who lust after human flesh, with a beastly passion, commit less grievous crimes because they devour something that is living? Are they less polluted with human blood and less dedicated to lewdness because they lap up that which is to turn into blood? No, they, of course, do not feast on babies, but rather on adults. (13) Let your unnatural ways blush before the Christians. We do not even have the blood of animals at our meals, for these consist of ordinary food. This is why we refrain from eating the meat of any animals which have been strangled or that die of themselves, lest we be in any way contaminated with blood, even if it is hidden in the flesh.[12]

(14) At the trials of Christians you offer them sausages filled with blood. You are convinced, of course, that the very thing with which you try to make them deviate from the right way is unlawful for them. How is it that, when you are confident that they will shudder at the blood of an animal, you believe they will pant eagerly after human blood? Is it, perchance, that *you* have found the latter more to your taste? (15) Human blood, then, and nothing else is certainly the very thing that ought to be employed as the touchstone of Christians, like fire or the incense box. Then they would be proved Christians by their appetite for human blood, just as they are at present by their refusal to offer sacrifice. On the other hand, they would have to be declared non-Christians if they did not taste it, just as if they had offered sacrifice. And, of course, you would have no shortage of human blood provided at the examination and condemnation of prisoners.

---

12 Cf. Acts 15.20, 29.

(16) Another point—Who are more expert at practising incest than those whom Jupiter himself has instructed? Ctesias relates that the Persians have intercourse with their own mothers. The Macedonians, too, were suspected of it because, the first time they attended the tragedy of *Oedipus,* they mocked the grief of the incestuous son, saying: 'He lay with his mother!' (17) Well, now! Consider how great chance there is for incestuous unions occasioned by mistaken identity. The promiscuousness of your wanton living affords the opportunity. In the first place, you expose your children to be taken up by some passerby out of the pity of a stranger's heart;[13] or you release them from your authority to be adopted by better parents. Sooner or later, the memory of the alienated family necessarily fades away. As soon as a mistake has occurred, the transmission of incest goes on, the stock spreading together with its crime. (18) Finally, then, wherever you are, at home, abroad, across the sea, your lust travels as your companion, and its outbursts everywhere—or even some slight indulgence—can easily beget children for you any place at all, though you may not know it. The result is that a brood thus scattered through illicit human intercourse may fall in with its own kindred and in blind ignorance fail to recognize it as begotten of incestuous blood.[14]

(19) As for us, an ever-watchful and steadfast chastity shields us from such an occurrence and, in so far as we refrain from adultery and every excess after marriage, we are safe, too, from the danger of incest. Some are even more secure, since they ward off the entire violence of this error by virginal continence, and as old men are still [as pure as] boys.

(20) If you would realize that these sins exist among yourselves, then you would perceive clearly that they do not exist

---

13 Cf. Lact., *Inst. div.* 6.20.21f.
14 Cf. Min. Fel., *Oct.* 31.4.

among Christians. The same eyes would tell you the facts in both cases. But, a two-fold blindness easily imposes itself, so that those who do not see what does exist seem to see what does not. I will point out that this is true in everything. Now I will speak of the more manifest crimes.

Chapter 10

(1) 'You do not worship the gods,' you say, 'and you do not offer sacrifice for the emperors.' It follows that we do not offer sacrifices for others for the same reason that we do not do it even for ourselves—it follows immediately from our not worshipping the gods. Consequently, we are considered guilty of sacrilege and treason. This is the chief accusation against us—in fact, it is the whole case—and it certainly deserves investigation, unless presumption and injustice dictate the decision, the one despairing of the truth, the other refusing it.

(2) We cease worshipping your gods when we find out that they are non-existent. This, then, is what you ought to demand, that we prove that those gods are non-existent and for that reason should not be worshipped, because they ought to be worshipped only if they were actually gods. Then, too, the Christians ought to be punished if the fact were established that those gods do exist whom they will not worship because they consider them non-existent. (3) 'But, for us,' you say, 'the gods do exist.' We object and appeal from you to your conscience. Let this pass judgment on us, let this condemn us, if it can deny that all those gods of yours have been mere men.[1] (4) But, if it should deny this, it will be refuted by its own documents of ancient times from which it has

---
[1] This idea, that the gods had once been mere men, was first proposed by Euhemerus, *ca.* 300 B.C. Cf. Cic., *De natura deorum* 1.42.119; Min. Fel., *Oct.* 21.1 n.1.

learned of the gods. Testimony is furnished to this very day by the cities in which they were born, and the regions in which they left traces of something they had done and in which it is pointed out that they were buried.

(5) And now, shall I quickly run through the list of deities, one by one, numerous and important as they are, the new and the old, barbarian and Greek, Roman and foreign, captive and adopted, private and public, male and female, belonging to the country, the city, the sailor, the soldier? (6) It would be wearisome even to call the roll! To sum up the whole situation—and this, not that you may become informed for the first time, but that you may recall what you already know (for you certainly act as though you had forgotten it)—before the advent of Saturn there was no god among you. With him starts the roster of all your divinities, or at least of those who are more powerful and better known. Hence, whatever is established about their beginnings will apply also to their posterity. (7) As for Saturn, as far as literature tells us, neither Diodorus the Greek, nor Thallus, nor Cassius Severus, nor Cornelius Nepos,[2] nor any other writer on antiquities of this sort has pronounced him other than a mere man. As far as arguments drawn from fact go, I find none more trustworthy than this: right in Italy itself, where Saturn finally took his abode after much traveling to and fro, and after enjoying the hospitality of Attica, he was welcomed by Janus[3]—or, as the Salii wish to call him, Janes. (8) The mountain which he made his home was called the Saturnian. The city which he founded is called, even to the present day,

---

2 Cf. Min. Fel., *Oct.* 21.4, and notes 11-14. Tertullian seems to have confused the orator, Cassius Severus, who flourished in the time of Augustus, with Cassius Hemina, the annalist, who wrote in the second century B.C.
3 Cf. Min. Fel., *Oct.* 21.5.

Saturnia.[4] Finally, all Italy, after being called Oenotria, was named Saturnia after him. The art of writing was first established there by him and coins were struck with his image. Hence, he presides over the treasury.

(9) However, if Saturn was a man, he certainly was born of man, and, because conceived by man, he was certainly not the child of Heaven and Earth. But, if his parents were unknown, it was easy for him to be called the child of those from whom all of us too may claim birth. For, who would not call heaven his father and earth his mother to pay them respect and honor? Even according to the custom all of us have, persons who are unknown, or even those who make an unexpected appearance, are said to have dropped from the sky. (10) Therefore, inasmuch as Saturn suddenly appeared everywhere, he happened to be called the 'Heavenly One,' for in popular speech people whose parentage is uncertain are called 'sons of Earth.'[5] I make no comment upon the actions of men who were still so uncivilized that they were moved by the quasi-divine appearance of some newcomer, since today men who by this time are civilized apotheosize human creatures who a few days before, with public mourning, they confessed were dead! (11) That is enough now about Saturn, brief though it is. We shall also prove that Jupiter was every bit as much a man, inasmuch as he was born of man, and thereafter the whole stock of his family was as mortal as the seed from which it came.

---

4 Cf. *ibid*. 21.6 n.16.
5 Cf. *ibid*. 21.7 n.18.

Chapter 11

(1) While you dare not deny that the gods were once men, yet you have made it your practice to affirm that after their death they became gods. Let us go back over the causes which have brought this about. (2) In the first place, you have to grant that there is some god more sublime, one who has, as it were, a rightful title to divinity, who has made gods out of men. The gods could not have assumed to themselves a divinity which they did not possess, nor could anyone supply it to them when they did not possess it, unless he had it in his own right. (3) On the other hand, if there were no one to make gods, you are offering a vain presumption that gods were made, while at the same time you do away with the maker. At all events, if they could have made gods of themselves, there never would have remained men with this power over a superior state of being.

(4) So, if there is someone who could make gods, I come back to examine the reasons why anyone would make gods out of men. I find no other reason except that the great god desired ministers and assistants in his divine functions.

But, in the first place, it would be beneath his dignity to need the services of anyone—least of all, a dead man! It would be more fitting for him to have made some god right from the start, if in due time he was going to need the services of a dead man. (5) I fail to see what service is needed. For, this whole fabric of the universe, whether it be unborn or unmade (as Pythagoras taught), or whether (as Plato believed)[1] born or made, was certainly arranged, equipped, ordered once and for all in its construction, and supplied with the complete guidance of reason. That which has perfected

---

[1] Cf. Cic., *Tusculanae disputationes* 1.28.70; *Academica priora* 2.37.118.

all things could not be imperfect. (6) Nothing awaited Saturn and Saturnia's tribe. Men would be fools if they were not convinced that from the beginning rain fell from the sky, the stars were bright, light shone, thunder rolled, and Jupiter himself trembled in fear of the thunderbolts which *you* place in his hand; if they were not certain that all crops came forth in abundance from the earth before Liber, Ceres, and Minerva, in fact, even before the first man (whoever he was), for nothing designed for the sustenance and preservation of man could be introduced after man. (7) Finally, the gods are said to have discovered, not devised, those things necessary to sustain life. But, whatever is discovered, was already in existence, and what was in existence is not to be considered the property of him who discovered it but of him who devised it; it existed before it could be discovered. (8) Now, if Liber is a god because he demonstrated the use of the vine, Lucullus fared badly in not having been deified as the originator of a new fruit, inasmuch as he was the discoverer of it; for it was he who first introduced the cherry from Pontus to Italy.[2] (9) Therefore, if from the beginning the universe has stood devised and arranged with fixed laws for exercising its functions, the argument from this viewpoint for admitting men into the ranks of divinity is void, because the positions and powers which you have attributed to them were in existence from the beginning, just as they would have been even if you had not made them gods.

(10) But, you turn your attention to another argument and reply that the conferring of divinity was a means of rewarding their services. On this point you grant, I suppose, that the god who makes gods possesses justice in a superior degree, since he has not recklessly nor undeservedly nor ex-

---
[2] Cf. Pliny, *Nat. hist.* 15.25.102.

travagantly bestowed such a great reward. (11) I would like to review these services, then, to see whether they are of a kind that would exalt these men to heaven and not rather plunge them into the abyss of Tartarus. (Such is the name you use, when it pleases you, for the prison of infernal punishment.) (12) It is there that the dead are relegated—those who are shameless toward their parents, who commit incest with their sisters, who seduce married women, rape young girls, and defile young boys, who commit sins of cruelty, murder, robbery, and fraud: all who are like anyone of your gods. No one of these, unless you deny that he was a man, can you prove to be free from crime or vice.

(13) Yet, just as you could not deny that they were once men, so these disgraceful marks upon them are an additional reason for our not believing that they afterwards became gods. For, if you sit in judgment to punish such persons, if such of you as are upright scorn fellowship, intercourse, intimacy with the wicked and depraved, while, on the other hand, it is men on their same level whom that god of yours has joined to himself to share in his majesty, why, then, do you condemn men whose associates you idolize? (14) Your injustice is an affront to heaven. Make all the worst reprobates into gods, that you may please your gods! It is an honor for them to have their equals deified.

(15) But—to omit further discussion of this disgraceful matter—supposing they were upright, blameless, and good! Yet, what a number of better men you have left in the underworld! For instance, a Socrates, renowned for wisdom, an Aristides for justice, a Themistocles for military ability, an Alexander for distinction, a Polycrates for good fortune, a Croesus for wealth, a Demosthenes for eloquence! (16) Which one of those gods of yours is more venerable or wiser than Cato, more just or more highly endowed with military

prowess than Scipio? Who surpasses Pompey in distinction, or Sulla in fortune, or Crassus in wealth, or Tully in eloquence? With how much more dignity might that god have waited to take such men as these into the ranks of the gods, since he surely knew ahead of time of their better qualifications! He acted hastily, I think, and closed the gates of heaven once and for all; he now blushes as the better men grumble about it in the world of the dead.

Chapter 12

(1) I am now finished with this matter. For, I am sure that on the basis of truth itself I shall have pointed out what these gods are not, when I have shown what they are. As for your gods, then, I see in them merely the names of certain men long dead. I hear their stories and recognize the sacred rituals arising from these myths. (2) As for their statues, I find no fault with them, except that the material used in them matches that in common pots and household utensils. Or if you will, they exchange their destiny, as it were, with those same pots and pans by being consecrated.[1] The free hand of art transforms them and treats them thereby with utmost insult, adding sacrilege in the very act of transformation. Actually, for us who are beaten because of these very gods, it could be a particular source of comfort in our punishments that they themselves, in order to become gods, undergo the same harsh treatment as ourselves.

(3) You hang the Christians on crosses and stakes. What idol does not first find its shape when clay is applied to a cross or stake? It is on a gibbet that the body of your god is dedicated in the first place. (4) With hooks of torture you scrape

---

1 Cf. Min. Fel., *Oct.* 22; Arnobius, *Adversus nationes* 6.14.

away the flesh from the flanks of Christians; with axes, planes, and files you fall to work upon all the parts of your gods with even greater gusto. We place our necks upon the block; before you use lead, glue, and nails, your own gods are headless! We are driven to the wild beasts—the same beasts, of course, which you associate with the service of Liber, Cybele, and Caelestis.[2] (5) We are burned in flames; this is the same treatment *they* receive right from the original lump of clay! We are condemned to the mines; that is where your gods get their start! We are relegated to the islands; it usually happens that on an island some god of yours was born or died! If such things as these constitute a measure of divinity, then those who inflict punishment on us consecrate us, and it should be said that the punishments have divine powers in them.

(6) Obviously, your gods are impervious to these injuries and the demeaning insults associated with their manufacture, even as they are impervious to your homage. O wicked words, O sacrilegious outcries! Gnash your teeth, foam with rage! You are the same ones who found [no] fault with a Seneca when, at greater length and with more bitter reproaches, he spoke about your superstitions.[3] (7) Therefore, if we do not adore cold statues and images made in the likeness of their dead originals, statues with which the kites and mice and spiders are well acquainted, is it not praise rather than punishment that we deserve for recognizing and repudiating the error? Can it seem that we are injuring those who, we are certain, have absolutely no existence? What is not in existence suffers nothing from any source, because it does not exist.

---

2 The chariot of Liber was drawn by tigers; that of Cybele, by lions. Caelestis, patroness of Carthage and identified with the goddess Astarte, was pictured riding a lion.
3 There is a textual difficulty here. Certainly, a negative is needed (unless the reading *probetis* of the *Codex Fuldensis* is accepted) in view of St. Augustine's remarks in *De civ. Dei* 6.10.

Chapter 13

(1) 'But, for us, the gods do exist,' you say. Then, how is it you are found to be wicked, sacrilegious, and irreligious toward your gods, neglect those whom you presume to exist, destroy those whom you fear, and make fun of those whom you champion? (2) Tell me if I am lying. In the first place, when some of you worship one set of gods, and others another set, you certainly offend the ones whom you fail to worship. There cannot be preference of one without causing insult to the other, because every choice implies a rejection. (3) You scorn those whom you reject, yet you do not fear to offend them by rejecting them. For, as we have mentioned before,[1] the status of any god depends on the Senate's opinion of him. He would not be a god whom a man, if consulted, would have rejected, and by rejecting would have cast aside.

(4) As for the household gods, whom you call the Lares, you treat them with a householder's power, pawning them, selling them, or changing them, sometimes making Saturn into a cooking pan or Minerva into a ladle,[2] according as each one of them becomes worn out and dented during its long worship, or as anyone finds out that a household necessity is holier [than the god]. (5) Similarly, under state law you disgrace the state gods and you treat them as sources of income at auction. You make your way to the Capitol just as you do to the vegetable market; it is at the same voice of the auctioneer, beneath the same hammer, under the same entry of the quaestor, that the deity is auctioned and goes to the highest bidder. (6) To make my meaning clearer, fields burdened with taxation are cheaper and persons subject to

---
1 Cf. *supra,* Ch. 5.1.
2 Saturn and Minerva are included in the term, Lares, since their statues were reserved in the lararium.

a head-tax are of lesser esteem (for this is a sign of subjection). On the other hand, gods who have a greater tax on them are of greater sanctity;[3] rather, one might say the greater the sanctity, the greater the tax. Their sovereignty results from their money-making. Religion goes around begging at all the shops. You demand a price for the ground in the temple, for the entrance to the holy place. It is forbidden to make the acquaintance of the gods gratis—they are to be had for a price.

(7) On the whole, what services do you perform in their honor that you do not perform also for your dead? You have shrines and altars for both alike; the same garb, the same decorations on the statues. As the talent and business of the deceased was, so also is the god. How does a funeral feast differ from a banquet of Jupiter, a mug from a sacrificial wine cup, an undertaker from an haruspex? For the latter, too, is in attendance upon the dead.

(8) It is fitting for you to proclaim divine honors for emperors after their death, since even in their lifetime you assent to it. Your gods will accept it gratefully; in fact, they will rejoice that their masters are now on the same level with themselves. (9) But, when you worship Larentina,[4] a public harlot (I might wish that at least it were Laïs or Phryne), together with your Junos, Cereses, and Dianas; when you set up Simon Magus with a statue and the inscription, 'Holy God';[5] when

---
3 Cybele, for example, paid tribute to the emperor. Regarding the begging priests of Cybele, cf. Min. Fel., *Oct.* 22.8 n.4 and Aug., *De civ. Dei* 7.26.
4 Concerning Acca Larentia (or Larentina), cf. Min. Fel., *Oct.* 25.8 n.12.
5 Tertullian confuses Simon Magus, whose encounter with the Apostles Peter and Paul is described in the Acts of the Apostles (8.9-24), with Semo Sancus, or, to give him his full Roman name, Semo Sancus Dius Fidius. In Rome, this ancient deity, who seems to occur also among the Oscans and Umbrians, appears in particular as a god of oaths. The error is found for the first time in St. Justin Martyr (*Apol.* I 26; cf. 56), who states that a statue had been erected to Simon Magus, with the inscription *Simoni Deo Sancto*, on the island of the Tiber in

you make a god of the Sacred Synod out of some favorite among the court pages[6]—even though your ancient gods are not more noble, at least they will deem it an insult on your part that you have granted this privilege to others which in days of old was conferred on them alone.

Chapter 14

(1) I would like to review your religious ceremonies, too. I say nothing of what you are like when you are sacrificing; anything that has been slain and is decaying and mangy you immolate. From rich and healthy animals you chop off any extra parts, like the head and hoofs, which at home you would have set aside for the slaves or dogs; on the altar of Hercules you place not even one-third of the tithes you owe him.[1] All the more should I praise your wisdom in that you salvage something from what is already a loss!

(2) Turning to your literature, whereby you are formed to wisdom and the duties befitting a gentleman, what utter absurdity do I find! On behalf of the Trojans and Greeks, the gods joined battle and fought it out among themselves like pairs of gladiators. Venus was wounded by the arrow of a mortal man because she wanted to rescue her son, Aeneas, who was almost killed by the same Diomedes.[2] (3) Mars

---

Rome. Afterwards, the error was repeated by a number of Christian writers; Irenaeus (*Adversus haereses* 1.23.1) and Eusebius (*Historia ecclesiastica* 2.13) both refer explicitly to St. Justin. The recovered inscription, however, reads *Semoni Sanco deo Fidio sacrum* (CIL VI 567), and so has nothing to do with Simon Magus.

6 The reference is to Antinous, a favorite of Hadrian, who committed suicide, moved by the superstitious idea that he could thus prolong the emperor's life. Hadrian then gave him a place among the gods.

---

1 The ancient writers frequently mention the custom of offering tithes to Hercules, and of sacrificing to him at least every ten days.
2 *Iliad* 5.330ff.

was almost worn out after thirteen months in chains.³ Lest Jupiter experience the same violence from the rest of the heavenly court, he was set free by the aid of a certain monster,⁴ and now weeps over the misfortune of Sarpedon,⁵ now lusts with a disgraceful passion for his sister, recounting to her the objects of his former amours who were never so beloved as she! (4) After this, what poet is to be found who is not a reviler of the gods, following the precedent of his leader?⁶ This one hands Apollo over to King Admetus to feed his flocks;⁷ another puts Neptune in charge of a building project for Laomedon.⁸ (5) There is even one well-known lyric poet —I mean Pindar—who sings of Aesculapius, who was punished for his avarice by a thunderbolt because in his practice of medicine he did injury to people's health.⁹ Jupiter was a wretch—if the thunderbolt is really his—who dishonored his grandson and envied the skilled practitioner! (6) If these tales are true, they ought not to have been recounted; if false, they should not have been invented by god-fearing men. But, as a matter of fact, neither tragic nor comic poets refrain from publicizing the calamities and errors in the household of any god.

(7) I pass over in silence the philosophers, satisfied merely to mention Socrates, who, as an insult to the gods, used to swear by an oak, a goat, or a dog. 'But,' you reply, 'Socrates was condemned for that very reason, since he undermined belief in the gods.' Yes, that is a fact; time and again—that means, always—truth is hated.¹⁰ (8) However, the Athenians

---

3 *Ibid.* 385-387.
4 *Viz.*, Briareus. Cf. *Iliad* 1.396ff.; *Aeneid* 10.567.
5 *Iliad* 16.458f.
6 Homer.
7 *Iliad* 2.766; Euripides, *Alcestis* (prologue).
8 *Iliad* 21.442f.
9 Pindar, *Pythian* 3.54ff.
10 Cf. Terence, *Andria* 68.

at last repented of this sentence, with the result that they later punished Socrates' accusers and placed a golden image of him in the temple. By repealing his sentence, they restored to Socrates his reputation.[11] (9) Diogenes, too, made some sportive remark or other in reference to Hercules, and the Roman Cynic, Varro, introduced three hundred Joves—or perhaps I should say Jupiters—minus their heads![12]

Chapter 15

(1) All the other lewd men of genius, too, revile the gods for your pleasure. Consider the attractive plays of men like Lentulus and Hostilius.[1] Is it the mimic actors you laugh at in their jokes and antics, or your gods? The program offers: 'Anubis, the Adulterer,' 'The Mannish Moon,' 'Diana Drubbed,' 'The Reading of the Late Jupiter's Will,' and 'Three Lean Herculeses—a Laughing-Stock.' (2) The text of your pantomimes, too, represents all the vileness of your gods. Sol mourns his son,[2] cast out of high heaven—it gives you a laugh; Cybele sighs passionately for her disdainful shepherd[3] —it causes you no blush of shame. You endure the songs which list the indictments against Jupiter and you let Juno, Venus, and Minerva be judged by a shepherd boy. (3) What of the fact that the face of your god covers the disgraceful and infamous head of the actor? That a lewd body, brought up with all the marks of effeminacy for this profession, represents a Minerva or a Hercules? Is not the majesty of your gods insulted and their godhead defiled by your applause?

---

11 Diog. Laert. (2.5.43).
12 Varro ridiculed the numerous gods of the Romans and reduced them all to one head, i.e., to one Jupiter.

---

1 Writers of mimes; only scant fragments of their writings are extant.
2 Phaëthon.
3 Attis.

(4) Of course, you are more devout in the seats of the amphitheater where, over human blood and the filth resulting from the tortures inflicted, your gods do their dancing and provide plots and stories for the guilty—except that the guilty, too, often assume the roles of your gods. (5) We once saw Attis, that god from Pessinus, castrated, and a man who was being burned alive played the role of Hercules. Then, too, at the gladiators' midday performance, in the midst of the cruelties of the entertainment, we laughed at Mercury testing the dead with his red-hot iron. We watched Jupiter's brother,[4] too, hammer in hand, dragging away the corpses of the gladiators. (6) Who could continue investigating all such details? If they disturb the honor of the godhead or sully the marks of majesty, they are to be explained as stemming from the contempt of those who do such things as well as of those for whom they do them.

(7) 'But,' you say, 'those are just public shows!' Then, I suppose, I should add facts which the conscience of everyone would just as readily recognize; namely, that adulteries are arranged in the temples, that pandering is carried on between the altars, that very commonly in the very abodes of the ministers and priests, and under their fillets and priestly caps and purple robes, while the incense is burning, they satisfy their lustful desires. Perhaps your gods have more fault to find with *you* than with the Christians. At any rate, those who are caught profaning the temples are always from your ranks, for the Christians have nothing to do with the temples, even in the daytime. Perhaps they themselves would despoil them if they, too, worshipped there.

(8) What is it that they worship, then, if they do not worship such things as these? This, certainly, is within your

---
4 Pluto, the god of the nether world.

power to understand: Those who do not worship falsehood worship Truth, and they no longer wander in an error wherein they have recognized their mistake and so have given it up. Grasp this point first and derive from it the whole system of our religion, after your false ideas about it have been first driven away!

Chapter 16

(1) Like certain others, you have talked foolishly about the head of an ass being our God. Cornelius Tacitus sowed the seed of such an idea as this. (2) In the fifth book of his *Histories,* he began the account of the Jewish War with the origin of this race; and, not only about the origin itself, but about the name and religion of the race, he used such arguments as he pleased. He states that the Jews who were liberated from Egypt, or, as he thought, exiled, were in the deserts of Arabia. While wasting away from thirst in regions absolutely devoid of water, they availed themselves of wild asses to guide them to a spring, since they thought the animals were perhaps coming from a pasture to seek a drink. In gratitude for this, they deified the head of an animal of this kind.[1]

(3) From this it was presumed, I suppose, that we, too, being closely related to the Jewish religion, are devoted to the worship of this same image.[2] But that same Cornelius Tacitus, certainly the most loquacious of falsifiers, relates in the same historical work that Gnaeus Pompey, after having captured Jerusalem, approached the temple to investigate the mysteries of the Jewish religion and found no statue there.[3] (4) Certainly, if what was worshipped was represented by some sta-

---
1 Cf. Tac., *Historiae* 5.3f. for the account of the wild asses.
2 Cf. Min. Fel., *Oct.* 9.3, and *infra,* note 9.
3 Cf. Tac., *Hist.* 5.9.

tue, nowhere would it be more likely to be on display than in its own shrine—all the more because that religion did not have to fear outside witnesses, however meaningless it might be. Only the priests were permitted to approach; moreover, a hanging curtain prevented others from observing what was within. (5) But you will not deny that all pack animals and whole mules, together with their patroness Epona,[4] are what *you* worship. Perhaps it is for *this* that we are condemned, because, of all those who worship all kinds of beasts and animals, we alone worship an ass!

(6) But, even one who considers us superstitious worshippers of a cross turns out to be, along with us, a devotee of the cross. When some piece of wood is worshipped, the appearance makes no difference, provided the quality of the material be the same; the form makes no difference, if the wood is itself the body of some god. Yet, how much difference is there between the shaft of a cross on the one hand and the Athenian Pallas or Pharian Ceres on the other?[5] The latter stands there, without any shape, on a rough stake of unpolished wood. (7) Every piece of wood which is fastened in an upright position is part of a cross. At any rate, if you insist on the point, we worship a god that is whole and entire. We have said[6] that the beginning of your gods can be traced to things fashioned by sculptors on a cross. Then, too, you adore trophies of Victory, although crosses constitute the trophies' inner parts. (8) The entire religion of Roman camp life consists of venerating standards, swearing by standards, plac-

---

4 The Celtic goddess of horses, mules, and asses. Cf. Min. Fel., *Oct.* 28.7.

5 Pausanias, *Arcadia* 32.4, recounts that Pallas was worshipped under the form of a square stone. Only Tertullian makes reference to the crude form of the statue at Pharis (Isis).

6 Cf. *supra*, Ch. 12.3.

ing standards before all the gods. All those rows of images on the standards are merely ornaments hung on crosses; the hangings of your flags and banners are but robes for crosses. I commend you for your caution: you did not want to worship crosses which were unadorned and naked.

(9) Others have an idea which is certainly more in accord with human nature and more likely; namely, that the sun is our god. If such is the case, we will be in a class with the Persians, although it is not the sun painted on a canvas that we adore, since we have it everywhere at present in its own orb. (10) To put it briefly, this suspicion started when it became known that we pray facing the East. But, even many of yourselves at times, with a pretense of adoring the heavenly bodies, move your lips toward the rising sun. (11) Likewise, if we devote Sunday to joyousness, for a reason other than that we worship the sun, still we take second place to those who set aside Saturday for resting and feasting; they themselves are far removed from the Jewish custom of which they know nothing.[7]

(12) A new representation of our god has quite recently been publicized in this city,[8] started by a certain criminal hired to dodge wild beasts in the arena. He displayed a picture with this inscription: '*Onokoites*, the god of the Christians.'[9] The figure had the ears of an ass, one foot was cloven,

---
7 Although the Romans had only confused ideas of Jewish observances, they set aside the Sabbath or Saturn's day as a day of rest. Cf. Horace, *Sermones* 1.9.69-72; Ovid, *Remedia amoris* 219f.
8 I.e., Carthage.
9 Among the *graffiti* on the Palatine is a crude picture of a crucified figure, having the head of an ass, and a man worshipping it. It bears the title, '*Alexamenos sebete theon*'—'Alexamenos worships his god' (cf. Min. Fel., *Oct.* 9.3 n.3). In *Ad nat.* 1.14, Tertullian describes the caricaturist of Carthage as a Jewish gladiator. *Onokoites* (from *onos* and *koites*) means 'he who lies in the manger of an ass,' 'the offspring of an ass.' Oehler, citing the glosses in Hesychius, writes *Onocoïetes*, 'the ass-worshipper.'

and it was dressed in a toga and carrying a book. We laughed at both the caption and the cartoon. (13) But our opponents should have adored this biform deity at once, because they have welcomed gods that had the head of both dog and lion conjoined,[10] the horns of a goat and a ram;[11] gods that had the loins of a goat,[12] the legs of a serpent,[13] and that had wings on foot and back. (14) These points I mention at length, lest it might seem that we had purposely passed over any rumor and left it unrefuted. Turning now to the explanation of our religion, we shall clear up all these matters.

Chapter 17

(1) The object of our worship is the one God, who, out of nothing, simply for the glory of His majesty, fashioned this enormous universe with its whole supply of elements, bodies, and spirits, and did so simply by the Word wherewith He bade it, the Reason whereby He ordered it, the Power wherewith He was powerful. Hence it is that even the Greeks apply the appropriate word 'cosmos' to the universe. (2) He is invisible, although He may be seen; intangible, although manifested by grace; immeasurable, although He may be measured by human senses. Therefore, He is so true and so great. However, what can be generally seen, touched, and measured is less than the eyes by which it is seen, the hands by which it is touched, and the senses by which it is discovered. But, what is infinite is known only to itself. (3) Thus it is that God can be measured, although He is beyond all measure;[1]

---

10 Anubis.
11 Pan.
12 The Satyrs.
13 The Chimaera.

---

1 Cf. Min. Fel., *Oct.* 18.8.

thus, the force of His magnitude makes Him known to men and yet unknown. And this is the gravest part of the sin of those who are unwilling to recognize Him of whom they cannot remain in ignorance.

(4) Do you wish us to prove His existence from His numerous, mighty works by which we are supported, sustained, delighted, and even startled? I repeat, do you wish us to prove Him from the testimony of the soul itself? (5) The soul, though it be repressed by the prison house of the body, though it be circumscribed by base institutions, weakened by lust and concupiscence, and enslaved to false gods, yet, when it revives, as from intoxication or sleep or some sickness and enjoys health again, names 'God' with this name alone because, properly speaking, He alone is true. 'Good God!' 'God Almighty!' and 'God grant it!' are expressions used by all mankind.[2] (6) That He is a Judge, also, is testified by the phrases: 'God sees,' and 'I commend it to God,' and 'God will reward me.' O testimony of the soul, which is by natural instinct Christian! In fine, then, the soul, as it utters these phrases, looks not to the Capitol but to heaven. It knows the abode of the living God; from Him and from there it has come.

Chapter 18

(1) But, in order that we might more fully and more energetically approach God Himself as well as His designs and desires, He has added the assistance of books, in case one wishes to search for God; and after searching, discover Him; and after discovering Him, believe in Him; and after believing in Him, serve Him. (2) From the beginning He sent into the world men who, because of their innocence and righteous-

---
2 Cf. *ibid.* 18.11; Tert., *De testimonio animae* 2.

ness, were worthy to know God and to make Him known to others. These men He filled with the Holy Spirit that they might teach that there is but one God who made the universe and formed man from the earth. He is the true Prometheus,[1] who has regulated the world with a fixed order and fixed endings for the ages. (3) Furthermore, what signs of His sovereign power to judge has He manifested by means of rain and fire! What regulations has He prescribed for placing men under obligation to Himself! What recompense has He determined for those who are ignorant of them, those who neglect them, and those who observe them; for, after the present life is ended, He will direct His faithful followers to the reward of eternal life, but the wicked to everlasting and unending fire. Then, all those who have died from the beginning of time will be revived. Their bodies will be reformed. There will be a general review, and everyone will be examined according to his own merits. (4) These are points at which we, too, laughed in times past. We are from your own ranks: Christians are made, not born!

(5) These teachers whom we mentioned are called prophets, because it is their function to foretell the future. Their words, as well as the miracles which they performed to win faith in their divine mission, are preserved in the treasures of literature and these are accessible. The most learned of the Ptolemies, surnamed Philadelphus,[2] well-versed in all literature, rivalled Pisistratus, I believe, in his interest in libraries. Among other memorable accounts whereby antiquity or research has given some support to his reputation, there is a

---

[1] For the story of Prometheus fashioning man, cf. Ovid, *Metamorphoses* 1.82f.
[2] Ptolemy II Philadelphus, 285-247 B.C.

story that at the suggestion of Demetrius of Phalerum,[3] the most highly-approved grammaticus of the time, to whom had been entrusted the position of head librarian, Ptolemy asked for books also from the Jews, their own literature written in their own tongue—books which they alone possessed.[4] (6) For, from the Jews had the prophets come and to the Jews they had always spoken, as to the race of God in accord with the favor shown to their fathers. In times past, those who are now Jews were Hebrews; therefore, their literature is Hebraic, too, and so is their speech. (7) But, lest the knowledge [of their books] lie idle, the Hebrew was also translated for Ptolemy by the Jews: seventy-two translators were assigned to him—men whom Menedemus, himself a philosopher,[5] the defender of belief in Providence, esteemed because of their agreement with his views. Aristaeus, too, has told this story to you.[6] (8) In this way he left these records completely translated into Greek; to this day in Ptolemy's library, the Serapeum, they are on display, together with the Hebrew originals. (9) Even the Jews read and reread them openly.

---

3 After governing Athens successfully, Demetrius was driven into exile by his enemies in 307 B.C. He fled to Egypt and was hospitably received by Ptolemy Soter, and, according to one version of the story, enjoyed the confidence of Philadelphus.

4 Clement of Alexandria (*Stromata* 1.22), following Aristeas, tells us that at the request of Philadelphus seventy learned scholars were sent by the Jews, and, although they worked privately, produced translations of their laws and their prophets which, upon comparison, were found to correspond perfectly with each other. Cf. St. Justin Martyr, *Apology* I 31; Philo, *Vita Moys.* 2.5; Josephus, *Ant. Jud.* 12.12ff.; Eusebius, *Praepar. ev.* 12.12.1.

5 Regarding Menedemus, disciple of Phaedo and others of Plato's friends, cf. Diog. Laert. (2.17).

6 Aristeas was an official in the court of Philadelphus. There is extant an apocryphal letter of his which is responsible for the origin of the story about the seventy translators at work in their private cells. Philo, Josephus, and Clement of Alexandria used the so-called Letter of Aristeas for their narrative on the origin of the Septuagint.

For that freedom they must pay a tax,[7] and generally they make use of it every Sabbath. He who listens will find God; he who exerts himself to understand will also be led to believe.

Chapter 19

(1) Their great antiquity claims prime authority for these records. Among you, too, it is in accord with your superstitious ideas to make faith depend on times past.[1]

[(1) Great antiquity provides authority for literature. Moses was the first of the Prophets; he wove from the past the account of the foundation of the world and the formation of the human race and afterwards the mighty deluge which took vengeance upon the godlessness of that age; he prophesied events right up to his own day. Then, by means of conditions of his own time, he showed forth an image of times to come; according to him, too, the order of events, arranged from the beginning, supplied the reckoning of the age of the world: Moses is found to be alive about 300 years before Danaus, your most ancient of men, came over to Argos. (2) He is 1,000 years earlier than the Trojan War and, therefore, the time of Saturn himself. For, according to the history of Thallus, where it is related that Belus, King of the Assyrians, and Saturn, King of the Titans, fought with Jupiter, it is shown that Belus antedated the fall of Troy by 322 years. It was by

---

7 After the capture of Jerusalem a tax was imposed upon the Jews by Vespasian. In return for this they were permitted to assemble in their synagogues and continue their own religion.

---

1 At this point, the text of the *Codex Fuldensis,* while preserving general ideas, is so differently phrased that it is usually printed for purposes of comparison. In spite of much research, no decision has been reached as to whether this version may be safely attributed to Tertullian or to an earlier apologist whom he and Minucius Felix used.

this same Moses, too, that their own true law was given to the Jews by God. (3) Next, other Prophets, too, have set forth many facts more ancient than your literature; even the last of the Prophets was either a little earlier or, at any rate, a contemporary of your wise men and lawmakers. (4) Zacharias lived in the reigns of Cyrus and Darius, at the time when Thales, first of the natural philosophers, in reply to the question of Croesus, said that nothing is certain regarding divinity, being disturbed, I suppose, by the words of the Prophets. After the manner of the Prophets, Solon told the same king that it is the end of a long life that one should envisage.

(5) Hence, it can be perceived that your laws as well as your learning were conceived from the law of God and divine teaching. What is first must of necessity be the seed. Thence you derive certain terms in common with us or very similar to ours: (6) the love of wisdom is called 'philosophy' from *sophia;* the striving after prophecy has derived the poetic term, 'vaticination,' from *prophetia.* Whatever glory men found, they have corrupted it to make it their own. Fruit has been known to deteriorate from its seed. (7) Still, in many ways I would maintain a very firm position about the antiquity of the Sacred Books, were there not at hand a consideration of greater weight in proving their trustworthiness which results from the power of their truth rather than from the evidence of their antiquity. For, what will more powerfully defend their testimony than their daily fulfillment throughout the whole world, when the rise and fall of kingdoms, the fate of cities, the ruin of nations, the conditions of the times, correspond in all respects just as they were announced thousands of years ago? (8) By this, too, our hope—which you deride—is animated, and our trust—which you call presumption—is strengthened. For, a review of the past is likely

to incline one to trust in the future: the same voices foretold both alike; the same books noted both. (9) In them, time—which to us seems to be split in two—is one. Thus, all that remains unproved has already been proved, as far as we are concerned, because it was foretold together with that which has been proved and with the things which at that time were yet to be. (10) You have, I know, a Sibyl, inasmuch as this name for a true prophetess of the true God has been everywhere appropriated for all who appeared to have the gift of prophecy; and just as your Sibyls have been deceitful regarding the truth in the matter of their name,[2] so also have your gods.]

(2) So, all the subject matter; all the material, origins, arrangements, sources of any of your ancient writings; even most of your races and cities, illustrious for their history and hoary, as far as records go; the very character of the letters whereby the events are indicated and preserved; and—I think we are still indulging in understatement—those very gods of yours, I say, and those temples, oracles, and sanctuaries —all are antedated by centuries by the writings of a single Prophet, in which it appears that there has been collected the store of knowledge of the entire Jewish religion and, from thence, of our own religion, too. (3) You may have heard, in the meanwhile, of Moses; he would be of the same age as the Argive Inachus; by nearly 400 years—actually, it was seven years less—he antedated Danaus, whom you consider the most ancient of your race; he lived about 1,000 years before the death of Priam; I might even say that he was about 1,500 years earlier than Homer, too, and I have reliable authorities to follow.[3] (4) As for the rest of the Prophets, too,

---

[2] For etymology of Sibylla, *dei mens,* cf. Isidore, *Origines* 8.8.1.
[3] This opinion regarding the age of Moses was generally held among the early Apologists. Cf. also, Lact., *Inst. div.* 4.5.6.

although they lived after Moses, are not their very latest representatives older than the earliest of your philosophers, lawgivers, and historians?

(5) The task would not be so difficult as it would be endless for us to explain by what means these points could be proved; the enumeration would not offer much trouble, but, in the present circumstances, it would take a long time. Many records, together with much mathematical calculation on the fingers, would have to be used. The archives of the most ancient of all peoples, the Egyptians, Chaldeans, and Phoenicians, would have to be laid open. (6) We would need to have recourse to the fellow citizens of those through whom this information has come to us, men like Manetho of Egypt, Berosus of Chaldea, and Hieromus of Phoenicia, King of Tyre; their followers, too—Ptolemy of Mendes, Menander of Ephesus, Demetrius of Phalerum, King Juba, Apion, Thallus, Josephus the Jew, the native defender of Jewish antiquities, and any other who either substantiates or refutes them.

(7) The Greeks' census lists, too, would have to be consulted to see what was done and when, that the time sequence might be made clear and the order of the records clarified; one would have to go through the foreign histories and literatures of the world. Yet, we have already introduced, as it were, a part of the proof when we have mentioned the names of some through whom all can be proved. (8) It is much better to postpone the proof, lest, in our haste, we either accomplish too little or digress too far from the point in accomplishing it.

Chapter 20

(1) We now will offer further details to compensate for this postponement: we draw attention to the high quality of

the Sacred Scriptures in case we do not prove them divine on the score of their antiquity or if there is still any doubt as to their age. This point is to be grasped at once and from no far distant source: that which will teach us is right at hand; namely, the world, all time, all events. (2) All that is now happening was foretold; all that is now seen was heard—that lands swallow up cities, that seas make off with islands, that wars abroad and at home tear the world asunder, that kingdoms contend with kingdoms, that famine, pestilence, and death resulting from local conditions and untold numbers of the slain everywhere render the land desolate, that the lowly are raised to lofty positions and the exalted brought low, (3) that justice fades away, that evil gains ground from day to day, that indifference to all cultural pursuits holds sway, that even the seasons and elements deviate in the performance of their regular functions, that the order of nature is disturbed by monsters and portents—all has been written with divine foresight. Even while we experience these happenings, they are being read; while we recall them, they are being fulfilled. The actual fulfillment of the prophecy is, I dare say, sufficient indication of its inspired nature. (4) In consequence of all this, it is safe for us to trust in the future, also, which we may consider already proved, since it has been predicted as well as events which each day are being proved true. The same voices give it utterance; the same literature records it; the same spirit animates it. All time is *one* to prophecy which foretells the future. (5) Among men, perhaps, time is considered in parts while it is finishing its course: from being future it is regarded as present and from present, past. What mistake do we make, I ask you, if we trust in the future, too, since by now we have learned, through two other divisions of time, to believe it true?

Chapter 21

(1) Since we have declared that this religion of ours depends upon very ancient Jewish records — although most people know it only as something of a novelty which came to birth during the reign of Tiberius (a fact which we ourselves acknowledge)—perhaps on this ground there should be further treatment of its status, as if, under the protecting name of a very well-known religion (and one that is, at any rate, lawful), it were concealing some claims of its own; (2) because, aside from the question of age, we have nothing to do with the Jews on any of these points: the taboo on certain kinds of food, the observance of certain holy days, the bodily 'seal,'[1] and the possession of a common name—matters upon which we certainly should agree were we subject to the same God. (3) However, by now, men in general know of Christ as [merely] one of mankind, as the Jews thought Him; a circumstance in virtue of which one may more readily think that we worship a mere man. But, we are not ashamed of Christ, since it is a pleasure to be designated by His name and condemned for it; nor do we have any different thoughts of God. Accordingly, it is necessary to speak briefly about Christ, inasmuch as He is God.

(4) At all times the Jews enjoyed favor with God and there also were outstanding justice and faith on the part of their original founders. As a result, their race multiplied and their kingdom rose to exalted power. Such good fortune was theirs that, by the words of God whereby they were taught, they were forewarned about serving God and not offending Him. (5) To what extent they failed, being so filled with presumptuous confidence in their ancestors as to stray from

---
1 Circumcision.

their teaching into the manners of the world—even if they did not acknowledge it themselves—the unhappy lot that today is theirs would indicate. Scattered, wandering about, deprived of land and sky of their own, they roam the earth without man or God as king, a race to whom there is not accorded the right granted to foreigners to set foot upon and greet one land as home. (6) The holy voices which warned them of this fate all insisted always on the same points: that the day would come in the last cycles of time when God would select for Himself worshippers from every race and people and place—worshippers much more faithful, to whom He would transfer His favor in fuller measure because they were receptive of a fuller doctrine.

(7) Consequently, there came the One who God had foretold would come to renew and shed light upon that doctrine; namely, Christ, the Son of God. It was proclaimed beforehand that the Lord and Master of this grace and doctrine, the Enlightener and Guide of the human race, would be the Son of God, yet His birth was not such that He must blush at the name of son or the thought of paternal seed. (8) Not as the result of incestuous intercourse with a sister or the violation of a daughter or another's wife has He for His Father a god with scales or horns or wings, nor one who, like the lover of Danaë, was turned into gold. Such are the human names which you have attributed to Jupiter; such are your deities.[2] (9) But the Son of God has no mother in any sense which involves the violation of her purity; in fact, she who is regarded as His mother did not marry [i.e. consummate her

---

2 Tertullian's scorn for the immoral features of the well-known myths to which he refers is unmistakable in spite of the confused condition of the text and the difficulty of a literal translation. *Nomina, numina,* and *humana* are all attacked and rejected or accepted by various editors of the *Apology*.

marriage]. But, let me discuss His nature first; then the manner of His birth will be understood.

(10) We have already said[3] that God fashioned this whole world by His word, His reason, His power. Even your own philosophers[4] agree that *logos,* that is, Word and Reason, seems to be the maker of the universe. This *logos* Zeno defines as the maker who formed everything according to a certain arrangement; the same *logos* (he says) is called Destiny, God, the Mind of Jupiter, and the inevitable Fate of all things. Cleanthes combines all these predicates into Spirit, which, according to him, permeates the universe.[5] (11) Moreover, we, too, ascribe Spirit as its proper substance to that Word, Reason, and Power by which, as we have said, God made everything. For, in Spirit giving utterance, there would be the Word; with Spirit arranging all things, Reason would cooperate; and in Spirit perfecting all things, Power would be present. This, as we have been taught, has been uttered by God and begotten by this utterance, and is, therefore, called the Son of God and God on account of the unity of nature; for God, too, is Spirit. (12) When a ray is shot forth from the sun, a part is taken from the whole; but there will be sun in the ray because it is a sun ray; its nature is not separated, but extended. Thus, spirit proceeds from spirit and God from God just as light is kindled from light. The source of the substance remains whole and unimpaired, although you may borrow from it many offshoots of its quality. (13) Thus, too, what proceeds from God is God and the Son of God, and both are one; similarly, Spirit proceeds from Spirit and God from God, making two by the measure of existence, plurality by

---
3 Cf. *supra,* Ch. 17.1.
4 The Stoics.
5 Seneca, *Quaestiones naturales* 2.45, sets forth these principles of Stoic teaching. Cf. Min. Fel., *Oct.* 19.2, and Cic., *De nat. deor.* 1.14.37.

gradation, but not by condition; He has not separated from, but proceeded from the producing cause.⁶

(14) This ray of God, then, as was ever foretold in the past, descended into a certain virgin and, becoming flesh in her womb, was born as one who is man and God united. The flesh, provided with a soul, is nourished, matures, speaks, teaches, acts, and *is* Christ.

For the moment, accept this account—it resembles your own tales—while we show how Christ is proved and who they are who have supplied you with contradictory stories which aim at the destruction of such truth. (15) The Jews, too, knew that Christ would come; in fact, they were the ones to whom the Prophets spoke. Even now they are expecting His coming, and there is no stronger bone of contention between them and us than their refusal to believe that He has already come. For His two comings have been made known: the first has already been fulfilled, when He came in the lowliness of human nature; the second is to come at the end of the world in the manifestation of the majesty of His Godhead. The Jews did not understand the first; the second, which was more clearly prophesied and for which they hope, they considered the only one. (16) That they should not believe the first coming—but they would have believed had they understood, and would have attained salvation had they believed—that was the result of their sins. They themselves read what has thus been written: they have been deprived of wisdom and understanding and the fruit of eyes and ears.⁷

(17) Therefore, since they considered Him merely a man, on the basis of His lowliness, it followed that they came to esteem Him as a wonder-worker because of His power. For, with a word He drove evil spirits from men, gave sight again

---

6 Cf. Tert., *Adversus Praxean* 2.
7 Isa. 6.9,10.

to the blind, cleansed lepers, healed paralytics, and finally, by a word, restored the dead to life; He reduced to obedience the very elements of nature, calming storms, walking upon the water, manifesting that He was the Word of God. In other words, He is that original, first-born *Logos,* endowed with power and reason and sustained by spirit, the same who, by a mere word, still creates and did create all things. (18) As for His teaching, whereby the teachers and elders of the Jews were refuted, they were so embittered, particularly because large numbers turned aside to follow Him, that they finally brought Jesus before Pontius Pilate, who at that time was governing Syria[8] in the interests of Rome, and by the violence of their demands they forced Pilate to hand Him over to them to be crucified. He Himself had foretold that they would do just this; that might be of slight account, had not the Prophets also foretold it long before. (19) Yet, fastened to the cross—the death appointed for Him—He manifested many signs which distinguished His death. For He anticipated the duty of the executioner[9] and, with a word, of His own accord, He breathed forth His spirit. At the same moment, although the sun was in the midst of her course, the daylight disappeared. Those who did not know that this, too, had been foretold of Christ thought that there was merely an eclipse. Yet, you have this disappearance of the sun all over the world related in your own archives.

(20) Then He was taken down [from the cross] and laid in a sepulcher. The Jews carefully surrounded the place with a large band of armed guards, lest—since He had foretold that on the third day He would rise from the dead—His disciples steal away His Body and thereby trick them for all

---
[8] Pilate was not governor of Syria, but procurator of Judaea, which belonged to the province of Syria.
[9] Cf. John 19.31ff.

their apprehension. (21) But, lo! on the third day the earth suddenly quaked and the massive stone which blocked the entrance to the sepulcher rolled back. The guards were scattered in fear and, although none of His disciples appeared on the scene, there was nothing to be found in the sepulcher except the winding sheets. (22) In spite of all this, since it was to the interest of the elders to spread a false story and reclaim from their faith in Christ the tribute-paying, service-rendering people, they spread the report that the body had been stolen by the disciples. For, Christ did not show Himself in public lest the wicked be freed from their blunder, and so that their faith, destined for no slight reward, might, by very reason of this difficulty, be firmly established. (23) However, He passed forty days with some of His disciples in Galilee, a province of Judaea, teaching them what they were to teach. Then, when they had been ordained for the office of preaching throughout the world, a cloud enveloped Him and He was taken up into heaven, a story that is much truer than the one which, among you, people like Proculus are wont to swear is true about Romulus.[10]

(24) All these facts about Christ were reported to Tiberius, the reigning emperor, by Pilate who was by now a Christian himself, as far as his conscience was concerned. And the Caesars, too, would have believed about Christ, had Caesars not been necessary for the world, or if Christians could have been Caesars. (25) The disciples, too, hearkening to the command of God, their Master, spread throughout the world, and, after enduring with constancy much suffering from the persecution of the Jews, finally, because of the savage cruelty of Nero, sowed the seed of Christian blood at Rome with joy, through their confidence in the truth.

---

10 According to Livy (1.16), Proculus, a Roman senator, swore that Romulus had appeared to him and requested that the Romans worship him under the title of Quirinus. Cf. Min. Fel., *Oct.* 21.9.

(26) But, we are going to show you that those very demons whom you adore are fit witnesses to Christ.[11] It is a matter of some moment if I employ those because of whom you do not believe the Christians as a means of making you believe the Christians. (27) For the present, you have a coherent outline [of the history] of our founding; we have explained here the origin of our religion and of our name in connection with its Founder.

Let no one any longer cast dishonor upon us, let no one think we have presented our case incorrectly, because it is not right for anyone to lie about his religion. For, if one says that he worships something other than he does worship, he denies what he worships. He transfers the worship and honor to another, and, in transferring it, no longer worships what he has denied. (28) We say—and we say openly—and, though covered with wounds and blood, we cry out to you, our torturers: 'It is God we worship, through Christ!' Think of Him as a Man; it is through Him and in Him that God wills to be known and worshipped. (29) To reply to the Jews: they themselves learned to worship God through a man, Moses. In answer to the objection of the Greeks: Orpheus in Pieria, Musaeus in Athens, Melampus in Argos, Trophonius in Boeotia bound men to religious duties through initiation cermonies. Glancing at you, too, the rulers of the nations: it was a man, Numa Pompilius, who burdened the Romans with their most wearisome superstitions. (30) Christ, too, might have expounded divinity, His own attribute, not in order to mold to refinement men who were rustics and still untamed by making them attentive to the tremendous number of deities to be served, as Numa did, but as one who would open to a recognition of the truth the eyes of men who were already refined and, by their very sophistication, de-

---

11 Cf. *infra,* Ch. 23.4-11.

ceived. (31) Examine, therefore, whether the divinity of Christ is true. If it is, and if its recognition remakes men for good, it follows that you must renounce the false, when in its full light the nature of what you believe is revealed to you. Concealed beneath the names of images of dead men, your false deities, by certain signs and wonders and oracles, bring about faith in their own divinity.

Chapter 22

(1) And so, we say that there exist certain spiritual natures. The term is not new; the philosophers know of evil spirits, like Socrates himself awaiting the will of his *daimon*. Why not; since it is said that a *daimon* was attached to him from the days of his childhood, which obviously held him back from the path of goodness.[1] (2) All the poets know of them; even the unlettered man of the street makes frequent use of a curse, for in the same tone of execration he pronounces the name of Satan, the leader of this wicked race—and does this as a result of the soul's instinctive knowledge. Again, Plato did not deny the existence of angels. As witnesses to the names of both [good and evil spirits], the magicians are at hand. (3) As for the details of how some of the angels, of their own accord, were perverted and then constituted the source of the even more corrupt race of devils, a race damned by God together with the originators of the race and him whom we have mentioned as their leader, the account is found in Sacred Scripture.[2]

---

1 Tertullian regarded the *daimonion* of Socrates as evil. To Socrates, however, the word had a very different meaning. Cicero rendered it correctly by translating it as something divine. The promptings of Socrates' *daimonion* were the dictates of conscience.
2 Tertullian alludes to Gen. 6.2, where, instead of 'Sons of God' the Cod. Alexandrinus of the Septuagint reads 'angels of God.'

(4) For the present, it will be sufficient to explain their mode of action. Their business is to corrupt mankind; thus, the spirit of evil was from the very beginning bent upon man's destruction. The demons, therefore, inflict upon men's bodies diseases and other bitter misfortunes, and upon the soul sudden and extraordinary outbursts of violence. (5) They have their own subtle, spiritual properties for assailing each part of human nature. Much power is allowed their spiritual faculties, with the result that, without being apprehended by sight or any of the other senses, they are more evident in the outcome of their activity than in the activity itself. So it is, for example, in the case of fruit or crops, when something imperceptible in the air casts a blight upon the flower, kills the bud, and injures the development; as if the air, tainted in some unseen manner, were spreading abroad its pestilential breath. (6) It is with the same mysterious power of infection that the breath of demons and [fallen] angels induces the corruption of the mind by foul passions, by dread derangements of the mind, or by savage lusts accompanied by manifold perversities. Of the latter, the greatest is that whereby those gods are foisted upon the seduced and deluded minds of men so that they may procure for themselves a proper diet of fumes and blood offered to their statues and images. (7) And what field of operation is more carefully watched for their benefit than that by which they might be enabled to turn man aside, by tricks of deception, from contemplation of the true God? I will explain, too, how these illusions are set in operation.

(8) Every spirit is [as though it were] winged. Both angels and demons have this property. Therefore, they are everywhere in a moment. For them, the whole world is but a single place; what happens and where it happened they can know and tell with the same ease. Their swiftness is considered a

divine power because their nature is not understood. Thus, too, they sometimes want to appear to be the authors of what they tell. Actually, they always are the authors of the evil, but never of the good. (9) They even have borrowed the counsels of God which the Prophets of old proclaimed, and today, as their prophecies continue to be declaimed, they continue to borrow. In this way and from these sources they derive information concerning certain fortunes of the times, and they strive to rival the divine power of God, while they try to steal His power to foretell.

(10) In the matter of oracles, moreover, people like Croesus and Pyrrhus know with what ingenuity they arrange their ambiguous answers to suit the events; why, in the manner we have just mentioned, the Pythian Apollo reported that a tortoise was cooking along with some mutton: a moment before he had been in Lydia.[3] From dwelling in the air[4] and being close to the stars and having communication with the clouds they know well of the proceedings going on in the skies, so that they can even promise the rain—which they already feel falling. (11) And they certainly are charitable regarding their care for your health! For, first they hurt you, then they prescribe remedies which are novel or even injurious; afterwards—so that there may be a miracle—they stop hurting and are considered responsible for the cure. (12) What, then, should I say of the rest of their cleverness or even of the powers of the deceitful spirits—the apparitions of the Heavenly Twins, the water carried in a sieve, the boat propelled with

---

[3] Herodotus (1.47.53) tells of the famous oracle given to Croesus, and Cicero, *De divinatione* 2.56.116, quotes the oracle which Pyrrhus received regarding his victory over the Romans.

[4] The earlier ecclesiastical writers repeatedly interpreted the phrase in Eph. 6.12 in this way, so that they thought the evil spirits were ever present in the lower regions of the air.

a belt, and the beard which turned red with a touch[5]—that stones are believed to possess divine power and that the true God is not sought?

Chapter 23

(1) Furthermore, if magicians evoke spirits and dishonor the souls of the dead, if they kill children to make an oracle speak, if, with quackish jugglers' tricks, they try to imitate many miracles, if they even send dreams, having always at hand to assist them the power of angels and demons whom they have solicited, through whom even goats and tables have become accustomed to utter prophecies, how much more eager would this power be, of its own will and for its own interests, to perform with all its strength what it now does in the affairs of another! (2) Or, if angels and demons do just what your gods do, then where is the superiority of divine power, which certainly should be considered superior to every other power? Will it not be more consistent to believe that they are the very ones who set themselves up as gods, since they do the same things as make men believe in gods, than to believe that gods are on a level with angels and demons? (3) The difference of location is stressed, I suppose, so that in the temples you may think of them as gods, although you do not call them gods anywhere else. Your idea is to create the impression that one who tries to fly through sacred towers[1] suffers from a mental derangement different from his who jumps from one neighbor's roof to another, and the power which belongs to one who castrates himself or slashes his

---
5 These stories may be found in Valerius Maximus (1.8.1;8.1 *absol.* 5); Livy (29.14.10-13); and Suetonius, *Nero* 1.

---
1 What Tertullian means by this phrase is unknown.

muscles[2] is declared to be different from that of one who cuts his own throat. The outcome of the madness is the same and it is one and the same motive which instigates it.

(4) But, that is enough on this point; there now follows a demonstration of the fact itself, whereby we shall point out that the nature of both terms is the same. Let there be produced right here before your tribunals someone who, it is well known, is beset by an evil spirit. If any Christian bids the spirit to speak, the same will confess that he is a devil, just as truly as elsewhere he will falsely proclaim himself a god. (5) In a similar way, let there be selected one of those who are thought to be under the influence of a god, who conceive the divine power from the fumes which they inhale at the altars, who are relieved by belching, and who prophesy by gasping for breath. (6) Take that maiden of yours, Caelestis,[3] the one who promises rain, or your Aesculapius, teacher of the healing arts, dispenser of life to Socordius, Thanatius, and Asclepiodotus,[4] who are to die another day; if they do not confess that they are devils—not daring to lie to a Christian—then right here and now shed the blood of that bold Christian!

(7) What is more revealing than such a performance? What more trustworthy than such a demonstration? Truth in its simplicity is right out in the open; its own virtue stands ready to defend it; there is no room for suspicion. 'But,' you would say—if your eyes and ears permitted you—'it is done

---

2 An ironical reference to the priests of Cybele.
3 Goddess of Carthage, often identified with Astarte of the Phoenicians. Tertullian, alone, in this passage refers to her power to send rain, but he has already (Ch. 22.10) referred to the pagans' belief that their deities (or devils) had this power.
4 Unknown names; guesses range from their being names of men to names of herbs.

by magic or some such trickery.' (8) What objection can be made against that which is displayed in its undisguised sincerity? On the one hand, if they really are gods, why do they lie and declare that they are devils? Is it that they may do us a favor? Ah! then, your divinity has become subject to the Christians! Certainly, that should not be considered divinity which is subject to a man, and—if anything can add to the humiliation—to its own enemies. (9) On the other hand, if they are devils or angels, why do they, in other places, reply that they represent the gods? Just as those who are considered gods would be unwilling to say they were devils if they were really gods, being, naturally enough, loath to degrade themselves from their position of majesty, so, too, those whom you know from first-hand information to be devils would not dare to represent gods at times if any of those whose names they use were actually gods at all. They would be afraid to abuse the majesty of those on high who, unquestionably, are to be feared. (10) So, there is nothing to that idea which you entertain about their divine power, because, if it really did exist, it would not be affected by devils in their open avowals, nor would it be disclaimed by the gods.

Therefore, since both groups agree on the statement and say that there are no gods, realize that there exists but one kind—devils—for both sides.

(11) Now, start looking for gods; for the ones whom you had presumed were gods you now recognize as devils. By this action of ours, since those gods of yours reveal not merely this fact, that neither they themselves nor any other beings are gods, you all at once realize this, too: namely, what God really is, whether He is the One and the only One whom we Christians acknowledge, and whether He is to be believed and worshipped in the way that the faith and practice of the Christians have set down. (12) Here, some might say: 'And

who is this Christ with His nonsense?' if He were merely a man of ordinary station in life, or a magician, or if after death He had been stolen from the tomb by His disciples and were now with the dead instead of being in heaven—from whence He is to come, amid the confusion of the whole earth, and the terror of the world, and the wailing of all save Christians, as the Power of God and the Spirit of God, as the Word and Wisdom and Reason of God, and as the Son of God.

(13) Whatever you laugh at, the devils may laugh at, too, along with you; let them deny that Christ is to judge every soul that has been from the beginning of time after its body has been restored to it; let them, if they like, say that Minos and Rhadamanthus have been assigned as a court for this purpose, according to the mutual agreement of Plato and the poets. (14) At least, let them refute the mark of their disgrace and condemnation; let them deny that they are unclean spirits, a fact which ought to be perceived even from the diet on which they feed—blood, and smoke, and fetid, burning heaps of animal flesh, as well as the unspeakably foul speech of their priests; let them reject the charge that for their wickedness they have been condemned in advance to the same day of judgment, with all their devotees and their works.

15) Yet, this whole mastery and power of ours over them derives its effectiveness from the mere mention of the name of Christ and the reminder of those punishments which they expect will come upon them from God through Christ, His Arbiter. Fearing Christ in God and God in Christ, they are subject to the servants of God and of Christ. (16) Thus, at a touch, a breath from us, rebuked by the thought and description of that fire, at our command, they quit the bodies of men—but against their will and grieving and blushing be-

cause you are present. (17) Believe them when they tell the truth about themselves, you who believe them when they lie! No one lies to bring disgrace upon himself, but rather for honor. We are more inclined to put faith in those who confess to their own disadvantage than in those who deny for their own advantage.

(18) Finally, these testimonials of your gods have habitually made converts to Christianity; by placing utmost trust in them, we show that we trust God in Christ. They themselves enkindle faith in our literature; they themselves build up confidence in our hope. (19) You worship them, as far as I know, even with the blood of Christians. They would be loath, therefore, to lose such profitable, such obliging devotees, lest at some later date, when you have become Christians, they be put to flight, if they are now allowed to lie while being examined by a Christian who wishes to prove the truth to you.

Chapter 24

(1) This whole confession of theirs, whereby they deny that they are gods and declare that there is no other god but the One whose subjects we are, is quite sufficient to repel the charge of treason to the Roman religion. For, if the existence of the gods is uncertain, then surely the existence of your religion is uncertain, too. If there is no religion, since you have no gods for certain, then it is certain we are not guilty of violating religion. (2) On the contrary, your charge will act as a boomerang upon yourselves. In worshipping falsehood you not only neglect—or, I should say (even more than this), do violence to—the true religion of the true God, you actually commit the crime of positive irreligion.

(3) Now, suppose the fact were established that gods exist: do you not acquiesce in the common opinion that some god is more sublime and more powerful, and, as it were, the ruler of this universe, a god of perfect majesty? That is the way most men apportion divine power; they would have the power of supreme command in the hands of one, but its exercise in the hands of many. Thus, Plato describes the mighty Jupiter in heaven attended by a host of both gods and demons;[1] so (they say) the procurators, prefects, and governors ought to be held in equal esteem. (4) Yet, what crime does one commit who, in order to render better service to Caesar, transfers his attention and his hope and declares that the title of God, like that of emperor, belongs to none other than the one sovereign, since it is considered a capital offense to call anyone Caesar but Caesar and to listen to such talk? (5) Let one worship God, and another Jupiter; let one extend his hands in supplication to heaven, and another to the altar of Fides; let one (if you so suppose), count the clouds[2] as he prays, and another the squares of the panelled ceiling; let one offer to his God his own soul, and another the soul of a goat.

(6) See to it, rather, that this, too, does not tend to confirm the reproach of irreligion; namely, for you to take away one's freedom of religion and put a ban on one's free choice of a god, with the result that it is not lawful for me to worship whom I will, but I am compelled to worship contrary to my will. No one, not even a man, will be willing to receive the worship of an unwilling client.

(7) Even the Egyptians were allowed the right—vain superstition that it was—to deify birds and beasts and to con-

---

[1] Plato, *Phaedrus* 246E.
[2] This was a charge made against the Christians because they assembled for prayer in open courts, without altars or statues, and raised their eyes to heaven. Juvenal (14.96ff.) ridicules the Jews on similar grounds.

demn to death anyone who killed a god of this sort. (8) Then, too, every province and city has its own god; for example, there is Atargatis in Syria, Dusares in Arabia, Belenus in Noricum, Caelestis in Africa, and the petty kings in Mauretania. The provinces which I have mentioned are, I believe, Roman, but the gods are not, because they are not worshipped at Rome any more than those gods who are listed on the roster of local deities all through Italy itself: Delventinus of Casinum, Visidianus of Narnia, Ancharia of Asculum, Nortia of Volsinii, Valentia of Ocriculum, and Hostia of Sutrium; Juno, among the Faliscans, even received a surname in honor of Father Curis.[3] (9) We are the only ones kept from having our own religion. We offend the Romans and are not considered Romans because we do not worship the god of the Romans. (10) It is well that there is one God of all, to whom we all belong whether we will or not. But among you it is lawful to worship anything you choose except the true God, as if He were not the God of all to whom we all belong.

Chapter 25

(1) It seems to me that I certainly have given sufficient proof of [the difference between] false and true divinity, now that I have pointed out how the proof depends not merely on discussion and argument, but also on the spoken testimony of those very ones whom you believe to be gods; so that there is no necessity of adding anything further to this topic. (2) However, since we made particular mention of the name of Rome, I will not avoid the issue which is provoked by that presumption on the part of those who say that the Romans, as

---

[3] Tertullian means that Juno Curitis was named after Curis, a Faliscan god; actually, the name is derived from *curis*, a spear, with which the goddess was represented as protectress of spearmen.

a result of their painstaking, scrupulous, religious observance, have been exalted to such sublime heights that they have become masters of the world;[1] and that, in consequence, their gods have brought it about that those surpass all others in prosperity who surpass all others in devotion to their deity. (3) You may be sure that the price was paid by the Roman gods to the name of Rome for the favor: Sterculus, Mutunus, and Larentina have exalted the Roman Empire. For, I would not expect gods from abroad to have been willing to do more for a race of foreigners than for their own, or to have surrendered to a race from across the sea their native soil where they were born, grew up, gained renown, and were buried. (4) Let Cybele account for it if she so ardently loved the city of Rome as the memorial of the race of Trojans who were, as you know, born and bred in her service, and whom she protected against the arms of the Greeks—if she looked forward to the prospect of going over to the avengers of Troy, knowing as she did that they would one day subdue Greece, the conqueror of Phrygia![2] (5) Why, even in our own day she has offered strong proof of the exalted dignity she conferred on our city. On March 17, near Sirmium, Marcus Aurelius was lost to the state.[3] On the 24th of the same month, the most devoted archigallus, after slashing his arms, offered his own impure blood[4] in sacrifice and then proceeded

---

[1] E.g., Cic., *De nat. deor.* 2.3.8; Val. Max. (1.1.8).
[2] Cf. Ovid, *Fasti* 4.191-348. In 204 B.C. by order of the Sibylline books, the Magna Mater, or Cybele, under the form of a black stone, was introduced from Pessinus into Italy in the hope of hastening the withdrawal of Hannibal.
[3] Cf. Cassius Dio (71.33).
[4] In the annual cycle of festivals in honor of Cybele, extending from March 15-27, March 24 was noted as *dies sanguinis*. On that day the mourning of the *mystai*, commemorating the sorrow of the Great Mother for the dead Attis, rose to its highest point, expressing itself in severe fasting and abstinence, self-laceration of the priests and self-mutilation of the neophytes. It probably was also the day on which the initiation of the new candidates took place.

to issue the usual recommendation to pray for the welfare of the Emperor Marcus—though death had already carried him off! (6) O tardy messengers, O sleepy dispatches! It was your fault that Cybele did not learn earlier of the demise of the emperor. Indeed, the Christians might well laugh at such a goddess! (7) Jupiter, too, should not have allowed his Crete to be immediately shattered by the Roman fasces, forgetting the familiar Idaean cave and the bronze cymbals of the Corybantes and the highly delightful odor of his nurse[5] there! Would he not have preferred that grave of his there to the entire Capitol, so that that land which covered the ashes of Jupiter might rather be pre-eminent in the world? (8) And would Juno want her beloved Punic city, 'preferred to Samos,'[6] wiped out, particularly by the race of Aeneas? As far as I know, 'Here were her arms, here her chariot; that this should be the realm of all peoples was the plan which the goddess was even then cherishing and fostering, should the fates allow.'[7] This poor soul, 'spouse and sister of Jupiter,'[8] had no power against the Fates! It is certainly true that 'On Fate depends Jupiter himself.' (9) Yet, the Romans did not surrender so much of their honor to the Fates which yielded Carthage to them, contrary to the design and prayer of Juno, as they did to that most wanton of prostitutes, Larentina.

(10) It is entirely settled that many of your gods were once kings. If, then, they have the right of conferring sovereign authority, since they once were kings, from whom did they receive this privilege? Whom did Saturn worship, and Jupiter? Some Sterculus, I suppose. But afterwards, the Romans, together with their countrymen, [came to worship him]. (11)

---

5 Amalthea.
6 *Aeneid* 1.16.
7 *Ibid.* 1.16-18.
8 *Ibid.* 1.47.

Moreover, if some of the gods were not kings, then they were ruled by others who were not yet their worshippers, inasmuch as they were not yet considered gods. Then, it lies within the province of others to bestow the right to rule, because power was exercised long before these gods of yours appeared on the scene.

(12) But, how senseless it is to attribute the dignity of the Roman name to their scrupulous religious observances, for it was after the institution of imperial, or, call it, still kingly power, that religion made advances. Although it was Numa who begot the superstitious punctiliousness, nevertheless divine service, with statues and temples, was not established among the Romans at that time. (13) Religious services were shabby, the rituals were unpretentious, and there was no Capitol struggling skyward; altars were improvised and built of sod, vessels were still made of clay from Samos, the odor from sacrifice was slight; the god himself had nowhere put in his appearance. At that time the genius of the Greeks and Tuscans for fashioning statues had not deluged the city. Consequently, the Romans' religious attitude did not precede their greatness, and, therefore, it was not for the fact that they were religious that they are great.

(14) On the contrary, how could their greatness be attributed to their religious attitude, since their greatness resulted from their indifference to religion? For, unless I am mistaken, every kingdom or empire is acquired by wars and extended by victories. Yet, wars and victories generally consist in the capture and destruction of cities. This business is not without its violence to the gods; there is indiscriminate destruction of city walls and temples, slaughter of citizens and priests without distinction, pillaging of treasures sacred and profane alike. (15) The sacrileges of the Romans are as numerous as their trophies; their triumphs over the gods as

many as those over nations; there is as much plunder as there are statues of the captured gods still on hand. (16) The gods, therefore, endure being adored by their enemies and decree 'empire without end'⁹ to those whose offences they should have requited, rather than their servile fawning. However, the injury of those who are devoid of feeling is as free from punishment as the worship of them is devoid of significance. (17) Certainly, the assumption cannot harmonize with truth that those people seem to have attained greatness on the merits of their religious service who, as we have pointed out, have either grown by giving offence to religion or have given offence by their growth. Even those whose realms were melted into the sum total of the Roman Empire were not devoid of religious attitudes when they lost their power.

Chapter 26

(1) Watch out, then, lest the one who dispenses kingdoms be the One to whom belong both the world which is ruled and man himself who rules it; lest He who existed before all time and who has made the world a unified system of times has ordained changes in the ruling powers during certain periods in the course of time; lest He under whom the race of men once lived before there were cities at all be the One who raises cities and destroys them. (2) Why fall into error? Rome in its woodland state existed earlier than certain of her own gods; she ruled before she developed such a pretentious Capitol; and the Babylonians had been in power before the pontiffs, the Medes before the quindecimviri, the Egyptians before the Salii, the Assyrians before the Luperci, and the Amazons before the Vestal Virgins. (3) In fine, if the religious ceremonies of the Romans confer kingdoms, never

---
9 *Ibid.* 1.279.

in times past would Judaea have been a kingdom, since she despised those divinities that are commonly worshipped; but you Romans at one time or another have honored her God with victims, have adorned her temples with gifts, have bound the nation with treaties; yet you would never have come to dominate Judaea had she not, in the end, sinned against God in the person of Christ.

Chapter 27

(1) Enough has been said to refute the charge of intending to offend divinity, since it cannot seem that we are offending that which we have shown does not exist. Therefore, when called upon to sacrifice, we take a firm stand against it because of the conviction of our knowledge, whereby we are certain whose services they are which reach us under the shameful misuse of images and the consecration of human names. (2) Some think it madness that, when we could offer sacrifice here and now and then go away unpunished, preserving the same attitude of mind as before, we prefer to be obstinate rather than safe. (3) You are, of course, offering advice whereby we may take advantage of you; but we realize the origin of such suggestions, who it is that prompts all this, and how at one time clever persuasion and then again harsh severity is employed to break down our perseverance.

(4) Actually, that spirit endowed with the nature of devils and angels, our enemy because of its separation from God, jealous of us because of the grace God gives us, wars against us, using as its battleground your minds which have been attuned to him by his secret insinuations and suborned to all the perverse judgment and wicked cruelty of which we spoke at the beginning. (5) Though the whole force of demons and similar spirits may be brought forward against us, yet, like

base servants, they sometimes mingle obstinacy with fear and they burn with the desire to injure those whom at another time they dread. Fear, too, inspires hatred. (6) Besides, those evil spirits, in the desperate condition resulting from their past condemnation, consider it a comfort, provided at times by the delay of their punishment, to derive enjoyment from their spitefulness.[1] Yet, when apprehended, they are subdued and sink down to their proper condition, and at close quarters they bow in petition at the feet of those whom from a distance they attack. (7) And so, like slaves rebelling against their enforced labor, whether in prison or in the mines, they break out from this kind of penal servitude against us, in whose power they actually are—though they know well that they are unequal to us and that for this very outbreak against us they are more thoroughly damned. But we, against our will, resist them, as ones who are a match for them. We fight back, persevering in that which they attack. And our triumph over them is never more brilliant than when, for our firm adherence to the faith, we are condemned.

Chapter 28

(1) Moreover, the injustice of forcing men of free will to offer sacrifice against their will is readily apparent, for, under all other circumstances, a willing mind is required for discharging one's religious obligations. It certainly would be considered absurd were one man compelled by another to honor gods whom he ought to honor of his own accord and for his own sake; in that case, it would not be his to say, in accordance with the rights of his liberty, 'I do not want

---

[1] It is evident from this that Tertullian believed that the evil spirits were not in hell until the end of the world, and did not yet suffer the penalty of fire. Justin, Irenaeus, and many others of the Fathers held the same opinion.

Jupiter propitious to me; who are you? Let Janus meet me in anger with whichever face he pleases. What have you to do with my affairs?' (2) Now, it is by the same spirits, assuredly, that you have been taught to force us to offer sacrifice for the well-being of the emperor; there has been imposed on you the necessity of using force, just as upon us is laid the obligation of exposing ourselves to danger.

(3) We have come, then, to the second charge alleged against us, that of offending a more august majesty. You pay your obeisance to Caesar with greater fear and craftier timidity than to Olympian Jupiter himself. And rightly so, if you but knew it! For, what living man—whoever he may be—is not more powerful than any of your dead ones? (4) But you do this, not for any logical reason, but out of regard for his manifest and perceptible power. In this point, too, it will be seen that you are lacking in religious feeling toward your gods, since you show more fear to a human lord. Finally, one is more ready among you to take a false oath by all the gods together than by the lone genius of Caesar.

Chapter 29

(1) First, then, let it be established whether those to whom sacrifice is offered can grant health to the emperor or to any man at all, and then proclaim the charge of treason against us if the angels or demons, who are by nature the most evil of spirits, work any good; if the lost can save and the damned grant freedom; if, finally, the dead, as you well know they are, can protect the living. (2) Certainly, they should first protect their own statues, images, and temples, which, I believe, the emperors' soldiers have to keep safe with guards. Moreover, those very materials for them come, I think, from the emperors' mines, and entire temples depend upon the nod

of a Caesar. (3) In fine, many gods have irritated a Caesar; it also has bearing on our case, that, if they have gained the good will of an emperor, he confers upon them some gift or privilege. If they are so completely in Caesar's power, and belong to him so completely, how can they have Caesar's welfare in their power? Would it seem that they can supply that which they themselves more readily obtain from Caesar? (4) So, we are committing a crime against the emperors because we do not subordinate them to their property, and we do not make a joke of our duty regarding their health, for we do not think it rests within hands that are soldered on with lead! (5) But then, *you* are the irreligious ones who seek health where it is not, who ask it from those who have no power to give it, and neglect the One in whose power it lies. And, in addition to all this, you assail those who know how to pray for it, and who can obtain it, too, since they know how to pray!

Chapter 30

(1) For, in our case, we pray for the welfare of the emperors to the eternal God, the true God, the living God, whom even the emperors themselves prefer to have propitious to them before all other gods.[1] They know who has given them power; they know—for they are men—who has given them life; they feel that He is the only God in whose power alone they are, commencing with whom they are second, after whom they stand first, who is before all and above all gods. Why not?—since they are above all men; since, as living beings, they surpass, at any rate, the dead. (2) They consider

---

1 For an example of such a prayer for rulers and governors, cf. the letter of St. Clement of Rome 60.4; 61.1-3.

to what extent power of empire avails and thus they come to understand God; against Him they cannot avail, through Him they know they do avail. Let the emperor [have a mind to] war against heaven, lead heaven in chains in his triumph, send his sentries to heaven, and on heaven impose his tax! He cannot do it. (3) So he is mighty, because he is less than heaven, for he is himself the property of Him to whom heaven and every creature belong. From Him comes the emperor, from whom came the man, also, before he became the emperor; from Him comes the emperor's power and his spirit as well. (4) Looking up to Him, we Christians—with hands extended, because they are harmless, with head bare because we are not ashamed,[2] without a prayer leader because we pray from the heart[3]—constantly beseech Him on behalf of all emperors. We ask for them long life, undisturbed power, security at home, brave armies, a faithful Senate, an upright people, a peaceful world, and everything for which a man or a Caesar prays. (5) Such petitions I cannot ask from any other save from Him, and I know that I shall obtain them from Him, since He is the only One who supplies them and I am one who ought to obtain my request. For, I am His servant; I alone worship Him; for His teaching I am put to death; I offer Him the rich—and better—sacrifice which He Himself has commanded, the prayer sent up from a chaste body, an innocent heart, and a spirit that is holy; (6) not grains of incense worth a mere

---

2 In the Roman ritual the head of the sacrificer was muffled or veiled (cf. *Aeneid* 3.405 and Lucretius 5.1198). Only in the worship of Saturn and in sacrificing to Hercules at the Great Altar was the head of the sacrificer uncovered (cf. Macrobius, *Saturn.* 1.8.2; 3.6.17).

3 Because of their superstitions, the Romans took exceeding precautions lest the formula of the prayer used at a sacrifice be in the slightest degree altered. Cf. Pliny, *Nat. hist.* 28.2.11; Cic. *De haruspicum responsis* 11.23.

penny, or tears of the Arabic tree, or two drops of wine, or the blood of a worthless ox that is longing for death, and, in addition to all this filth, a polluted conscience—so that I wonder when, among you, victims are examined by the most vicious of priests, why it is the hearts of the slain animals are examined rather than those of the priests themselves. (7) So, then, as we kneel with arms extended to God, let the hooks dig into us, let the crosses suspend us, the fires lick us, the swords cut our throats, and wild beasts leap upon us: the very posture of a Christian in prayer makes him ready for every punishment. Carry on, good officials, torture the soul which is beseeching God on behalf of the emperor! Here will lie the crime, where there reigns truth and devotion to God!

Chapter 31

(1) Well, now, we have been flattering the emperor and have lied about the prayers we said just to escape rough treatment! That ingenious idea of yours is certainly of advantage to us, for you permit us to prove whatever we allege in our defense. If you think that we have no interest in the emperor's welfare, look into our literature, the Word of God. We ourselves do not keep it concealed; in fact, many a chance hands it over to outsiders. (2) Learn from this literature that it has been enjoined upon us, that our charity may more and more abound, to pray to God even for our enemies, and to beg for blessings for our persecutors.[1] Now, who are any greater enemies and persecutors of Christians than those on whose account we are charged with the crime of treason? (3) But it is clearly and expressly said: 'Pray for kings, for princes and for rulers, that all may be peaceful for you!'[2] For, when

---
1 Matt. 5.43-45.
2 1 Tim. 2.2.

the empire is shaken, and its other members are shaken, we, too, although we are considered outsiders by the crowd, are naturally involved in some part of the disaster.

Chapter 32

(1) There is also another, even greater, obligation for us to pray for the emperors; yes, even for the continuance of the empire in general and for Roman interests. We realize that the tremendous force which is hanging over the whole world, and the very end of the world with its threat of dreadful afflictions, is arrested for a time by the continued existence of the Roman Empire.[1] This event we have no desire to experience, and, in praying that it may be deferred, we favor the continuance of Rome.

(2) Then, too, we take an oath not by the *'genii* of the emperors,' but by their prosperity—which is more august than any *genius* at all. Are you not aware that *genii* are evil spirits and, thence, to use a diminutive term, are called *daemonia?* We respect in the emperors the decision of God, since He has placed them over the people. (3) We know that in them is that which God has willed, and so we wish that what God has willed be safe and sound, and we consider this an important oath. As for evil spirits, that is, *genii*, we are in the habit of exorcising them in order to drive them out of men, but not to swear by them in a manner that would confer upon them the honor of divinity.

Chapter 33

(1) Why should I say more about the respect and the

---

1 The phrase in 2 Thess. 2.7, *'ho katéchon,'* was understood by Tertullian and others to refer to the Roman Empire, which they believed would last until the end of the world. Cf. *infra, Ad Scapulam* 2, and note 3.

loyalty of Christians toward the emperor? We are under obligation to look up to him as one whom our Lord has chosen. So, I might well say: 'Caesar belongs more to us, since he has been appointed by our God.' (2) And so, as he is mine, I do more for his welfare, not only because I pray for it to Him who can really grant it, or because I am such that I deserve to be heard, but also because, as I set the dignity of Caesar below that of God, I commend him the more to God to whom alone I subordinate him. However, I do subordinate him to God; I do not make him His equal. (3) I will not call the emperor God, either because I do not know how to lie,[1] or because I dare not make fun of him, or because even he himself does not want to be called God.[2] If he is a man, it is to his interest as a man to yield precedence to God. Let him consider it enough to be called emperor. That, indeed, is a title of dignity which God has given him. One who says he is God says he is not the emperor; unless he were a man he could not be emperor. (4) Why, even during his triumph, right in his lofty chariot, he is reminded that he is a man. For, someone behind him whispers: 'Look behind you! Remember you are a man!' And certainly, he rejoices all the more in this, that he shines forth in such great glory that he needs a reminder of his condition. He would be of less importance were he then called 'God,' because it would not be true. He is of greater importance who is called to look back, lest he think that he is God.

Chapter 34

(1) Augustus, who formed the empire, did not even want

---
1 Is Tertullian echoing Juvenal's ironical *'mentiri nescio'* of *Sat.* 3.41?
2 Cf. Min. Fel., *Oct.* 21.10.

to be called 'Lord';[1] for this title, too, belongs to God. Of course, I will call the emperor Lord, but only in the customary meaning of the word, if I am not forced to call him Lord in place of God. So far as he is concerned, I am a free man. For, I have one Lord, the omnipotent and eternal God, the same who is his Lord, too. (2) As for the one who is 'Father of his country,' how can he be its Lord? Yet, this title is an acceptable one, too, implying paternal responsibility rather than power. Even in the family, we speak of 'fathers' rather than 'lords.' (3) All the more improper is it that the emperor should be called God, which is unthinkable save in terms of a most disgraceful and pernicious flattery. Just as if you already had an emperor and were to call another man by that name, would you not incur the severe and inexorable displeasure of the real emperor whom you had, a displeasure which must be feared even by him whom you called emperor? Be reverential toward God if you wish Him to be propitious to the emperor. Stop believing in another god and, so, stop calling this one god who has need of God. (4) If flattery like this, which addresses a man as god, does not blush for its hypocrisy, let it at least have fear of misfortune. It is blasphemous to call Caesar god before his apotheosis.

Chapter 35

(1) So, this is why Christians are public enemies, because they do not proclaim meaningless, false, and wanton honors for the emperors; for, as men who belong to the true religion, they celebrate the feasts of the emperors[1] with realization rather than with self-gratification. (2) There is no question

---

1 Cf. Suet., *Augustus* 53.

1 Their birthdays and anniversaries.

about it: it is a splendid ceremony to bring out in public the braziers and banquet couches, to dine in the streets, to make the city smell like a tavern, to make mud with the wine, to chase around in bands in order to commit crimes, effrontery, and the seductive pleasures of lust.[2] Is it in such fashion that the public expresses its delight, with public degradation? Are such actions as these becoming on solemn festivals of the emperors, though they are not becoming on other days? (3) Are those who keep order out of respect for the emperor to abandon it because of the emperor? And shall their immoral licentiousness be considered loyalty; the opportunity for excessive indulgence, religious respect? (4) Oh, how rightly are we to be condemned! Why do we perform our ceremonies and express our joys for the Caesars in a way that is chaste, sober, and decent? Why, on a festive day, do we not overshadow our doorposts with laurel branches and infringe upon the daylight with lamps?[3] It is an honorable practice, indeed, when a public festival demands that you deck out your home with the appearance of a new brothel!

(5) Now, on this question of religious worship rendered to a less august majesty,[4] the point on which action is brought against us Christians as a second charge of sacrilege,[5] inasmuch as we do not celebrate with you the festivals of the emperors in a manner which neither modesty, self-respect, nor virtue permits, a manner urged by the opportunity for self-

---

2 Tertullian is not exaggerating the degradation. Tacitus, *Ann.* 15.37, gives a comparable picture of Nero's excesses.
3 Such were the signs of public rejoicing. Cf. Juv. (6.79, 227; 12.91).
4 Cf. *supra*, Ch. 28.2. The terminology is confusing and the meaning somewhat obscure.
5 From this passage it is evident that to Tertullian the charge of treason and sacrilege are the same. But the Christians were accused of a twofold sacrilege or treason, *laesae religionis*, and *laesae pietatis in Caesarem*.

indulgence rather than any worthy motive—in this regard I would like to point out your loyalty and sincerity, in case here, too, those who want us to be considered not Romans, but enemies of the Roman emperors, may prove, perchance, to be worse than Christians. (6) It is the Romans themselves, the very people born and bred on the Seven Hills, that I arraign: does that Roman tongue spare any emperor of its own? As witness, there is the Tiber, and the training schools for wild beasts. (7) If only nature had enclosed our breasts with some kind of glass-like material to make them transparent, whose heart would not appear engraved with the scene of one new Caesar after another presiding over the distribution of the dole, even in that hour when they shout in applause: 'From our years may Jupiter multiply for thee thine own!' A Christian can no more make such remarks than he can hope for a new emperor.

(8) 'But, that's the rabble,' you say. Perhaps it is the rabble; still, they are Romans, and none is more clamorous in their demands for punishment of the Christians than the rabble. Yes, of course, the other classes of society are conscientiously loyal, as their position of authority requires. There is never a hostile whisper from the Senate, the knights, the camp, or the palace itself.[6] (9) Whence come men like Cassius and Niger and Albinus? Whence, those who between the two laurels lay hands on Caesar?[7] Whence, those who practise the art of wrestling in order to choke him to death? Whence, those who burst into the palace in arms, bolder than any Sigerius or Parthenius?[8] From the ranks of the Romans, unless I am

---

[6] Bitter irony, inasmuch as the basest traitors came from these ranks.
[7] The place called 'between the two laurels' was situated in the thirteenth region of Rome.
[8] Tertullian recalls some of the violent assaults upon the emperors. Cassius, in the reign of M. Aurelius, usurped imperial power; Niger (in 193) was hailed as emperor after the murder of Commodus, as

mistaken—that is, from among non-Christians. (10) And so, all of them, right until the very outbreak of their disloyalty, offered sacrifices for the well-being of the emperor and swore by his *genius,* some publicly, others privately; naturally, they gave Christians the name of public enemies.

(11) But, even those who now are being brought to light each day as associates or acclaimers of the criminal parties, the gleanings which are left after a whole harvest of parricides—how they used to deck their doorposts beforehand with the freshest and fullest laurel branches! How they used to shadow their halls with the loftiest and brightest lamps! How they apportioned the forum among themselves with the most elegant and magnificent couches! And all this, not to celebrate an occasion of public joy, but to express what was already their own wish on the festivity of another emperor and to set up the model and image of the object of their own hopes, while changing the name of the emperor in their hearts. (12) The same type of service is rendered by those who consult astrologers, soothsayers, fortune-tellers, and magicians regarding the life of the emperors. But these wiles, which have been made known by the rebel angels and which are forbidden by God, Christians do not use even in their own personal affairs. (13) Moreover, who has to inquire about the emperor's health except one who is plotting or desiring something against it, or who is hoping for or expecting something after his death? For, it is not with the same attitude of mind that one seeks information regarding his loved ones and his masters! There is one kind of concern shown in uneasiness about one's family; another, about one's enslavement.

---

also Albinus (cf. *infra, Ad Scapulam* 2 n. 1). Commodus suffered several attacks in his life, and was finally strangled by his wrestling partner, apparently by accident. Pertinax was murdered in the Palace; Domitian, by conspirators among whom were Sigerius and Parthenius.

Chapter 36

(1) If such is the case, and those who once were called Romans are now found to be enemies, why is it that we who are considered enemies are refused the name of Romans? It cannot be that we are non-Romans because we are enemies, since it is discovered that those are really enemies who once were considered Romans. (2) Furthermore, the loyalty, the reverence, the fidelity due the emperors consists not in such services as even hostile minds can render to cloak their thoughts, but, on the contrary, it consists in that moral behavior which God demands be shown the emperor just as truly as necessarily is to be shown to all men. (3) These indications of good will are not due on our part to the emperors alone. In no good that we perform do we show preference for certain persons, since we actually are doing it for ourselves; we are striving for a just recompense either of praise or of reward not from man, but from God who demands and repays goodness that is impartial. (4) We are the same toward the emperors as we are toward our neighbors. For, to desire evil, to do evil, to speak evil, to think evil of anyone—all are equally forbidden to us. Whatever we may not do to the emperor, we may not do to anyone else; whatever is forbidden with regard to anyone is, perhaps even to a greater degree, forbidden with regard to that one who, through God, is so great a personage.

Chapter 37

(1) If, as I have said above, we are commanded to love our enemies, who is there for us to hate? Likewise, if we are forbidden to return an injury, lest, through our action, we become wrong-doers like them, who is there for us to injure?

(2) Examine yourselves on this point! How often do you rage furiously against the Christians, partly in response to your own feelings, partly out of respect for the laws? How often, too, has a hostile mob, without consulting you, attacked us on their own initiative, with stones and torches in their hands? Why, with the very fury of Bacchanals, they spare not even the corpses of Christians, but drag them from the repose of the grave, from that resting place, as it were, of death; although they are already changed and by now rotting in corruption, they cut them into bits and tear them limb from limb. (3) Yet, what fault do you ever find with people who are bound together by such intimate ties, what retaliation for injury do you ever experience from those who are so disposed even to death, though even a single night, with a few little torches, could produce such rich vengeance, if it were permitted us to requite evil with evil? But, far be it from us that our God-given religion avenge itself with human fire or that it grieve to endure the suffering whereby it is put to the test.

(4) If we wanted to act as open enemies and not merely as secret avengers, would we lack the strength of numbers and troops? Take the Moors and Marcomani and the Parthians themselves or any tribes at all who, even if they are numerous, still live in one place and inhabit their own territories—are they really more numerous than the Christians who are scattered over the whole world? We are but of yesterday, yet we have filled every place among you[1]—cities, islands, fortresses, towns, marketplaces, camp, tribes, town councils, the palace, the senate, the forum; we have left nothing to you but the temples of your gods. (5) For what war would we not have been fit and ready, even though un-

---

1 Tertullian here testifies to the rapid spread of Christianity, but he is doubtless indulging to some degree in hyperbole.

equally matched in military strength, we who are so ready to be slain, were it not that, according to our rule of life, it is granted us to be killed rather than to kill?

(6) Even unarmed and without any uprising, merely as malcontents, simply through hatred and withdrawal, we could have fought against you. For, if such a multitude of men as we are had broken loose from you and had gone into some remote corner of the earth, the loss of so many citizens, of whatever kind they might be, would certainly have made your power blush for shame; in fact, it would even have punished you by this very desertion. (7) Without a doubt, you would have been exceedingly frightened at your loneliness, at the silence of your surroundings, and the stupor, as it were, of a dead world. You would have had to look around for people to rule; there would have been more enemies than citizens left to you. (8) For, now, the enemies whom you have are fewer because of the number of Christians, inasmuch as nearly all the citizens you have in nearly all the cities are Christians. But, you have preferred to call them the enemies of the human race[2] rather than of human error.

(9) But, who would snatch you away from those secret enemies that are constantly destroying your spiritual and bodily health—I mean, from the attacks of demons which we ward off from you without any reward and without pay? This alone would have been sufficient revenge for us, if from then on you were left open and exposed to the possession of the impure spirits. (10) Furthermore, instead of thinking of any compensation for so great a protection, you have preferred to consider as enemies a class of men, who, far from being a troublesome burden to you, are actually indispensable. To tell the truth, we are enemies, not, however, of the human race, but rather of human error.

---

2 Cf. Tacitus, *Ann.* 15.44.

Chapter 38

(1) Accordingly, ought not this religion to be regarded with somewhat milder judgment among those societies which cannot legally exist? Its members commit no such crimes as are regularly feared from illegal associations. (2) For, unless I am mistaken, the motive for prohibiting associations rests on the prudent care for public order, lest the state be split into parties, a situation which would easily disturb voting assemblies, council meetings, the Senate, mass meetings, and even public entertainments by the clash of rival interests, since by now men have even begun to make a business of their violence, offering it for sale at a price. (3) But, for us who are indifferent to all burning desire for fame and honor, there is no need of banding together. There is nothing more unfamiliar to us than politics. There is only one state for all which we acknowledge—the universe.

(4) Likewise, we renounce your public shows just as we do their origins which we know were begotten of superstition, while we are completely aloof from those matters with which they are concerned. Our tongues, our eyes, our ears have nothing to do with the madness of the circus, the shamelessness of the theater, the brutality of the arena, the vanity of the gymnasium. (5) How, then, do we offend you? If we prefer different pleasures, if, in fine, we do not want to be amused, that is our loss—if loss there be—not yours. We reject the things that please you. And ours give you no pleasure. But the Epicureans were allowed to decide upon a different truth regarding the nature of pleasure, namely, tranquillity of mind.

Chapter 39

(1) Now I myself will explain the practices of the Christian Church, that is, after having refuted the charges that they are evil, I myself will also point out that they are good. We form one body because of our religious convictions, and because of the divine origin of our way of life and the bond of common hope. (2) We come together for a meeting and a congregation, in order to besiege God with prayers, like an army in battle formation. Such violence is pleasing to God. We pray, also, for the emperors, for their ministers and those in power, that their reign may continue, that the state may be at peace, and that the end of the world may be postponed. (3) We assemble for the consideration of the Holy Scriptures, [to see] if the circumstances of the present times demand that we look ahead or reflect. Certainly, we nourish our faith with holy conversation, we uplift our hope, we strengthen our trust, intensifying our discipline at the same time by the inculcation of moral precepts. (4) At the same occasion, there are words of encouragement, of correction, and holy censure. Then, too, judgment is passed which is very impressive, as it is before men who are certain of the presence of God, and it is a deeply affecting foretaste of the future judgment, if anyone has so sinned that he is dismissed from sharing in common prayer, assembly, and all holy intercourse. (5) Certain approved elders preside, men who have obtained this honor not by money, but by the evidence of good character. For, nothing that pertains to God is to be had for money.

Even if there is some kind of treasury, it is not accumulated from a high initiation fee as if the religion were something bought and paid for. Each man deposits a small amount on a certain day of the month or whenever he wishes, and only on condition that he is willing and able to do so. No one is forced; each makes his contribution voluntarily.¹ (6) These are, so to speak, the deposits of piety. The money therefrom is spent not for banquets or drinking parties or good-for-nothing eating houses, but for the support and burial of the poor, for children who are without their parents and means of subsistence, for aged men who are confined to the house; likewise, for shipwrecked sailors, and for any in the mines, on islands or in prisons. Provided only it be for the sake of fellowship with God, they become entitled to loving and protective care for their confession. (7) The practice of such a special love brands us in the eyes of some. 'See,' they say, 'how they love one another'; (for *they* hate one another), 'and how ready they are to die for each other.' (They themselves would be more ready to kill each other.)

(8) Over the fact that we call ourselves brothers, they fall into a rage—for no other reason, I suppose, than because among them every term of kinship is only a hypocritical pretense of affection. But, we are your brothers, too, according to the law of nature, our common mother, although you are hardly men since you are evil brothers. (9) But, with how much more right are they called brothers and considered such who have acknowledged one father, God, who have drunk one spirit of holiness,² who in fear and wonder have come forth from the one womb of their common ignorance to the one light of truth! (10) Perhaps this is why we are considered less legitimate brothers, because no tragic drama has our brotherhood as its theme, or because we are brothers who use the same family substance which, among you, as a rule, destroys brotherhood.

(11) So, we who are united in mind and soul have no hesi-

---
1 Cf. 2 Cor. 9.7; St. Justine Martyr, *Apology* I 14.2; 67.6; St. Cyprian, *Ep.* 2.1.
2 Cf. 1 Cor. 12.13.

tation about sharing what we have. Everything is in common among us—except our wives. (12) In this matter—which is the only matter in which the rest of men practise partnership—we dissolve partnership. They not only usurp the marriage rights of their friends, but they even hand over their own rights to their friends with the greatest equanimity. This results, I suppose, from the teaching they have learned from those who were older and wiser, the Greek Socrates and the Roman Cato, who shared with their friends the wives whom they had married, so that they could bear children in other families, too. (13) As a matter of fact, perhaps the wives were not exactly unwilling. For, why should they care about a chastity which their husbands had so readily given away? Oh, what an example of Attic wisdom and Roman dignity! The philosopher a pander, and the censor, too![3]

(14) Why wonder, then, if such dear friends take their meals together? You attack our modest repasts—apart from saying that they are disgraced by crimes—as being extravagant. It was, of course, to us that Diogenes' remark referred: 'The people of Megara purchase supplies as if they were to die tomorrow, but put up buildings as though they were never to die.' (15) However, anyone sees the bit of straw in another's eye more easily than a mote in his own. With so many tribes, courts, and sub-courts belching, the air becomes foul: if the Salii are going to dine, someone will have to give a loan; the city clerks will have to count up the cost of the tithes and extravagant banquets in honor of Hercules; for the festival of the Apaturia, for the Dionysiac revels, for the mysteries of Attica, they proclaim a draft of cooks; at the

---

3 Tertullian confuses Cato the Censor (184 B.C.) with the younger Cato Uticensis (d. 46 B.C.) who was guilty of this offense, as Quintilian (10.5.13) relates. As for Socrates, the passage in Plato, *Republic* 457C-D, may have given origin to the story, found in Diogenes Laertius (2.5.26).

smoke of a feast of Serapis the firemen will become alarmed. But, only about the repast of the Christians is any objection brought forth.

(16) Our repast, by its very name, indicates its purpose. It is called by a name which to the Greeks means 'love.'[4] Whatever it costs, it is gain to incur expense in the name of piety, since by this refreshment we comfort the needy, not as, among you, parasites contend for the glory of reducing their liberty to slavery for the price of filling their belly amidst insults, but as, before God, greater consideration is given to those of lower station. (17) If the motive of our repast is honorable, then on the basis of that motive appraise the entire procedure of our discipline. What concerns the duty of religion tolerates no vulgarity, no immorality. No one sits down to table without first partaking of a prayer to God. They eat as much as those who are hungry take; they drink as much as temperate people need. (18) They satisfy themselves as men who remember that they must worship God even throughout the night; they converse as men who know that the Lord is listening. After this, the hands are washed and lamps are lit, and each one, according to his ability to do so, reads the Holy Scriptures or is invited into the center to sing a hymn to God. This is the test of how much he has drunk. Similarly, prayer puts an end to the meal. (19) From here they depart, not to unite in bands for murder, or to run around in gangs, or for stealthy attacks of lewdness, but to observe the same regard for modesty and chastity as people do who have partaken not only of a repast but of a rule of life.

(20) Such is the gathering of Christians. There is no question about it—it deserves to be called illegal, provided it is like those which are illegal; it deserves to be condemned, if

---

4 I.e., *agápe*.

any complaint is lodged against it on the same ground that complaints are made about other secret societies. (21) But, for whose destruction have we ever held a meeting? We are the same when assembled as when separate; we are collectively the same as we are individually, doing no one any injury, causing no one any harm. When men who are upright and good assemble, when the pious and virtuous gather together, the meeting should be called not a secret society but a senate.

Chapter 40

(1) On the other hand, those men deserve the name of a secret society who band together in hatred of good and virtuous men, who cry out for the blood of the innocent, at the same time offering as a justification of their hatred the idle plea that they consider that the Christians are the cause of every public calamity and every misfortune of the people. (2) If the Tiber rises as high as the city walls, if the Nile does not rise to the fields, if the weather will not change, if there is an earthquake, a famine, a plague—straightway the cry is heard: 'Toss the Christians to the lion!' So many of them for just one beast?

(3) I ask you, before the reign of Tiberius, that is, before the coming of Christ, what great misfortunes befell the world and its cities? We read that the islands of Hiera, Anaphe, Delos, Rhodes, and Cos were swallowed up with many thousands of men. (4) Plato, too, relates that a land larger than Asia or Africa was washed away by the Atlantic Ocean.[1] An earthquake emptied the Corinthian Sea, and the might of the waves wrested Lucania away [from Italy] and left it

---
1. Cf. Plato, *Timaeus* 24E.

separate under the name of Sicily. Naturally, these happenings could not fail to be attended by injury to the inhabitants.

(5) In those days, when the great flood poured its waters over the whole world, or, as Plato thought, merely over the plains, where then were—I shall not say the Christians who scorn your gods—but your gods themselves? (6) For, that your gods belong to a later date than that calamity of the deluge is attested by the very cities in which they were born and died, as well as by those which they founded. Otherwise, they would not exist until the present day unless they themselves had come into existence after that disaster.

(7) Palestine had not yet received a swarm of Jews from Egypt nor had the nucleus of the Christian Church settled there, when a rain of fire burnt up the neighboring regions of Sodom and Gomorrah.[2] The earth still smells from burning; if any fruit tries to grow on the trees there, it is only a promise to the eyes, for, as soon as it is touched, it turns to ashes. (8) Moreover, neither the people of Etruria nor of Campania voiced complaints about Christians at the time when fire from heaven poured upon Volsinii and fire from its own neighboring volcano overwhelmed Pompeii. No one at Rome had yet come to adore the true God when Hannibal, near Cannae, measured his slaughter by bushels of Roman rings. All your gods used to be worshipped by everyone when the Senones seized the Capitol.[3]

(9) It is to be noted, in connection with such misfortune, that if any disaster befell the cities, the same destruction was visited upon temples as upon city walls; hence, I can clearly demonstrate that the gods were not the cause of the misfortunes, inasmuch as similar misfortunes befell them, too.

(10) At all times the human race has deserved ill at God's

---
2 Cf. Gen. 19.24.
3 The Gauls did not actually seize the Capitol.

hands. In the first place, because it failed in its duties toward Him; although it knew Him in part, it did not seek and find Him, but actually invented for itself other additional gods to worship; in the second place, because, by not seeking the Teacher of innocence and the Judge and Avenger of guilt, it became hardened in all vices and crimes. (11) But, if it had sought Him, it would have followed that it would recognize Him who was sought, would worship Him when recognized, and, if it worshipped Him, it would experience His mercy rather than His wrath. (12) So, the race now must experience the anger of this same God just as [it did] also in times past, before the name of Christian was even mentioned. His were the blessings men enjoyed, bestowed before they fashioned any of their own deities; why do they not realize that the misfortunes as well come from Him whose blessings they have failed to recognize? They are guilty before Him toward whom they have been ungrateful.

(13) Yet, if we take into consideration the misfortunes of earlier times, those of the present time are less serious, now that the world has received the Christians from God. For, since that day, their innocence has tempered the wickedness of the world, and there have begun to be intercessors with God. (14) In a word, when summer days keep away the winter rain and men become anxious about the year's crops, this is your procedure: you eat your fill each day and are straightway ready to eat again; you keep the baths, taverns, and brothels constantly busy; you offer to Jupiter the so-called Aquilicia; you announce barefoot processions for the people; you investigate the sky near the Capitol; you watch for clouds from the panelled temple-ceilings—while you turn your back on heaven and God Himself. (15) Whereas we, grown lean with fastings and emaciated from all forms of self-restraint, abstaining from all the enjoyments of life, rolling in sack-

cloth and ashes, assail heaven with eager importunity and touch God's heart. And, when we have wrung from Him divine compassion, Jupiter gets all the honor!

Chapter 41

(1) You are the ones, then, who cause trouble in human affairs; you are always the ones who bring down public calamities—you, who scorn God and adore statues. For, it ought to be easier to believe that He who is neglected is angry, rather than those gods who are worshipped; (2) or else those gods of yours are certainly most unfair if, because of the Christians, they also harm their own worshippers—whereas they ought to exempt them from the punishment of the Christians!

'One may,' you say, 'cast this reproach against your God, too, inasmuch as He allows His worshippers to suffer misfortunes because of the wicked.' First, admit His divine dispensation, and you will not make this accusation against Him. (3) For, He who has, once and for all, appointed eternal judgment after the end of this world does not anticipate the separation, which is a preliminary condition of the judgment, before the end of the world.[1] Until that time He maintains an impartial attitude toward the entire human race, both indulging and disciplining them. He has willed that all things be shared by all: good fortune by the wicked and misfortunes by His own, so that by common participation we might all experience His mildness and His severity. (4) Because we have thus learned these things from Him, we love His mildness and fear His severity; you, on the other hand, despise them both. It follows that all the afflictions here below, whatever befall

---
1 Cf. Matt. 13.29ff., 37ff.; 25.32.

us, come to us from God as a warning; to you they come as a punishment.

(5) Nevertheless, we in no way suffer harm; in the first place, because nothing is of importance to us in this world, except to leave it as quickly as possible; secondly, because, if any misfortune is inflicted upon us, it is attributed to your sins. But, even if some things also touch us, inasmuch as we are in close association with you, we rejoice the more, remembering the divine predictions, which strengthen our confidence and the firm foundation of our hope. (6) But, if all these misfortunes befall you from those gods whom you worship, and if they happen because of us, why do you persist in worshipping gods who are so ungrateful and so unfair, gods who should have been more help and protection to you in the afflictions which the Christians suffer?

Chapter 42

(1) But, on still another charge of misconduct are we arraigned: They say that we are worthless in business. How can they say that? Are we not men who live right with you, men who follow the same way of life, the same manner of dressing, using the same provisions and the same necessities of life? We are not Brahmans or Indian ascetics who dwell in forests, withdrawn from life. (2) We bear in mind that we owe thanks to the Lord our God who created us; we disdain no fruit of His works; obviously, we do restrain ourselves from an immoderate or excessive use of them. So, it is not without a Forum, not without a meat market, not without baths, shops, factories, inns, market days, and the rest of your business enterprises that we live with you—in this world. (3) We are sailors along with yourselves; we serve in the army; we engage in farming and trading; in addition, we share with

you our arts; we place the products of our labor at your service. How we can appear worthless for your business, when we live with you and depend on you, I do not know.

(4) If I do not attend your ceremonials, nevertheless, even on that day, I am a man. I do not bathe in the early dawn on the Saturnalia, lest I should waste both night and day; still, I do bathe at the hour I should, one which is conducive to health and which protects both my temperature and my life's blood. To become stiff and ashen after a bath—I can enjoy that when I'm dead! (5) At the feast of Bacchus I do not recline at table in public, a custom which belongs to gladiators eating their last meal; but wherever I do dine, I dine from your supplies. (6) I do not buy a wreath for my head; what business of yours is it how I use flowers as long as I bought them? I think they are more pleasing when free, unbound, and hanging loosely everywhere. But, even if the flowers are bound into a wreath, we know a wreath by our noses; let them look to it who smell through their hair![1] (7) We do not attend the public games; yet, the things which are for sale at those gatherings I could, if I so desired, pick up more freely in their own proper places. Of course we do not buy incense; if the Arabians complain, let the people of Saba know that more of their wares and dearer ones are spent on burying Christians than on fumigating the gods.

(8) 'At all events,' you say, 'the income of the temples is daily melting away. How few there are who still cast in a contribution!' Of course; for we cannot afford to help both men and those gods of yours, though both are begging, and we do not think that aid should be given to others than those who ask. So, then, let Jupiter hold out his hand and receive! In the meanwhile, our mercy spends more from street

---
1 Cf. Min. Fel., *Oct.* 38.2.

to street than your religion does from temple to temple. (9) But the rest of the taxes will acknowledge a debt of gratitude to the Christians who pay their dues with the same good faith that keeps us from defrauding another; so that, if the records were checked as to how much the state treasury has lost through the deceitfulness and dishonesty of your declarations, the account could easily be calculated: the deficit on one side is balanced by the gain in the rest of the accounts.

Chapter 43

(1) I will frankly acknowledge, then, what group may, perhaps with good reason, complain about the unprofitable Christians. First of all, there are the pimps, panders, and their agents; secondly, the assassins, poisoners, and magicians; thirdly, fortune-tellers, soothsayers, and astrologers. (2) To be unprofitable to these is a tremendous profit. Yet, whatever loss your business suffers through this group of ours, it can be balanced by a certain protection. Of what worth do you consider—I do not say now, men who drive the evil spirits out of you; I do not say now, men who offer prayers for you to the true God, because, perchance, you do not believe that—men, I say, from whom you can have nothing to fear?

Chapter 44

(1) Yet there is a loss to the state, as great as it is real, and no one pays any attention to it; an injury to the state, and no one considers it—when so many upright men, such as we, are sacrificed, when so many of us, men of blameless character, are executed. (2) We now call to witness your actions, you who preside each day to pass judgment on prisoners, you who clear the criminals' records by passing sentences. So many guilty men are examined by you with various

charges against them: the man arraigned there as a murderer, a pickpocket, a profaner of temples, a seducer or robber of those in the baths—which one of them is charged also as a Christian? Or, when Christians are brought forward with their own charge, which one of them is also of such a character as are so many of those guilty ones? (3) It is with men from your own midst that the jail is always bulging, with your own that the mines are always humming, with your own that the wild beasts are always fattened, with your own that the producers of gladiatorial shows feed the herds of criminals. No one there is a Christian—unless he is *merely* that; if he is something else, too, then he is no longer a Christian.[1]

Chapter 45

(1) We, then, are the only ones who are innocent! What wonder if this must necessarily be the case? For it really must be. We have been taught our innocence by God; we understand it perfectly, as something revealed by a perfect Teacher; we guard it faithfully as something entrusted to us by a Judge who is not to be despised. (2) On the other hand, it is man's judgment that has handed over to you your [idea of] innocence; man's authority has enjoined it; therefore, you are not possessed of a moral system fully and sufficiently formidable to produce true innocence. Man's wisdom in pointing out good is in proportion to his power to exact it. It is as easy for the former to be mistaken as it is for the latter to be scorned. (3) And so, which is more complete, to say: 'Thou shalt not kill,' or to teach: 'Be not even angry'?[1] Which is more perfect, to forbid adultery, or to guard against even a single

---

1 Cf. Min. Fel., *Oct.* 35.6.

---

1 Cf. Matt. 5.21f.

glance of concupiscence?[2] Which is more learned, to forbid evil-doing, or even an evil word? Which is more wise, not to permit an injury, or not even to allow one to reciprocate an injury?[3] (4) Moreover, you should know that those laws of yours, too, which seem to tend toward innocence, were borrowed from the divine Law, as from an older pattern. We have already spoken of the Age of Moses.[4]

(5) But, how much authority have human laws, when it may happen that a man may evade them, time and again remaining concealed in his crimes, and that he sometimes despises them as he transgresses them of his own free will or through necessity? (6) Consider these things and also the short duration of every punishment, which at any rate is not going to last beyond the grave. Thus, even Epicurus would consider of slight account every pain and sorrow, expressing the opinion that a small pain is to be despised and a great one is something that will not last long.[5] (7) But we alone who are examined under the eyes of an all-seeing God, we who foresee an eternal punishment from Him, deserve to attain to innocence because of the fullness of our wisdom and the difficulty of finding a hiding place, and because of the greatness of the torments which are to be not simply of long duration but eternal; we are in fear of Him whom he, too, will have to fear—I mean, the very one who sits to pass judgment on us, the fearful; in a word, we fear God, not the proconsul.

---

2 *Ibid.* 5.28.
3 *Ibid.* 5.39.
4 Cf. *supra,* Ch. 19.3.
5 Cf. Cic., *De finibus* 2.7.22.

Chapter 46

(1) We have, I believe, held our ground against all the crimes imputed to our charge which demand the blood of Christians. We have pointed out our whole position and the means by which we can prove that it is just as we have indicated, namely, by the evidence and antiquity of the Sacred Scriptures, and by the testimony of the spiritual powers. Who will dare to refute us, not by skill in eloquence, but by the same form with which we have established our proof: by means of truth? (2) But, while the truth which is ours becomes manifest to each and all, meanwhile, disbelief, though it be convinced of the goodness of this religion, because it has already become known through experience and communication, does not consider our doings as divinely inspired at all, but merely as a sort of philosophy. 'The philosophers,' it says, 'teach the same virtues, and they, too, profess morality, justice, patience, moderation, and chastity.' (3) If, then, we are compared to them on the basis of our teaching, why are we not, accordingly, treated the same as they regarding the free and unmolested practice of our teaching? Or why, as our equals, are they, too, not forced to carry out the duties to which we have to submit or become involved in trouble? (4) For, who compels a philosopher to offer sacrifice, or to take an oath, or, in broad daylight, to set forth lamps that serve no purpose? Why, in fact, they even destroy your gods openly; in their writings they attack your superstitions—and you praise them for it. The majority of them even rant against the emperors, while you uphold them; and they are more readily rewarded with statues and salaries than with a sentence of condemnation to the wild beasts. (5) That is as it should be, for they bear the name 'philosophers,' not 'Christians.' This name of 'philosophers' does not chase away

demons. And why not, since the philosophers consider the demons rank second to the gods? There is a saying of Socrates: 'If the *daimon* permit.'[1] And this same Socrates—although he knew something of the truth, in so far as he denied the existence of the gods—nevertheless, right at the end, bade that a cock be sacrificed to Aesculapius, I suppose in honor of the father of Aesculapius, because Apollo had praised Socrates as the wisest of all men.[2] (6) O foolish Apollo! He bore witness to the wisdom of that man who said that the gods do not exist!

The degree of hatred that truth enkindles is the degree of offense given by one who maintains truth in accordance with his belief. The one who corrupts and makes a pretense of it, however, for the most part wins favor on this ground among the persecutors of truth. (7) It is this same truth that the philosophers mock and corrupt. They make a pretense of truth with an actor's skill[3] and, by pretending, they corrupt it, as men who are eager only for glory. Christians seek truth of necessity and they maintain it uprightly, as men who are concerned about their own salvation. (8) Hence, we are not their equals, as you think, with regard to knowledge or way of life. What definite answer did Thales, first of the natural philosophers, give to Croesus when the latter questioned him about divinity? One extension of time for reflection after the other proved vain.[4] (9) Any Christian workman at all finds God, makes Him known, and consequently assigns to Him in

---

1 Cf. Plato, *Apology* 31D.
2 Cf. Plato, *Phaedo* 118A; *Apology* 21A.
3 The readings *inimice* and *minice* are both attested by the MSS. The latter has been preferred here, although the reading of the *CSEL* text is *inimice*. There is a reminiscence here also of a verse from Terence, *Andr.* 68 (cf. Ch. 4 n.2; 7 n.2, *supra*).
4 Tertullian's memory appears to have failed him on this point, since the incident which he mentions here and in *Ad nat.* 2.2 regarding Thales and Croesus is referred to Simonides of Ceos and King Hiero by Min. Fel., *Oct.* 13.4, and Cic., *De nat. deor.* 1.22.60.

actual deed everything which man seeks in God; though Plato asserts that the maker of the universe is not easily found, and, when found, is with difficulty made known to all men.[5]

(10) Furthermore, if we should be challenged on the ground of chastity, I read part of the sentence the Athenians pronounced on the Socrates who was proclaimed the corruptor of young boys. A Christian makes no perversion even of the female sex. I know about Phryne, the courtesan, submitting to the passion of Diogenes; I have heard, too, of a certain Speusippus of Plato's school, who was killed in the act of adultery. A Christian is born male for his own wife alone. (11) Democritus, who blinded himself because he could not look at women without lustful desires and was in distress if he could not realize them, confessed his incontinence by the means he took to cure it. A Christian, however, keeps his eyes but does not look [with lust] upon women; it is his mind he has blinded against lust.

(12) If I am to answer regarding modesty of behavior, see how Diogenes, with muddy feet, tramples upon the proud couches of Plato with pride of a different kind. A Christian manifests no insolent pride even toward a pauper. (13) If I must argue about freedom from ambition, see how Pythagoras at Thurii and Zeno at Priene strive for the office of tyrant; whereas a Christian does not even strive for aedileship. (14) If it is on the question of evenness of mind I must meet you, Lycurgus hoped to starve himself to death because the Spartans had amended his laws; a Christian, even when condemned, gives thanks. If I draw a comparison regarding honesty, Anaxagoras refused to restore to his guests the goods they had placed in his trust. A Christian is called honest even

---

5 Cf. Plato, *Timaeus* 28C; Min. Fel., *Oct.* 19.14.

by those outside his religion. (15) If I should enter upon the question of straightforwardness, Aristotle shamelessly made his friend, Hermias, yield him place; a Christian does not hurt even his enemy. This same Aristotle is as shameful in his base flattery of Alexander, who was rather to be directed, as is Plato, who sells himself to Dionysius for the gratification of his belly. (16) Aristippus luxuriates in purple under the impressive veneer of dignity, and Hippias,[6] while laying plans for a conspiracy against the state, is killed. No Christian has ever attempted such a thing for his own friends, no matter with what cruelty they had been scattered.

(17) Someone will say that even some from our own ranks fall away from the rule of our way of life. They cease, however, to be considered Christians by us; but those philosophers we mentioned, in spite of such deeds, continue to keep the name and reputation of being wise. (18) What is there, then, about them that is alike, the philosopher and the Christian—the disciple of Hellas and the disciple of Heaven—the dealer in reputation and the dealer in salvation—one occupied with words and one with deeds—the creator of error and its destroyer—the friend of error and its foe—the despoiler of truth and its restorer—its robber and its warden?

Chapter 47

(1) Truth is older than anything, unless I am mistaken. Here, the antiquity of Sacred Scripture, as shown above,[1] assists me, for, because of this, one may easily believe that it served as a treasure-chest for every subsequent system of philosophy. And now, were I not keeping the weight of my

---
6 The reading of the MSS. is corrupt.

---
1 Cf. *supra,* Ch. 19.

book within limits, I might also make a disgression into this proof. (2) Which of the poets, which of the sophists is there who has not drunk from the fount of the Prophets? So, from this source have the philosophers watered their thirsty spirit,[2] so that which they possess from our books places us in a position to be compared with them. It is for this reason, I suppose, that philosophy was banned by certain people; namely, the Thebans, Spartans, and Argives. (3) Since they were striving for our doctrines and, as we have said, were men with a passion solely for reputation and eloquence, if they discovered anything in the sacred writings, they appropriated it for their own works, as a result of their instinctive desire for knowledge. Either they had not sufficient belief in the divinity of those passages so as not to interpolate them, or they did not sufficiently understand that at times these passages were somewhat obscure and beclouded even to the Jews themselves, whose property they seemed to be. (4) But, wherever the truth was easy to understand, there all the more did human skepticism scorn it and change it. And through this means they have mixed into their uncertainty even what they had found that was certain.

(5) They merely found God, but they did not examine Him as they found Him, so that they must debate about His quality, His nature, and His abode. (6) Some claim that He is incorporeal, others that He is corporeal—as, for example, the Platonists, and the Stoics; some assert that He is constituted of atoms, others of numbers—as Epicurus and Pythagoras; another says He consists of fire, as it seemed to Heraclitus; while the Platonists attribute to Him concern for the world, on the other hand, the Epicureans say that He lives in a world of repose and inactivity, being, so to say, a non-

---

2 Cf. Min. Fel., *Oct.* 34.5.

entity in human affairs; (7) the Stoics, however, say His position is outside the world, in the manner of a potter, who twirls this mass around from the outside, while Plato's followers place Him within the world, in the manner of a pilot, who remains within that which he directs. (8) So, too, they disagree about the world itself, whether it came into being or had no beginning; whether it will come to an end or continue in existence. Thus, too, they argue about the condition of the soul, which some declare is divine and eternal, and others say is subject to dissolution. According to his own feelings, each has introduced and formulated his doctrine.

(9) No wonder, then, if the talents of the philosophers have distorted the Old Testament. Men of their breed have even adulterated this new little dispensation of ours[3] with their own ideas to match the opinions of the philosophers, and from the one way they have split into many bypaths and blind alleys. I would add this, lest the well-known variety within this Christian religion should seem to anyone to put us in the same class with the philosophers on this point, also, and from the variety of defense should condemn the truth. (10) But, we promptly place against our corruptors the formal reply that there is one rule of truth, which proceeds from Christ and has been transmitted through His companions; and these conflicting interpreters will be found to be of somewhat later date than they.

(11) Everything against truth has been constructed from truth itself. The spirits of error effect this rivalry. By them has this kind of corruption of our life-giving doctrine been instigated; by them, too, have certain tales been started, which, by virtue of their resemblance to the truth, would weaken faith in the latter, or rather, would win it over for themselves, so

---

3 The New Testament.

APOLOGY   117

that anyone may consider that Christians must not be believed because poets and philosophers must not be—or he may think that poets and philosophers should be believed all the more because they are not Christians.[4]

(12) Hence, we are ridiculed when we proclaim that God will hold a final judgment. Yet, in like manner the poets and philosophers establish a tribunal in the underworld. And, if we threaten hell, which is a subterranean storehouse of punishment consisting of a mysterious fire, we are laughed to scorn for it. Yet, Pyriphlegethon is also called a river among the dead. (13) If we mention paradise, a place of supernatural beauty destined to receive the souls of the blessed, separated from knowledge of the ordinary world by the wall, as it were, of that fiery zone, the Elysian Fields have already won belief. (14) Whence, I ask you, comes such close resemblance with the philosophers and poets? From no place else but from our own doctrines. If from our doctrines as their primary source, then our doctrines are more reliable and more worthy of belief than the copies of them which also find belief. But, if from their own ideas, then our doctrines will be considered copies of things subsequent to themselves—something which the nature of things precludes. For, no shadow ever exists before the body nor does a copy precede the original.

Chapter 48

(1) But, come now, suppose some philosopher should declare, as Laberius says, starting from the view of Pythagoras, that a mule becomes a man, and a woman a snake;[1] and

---
4 Cf. Justin, *Apol.* I 54.

---
1 Cf. Min. Fel., *Oct.* 34.7.

suppose he should twist all arguments by virtue of his eloquence, to support this idea—might he not meet with favor and inspire belief? Might not someone even be persuaded by this argument to abstain from meat, lest by any chance he feast upon a piece of beef that was part of his own great-grandfather? Yet, if a Christian promises that from a man a man will rise again, and Gaius himself will return from Gaius, the people will drive him away with stones, not just with shouts.

(2) If there is any reason which controls the re-entry of souls into bodies, why would they not return into the same substance, since this term, 'to be restored,' means that the thing becomes what it was formerly? But, they are not now what they were—because they could not be what they were not before, unless they cease to be what they had been. (3) We also would need, at leisure, a great many passages, if we wished to indulge in such a waste of time, [to decide] who seemed to turn into which beast. But, this point is better support for the argument which we propose; it is certainly more deserving of belief that man will rise again from man, man for man, provided he be a *human,* so that the same quality of the soul is to be restored into the same condition, although not in the same form. (4) But, since the reason for restoring the soul is that it is destined for judgment, necessarily, then, the same man who once was will be restored so that he may receive from God the judgment which he has deserved for his good or bad deeds. And for this reason the bodies, too, will be brought forth, because the soul cannot endure anything without a firm substance, that is, the flesh;[2] and what souls generally have to suffer from the judgment of God they have not deserved without the flesh, within which they committed

---

2 Cf. Tert., *De test. anim.* 4.

all their actions. (5) 'But how,' you say, 'can matter that has decomposed be brought forth?' Consider the case of yourself, man, and you will find grounds for believing it. Recall what you were before you were you. Absolutely nothing! You would remember, if you were anything. So, if you were nothing before your present state, and likewise become nothing when you cease to be, why can you not have another existence from nothing by the will of that same Creator who willed you to exist from nothing? (6) What novelty would happen to you? You did not exist; you came into being; and, when you no longer exist, you will again come into being. Give me, if you can, an explanation of how you came into being and then look for one as to how you will come into being again! Yet, you will certainly come quite easily to be what you once were, because it was with corresponding ease that you came to be what you had never been at any time.

(7) Someone, I suppose, will have a doubt about the power of God who has produced this great body of the world out of what did not exist, which is no less than to produce it out of the death of emptiness and void, vivified by the spirit which is the principle of life of all souls, a manifest example, too, of the resurrection of man given as a testimony to you. (8) The light of day, after it has passed away each twilight, again shines brightly; darkness in turn gives way to light and then follows it; the stars wane and come to brightness again; as soon as the seasons are over they begin again; fruit withers away but returns; seeds spring up with greater fruitfulness only when they have rotted and are destroyed;[3] all things are preserved by dying. All things, from their destruction, are restored. (9) And you, man—so great is your name!—if you know yourself, or if you learn yourself, according to the in-

---

3 Cf. Tert., *De resurrectione carnis* 12; Min. Fel., *Oct.* 34.11.

scription of the Pythia, will you, the master of all things that die and rise again, will you die only to this end, that you perish utterly? Wherever you died, whatever matter destroyed you, consumed you, devoured you, and reduced you to nothing shall restore you. To Him belongs the very nothingness to whom belongs also the whole.

(10) 'So then,' you ask, 'is there always to be death and always resurrection?' If the Lord of all things had intended it thus, you would unwillingly experience the law of your being. But, He has intended it just as He foretold. (11) The same Reason which arranged the universe out of diverse elements, so that all things should consist of rival substances under the reign of unity—void and solid, animate and inanimate, tangible and intangible, light and darkness, life itself and death—this same Reason also has so distributed the duration of the world and formed it into a whole on the condition of this distribution that this first part, which from the beginning of things we have been inhabiting, passes on toward its end in an age subject to time; but the subsequent one, which we hope for, will be prolonged into an eternity without end.

(12) So, when the limit and boundary line which gapes widely in the midst is at hand, so that even the temporal aspect of this world is changed, which is stretched out like a curtain against the disposition of eternity, then shall the entire human race be restored to settle the account for the good or the evil it has merited in this world, from then on to be requited for a limitless and unending eternity. (13) And so, no longer will there be death or resurrection again and again, but we will be the same as we now are and not someone else afterwards; being really worshippers of God, we will always be with God, clad in the eternity of our own proper substance which we have put on. But the profane, and those who have

not turned wholly to God will be in the punishment of perpetual fire, and they shall have from the very nature of this fire a divine supply, as it were, of incorruptibility.

(14) Even the philosophers knew of the difference between this mysterious fire and ordinary fire. That which serves mankind's use is far different from that which serves the judgment of God, whether it casts thunderbolts from heaven or belches forth from the earth through the mountain peaks. It does not consume what it burns, but, while it destroys, it restores.[4] (15) So it is that volcanoes remain, though they are always on fire, and one who has been struck by lightning is safe, for now no fire can ever reduce him to ashes.[5] This is a proof of the fire of eternity, this a foreshadowing of the eternal judgment which renews its punishment: mountains burn, but continue to exist. How will the guilty and the enemies of God fare?

Chapter 49

(1) These are the beliefs which in our case alone are called prejudices; in the case of philosophers and poets they are deemed the height of wisdom and extraordinary genius. They are thought prudent—we, fools; they deserve to be honored —we, to be mocked; rather, more than this—we deserve to be punished! (2) Granted, now, that these beliefs which we maintain are false and even may be justly called prejudices. Still, they are necessary; granted that they are stupid, they

---
[4] Cf. Min. Fel., *Oct.* 35.3.
[5] Tertullian is of the opinion that the body of a person struck by lightning is fireproof. This may be a reminiscence of the superstitious belief that the bodies of persons killed by lightning do not decay and are not devoured by wild beasts (Plutarch, *Quaestiones convivales* 4.2.3), or of a custom, mentioned by Pliny the Elder (*Nat. hist.* 2.54.145), according to which the bodies of such persons are not cremated.

still are of advantage; for men who believe them are bound to become better through the fear of eternal punishment or the hope of eternal consolation. Hence, there is no use in calling those beliefs false or in considering them stupid, while there is some use in accepting them as true. Under no pretext may things be subjected to wholesale condemnation when they serve some advantage. So, it is in yourselves that there is this prejudice which condemns things that are of advantage. It follows, then, that our teachings cannot be stupid, either. (3) At least, even if they are false and stupid, they are certainly not harmful to anyone. For, they are like many other beliefs upon which you impose no punishment, which, though vain and fictitious, go unaccused and unpunished as being harmless. In the case of such things, if one must pass judgment at all, he must judge that they deserve ridicule, but not swords, fire, crosses, and wild beasts. (4) Not only the blind mob exults and heaps insults upon them with this wicked type of savagery, but even certain of your own number, who gain their popularity with the mob through wrong-doing, glory in it, as though everything which you can do to us were not a matter of our free will! (5) Certainly, only if I want to be, am I a Christian. And only then will you condemn me, if I am willing to be condemned. But, since you cannot do anything to me unless I am willing, what you can do is a matter of my own will, not of your power. (6) Consequently, even the mob takes an empty delight in our torture. So, too, ours is the joy which takes its own vengeance, since we prefer to be condemned rather than to fall away from God. On the other hand, those who hate us ought to grieve rather than rejoice when we have attained that which was the object of our choice.

Chapter 50

(1) 'Why, then,' you say, 'do you complain because we persecute you, if you desire to suffer, since you ought to love those through whom you suffer what you desire?' Certainly, we are willing to suffer, but in the way that a soldier endures war. No one actually has a liking for suffering, since that inevitably involves anxiety and danger. (2) However, a man fights a battle with all his strength and, though he complained about there being a battle, he finds delight in conquering in battle, because he is attaining glory and reward. There is a battle for us, because we are called to trial in court so that we may fight there for the truth while our life hangs in the balance. And the victory is to hold fast to that for which we have fought.[1] This victory has attached to it the glory of pleasing God and the reward of eternal life.

(3) But, we are cut down. Certainly, when we have held fast. We have won the victory when we are killed; we escape at last when we are led forth. So you may call us 'faggot fellows' and 'half-axle men,' because we are bound to a half-axle post and burned in a circle of faggots. This is the garb of our victory; this is our robe embroidered with palms; in such a chariot do we celebrate our triumph. (4) Quite rightly are we a source of displeasure to the vanquished, for on this account we are considered desperadoes and profligates. But, such recklessness and depravity, for the sake of glory and renown, raise aloft among you the banner of courage.

(5) Mucius willingly left his right hand on the altar:[2] oh, what nobility of soul! Empedocles made an offering of his entire self to the flames of Aetna:[3] oh, what strength of mind!

---
1 Cf. Min. Fel., *Oct.* 37.1.
2 Cf. Livy (2.12); Min. Fel., *Oct.* 37.3 n.1.
3 Cf. Diog. Laert. (8.2.69).

That well-known foundress of Carthage surrendered on the funeral pyre a second marriage:[4] oh, what a glorious mark of chastity! (6) Regulus, lest he alone might be spared his life in comparison with many of the enemy, endured tortures in his entire body:[5] oh, what a man of fortitude, victorious even in his captivity! While Anaxarchus was being pounded to death with a pestle used for barley groats, he cried out: 'Pound, pound away at the shell of Anaxarchus, for you are not pounding Anaxarchus!'[6] Oh, the lofty soul of that philosopher, who even joked about such a death as his! (7) I pass over those who by their own sword or by some other gentler manner of death made sure of their fame after death. See, even the struggles against the torturers are awarded a crown by you. (8) The Athenian courtesan, when her executioner was at length weary, bit off her own tongue and spit it into the face of the raging tyrant, that she might thereby spit out her voice, too, and not be able to confess the names of the conspirators, even if she should want to, being finally won over.[7] (9) When Zeno, the Eleatic, was asked by Dionysius what benefit philosophy offered, and replied: 'A contempt of death,' he was subjected to the unbearable scourge of the tyrant and sealed his opinion with his death.[8] Certainly, the lashes of the Spartans, intensified as the relatives stood watch-

---

[4] According to Timaeus of Tauromenion (frg. 23 Müller), Dido committed suicide after the death of her husband, lest she be forced to marry the King of the Lybians. On the plea that she had to perform a sacrifice solemnly promised, she erected a pyre and, after having kindled it, leaped into the flames. The same story is found in Justinus, *Trogi Pompei Historiarum Philippicarum Epitoma* 18.4-7.

[5] Cf. Cic., *De officiis* 3.26-27.

[6] Cf. Diog. Laert. (9.10.59).

[7] Pausanias (1.23.1) and Pliny, *Nat. hist.* 7.23.87, cite this example of female fortitude. The courtesan's name was Leaena, and Harmodius and Aristogiton were the conspirators.

[8] Cf. *De anima* 58.5.

ing and giving encouragement, confer honor on the family which endures it in proportion to the blood shed.

(10) Oh, what glory, which is permitted because it is man's! To it neither a depraved prejudice nor a reckless intention is attributed when it scorns death and every kind of cruelty. In this case it is permissible to suffer for one's country, one's empire, or for friendship everything which it is not permissible to suffer for God! (11) Yet, for all those men you mold statues, you put inscriptions on their busts, and you engrave their titles of distinction for all time. To the extent that you can, by means of monuments, you yourselves, in a manner of speaking, grant a resurrection to the dead. But, the man who hopes for a true resurrection at the hand of God, if he suffers for God, is a madman!

(12) But, carry on, good officials; you will become much better in the eyes of the people if you sacrifice the Christians for them. Crucify us—torture us—condemn us—destroy us! Your iniquity is the proof of our innocence. For this reason God permits us to suffer these things. In fact, by recently condemning a Christian maid to the *pander* rather than to the *panther* [in the arena],[9] you confessed that among us a stain on our virtue is considered worse than any punishment or any form of death.[10] (13) Yet, your tortures accomplish nothing, though each is more refined than the last; rather, they are an enticement to our religion. We become more numerous every time we are hewn down by you: the blood of Christians is seed.

(14) Many among you urge men to endure suffering and death, as Cicero does in his *Tusculans,* Seneca in his essay

---

9 The Latin, *ad lenonem . . . quam ad leonem,* is typical of Tertullian's powerful sound effects, but is difficult to imitate in translation.
10 As, for example, in the case of St. Agnes. Cf. Ambrose, *De virginibus* 2.4.19.

on chance, Diogenes, Pyrrho, and Callinicus; yet, their words do not discover such disciples as do the Christians who teach by deeds. (15) That very obstinacy which you rebuke is the teacher.[11] For, who is not stirred by the contemplation of it to inquire what is really beneath the surface? And who, when he has inquired, does not approach us? Who, when he has approached, does not desire to suffer so that he may procure the full grace of God, that he may purchase from Him full pardon by paying with his own blood? (16) For, by this means, all sins are forgiven. That is why we thank you immediately for your sentences of condemnation. Such is the difference between things divine and human. When we are condemned by you, we are acquitted by God.

---

11 Cf. Pliny, *Epist.* 10.96.

TERTULLIAN

THE TESTIMONY OF THE SOUL

Translated
by
RUDOLPH ARBESMANN, O.S.A., Ph.D.
Fordham University

IMPRIMI POTEST

TARCISIUS A. RATTLER, O.S.A.
Vicar Provincial

New York
February 26, 1950

INTRODUCTION

ONE OF THE METHODS employed by the Christian Apologists for gaining a hearing for their faith was to show that, in a number of fundamental questions, many pagan philosophers and poets were in agreement with Christian teaching. In his *Testimony of the Soul,* Tertullian acknowledges the failure of this approach, because the foes of Christianity reject even their most admired teachers whenever they seem to uphold the truth contained in Christianity. The use of the Holy Books as a basis for argument is of no avail, because no one believes in them unless he is already a Christian. Tertullian, using a bold innovation, introduces a new method, by calling as a witness the simple, unsophisticated human soul not yet deformed by any learning. In the mouth of the common people, he argues, there are found a number of expressions which clearly reveal a notion of Christian truths, such as the belief in the one God, the belief in His goodness and uncompromising justice in rewarding and punishing beyond the grave, the belief in the existence of demons, and the belief in immortality. These expressions are spontaneous testimonies of the human soul; hence, of nature and of God Himself as its Creator.

Though in some places the author offers assertions rather than proofs, his little work possesses great charm because of the warmth of feeling with which it is written. Especially effective is the way in which the soul is addressed.

The Testimony of the Soul must be dated shortly after the *Apology* (197), to which Tertullian refers in Chapter 5: 'As we have shown in its proper place.'[1] As a matter of fact, *The*

---
1 Cf. *Apol.* 19.

Testimony of the Soul is little more than a further development of a sentence in the *Apology* (17.6) : 'O testimony of the soul, which is by natural instinct Christian.'

The text followed in the present translation is that of A. Reifferscheid and G. Wissowa (*CSEL* 20 Vienna 1890) 134 ff.; the edition by W. A. J. C. Scholte (Amsterdam 1934) was consulted throughout.

SELECT BIBLIOGRAPHY

Texts:

    F. Oehler, *Quinti Septimii Florentis Tertulliani Quae Supersunt Omnia* I (Leipzig 1853) 399 ff.
    A. Reifferscheid and G. Wissowa, *CSEL* 20 (Vienna 1890) 134 ff.
    W. A. J. C. Scholte, *Q. S. Florentis Tertulliani libellum De testimonio animae praefatione, translatione, adnotationibus instructum edidit* (Amsterdam 1934).

Translations:

    S. Thelwall, *The Ante-Nicene Fathers* (American reprint of the Edinburgh edition) III (New York 1903) 175ff.
    K. A. H. Kellner, *Tertullians ausgewählte Schriften* I (Bibl. d. Kirchenväter 7, Kempten and Munich 1912) 203ff.

Other Sources:

    G. Esser, *Die Seelenlehre Tertullians* (Paderborn 1893) 166-176.
    A. Miodonski, 'Tertullian de testimonio animae,' *Eos* 5 (1904) 117ff.

THE TESTIMONY OF THE SOUL

Chapter 1

GREAT LOVE for research and an even greater memory are required of a student who would gather, from the most accepted works of the philosophers, poets, and any other teachers of secular learning and wisdom, proofs for the truth of Christianity, in order to convict its rivals and persecutors by their own learned apparatus of error in themselves, and, thus, of their injustice toward us. Indeed, some of our brethren, who, from their former literary pursuits, have kept their liking for laborious research as well as their retentiveness of memory, have composed small treatises of this kind.[1] In these they have related and at the same time attested point by point to the reason, origin, and tradition of our opinions and their proofs. From all this it may clearly be seen that we have embraced nothing new or revolting, nothing in which even the common and public literature would not support us with approbation, whether we have rejected something as erroneous or accepted something as justified. Unfortunately, however, the stubbornness of men in disbelieving has denied credence even to their own teachers, who otherwise are widely approved and read, whenever they touch upon the proofs of Christian apologetics. Then, the poets are fools when they depict the gods with human passions and as fabu-

---

[1] Tertullian has in mind Christian Apologists who wrote before him, men like Quadratus, Miltiades (probably from Asia Minor), Apollinaris (Bishop of Hierapolis in Phrygia), Melito (Bishop of Sardis), Aristides, Athenagoras (both Athenian philosophers), St. Justin Martyr, Tatian (from Assyria), Theophilus of Antioch, St. Irenaeus, and Clement of Alexandria.

lous characters; then, the philosophers are harsh when they knock at the gates of truth. A man who pronounces near-Christian doctrines will still be considered wise and prudent, while, if he should strive earnestly for knowledge and wisdom either by rejecting pagan ceremonies or by denouncing the world, he is sure to be branded as a Christian. Therefore, we will no longer have anything to do with the literature and instruction of a perverted felicity, to which is given more belief in its errors than in its truth. Let them see for themselves whether some of their authors have made a pronouncement concerning the one and only God. Let us even assume that nothing at all has been reported by them which a Christian may acknowledge without being able to disprove. For, that which has been reported[2] not all men know, nor do those who know feel confident that it is sufficiently established. So far are men from assenting to our writings, to which no one comes unless he is already a Christian.

I call to our aid new testimony, even better known than all literature, more discussed than all doctrine, more familiar to the masses than any publication, greater than the whole man, that is, all that is peculiar to man. Stand, then, in the middle, O soul. If thou art a divine and eternal thing, in accordance with the opinions of many philosophers—so much more reason thou wilt not lie. Or, if thou art not divine at all, because thou art mortal, as it seems to Epicurus alone—all the more reason thou wilt not be obligated to lie. Whether thou art received from heaven or conceived from earth, whether thou art composed of numbers or of atoms, whether thou takest thy beginning with the body or whether thou comest in after the body—from whatever source and in whatever way thou didst come into existence—it is thou that makest man a ra-

---

2 In pagan literature.

tional being with the greatest capacity for understanding and knowledge.

I do not call upon thee who art formed in the schools, practiced in the libraries, nourished in the Attic academies and porticoes—thou who dost belch forth wisdom. I address thee who art simple, unskilled, unpolished and uneducated, that is, of such a nature as they have thee who have thee alone, that very soul in its entirety coming from the crossroad, public square and workshop. It is thy inexperience that I need, since no one has any faith in thy little bit of experience. I shall demand from thee an answer concerning those things which thou bringest with thee into man, which thou hast learned to perceive, either from thyself or through thy author—whoever he may be. Thou art not a Christian, as far as I know, for, as a rule, the soul is not born Christian; it becomes Christian. Nevertheless, the Christians are now pleading for testimony from thee, an alien, against thine own, so that they may blush even before thee, because they hate and ridicule us for things the guilty knowledge of which makes thee an accessory.

Chapter 2

We do not receive applause by proclaiming that there is but one God, called by this name alone, from whom all things come and to whom the universe is subject. Give testimony, if this is thy knowledge. For, we hear thee openly, and with a complete freedom which is not allowed to us, use in private and in public such expressions as, 'God willing' and 'May God grant this.' By these expressions thou dost indicate that someone does exist, and thou dost confess that all power belongs to him for whose will thou dost have regard.

At the same time, thou dost deny that there are other gods, while thou dost call Saturn, Jupiter, Mars, and Minerva by their own names. For, thou dost confirm that He alone is God whom alone thou dost name God; so that, when thou dost sometimes call the other gods, thou dost seem to use a foreign and, as it were, a borrowed expression.

Furthermore, the nature of the God whom we proclaim is not hidden from thee. 'God is good' and 'God does good' are expressions of thine. And, plainly, thou dost add, 'But man is evil.' By this contrary proposition, thou indirectly and figuratively dost accuse man of being evil, for the very reason that he has departed from God who is good. Moreover, since in the power of the God of goodness and benignity every blessing among us becomes the highest consecration of our moral life and conduct, thou dost utter just as easily as a Christian must, 'May God bless thee.' But, when thou turnest the blessing of God into a curse, then by this very word thou dost confess in the same manner as we that all power over us belongs to Him.

There are those who do not deny that God exists, but plainly do not regard Him as the Searcher, Arbiter and Judge of our actions. It is on this point that they especially despise us who throw ourselves into the arms of this doctrine because of fear of the predicted judgment. Thus do they wish to honor God, while they separate Him from the cares of observation and the annoyances of chastisement, Him to whom they do not attribute even wrath. For, they say, if God becomes angry, He is subject to corruption and passion. Moreover, that which is subject to suffering and to corruption is also subject to annihilation, which God is not. But, these very men, who elsewhere declare that the soul is divine and bestowed by God, fall upon the testimony of the soul itself, which has to be turned back against their former opinion. For, if the soul is either divine or given by God, it undoubtedly knows its giver, and, if it knows Him, it certainly fears Him, too; especially, since this augmenter is so great. Or does it not fear the One whom it wishes to be propitious rather than angry? Whence, therefore, is this natural fear of the soul toward God, if God is incapable of wrath? How is it that He is feared who cannot be offended? What is feared, if not anger? Whence does anger arise, if not because of punishment? Whence punishment, if not as a result of judgment? Whence judgment, if not as a result of power? And whose is the highest power, if not God's alone? Hence, O soul, because of thy knowledge thou art justified in proclaiming in private and in public without fear of scorn and prohibition: 'God sees all' and 'I commend thee to God' and 'God will reward you' and 'God will judge between us.' Whence does this come to pass, if thou art not a Christian? And this happens often, even when thou has wound around thy head the fillet of Ceres,[1] and when thou art clad in the scarlet mantle of Saturn[2] or the linen garment of the goddess Isis;[3] in a word, in these very temples thou dost implore God as judge. Thou dost stand beneath the statue of Aesculapius and adorn the bronze statue of Juno and furnish the helmet of Minerva with dusky fig-

---

1 Tertullian, like Juvenal (*Satires* 6.50), seems to refer to the procession on the *sacrum anniversarium Cereris*, a festival celebrated in August by the Roman matrons in special costumes. The fillets seem to have been worn not only by the priestesses of Ceres, but also by all those who had been initiated. We have no proof, however, that the festival, introduced shortly before the Hannibalic War, was still in existence after the time of Augustus.
2 The priests of Saturn wore a toga with an especially broad purple border, and a loose outer garment of a color called Galatian red (cf. Tertullian, *On the Pallium* 4); the best scarlet dyes came from Galatia and Armenia.
3 Apuleius, a second-century African writer, describes, in his romance *Metamorphoses* or *The Golden Ass* (11.10), the procession on the festival of Isis: 'Then there came streaming the crowd of those who had been initiated into the divine mysteries, men and women belonging to every position in life and of every age, shining in the clean brightness of their linen garments.

ures,[4] and then thou dost call upon no one of the gods who are present as witnesses. In thy forum thou dost appeal to a judge from somewhere else; in thy temples thou dost suffer another god. O testimony of truth, which in the very midst of the demons makes thee a witness for the Christians!

Chapter 3

Verily, some follower of Chrysippus[1] ridicules us when we assert that demons exist just as if we did not prove their existence, we who alone drive them out of bodies. Thy curses answer that they exist and are filled with horror. Thou dost call a man a demon who, either because of his uncleanness or wickedness or insolence or of whatever stain we attribute to the demons, is repulsive according to the inevitable law of hatred. Finally, in every instance of annoyance and in every expression of contempt and detestation, thou dost utter the word 'Satan.' This is the one whom we call the angel of wickedness, the artificer of every error, the corrupter of the whole world; through him, man was deceived from the beginning so that he transgressed the commandment of God and, therefore, having been given unto death, made the whole human race, which was infected by his seed, the transmitter of condemnation. Thou dost then perceive who thy perverter is, and, although the Christians alone and whatever group profess the Lord know him, thou, too, knowest him in thy hatred of him.

---

4 This obscure passage may allude to an unknown rite on a festival of Minerva, or to the black fleece which the priests of Bellona wore on their heads; cf. F. Oehler's note to the passage in his edition of Tertullian's works, I (Leipzig 1853) 404.

---

1 Chrysippus of Soli, one of the most distinguished of the Stoic philosophers, a pupil of Zeno and Cleanthes. It was the specifically Christian (and Jewish) notions of demons and demoniacal possession to which the later Stoics objected.

Chapter 4

Now, with regard to thy opinion in a matter which most closely concerns thee, inasmuch as it refers to thy very condition of existence: We affirm that thou dost continue to exist after the extinction of life and to await the day of judgment; and that, according to thy deserts, thou wilt be delivered either to torture or to bliss, both eternal; and that, in order to be capable of it, thy former substance must necessarily return to thee, the matter and memory of the same human being. For, thou couldst feel neither evil nor good without the agency of the sensitive body, and there would be no reason for judgment without the presentation of the very one who deserved the severity of judgment. This is the Christian opinion. Although it is much more honorable than the Pythagorean—since it does not transfer thee into beasts, and more complete than the Platonic—since it even returns to thee the dowry of the body, and more serious than the Epicurean—since it defends thee from annihilation, yet, because of its name, it is considered a mere delusion and folly, and, as men say, a presumption. But, we do not blush at our presumption if thou dost share it.

For, to begin with, when thou dost mention someone who has died, thou dost call him 'poor man,' not, of course, because he is snatched away from the good of life, but because he has already been delivered to punishment and judgment. But, at other times, thou dost say of the dead that they are well taken care of. By this, thou dost testify that life is a burden and death a blessing. Thou dost say they are well taken care of even when thou dost visit their graves, and dost make offerings of viands and dainties to thyself rather than to them, or when thou dost return home from the graves half tipsy.¹ But, I demand thy sober opinion. Thou dost call the dead poor when thou speakest thy own thoughts, when thou art far away from them. For, thou art unable to criticize their lot at their banquets where they are, as it were, present and reclining. Of course, thou must shower compliments on those on whose account thou art feasting more gaily. Dost thou call a man poor, then, who does not feel anything? But, how is it that thou cursest a man whose memory comes back to thee with the sting of an old offense, as if he could feel? On him thou dost wish that the earth may lie heavy,² and his ashes be tormented in the realm of the lower world. In like manner, when thou dost feel kindly disposed toward a man to whom thou owest thanks, thou wishest consolation for his bones and ashes, and that he may rest in peace among the dead.

If thou art incapable of suffering after death, if no power of feeling remains, if, finally, thou art nothing after having left the body, why dost thou lie to thyself as if thou wert capable of enduring anything further? Indeed, why dost thou fear death at all, if thou must fear nothing after death— since nothing is to be experienced after death? For, although it can be said that death is feared, not for anything it threatens in the beyond, but in that it deprives man of the comforts of life, yet, since thou dost depart equally from the discomforts of life which are far more numerous, thou dost remove the fear by gaining the better part; nor must the loss of

---

1 Tertullian refers to the *Parentalia* in February, a festival of dead kinsfolk, and especially of dead parents. Ovid, in his commentary on the calendar (*Fasti* 2.533ff.), gives an account of the ritual of the occasion, including the offering made to the spirits of the dead.
2 *Sit tibi terra levis*—'May the earth lie lightly upon thee'—is a very common inscription on Roman tombs and was often shortened to S.T.T.L. The formula occurs also in the works of the Roman poets Tibullus, Martial, and Juvenal.

goods be feared which is outweighed by another good, namely the relief from discomforts. Nothing is to be feared from that which sets us free from all fear. If thou art afraid to depart from life because thou dost know it to be the highest good, thou certainly ought not fear death, since thou dost not know it to be an evil. But, when thou dost fear, thou dost know that it is an evil. Moreover, thou wouldst not know that it is an evil and be afraid of it, if thou didst not know that there exists something after death which makes it an evil, so that thou art afraid of it.

Let us now pass over that natural way of fearing death. No one should fear that which he cannot escape. I shall attack the problem from the other direction, that is, by arguing on the ground of a happier hope after death. It would be tedious to relate again the stories of men like Curtius,[3] and Regulus,[4] or the Greek heroes. The high praises they received as a result of their contempt of death, for the sake of posthumous fame, are innumerable. Who today does not take good care to have his memory celebrated after death by endeavoring to perpetuate his name either by works of literature or by praise of his sincere character or even by the display of his tomb? How is it that the soul today strives for something which it desires only after death, and prepares so carefully that which it will use only after departure from life? Certainly, it would care nothing about the future, if it knew nothing about the future. But, perhaps you feel more sure

---

3 A legendary hero of Rome, who, according to one story, sacrificed himself by jumping, fully armed and on horseback, into a gulf which had suddenly opened in the Roman Forum, and which, according to the seers, the Romans could close only by sacrificing their most precious possession. Curtius considered nothing more precious than a brave citizen.

4 A Roman general and consul who was taken prisoner during the First Punic War. According to tradition, he was sent to Rome on parole to negotiate a peace, but urged the Senate to refuse the proposals of the Carthaginians; on his return to Carthage, he was tortured to death.

about the capability of feeling after death than you are about the future resurrection, a doctrine of ours which is branded as a reckless supposition. Yet, this also is proclaimed by the soul. For, if someone inquires about a person who has died long ago as though he were alive, the following answer readily comes to our lips: 'He has already gone.' He is supposed to return, then.

Chapter 5

These testimonies of the soul are as true as they are simple, as simple as they are common, as common as they are universal, as universal as they are natural, as natural as they are divine. I do not think that they can seem worthless and unimportant to anyone, if he should deliberate upon the majesty of nature by which the authority of the soul is appraised. As much as you will give to the teacher, so much you will award to the pupil. Nature is the teacher; the soul is the pupil. Whatever either the one has taught or the other has learned has come from God, that is, the Teacher of the teacher. What the soul can divine with regard to its chief teacher, you are able to judge from that which is within you. Learn to perceive that which makes you perceive. Consider how it operates: a prophet in forebodings, an augur in omens, a foreseer in [fortunate and unfortunate] events. Is it something to be wondered at, if, being a gift of God, it knows how to divine? Is it really something strange if it knows Him by whom it was bestowed? Even deceived by its adversary, it remembers its Author, His goodness and law, its own end, and its adversary. Is it so extraordinary, then, if, being a gift of God, it proclaims the same things which God has given to His own people to know?

But, he who does not consider such outbursts of the soul

as the doctrine of nature and the silent deposit of a congenital and inborn knowledge will rather say that the practice and, as it were, the vice of speaking in this fashion have been strengthened by the opinions of published books which have been widely spread among the common people. At all events, the soul was prior to letters; speech, prior to books; ideas, prior to setting them down in writing; and man himself, prior to the philosopher and poet. Are we to believe, therefore, that before literature and its dissemination men lived without making utterances of this sort? That no one should have spoken of God and His goodness, no one of death, no one of the lower world? Speech went abegging, I suppose, or rather could not exist at all, since those things were lacking without which it cannot exist even today, although it has become more perfect, more rich, and more refined. Indeed, it could not have existed, if those things which are today so simple, so constantly present, so obvious, and born somehow on our very lips, did not exist in the past—before letters had sprung up in the world, before Mercury,[1] I suppose, was born. And whence, I ask, did it happen that letters came to know and disseminate for the use of speech things which no mind had ever conceived, or tongue had ever expressed, or ear had ever heard? For, since the books of Divine Scripture, which belong to us or to the Jews, upon whom, as on a wild olive tree, we have been grafted,[2] are much older than secular letters, or at least by some short period of time—as we have shown in its proper place[3] in proving their credibility—and if the soul has appropriated these utterances from letters, then one must believe it has taken them from ours, not yours. For, earlier

---

[1] Mercury, the god of trade and divine exponent of success of every kind, was also given credit for having invented letters.
[2] Cf. Rom. 11.24.
[3] Tertullian refers to Ch. 19 of his *Apology*.

works are more fitted for the instruction of the soul than later ones which, for their part, had to submit to instruction by the earlier ones. Even if we should grant that the soul has been instructed from your writings, the tradition would reach back to the principal source, and whatever you were so fortunate to have taken and handed down from our writings would be entirely ours. It matters little, therefore, whether the knowledge of the soul has been formed by God or by the letters of God. Why, then, O man, do you wish that these things have proceeded from the human opinions of your literature into the well-established and common usage of language?

Chapter 6

Therefore, trust your own books. As to our Scriptures, trust them all the more because they are divine. As to the judgment of the soul itself, trust nature in like manner. Of these, choose the one whom you observe to be the more faithful sister of truth. If you distrust your own literature, neither God nor nature is capable of lying. In order to trust nature as well as God, trust the soul. It will bring it about that you trust yourself. It certainly is the soul which you value in proportion to the greatness it gives to you; to which you belong totally; which is all to you; without which you cannot live or die; for the sake of which you neglect God. When you are afraid to become a Christian, question the soul. Why does it take the name of God in its mouth, while it worships another? Why does it speak of demons, when it means to denote spirits held to be accursed? Why does it utter protestations heavenward, and its curses earthward? Why does it render service in one place, and call upon an avenger elsewhere? Why does it pass judgment on the dead? Why does it have expressions from the Christians, whom it desires neither to hear nor to see? Why has it either handed over these words to us, or received them from us? Why has it either taught, or learned them? Look with distrust at the accordance in doctrine, while there is so great a discordance in the mode of life. You are foolish if you attribute such expressions to our language alone, or to the Greek which is considered closely related, thus denying the universality of nature. It is not to the Latins and Greeks alone that the soul comes as a gift from heaven. Among all the nations man is one and the same, though the name varies; there is one soul, though many tongues; one spirit, though many sounds. Each people has its own language, but the subject matter of every language is common to all. God and the goodness of God are everywhere, and everywhere is the testimony. Every soul justly proclaims those things which we are not allowed even to hint at. Deservedly, then, every soul is a defendant as well as a witness of the truth, and it will stand before the forecourts of God on the day of judgment without anything to say.

O soul, thou always didst proclaim God, yet not seek Him; didst detest the demons, yet adore them; didst invoke the judgment of God, yet not believe in its existence; didst foresee the infernal punishments, yet not guard against them. Thou didst know about the Christian name, yet didst persecute it.

TERTULLIAN

TO SCAPULA

*Translated
by*
RUDOLPH ARBESMANN, O.S.A., Ph.D.
Fordham University

INTRODUCTION

During the last years of the reign of Septimius Severus (A.D. 193-211), and under his immediate successors, the Church enjoyed relative tranquility. She made considerable progress in expansion and was able to consolidate her organization. However, the attitude of high imperial officials toward Christianity continued to be hostile. About A. D. 215, for instance, the outstanding and influential Roman jurist Domitius Ulpianus made a collection of the imperial rescripts which had been issued against the Christians. The collection itself has not come down to us, but is referred to by Lactantius in his *Divine Institutions* (5.11.19): 'In the seventh book of his work, *The Office of the Proconsul*, Domitius has collected the vicious rescripts of the emperors in order to show what punishments ought to be inflicted on those who professed to be worshippers of God.' Since the general prohibition of the Christian religion was not revoked, the legal situation remained the same, and the application of the persecuting edicts rested with the individual provincial governors.

This is the background of the small apologetic writing which Tertullian addressed in the form of an open letter to Scapula, governor of proconsular Africa between 211 and 213. Scapula had taken action and started a bitter persecution.

Tertullian begins by stating that, in appealing to the governor, he is not motivated by fear, but by the Christian precept of loving one's enemies. He continues by laying down and defending the fundamental principle of liberty of conscience: that each individual has the natural right to worship what he thinks good and that religion should be embraced of one's own free will and not through force. Moreover, any doubt regarding the loyalty of the Christians toward the emperor is unfounded, since they know that his authority comes from God. Hence, they love and honor him, desiring and praying for his well-being and the welfare of the Empire. The author's main argument, however, consists in enumerating the terrible punishments meted out by divine disposition to all those who had persecuted the faithful. Moreover, a certain number of recent events—devastating rainfalls, fires which hung over the walls of Carthage, the eclipse of the sun, the governor's own illness—are warning signs from Heaven. Tertullian appeals to the governor 'not to fight against God,' but to act humanely, as many of his colleagues had done before. He concludes by raising the question as to what the governor would do with the great number of Christians if they all gave themselves up to the authorities. With his main argument, Tertullian anticipated by a hundred years a work of Lactantius, *On the Deaths of the Persecutors* (*De mortibus persecutorum*), written in the same strain, though on a larger scale.

The work must have been written shortly after August 14, 212, since Tertullian refers to the eclipse of the sun, which took place on that date, as a recent event.

The text followed in the present translation is that of F. Oehler (Leipzig 1853); the edition by T. H. Bindley (Oxford 1893) was consulted throughout.

SELECT BIBLIOGRAPHY

Texts:

F. Oehler, *Quinti Septimii Florentis Tertulliani Quae Supersunt Omnia* I (Leipzig 1853) 539ff.

T. H. Bindley, *Quinti Septimi Florentis Tertulliani De praescriptione haereticorum, Ad Martyras, Ad Scapulam*, with introduction and notes (Oxford 1893) 127ff.

Translations:

S. Thelwall, *The Ante-Nicene Fathers* (American reprint of the Edinburgh edition) III (New York 1903) 105ff.

K. A. H. Kellner and G. Esser, *Tertullians ausgewählte Schriften* II (Bibl. d. Kirchenväter 24, Kempten and Munich 1915) 264ff.

Other Sources:

J. Schmidt, 'Ein Beitrag zur Chronologie der Schriften Tertullians und der Prokonsuln von Afrika,' *Rhein. Museum* 46 (1891) 77-98.

TO SCAPULA

Chapter 1

WE ARE, INDEED, neither dismayed nor greatly disturbed at the persecutions which we suffer from ignorant men, since we joined this way of life with the understanding that we pledged ourselves to enter into the present conflicts at the risk even of our lives, wishing to obtain those things which God promises in return, and fearing to suffer those things which He threatens for any contrary course of life. Accordingly, we battle against all your cruelty, even rushing voluntarily to the contest, and we rejoice more when condemned than when acquitted. We have therefore presented this petition to you, not fearing for ourselves, and by no means for our friends, but for you and for all our enemies. For, we are commanded by the teachings of our religion to love even our enemies and to pray for those who persecute us:[1] so that our goodness may be perfect and peculiar to us, and not that of the run of the world. To love friends is the custom for all men, but to love enemies is customary only for Christians. We, then, who are saddened by your ignorance, have compassion on human error, and look ahead into the future, seeing signs of it threatening daily—we, I say, must proceed to set before you in this way what you do not wish to hear openly.

Chapter 2

We worship one God, whom you all know, since nature is your teacher, at whose lightning and thunder you tremble, at

---

1 Cf. Matt. 5.44; Luke 6.27,35; Rom. 12.14.

whose benefits you rejoice. The rest you yourselves think to be gods, but we know to be demons. It is the law of mankind and the natural right of each individual to worship what he thinks proper, nor does the religion of one man either harm or help another. But, it is not proper for religion to compel men to religion, which should be accepted of one's own accord, not by force, since sacrifices also are required of a willing mind. So, even if you compel us to sacrifice, you will render no service to your gods. They will not desire sacrifices from the unwilling unless they are quarrelsome—but a god is not quarrelsome. Finally, He who is the true God bestows all His gifts equally—on the unholy as well as on His own. This is why He also appointed an eternal judgment for those who are thankful and for those who are not. You have never caught us, whom you consider sacrilegious, in theft; much less, in committing sacrilege. But, all those who rob the temples both swear by the gods and worship the same; they are not Christians, yet they are caught in committing sacrilege. It would be tedious to relate in what other ways all the gods are ridiculed and despised, even by their own worshippers.

So, too, we are defamed regarding the majesty of the emperor, yet never could the followers of Albinus, or of Niger, or of Cassius[1] be found among the Christians; but, those same men who, up to the very day before, had sworn by the genii

---

[1] When the Emperor Commodus (A.D. 180-193) died without a successor, L. Septimius Severus was proclaimed Emperor by the Danubian legions, D. Clodius Albinus by the legions in Britain and on the Rhine, and C. Pescennius Niger by the Syrian legions. In the civil war which followed, Niger was defeated and killed in 194; Albinus, in 197. The followers of both were cruelly persecuted by Septimius Severus. Avidius Cassius, a Roman general under Marcus Aurelius (161-180), rebelled in 175, after he had been falsely informed of the Emperor's death. Though proscribed by the senate, he won many followers in the East, but was assassinated in August of the same year. Unlike Septimius Severus, Marcus Aurelius showed great clemency toward the followers of Cassius.

of the emperors,[2] who had both offered up and vowed sacrifices for their health, who had often condemned the Christians, were found to be enemies of the emperors. A Christian is an enemy of no one, much less of the emperor. Since he knows him to be appointed by his own God, he must love, reverence, honor, and wish him well, together with the whole Roman Empire, as long as the world shall last. For, so long the Roman Empire will last.[3] In this way, then, do we honor the emperor, as is both lawful for us and expedient for him, as a man next to God: who has received whatever he is from God; who is inferior to God alone. This, too, he himself will desire. For, in this way he is greater than all, since he is inferior only to the true God. Thus, he is even greater than the gods themselves, since they, too, are also in his power. This is why we also offer sacrifice for the welfare of the emperor, but to God, who is our God and his—and in the way God commanded us, with pure prayer. God, the Maker of the universe, does not need any odor or blood. These are the food of demons. And the demons we not only reject, but convict; we daily expose them, and cast them out of men, as is well known to many. Therefore, we pray in a better way for the welfare of the emperor, asking it from Him who is able to give it. Surely, it can be sufficiently clear to you that we act according to the teachings of godly patience,

---

2 By the end of the first century A.D, the worship of the genius of the Emperor had become the most characteristic feature of Roman religion. The oath by his genius served as the symbol of national unity and the criterion by which the loyalty and patriotism of the individual were tested.

3 The same idea is expressed by Lactantius in his *Divine Institutions* (7.25.7f.). It became a proverbial saying:
> 'As long as the Colosseum stands, Rome shall stand;
> When the Colosseum falls, Rome will fall;
> When Rome falls, the world will fall.'

(*Excerptiones Patrum, Collectanea,* mistakenly attributed to the Venerable Bede, *PL* 95.543.)

when, as such a great multitude of men—almost the majority in every city—we live in silence and loyalty, known, perhaps, more as individuals than as a group, and knowable in no other way than by the reformation of our former vices. For far be it from us to take it ill that we suffer things for which we long, or to plot of ourselves any vengeance which we await from God.

Chapter 3

Nevertheless (as we have said before), we must grieve, because no city will go unpunished for the shedding of our blood, as was the situation under the governorship of Hilarian,[1] when they had cried out concerning our burial grounds: 'Let them have no *areae*—no burial grounds!' But, the result was that they themselves had no *areae*—no threshing-floors:[2] they did not gather their harvest. Moreover, with regard to the rains of the past year, it has become clear of what they have reminded mankind, namely, that there was a deluge in ancient times because of the unbelief and wickedness of men. What the fires which lately hung all night over the walls of Carthage threatened is known to those men who were eye witnesses. Of what message the sounds of the preceding thunders were portents is known to those men who hardened themselves against them. All these are signs of the impending wrath of God, which we must, in whatever way we can, both announce and proclaim, and in the meanwhile

---

1 This is the same procurator Hilarian under whom the famous martyrs of the North African Church, SS. Perpetua and Felicitas, suffered martyrdom, in company with a group of their fellow countrymen, at Carthage on March 7, 203. Hilarian administered the province of Africa as procurator after the death of the proconsul Minucius Oppianus.

2 A play upon words: Lat. *area* may mean both the threshing floor and the cemetery.

pray that it may be only local. The universal and final wrath will be felt in due time by those who interpret these samples of it in another fashion. The well-known strange appearance of the sun, when its light was almost extinguished,[3] during the meeting of the court[4] at Utica, also was an omen, inasmuch as the sun could not have suffered this from an ordinary eclipse, since it was situated in its own height and abode in the heavens. You have astrologers; consult them about it.

We can likewise call to your attention deaths of certain governors who at the close of their lives realized that they had sinned by tormenting the Christians. Vigellius Saturninus, who was the first to draw his sword against us in this province,[5] lost his eyesight. In Cappadocia, Claudius Lucius Herminianus,[6] taking it ill that his wife had become a convert to our mode of life, had treated the Christians cruelly. Left alone in his palace, and wasted by the plague, even to the point of breaking out with worms, he said while still alive: 'Let no one know it, lest the Christians rejoice and Christian wives conceive new hopes.' Afterwards, he recognized his error in having caused some to fall away from their resolution because of torture, and died, almost a Christian. Caecilius Capella, during the well-known doom which overtook Byzan-

---

3 This eclipse of the sun took place, according to the calculations of modern astronomers, on August 14, 212.
4 The Latin word is *conventus*. When a Roman province was created, a civil constitution was drawn up, dividing it into districts for the collection of imperial taxes, into assizes (*conventus*) for judicial purposes and into units of local administration. The governor not only sat in judgment in the capital of his province, but also held assizes in its principal towns.
5 The name of the proconsul Vigellius Saturninus is preserved in another document of the early Church, the Acts of the first African martyrs of whom we know. They were from Scilli, a town in proconsular Numidia, and suffered martyrdom on July 17, 180.
6 Nothing certain is known of this provincial governor. The MSS. vary regarding his last name.

tium,[7] cried out: 'Christians, rejoice.' But, even those persecutors who believe that they have gone unpunished will come to the day of divine judgment. To yourself, also, we wish it may have been only as a warning that, after you condemned Mavilus of Hadrumetum[8] to the beasts, this recent calamity immediately followed.[9] And, now, this hemorrhage[10] of yours is for the same reason. But, think of the future.

Chapter 4

We who are without fear ourselves do not wish to frighten you, but I would that we could save all men by warning them 'not to fight against God.'[1] You can perform the duties of your office as a judge, yet keep in mind the rights of humanity—even if for no other reason than that you are also under the law of the sword. For, what other command do you have than to condemn the guilty who confess, and to bring to torture those who deny? You see, then, how you yourselves act against your orders by forcing those who have confessed to deny. By this, you confess that we are innocent, whom you are willing to condemn at once from our own confession. But, if you strive to destroy us, it is our innocence that you are attacking.

---

7 Caecilius Capella was one of the generals of Niger (cf. Ch. 2, n.1), and acted as provincial governor at Byzantium. In his campaign against Niger and Albinus, Septimius Severus destroyed Byzantium in 196, and put its principal inhabitants to the sword.
8 In the Roman Martyrology, the African martyr Mavilus is listed on January 4th. Today the site of ancient Hadrumetum is occupied by Sousse, a city one hundred miles south of Carthage.
9 This probably refers to the torrential rains, mentioned at the beginning of this chapter, which destroyed the crops and led to a serious shortage of grain.
10 *interpellatio sanguinis* is translated as hemorrhage, according to Forcellini, *Totius Latinitatis Lexicon*, s. v. *interpellatio*; cf. Bindley's edition, p. 135, n.4 and n.5.

---

1 Cf. Acts 5.39.

How many governors, more determined and cruel than you, have made allowances in order to rid themselves of such cases! Cincius Severus[2] did so, who himself furnished a plan of escape at Thysdrus,[3] whereby the Christians might make such an answer that they would be set free; so did Vespronius Candidus,[4] who, in order to satisfy the wishes of his citizens, first punished a Christian as a disturber of the peace and then dismissed him; so did Asper,[5] who, when a man was slightly tortured and immediately fell from the faith, did not compel him to offer sacrifice, for he had previously declared in the presence of the advocates and assessors that he was sorry that he had come upon this case. Pudens[6] also dismissed a Christian who had been sent to him, perceiving from the indictment that the man was the victim of a vexatious countercharge. He tore up this very indictment, saying that according to his instructions[7] he was not to hear a man without an accuser.

All these things you may learn from the officials on your staff, from the same advocates who themselves have benefitted from the Christians, although in court they vote as they like.

---

2 Cincius Severus was governor of the province of Africa under Commodus (180-193). In 197, he came under false suspicion of plotting against Emperor Septimius Severus, and was put to death.
3 Thysdrus, in North Africa, was important as the meeting place of several highways. Today its site is occupied by a poor Arab village, El Djem.
4 L. Vespronius Candidus was proconsul of the province of Africa toward the end of the reign of Commodus (180-193).
5 C. Julius Asper was consul, the first time under Commodus, the second time, with his son C. Julius Galerius Asper, in 212. Between his two consulates, he was proconsul of the province of Africa.
6 C. Valerius Pudens was proconsul of the province of Africa *ca.* 212.
7 Pudens probably refers to an imperial rescript of about the year 125. Hadrian wrote to several provincial governors, notably a letter to the proconsul of Asia, C. Minucius Fundanus, ordering the prosecution of those who denounced Christians or staged riots against them and insisting on orderly court trials in such cases. A similar attitude was taken by the Emperor Antoninus Pius (138-161).

For, the secretary of a certain gentleman, when he was suffering from falling sickness caused by a demon, was freed from it; so also were a relative of some of the others and a certain little boy. And heaven knows how many distinguished men, to say nothing of common people, have been cured either of devils or of their sicknesses. Even Severus himself, the father of Antoninus,[8] graciously remembered the Christians. He searched for Proculus[9]—a Christian whose surname was Torpacion, a manager in the employ of Euhodia—who had cured him once by means of oil, and kept him in his palace until his death. Antoninus also knew him very well, brought up as he was on Christian milk. Moreover, Severus did not harm prominent women and prominent men, even though he was aware that they belonged to our group. Even more, he honored them by his own testimony and openly resisted the populace when they were raging against us.[10] Marcus Aurelius, during his German expedition, after prayers had been

---

8 The Emperor Septimius Severus, a Punic-speaking African, pretended to have been adopted into the family of the great Antonine emperors of the second century. Though he retained his own name, he renamed his son Septimius Bassianus, commonly known as Caracalla (211-217), Marcus Aurelius Antoninus.

9 Nothing certain is known of this Proculus; cf. *Prosopographia Imperii Romani Saeculi I II III* (edd. E. Klebs, H. Dessau, P. de Rohden, Berlin 1897-98) 3.101, F. Oehler's note to the passage in his edition of Tertullian's works, I (Leipzig 1853) 547, and Bindley's edition, p. 138, n.5.

10 At first, Septimius Severus continued the mild policy of his predecessor Commodus, in whose wife Marcia the Christians had had a powerful advocate. Later, however, he changed, probably made suspicious by the growing number of upper class Christians. In 202, a rather severe persecution began and we know of martyrdoms in Egypt and Africa (cf., for instance, Ch. 3, n. 1). After 208, the Church again enjoyed tranquility, though the unfriendly attitude among the high imperial officials continued and, because of the legal situation, local persecutions were possible. The tolerance of his son (Caracalla or Marcus Aurelius Antoninus) was probably due to impressions received in his youth; hence Tertullian's expression, 'brought up as he was on Christian milk.'

offered to God by his Christian soldiers, also obtained rain during the well-known drought.[11] When have droughts failed to be removed by our kneelings and fastings? Then, too, the people cried to the God of gods who alone is mighty and gave testimony to our God, though they did so under the name of Jupiter.

Besides this, we do not misuse any trust funds deposited with us, we defile the marriage of none, we treat our orphans affectionately, we succor the needy, to no one do we return evil for evil. What does it matter that there are some who falsely claim to belong to our religion and whom we ourselves disown? Finally, who makes a complaint in court against us on other grounds? What other trouble does a Christian suffer, except that which comes to him because of his religion? And no one in all this time has proved this religion to be marred by incest and cruel deeds. It is for so much innocence, for so much uprightness, for justice, for chastity, for faith, for love of truth, for the living God, that we are burned at the stake: a punishment which you are wont to inflict neither on those guilty of sacrilege, nor on real public enemies, nor on those guilty of high treason. Even now, this name of Christian is persecuted by the governors of Numidia[12] and Mauretania, though, in pronouncing death sentences, they limit them to beheading, that is, to that kind of punishment

---

[11] This refers to the famous incident of the Thundering Legion (*legio fulminatrix*) during the campaign of Marcus Aurelius against the Quadi and Marcomanni. While the Roman army was surrounded on all sides, a storm broke, refreshing the Roman soldiers and scattering the enemy. Pagan authors attributed the emperor's escape and victory to magic or his own prayers, while Christian writers ascribed it to the prayers of the Christian soldiers. The legend soon developed that the Emperor, as a result of the miraculous rain, put a stop to the persecution of the Christians.

[12] By *Legionis*, no doubt, is meant Numidia where the third Augustan Legion had its camp at the town of Lambaesa.

which from the very beginning was officially ordered to be inflicted on the Christians. But, the greater the contests, the greater the rewards to follow.

Chapter 5

Your cruelty is our glory. Only, see to it whether, just because we endure such things, we do not appear to burst out for this one purpose alone, namely, to prove that we do not fear these things, but willingly call them down upon ourselves. When Arrius Antoninus[1] was carrying out a vehement persecution in Asia, all the Christians of the city appeared in a body before his tribunal. After ordering a few to be led away to execution, he said to the rest: 'Wretched men, if you wish to die, you have precipices and ropes to hang yourselves.' If it should come into our mind to do the same thing here, also, what will you do with so many thousands of human beings, so many of both sexes—men and women—of every age, of every station, giving themselves up to you? How many stakes, how many swords, will you need? What will Carthage itself endure, which you will have to decimate, when every man will recognize his own relatives and companions among them, when, perhaps, he will see even men of your own rank among them, noble ladies, and all the outstanding persons of the city, and the relatives or friends of your own friends? Spare yourself, then, if not us. Spare Carthage, if not yourself. Spare the province which, when your intention became manifest, fell victim to the vexatious accusations both of the soldiers and each man's private enemies.

We have no master but God alone. He, to whom you can do nothing, is before you and cannot be hidden. But, those whom you regard as masters over you are men, and they

---

1 C. Arrius Antoninus was governor of the province of Asia *ca.* 184-185.

themselves one day will die. Our religion, however, which you know is growing stronger at the very moment when it seems to be cut down, will never perish. For, whoever beholds such noble endurance will first, as though struck by some kind of uneasiness, be driven to inquire what is the matter in question, and, then, when he knows the truth, immediately follow the same way.

TERTULLIAN
ON THE SOUL

Translated

by

EDWIN A. QUAIN, S.J., Ph.D.

Fordham University

IMPRIMI POTEST

JOHN J. McMAHON, S. J.
Provincial

New York
March 3, 1950

INTRODUCTION

TERTULLIAN'S TREATISE *On the Soul* is the first work in the long series of Christian contributions to psychology. In entering this field, however, the most learned personality of the early Church was not deserting his dual function as apologist for Christianity against the pagans and as staunch defender of the apostolic faith against the machinations of heretics. He had written a work, *On the Origin of the Soul* (which has not survived), against the materialist Hermogenes, and in the present treatise he turns to a complete treatment of the other matters in which philosophical speculation about the soul impinged upon the teaching of Revelation.[1]

His reason for undertaking this task is made clear from the outset. The defense of Christian teaching against the heretics is best furthered by attacking the basis of heresy—the errors of philosophy—for 'The philosophers are the patriarchs of the heretics.' Consequently, we should not look to Tertullian primarily for philosophical speculation, which was hardly the dominant characteristic of his mind. His vast erudition in the fields of ancient philosophy, religion and physiology are here forged into arms for the defense of divine Truth. Tertullian is composing the theological answer to pagan and heretical teachings on the soul rather than constructing a system of Christian psychology. He makes use of

---

[1] The translator was fortunate in being able to use the excellent edition of J. H. Waszink, *Quinti Septimi Florentis Tertulliani De Anima* (Amsterdam 1947) X 49* 651.

ancient philosophy, sometimes to agree with it, but generally to condemn its teaching and always to compare it with what God has revealed about His masterpiece of earthly creation, the soul of man.

After an introduction in which he describes the faulty methods of the philosophers and warns against the dangers of their teaching,[2] he analyzes the questions that arise as to the qualities of the soul. Against Plato, who held the eternity of the soul, actuated from time to time in different incarnations, he declares that it had a beginning in time, its origin being in the breath of God.[3] He then joins the Stoics in asserting the fact that the soul is corporeal, against Plato who held that it was incorporeal, and fortifies his view from the parable of Lazarus and Dives, which, he insists, must be understood literally. It is clear from Tertullian's extended treatment of this point that he cannot conceive of a spiritual entity and he fears that an admission of incorporeality may endanger the substantial reality of the soul. To be sure, he insists that the the soul is a body, but a body of a peculiar kind, and one that will, of its very nature, lack many of the attributes of a material body. Thus, in spite of its invisibility, it is still corporeal.[4]

Because of his assertion of corporeality, Tertullian is forced to say that the soul has a definite shape—the same as that of the contours of the body. In support of this he adduces a vision enjoyed by a woman of the Montanist sect who had 'seen' a human soul, together with the account in Genesis[5] of the divine inbreathing of the soul of Adam.[6]

The unity of the soul next engages his attention, and he

---

[2] Chs. 1-3.
[3] Ch. 4.
[4] Chs. 5-8.
[5] Gen. 2.7.
[6] Ch. 9.

must oppose the view of some early anatomists who believed that life could exist (and did, in small insects) without breathing. Thus he asserts the identity of life, breath and the soul. The mind, again, is identical with the soul, intelligence being its second function, after that of giving life to man. Finally, he denies the various divisions of the soul into parts excogitated by philosophers and claims the activities of the soul are merely functions exercised throughout the parts of the body by the soul diffused through the whole.[7]

Allied to the question of the unity of the soul are a number of points concerned with its activity. Thus, the soul has its principle directive faculty seated in the heart; the irrational element of which Plato spoke is not a part of the soul, but arose from sin as a result of the temptation of the Devil and the consequent effects of Original Sin.[8] He asserts the infallibility of sense perception, except when other factors impede the senses in their normal function. These senses, together with the mind, are the soul's source of knowledge.[9] The life and development of the soul begins from the moment of conception and, while the essential nature of the soul is identical with the soul of Adam, all changes are due to external circumstances.[10]

The second part of the work treats of the origin of the soul, beginning with a refutation of Plato's doctrine of 'reminiscence'[11] and the assertion that the embryo is a living being and that body and soul come into being at the same time.[12] There follows a digression, in which all the resources of Tertullian's irony are called into play, attacking the Pythagorean and Platonic theory of transmigration of soul.[13] The sex of the

---

7 Chs. 10-14.
8 Chs. 15-16.
9 Chs. 17-18.
10 Chs. 19-21.
11 Chs. 23-24.
12 Chs. 25-27.
13 Chs. 28-35.

soul and its development up to the time of birth conclude this section.[14]

The concluding portion of the work deals with the topics which were most important for Tertullian's main purpose: the growth of the soul along with the body, his curious notion of an age of puberty for the soul as well as for the body, and the influence of sin on the soul. The attacks of the Devil upon the soul begin at birth and continue through life, and Original Sin is removed by Baptism.[15] The questions of sleep and dreams were of great interest to Tertullian, who, now in his Montanist period, looked to the influence of 'ecstasy' as a means of divine communication with the soul.[16]

The philosophic and heretical views of death are next dealt with and it is declared to be the permanent separation of soul and body.[17] The final topic, the fate of the soul after death, strongly reflects Tertullian's millenarian views when he declares that only the souls of martyrs go immediately to Heaven, all others being detained in Hell until the resurrection, for reward or punishment in accordance with their deeds. Without using the word, Tertullian is here describing the state of Purgatory; the final punishment or reward of the soul must await the resurrection of the body, its companion in sin or virtue.[18]

At every step of the way, Tertullian has stated and analyzed the views of the philosophers and pagans, and his work would have been an arsenal of argument for subsequent Christian writers. The learning, both divine and human, manifested in the treatise give credence to the fulsome praise accorded

---

14 Chs. 36-37.
15 Chs. 38-41.
16 Chs. 42-49.
17 Chs. 50-53.
18 Chs. 54-58.

him by Vincent of Lerins and St. Jerome.[19] Such praise is surely the more deserved when we realize that those who laud his gifts must bemoan the tragedy that led so brilliant a mind into the heresy of Montanism.

The main source for the origins of Montanism is Eusebius,[20] who tells of the disturbance of the Church in Asia Minor caused by the alleged prophecies of Montanus and his associates, Priscilla and Maximilla. The essential point of this movement was the reliance on personal *charismata* of prophecy as a guide for the government of the Church. Eusebius considered them agents of the Devil for the perversion of truth. Their 'new prophecy' had the faithful in a turmoil for a time, but the movement, after a brief appearance in Rome, where it was immediately condemned, seems to have faded away. In some fashion not ascertainable, it moved into North Africa, and at Carthage Tertullian became acquainted in great detail with its teaching and practices.

Tertullian is thenceforward the source of our information as to the ideas of Montanism and it is not clear how much of this development was the result of his own additions to the curiously undogmatic heresy from the East.[21] For it appears to have adhered strictly to traditional teaching with the exception of a belief in an early end of this life, which

---

19 Vincent of Lerins, *Commonitorium* 24: 'There is no one more learned than this man, none better informed in all human and divine sciences. He is at home in philosophy; he knows all the philosophic schools and their founders; by the amazing breadth of his mind he was able to encompass all the variety of the arts and human history.' St. Jerome, *Epistola* 70.5: 'When we turn to those who wrote in Latin, there is no man more learned or more effective then Tertullian. His *Apology* and his work, *Against the Pagans*, contain all the learning of the ancient world.'
20 *Ecclesiastical History*, trans. K. Lake, 2v. (Loeb Classical Library, Cambridge, Mass. 1926) 5.14.19.
21 Cf. the works of Labriolle, listed in Select Bibliography.

would be followed by the resurrection of the just and the thousand-year reign of Christ on earth. This Millenarianism was a survival of the materialistic Jewish ideas as to an earthly Messias-King and it had affected a certain number of Christians until it was attacked by Origen and effectively destroyed by St. Augustine.

The influence of Montanist ideas is to be found in the works of Tertullian for some years before he made his formal break with the Church. Thus, he shows a belief in Millenarianism, an increasing severity in his moral teaching such as the condemnation of second marriages, and a denial to the Church of the power of forgiving the sins of murder, fornication and idolatry. He obviously became persuaded of the truth of Montanist 'oracles' and, on this point, according to St. Augustine, lapsed into formal heresy. He envisaged God's dealing with mankind in successive stages of clearer revelation. 'The Old Law was born in the reign of fear, mankind passed its infancy under the direction of the Law and the Prophets, the Gospel brought it to the bloom of youth until finally, in the reign of the Paraclete, it came full maturity.'[22] In discussing his condemnation of second marriages, he asks: 'If Christ could change what had been permitted by the Law of Moses' [divorce for adultery] 'why cannot the Paraclete deny the concession allowed by St. Paul?'[23]

From St. Augustine we know that Tertullian was at first opposed to Montanism, and it is a fascinating problem to consider how a man of his learning and training could have been attracted to a movement so contrary to his type of mind and the principles on which his early work was based.

Many things about Montanism should have repelled him.

---
22 *De virginibus velandis* 1.
23 *De monogamia* 14.

Even in his treatise *On the Soul* (when he was strongly under Montanist influence) he shows scant respect for Phrygians.[24] The high position in the sect accorded to women would also have gone against the grain but the strongest deterrent would surely lie in the anarchical tendency of Montanism. The methodical and legal mind of Tertullian clearly shows his predilection for orderly organization with a clear delineation of the lines of authority. The rule of faith was for him all-important and his main point in his controversy with the heretic Marcion is the succession and fidelity to apostolic teaching.[25] The mind must accept the Church's teaching and strict discipline will act as a curb on the will. How such a mind could have embraced Montanism, in which teaching and discipline were liable to daily variation on the strength of the latest 'oracle,' is one of the psychological mysteries on which his *On the Soul* throws no light.

On the other hand, certain features of Montanism would have been attractive to Tertullian. His moral teaching always leaned to the rigoristic side, and Montanist stress on mortification and martyrdom as a preparation for the proximate Second Coming of Christ would have appealed to him. He surely disliked vague and general moral prescriptions, preferring a clear and definite statement of obligation to any apparent compromise with human weakness. On the word of the Paraclete, he made obligatory for all what had been matters of devotion in the question of fasting. Early in his career he condoned the weakness of the counsel of prudent flight in the face of persecution, but later he condemned it as a refusal of the grace of martyrdom.[26] Christ may have allowed the Apostles to escape, but that permission had been

---

[24] Ch. 20.3.
[25] *De pudicitia* 21.
[26] *De fuga* 1, 9, 11, 14.

abrogated by the Paraclete. In the years 200-203 he would allow remarriage of a widow, but considered it more perfect to remain unmarried.[27] At his first exposure to Montanism he recanted and later went so far as to say that as there was only one God, there could only be one marriage.[28] Life was simpler for Tertullian when peremptory command made nicety of moral judgment unnecessary. This desire that the practical conduct of life should ever be determined by definite rules was fostered by the promise, implicit in Montanism, of continual guidance and direction by the Spirit. The 'living voice' of apostolic teaching soon appeared defective and he gave an enthusiastic welcome to the sect that promised ever more explicit revelation in practical matters. With the overemphasis on one consideration to the neglect of others so typical of all heresy, he made St. Paul's mention[29] of the *charismata* of prophecy the touchstone of all truth and discipline.

Furthermore, it is clear from all of Tertullian's writings that he had held none of his opinions lightly. His polemical works against pagans and heretics all manifest a violent and passionate temperament. The more his opinions were opposed, the more he had to win the argument; pride finally overcame judgment. The staunch defender of the *magisterium* founded by Christ became the preacher of a doctrine that would supersede the teaching of the Master whom Tertullian undoubtedly loved and revered after his fashion, even to the end of his unhappy life.

---

27 *Ad uxorem* 1.7.
28 *De monogamia* 1.
29 1 Cor. 14.

SELECT BIBLIOGRAPHY

Text:

J. H. Waszink, *Q.S.F. Tertulliani De Anima*, edited with [English] introduction and commentary (Amsterdam 1947).

Other Sources:

A. d'Alès, *La Théologie de Tertullien* (Paris 1905).

G. Esser,, *Die Seelenlehre Tertullians* (Paderborn 1893).

Pierre de Labriolle, *La Crise Montaniste* (Paris 1913).

———, *Histoire de la littérature latine chrétienne*, 2v. 3rd ed., G. Bardy (Paris 1947).

———, *Les Sources de l'historie du Montanisme* (Fribourg-Paris 1913).

J. Lebreton and J. Zeiller, *History of the Church*, trans. E. C. Messenger, III (London 1946).

CONTENTS

Chapter *Page*

1 The discussions about the soul by the philosophers, especially Plato in the *Phaedo*, are of no value. . 179
2 Beware of the philosophers who have distorted the truth. We learn of the soul from God 182
3 The philosophers are the patriarchs of the heretics. The soul comes from the breath of God 185
4 The soul had a beginning in God 187
5 The soul is corporeal 187
6 Refutation of Plato on incorporeality of the soul . . 189
7 The Gospel proves the soul is corporeal 193
8 The soul is corporeal even though invisible 194
9 The shape of the soul 196
10 The identity of life, breath, and soul 199
11 The difference between soul and breath 202
12 Soul and mind 205
13 The superiority of soul over mind 207
14 The soul has no parts 208
15 The directive faculty of the soul 209
16 Plato's division of the soul 212
17 The reliability of sense perception 214
18 Mind should not be separated from the senses . . . 218
19 The soul is complete from its very beginning . . . 223

Chapter	Page
20 The uniformity of the human soul	226
21 Refutation of the Valentinians	228
22 Summary of preceding chapters	230
23 Heretical theories on the soul stem from Plato	231
24 Refutation of Plato's doctrine of reminiscence	232
25 The soul is present even in the smallest embryo	236
26 Holy Scripture testifies that the fetus has a soul	240
27 The simultaneous origin of body and soul	242
28 Pythagoras the inventor of the doctrine of transmigration of souls	245
29 Plato's doctrine of 'opposites' is no proof of transmigration	247
30 According to Plato, the number of souls in the human race must always remain constant	249
31 Various arguments against the doctrine of transmigration	251
32 Refutation of the doctrine of Empedocles, that a human soul may return to the body of an animal	252
33 Transmigration neither necessary nor adequate as punishment or reward for former sins	256
34 Refutation of Simon Magus, who taught a kind of transmigration	260
35 Refutation of the theory of Carpocrates	262
36 The sex of the soul is determined at the moment of conception	265
37 Stages in the development of the body and soul	266

Chapter	Page
38 Puberty of the soul	268
39 The influence of the Devil on the new-born soul	270
40 Body and soul with relation to sin	271
41 Original sin and baptism	273
42 Relation of the soul to death	274
43 The nature of sleep	275
44 The story of Hermotimus	279
45 A dream is the result of 'ecstasy'	280
46 The significance of prophetic dreams	281
47 The causes of dreams	285
48 The influence of seasons, bodily position, and food on dreams	286
49 Everyone has dreams	288
50 All things living will die	288
51 Death is the separation of body and soul	290
52 Every death is violent and contrary to nature	293
53 A lingering death is no argument for divisibility	294
54 Refutation of the theories of philosophers as to the abode of souls after death	296
55 The Christian view of Hell	298
56 Immediately after death, souls go down to Hell	300
57 The dead cannot come back to earth	303
58 The reward and punishment of souls during their temporary stay in Hell	307

ON THE SOUL

Chapter 1

IN MY DISCUSSION with Hermogenes concerning the nature of the soul, I deliberately restricted myself to the single point of its origin, in as much as he assumed this origin to be a result of an emanation from matter rather than of the divine inbreathing.[1] Now we may turn to some other related questions in which I feel sure I shall have to contend with the philosophers.

(2) Even in the prison cell of Socrates[2] they skirmished as to the immortality of the soul. I am not sure that was quite the best moment for an official statement of the master's opinion, though the fact the discussion took place in jail is not the important one. For, how could Socrates have a clear perception of anything at such a time? The sacred ship had returned from Delos; by his formal condemnation he had, in anticipation, already drained the cup of poison; he stood on the brink of death. Obviously, any natural emotion would have terrified him in such circumstances, and any unnatural reaction

---

1 This cannot refer to the extant treatise *Against Hermogenes* since the origin of the soul is not discussed therein. Tertullian is here alluding to his (lost) work *On the Origin of the Soul against Hermogenes*, knowledge of which is assumed throughout the *De anima*. He refers to it nine times, often curtailing his treatment of important topics (e.g., the immortality of the soul, *De anima* 22.2; 24.2) because he had established them in the earlier treatise. Hermogenes came from the East and settled in Carthage as a painter where he came to the attention of Tertullian. Hermogenes believed in the eternity of matter and hence denied Creation out of nothing. Cf. Waszink, *op. cit.* 7*-14*.

2 Tertullian here attacks Socrates as the leader of all the philosophers, whose main defect is that they have examined the soul without the help of divine Revelation. Elsewhere, he expresses agreement and admiration for Socrates and his pupil and spokesman, Plato.

would have left him entirely beside himself. Even though he were calm and peaceful, totally unshaken, either by the tears of his wife, soon to be a widow, or by the sight of his children, forthwith to be orphans, and so rose superior to affection's claims, he yet would be disturbed in mind by the effort to maintain his composure; this composure, in turn, would have been ruffled by the struggle he made to overcome his natural trepidation in such a situation. No man, thus unjustly condemned, could bring himself to think calmly of anything but what would console him in his misfortune. Much less could the philosopher who lives for glory, and, in trouble, must not seek consolation for the injustice he suffers, but rather must show contempt for it.

(3) So, when Socrates had been sentenced and his wife came to him crying that he had been unjustly condemned, he seemed almost cheerful as he asked her: 'Would it have been all right had I been justly condemned?' Therefore, it is not surprising that even in prison he tried to take some of the glory from the discreditable victory of Anytus and Melitus by thus asserting the immortality of the soul. For, in that way, he could set at naught the wrong they had perpetrated.

(4) The result is that, at that moment, all the famous wisdom of Socrates was more concerned with maintaining an outward appearance of equanimity than of asserting his conviction of solemn truth. For, who can know truth without the help of God? Who can know God without Christ? Who has ever discovered Christ without the Holy Spirit? And who has ever received the Holy Spirit without the gift of faith? Socrates, as we know, surely was guided by a far different spirit. He claimed that he had been directed from his youth by a *daimon*—the worst kind of teacher surely—in spite of the fact that the poets and philosophers speak of such as though they were gods or very close to gods.

(5) But, at that time the power of Christian teaching was not yet known. Christian truth alone can give the lie to this most dangerous and pernicious devil, the father of all falsehood and the destroyer of all truth. Now, if the voice of the demon who spoke from the Pythian shrine (thus conveniently promoting the work of his colleague)[3] proclaimed him the wisest of all men, how much more admirable and trustworthy is the voice of Christian wisdom before whose breath the whole host of demons is scattered!

(6) The wisdom of the school of Heaven calmly denies the existence of the gods of this world and is never caught in the inconsistency of offering a cock to Aesculapius.[4] Christian wisdom invents no new gods, but destroys the old; it never corrupts the youth, but trains them in goodness and purity. Therefore, it stands condemned not merely in one city but in all the world and in the cause of truth; it incurs the greater hatred in proportion to the fullness of the wisdom it cherishes. Hence, it does not die by emptying a cup in convivial fashion, but it perishes on the cross, by being burned alive or by whatever other horror human ingenuity can devise. And so, when there is question of examining the soul here in the dungeon of this world (far darker than the prison where Socrates met with Cebes and Phaedo), let us study the question in accordance with the teachings of God, sure that no one can tell us more of the soul than its Creator. Learn from God about that which you have received from God; if you don't learn it from God, you never will from anyone else. For, who can reveal what God has concealed? Whom would we ask? If we are ignorant, let us be content. It is safer and

---

3 The personal *daimon* of Socrates.
4 At the end of Plato's *Phaedo*, after a discussion of the immortality of the soul which took place on the day of Socrates' death, Socrates takes the poison and asks one of his friends to pay in his name the debt of a cock to the god, Aesculapius.

better to be ignorant, if God has not revealed it, than to know something which human presumption has discovered.

Chapter 2

(1) Of course, I would not deny that the philosophers occasionally happen upon the truth;[1] the very fact that they do testifies to the truth itself. Sometimes in the midst of a storm when the sailor can't tell sea from sky, by sheer luck the ship will sail into a safe harbor. At night by blind chance we will often find the right door in the dark. Most of our ideas about nature, however, are suggested by a kind of common sense with which God has endowed the soul of man.

(2) This good sense has been appropriated by philosophers and, with a view to enhancing that glory of their own profession, they have blown it up to great size (in the context, the expression comes to me quite naturally), straining after that subtlety of expression which is more adapted to tearing down than to building anything up and which is cleverer at persuading men by talking than by teaching. Philosophy invents general laws for things and declares some universally applicable and some only partially so. She makes incertainties out of certainties, appeals to examples, as if all things could be compared; she defines anything, allotting different properties to the same objects; she grants nothing to divine power and treats her own private theories as if they were laws of nature. All this I could tolerate if only philos-

---

[1] Philosophers sometimes attain truth by pure chance, by using common sense which is a gift of God. They also use certain so-called sacred books, apocryphal books (not acknowledged as part of the canon of Sacred Scripture) and, occasionally, portions of the Old Testament, which they either falsified or wrongly applied. Hence, they cannot arrive at the truth.

ophy were faithful to nature and would admit that it sprang from the same source.

(3) Philosophy imagines that she draws her wisdom from sacred books because in ancient times they thought all writers were gods, or at least somehow divine. For instance, Plato followed closely the teachings of Egyptian Mercury [Hermes]; in Phrygia they honored Silenus, to whom Midas gave his long ears when the shepherds brought his to the god; Clazomenians built a temple to Hermotimus after his death; and they had the same attitude toward Orpheus, Musaeus and Pherecydes the teacher of Pythagoras. Why, the philosophers have even adopted the teachings of those works which we condemn as spurious. For we know these works are not to be accepted unless they agree with the true system of prophecy which has arisen in our times.[2] We never forget that there have been false prophets, yes, and fallen angels, too, who have taught the whole world by this same kind of deceitful cleverness.

(4) I suppose it is conceivable that some ancient searcher for wisdom might, out of honest curiosity, have consulted the writings of the Prophets. But among the philosophers you will certainly find more discord than harmony in their doctrines. In fact, in their points of agreement they betray the discord between the various schools. When you find in their works something true and in accord with the teaching of the Prophets, they claim it was obtained from some other source or they twist it in some other fashion, thus perverting the original truth which they pretend is bolstered by falsehood or itself supports what is not true.

(5) One of the principal points of difference between philosophers and ourselves in this matter is that they frequently

---

2 The teaching on Montanus, founder of the Phrygian sect of the Montanists.

clothe sentiments that are common to both of us in arguments they have themselves invented, which are in some respects contrary to our teaching. In other cases, to prove their own views they will use arguments which both of us admit to be valid but which are more allied to their opinions. The result is that truth is not to be found among the philosophers because of the poison with which they have infected it. Therefore, it is incumbent upon us to free ourselves from agreement with the philosophers under both of these specious appearances which are ultimately destructive of truth. Hence, we must separate the points on which we agree from the arguments of the philosophers and the arguments which both accept from their erroneous conclusions. To this end we must submit all questions to God's teachings, with the clear exception of those obvious points which we can accept as plain truth without committing ourselves to a favorable judgment on philosophy in general. For, in such cases, we may accept proof from our opponents when to do so will be useful to such as are not our enemies.

(6) Now, I am quite aware that the philosophers have gathered a vast mass of material on the soul in their own treatises. There are all sorts of opinions on the soul, many sharp disagreements, countless questions are asked and all kinds of intricate solutions are offered. Besides, I have also studied the sister-science to philosophy, medicine, which claims through its ability to cure the body a special competence as to the doctrine on the soul. This causes a disagreement between philosophy and medicine, for the latter claims to know more because it deals with the habitation of the soul. But, let them settle their own quarrel as to which is the greater. In pursuing their researches in the soul, philosophy has exercised the full scope of her genius, while medicine has been restricted

to the techniques of that profession. Probabilities leave a broad field for speculation and one can argue forever about possibilities. The harder it is to prove something, the more difficult it is to persuade a man of your view. Hence, I am not surprised that the gloomy old Heraclitus became bored with their interminable questions when he saw how little light they shed on the subject. He told the philosophers: 'You'll never explore the furthest reaches of the soul, no matter how many roads you travel.'

(7) The Christian, however, can plumb the depths of this topic with the aid of a few simple words. Things that are absolutely certain are always simply explained and his investigations should go no further than we are permitted. The Apostle has forbidden us to indulge in endless questions. We can learn no more about the soul than God has revealed and His revelation is the sum and substance of the whole matter.

Chapter 3

(1) I have often wished that the clarification of approved doctrines did not, in a sense, demand the existence of heresies. For we thus would have no need of arguments about the soul with the philosophers, those patriarchs of the heretics.[1] Even in the time of the Apostles, St. Paul foresaw there would be trouble between philosophy and the truth. He felt it necessary to issue that warning after he had visited Athens, that city of

---

1 Tertullian's purpose in this treatise was to combat heretics; by refuting the philosophers, the ultimate teachers of heresy, he could destroy the basis of any heretical teaching on the soul. Thus, Tertullian wrote a treatise (not extant) on the origin and essence of the soul against Hermogenes, who taught that matter was eternal and creation impossible. Certain ideas of Aristotle and Plato may have influenced his thought. Cf. Waszink, *op. cit.* 9*-14*.

babblers, with its horde of hucksters of 'wisdom' and 'eloquence.'[2]

(2) The doctrines about the soul concocted by these pseudo-philosophers remind me of men who mix water with wine. Some of them deny the immortality of the soul, while others claim it is even more than immortal. They argue about its substance, its form, or its individual faculties. They hold various views as to its origin and they disagree as to its ultimate fate. I think their views stem from the characters of their leaders. Thus, they speak of the idealism of Plato, the vigor of Zeno, the calmness of Aristotle, the pessimism of Epicurus, the sadness of Heraclitus, the madness of Empedocles.

(3) It's too bad, I suppose, that the Law has come forth from Sion and not from Greece. It is regrettable, too, that Christ chose fisherman instead of sophists to preach His doctrine. The philosophers with their vaporings becloud the clear sky of truth. These must Christians disperse, scattering the teachings of the philosophers about the origin of things by using the heavenly teachings of the Lord. Thus, the doctrines by which the pagans are deceived and the faith of Christians weakened will be destroyed.

(4) As we said at the beginning, we established one point in our discussion with Hermogenes—that the soul has its origin in the 'breath' of God and did not come from matter. We base that statement on the clear assertion of divine Revelation, which declares that 'God breathed the breath of life into the face of man and man became a living soul.'[3] On the origin of the soul, then, there is no further need of discussion.

---

2 Cf. Acts. 17.16-34, for St. Paul's address to the Athenians. Col. 2.8: 'See to it that no one deceives you by philosophy and vain deceit, according to human traditions, according to the elements of the world and not according to Christ.'
3 Gen. 2.7.

There is a treatise on that and there is a heretic who denies it. Let that be the introduction to my other ideas on the subject.

Chapter 4

(1) Now that we have decided on the origin of the soul, the next question is as to its nature. When we say that it has its own origin in the breath of God, we obviously hold that the soul had a beginning. Plato denies this, since he believes it to be unborn and uncreated.[1] Since it had a beginning, we teach that it was born and made. In this we make no mistake, either, for there is a distinction between being born and being made, and the former term we generally apply to living things. Though such distinctions sometimes indicate that things are mutually exclusive, they may also hint at a certain similarity of meaning. Thus, when we say that something is 'made' we mean that it is 'brought forth,' for anything that receives being in any sense can be said to be generated. Obviously, the maker of anything can be referred to as its parent, and even Plato uses this terminology.[2] So, our faith tells us that souls are made or born. Besides, Plato's opinion is contradicted by Revelation.[3]

Chapter 5

(1) If we were to question Eubulus on this matter, and Critolaus, Xenocrates, and Aristotle, who here happens to agree with Plato, we might be inclined to deny that the soul is in any sense corporeal, forgetting that a considerable number of philosophers believe the soul to be a body.

---

1 *Phaedrus* 245D.
2 *Timaeus* 28C.
3 I.e., his opinion that the soul is eternal.

(2) And, I am not speaking of those who say that it is made of things obviously material as do Hipparchus and Heraclitus [Fire], Hippo and Thales [Water], Empedocles and Critias [Blood], and Epicurus [Atoms] (*if* [sic.] as a matter of fact atoms do form bodies by their unions), or Critolaus and his Peripatetics who say it is made of some fifth substance, if that is necessarily a body which includes corporeal substances. It is the Stoics[1] I am speaking of, who will easily prove that the soul is a body, even though they almost agree with us in saying that the soul is a spirit; for spirit and breath are very nearly the same thing.

(3) Zeno, defining the soul as a spirit that is generated with the body, argues in the following fashion. Anything that by its departure causes a living being to die is a body. But, on the departure of this spirit which is generated with the body, the living being dies. Therefore, this spirit which is generated with the body is a body. But, this spirit of which we speak is the soul. Hence, we must conclude that the soul is corporeal.

(4) In much the same way, Cleanthes believed that just as there are bodily resemblances between parents and their children, so also qualities of soul are directly transmitted from the souls of the parents. Thus, he holds that both soul and body of the child would be the reflection of the individual manners, characteristics, and qualities of the bodies and souls of each of the parents.

---

[1] Tertullian's insistence that the soul is a *body* is understandable in view of his early position in the development of philosophical terminology. In his view, *body* is equivalent to *substance,* and the only way in which he could defend the substantiality of the soul was to call it a body. For, unless it were a *body,* it would be *nothing.* Cf. *On the Flesh of Christ* 11; *Against Hermogenes* 35; *On the Soul* 7.3. His general principle, 'Everything that is, is in some fashion, a body,' is to be understood in this sense. In this he was strongly influenced by Stoicism. Cf. A. d'Alès, *La Théologie de Tertullien* (Paris 1905) 137, and G. Esser, *Die Seelenlehre Tertullians* (Paderborn 1893) 65f.; 111f.

(5) But it is as being corporeal that the soul can be called like or unlike, since corporeal and incorporeal things do not share the same characteristics. Further, the soul shares the pain of the body when the latter suffers from bruises, wounds, or sores, and the body will reflect the disabilities of the soul under the influence of anxiety, worry, or love by a parallel weakness, as when the body testifies to the presence of shame and fear in the soul by blushing or growing pale. This mutual influence, then, proves the soul to be corporeal.

(6) Chrysippus agrees with Cleanthes when he declares that it is impossible for corporeal things to be separated from incorporeal substances because there is no medium of contact between them. For, as Lucretius says: 'Nothing can touch or be touched unless it be a body.'[2] As a matter of fact, when body and soul are separated, a man dies. Hence, we see that the soul is corporeal; unless it were, it could not be separated from the body.

Chapter 6

(1) There is more subtlety than truth in Plato's attempt to refute this position. All bodies, he says, are either living or non-living. If they be non-living, they receive motion from without, while living bodies have an intrinsic principle of activity.[1] Now, the soul is not moved from without since it is living, nor from within, since the soul itself is the cause of the movement of the body. Hence, it would appear not to be a body, since its motion is not goverened by the laws of bodily motion.

(2) Our first stricture on this argument is the incongruity

---

[2] Lucretius, *On the Nature of Things* 1.305.

[1] *Phaedrus* 245E.

of a definition which is drawn from things which have no relation to the soul. Why does he say that the soul is either a living or a non-living thing when, as a matter of fact, a man's body is said to be living or dead because of the presence or absence of the soul? That which produces an effect cannot be said to be that effect in such a way that you could say it is *either* living *or* non-living. The soul is so called by virtue of its substance. If, then, the soul cannot be spoken of as either a living or a non-living substance, why reduce it to categories which embrace living and non-living things?

(3) Let us admit for the sake of argument that it is a law of bodies that they are moved from without. Have we not shown in another work[2] that the soul is moved by another in prophecy and madness and, therefore, from without? It is clear according to my major premise, then, that I must assert the soul to be corporeal. Now, if it be a law of bodies that they receive motion from without, it is to a greater extent their characteristic to move others. The soul moves the body and the effect of its influence appears externally. For, it is the soul which moves the feet in walking, the hands in touching, the eyes in seeing, and the tongue in speaking, as a sort of internal image which moves within and stirs the surface. How could an incorporeal soul have this power to move solid bodies if it were itself incorporeal?

(4) How would you say the corporeal and intellectual powers of sensation are divided in man? The Platonists[3] tell us that physical substances such as earth and fire are perceived by the bodily senses of touch and sight, while immaterial things such as kindness or meanness are apprehended by the intellectual powers. Therefore, they conclude that the soul is in-

---
2 Probably in the lost treatise on the origin of the soul written against Hermogenes.
3 Cf. *Phaedo* 79A.

corporeal since its properties are perceived by the intellectual and not by the bodily senses.

(5) All this would be fine, except that I shall now upset the basis of their argument. For, you see, incorporeal objects *can* be perceived by the bodily senses: thus, sound by the hearing, color by the sight, odors by the sense of smell, in all of which cases the soul has contact with the body. Note that I am not saying that these things are perceived by bodily senses because they have physical contact with material things. Since, as we see, incorporeal things are perceived by corporeal organs, what is to prevent the soul which is corporeal from being understood by incorporeal faculties? Thus, surely, is their argument refuted.

(6) Another one of their favorite arguments goes like this: All bodies are nourished by bodies, but the incorporeal soul by incorporeal things such as the study of wisdom. But, even this argument will not stand up, since we are told by Soranus,[4] a learned medical authority, that material food also benefits the soul and when in a state of weakness it is frequently refreshed by food. Naturally, since if it is deprived of all food, it departs from the body. This same Soranus has written four volumes of exhaustive commentary on the soul and he has examined all the theories of the philosophers, too, though in the process of establishing the corporeality of the soul he has robbed it of its immortality. Unfortunately, it is not granted to all men to believe the truth which Christians hold.

(7) Therefore, just as Soranus has adduced facts to prove

---

[4] Soranus, a Greek physician of the early second century A.D., wrote four books on the soul, in which he quoted from the works of Plato, Aristotle, Chrysippus, and Heraclides of Pontus. He was keenly interested in the history of medicine and in etymology. Much of Tertullian's information about medical matters and ancient Greek religion is apparently borrowed from Soranus.

that the soul is fed with material food, let Plato bring forward the same kind of argument to prove it is fed with incorporeal substances. But no one has ever injected into the soul that was hesitating on the brink of death some honeyed drops of Platonic eloquence or stuffed it with crumbs of Aristotelian subtlety. How do the souls of all those hardy barbarians manage to live? They have never been privileged to drink of the fountains of wisdom, and yet, while uneducated, they show very good sense. Poor ignorant fellows, they have never strolled in the Academic gardens or Stoic porches nor have they ever visited the prison of Socrates. In a word, though philosophy forms no part of their diet, they still manage to live. For, the substance of the soul is not increased by intellectual discipline, but it is rendered more cultivated. Learning will not add to the soul's girth, but only to its embellishment. I like the Stoic opinion that the arts, too, are corporeal; if they are right, then the soul would receive corporeal nourishment from wisdom and that would be a proof that the soul was corporeal.

(8) But the philosophers are so marvelously abstracted in their speculations that they can't see what is in front of them. You recall the story of Thales, who fell into the well. It often happens that, through a misunderstanding of their own doctrines, they suspect a failure of their own health; that was the trouble with Chrysippus when he took hellebore. Some such hallucination, I imagine, must have occurred to Plato when he asserted that two bodies could not be contained in one. Apparently, he was forgetting that pregnant women quite often carry not only one, but two or three bodies within the confines of one womb. In the records of civil law, there is the case of the Greek woman who bore quintuplets at one birth. Clearly, she was the mother and parent of the whole brood, all of a single brood, and thus she bore within

herself this numerous progeny—I almost said 'race'—and she herself was the sixth.

(9) Nature in general testifies that bodies destined to be born from other bodies are already contained in the one from which they are delivered. That which in any way proceeds from another is distinct from the first. Nothing, however, proceeds from another except by generation and the result of such a process is always two beings.

Chapter 7

(1) Let that suffice for the philosophers, since we have plenty of evidence from our own side. The corporeal nature of the soul is asserted all through the Scriptures. A soul is said to suffer in Hell; it is punished in the flames, its tongue is so parched that it begs from a more fortunate soul the comfort of a drop of cold water.

(2) Don't tell me that the story of the joy of Lazarus and the torments of Dives is merely a parable.[1] Why was the name of Lazarus mentioned if the story were not true? But, even if we are to take it all as imaginary, it still proves my position. For, unless the soul really were corporeal, bodily qualities would not be attributed to the soul, nor would Scripture make up a statement about parts of the body if they did not exist in Hell.

(3) Tell me: What goes to Hell after the separation of soul and body? What is imprisoned there till the Day of Judgment? To what did Christ go after His death on the Cross? To the souls of the patriarchs? Well, why all this, if

---

[1] Tertullian to the contrary, the story of Lazarus and Dives was not intended to be taken literally; cf. *Luke* 16.20-31. Tertullian assumes that the use of the name 'Lazarus' must refer to the brother of Mary and Martha, although nothing in the Gospel would lead us to suspect that he was a beggar.

in Hell souls are *nothing?* For, they certainly are *nothing* if they have no bodily substance. An incorporeal thing cannot be guarded in any way and it is incapable of punishment or refreshment. Anything that can undergo punishment or reward must be a body. But I'll deal with that more fully at the proper time.

(4) For the present, we may say that whatever torment or comfort the soul experiences in its prison or temporary lodging in the lower regions, whether in the fire or resting in the bosom of Abraham, it all proves that the soul is corporeal. An incorporeal thing can't suffer, since it hasn't got that which would make it capable of suffering. If it has, it's a body. Now, if anything corporeal is thereby capable of suffering, it follows that anything capable of suffering must necessarily be corporeal.

Chapter 8

(1) Besides, it is an altogether foolish procedure to deny that a thing is corporeal because it is not exactly like all other corporeal things. And, when we find something with a great variety of special natures, isn't that really a sign of the omnipotence of the Creator that He can thus combine like and unlike in such friendly rivalry? The philosophers themselves teach us that the universe is made up of a system of harmonious opposites, according to Empedocles' doctrine of strife and love.

(2) So, although corporeal things are opposed to the incorporeal, yet the former differ among themselves in such fashion as to broaden the extension of the species without at all changing the genus, all remaining corporeal. Their very variety enhances the glory of God. They vary because of their differences; they differ according to their varying

modes of perception; they have different foods; some are visible, others invisible, some light, some heavy.[1]

(3) The philosophers would tell us that a body from which the soul has departed is heavier than it was before and thence they conclude that the soul must be incorporeal. And, if the soul were corporeal, then a corpse should be lighter than before, since presumably it has lost the weight of something corporeal. In answer to this, Soranus says that we might as well conclude that the sea is incorporeal since a ship out of water is a heavy and motionless hulk. In fact, is not the corporeal essence of the soul all the stronger since with the slightest effort it is able to move the great bulk of the body?

(4) The fact that the soul is invisible flows from the nature of its corporeal substance and is determined by its own nature. Besides, of its very nature it is destined to be invisible to certain things. Owls cannot endure the light of the sun whereas eagles are so capable of gazing at its light that the parent eagle judges the nobility of its young by the way in which the eaglet stares at the sun. An eaglet that turns its eyes away from the sun is cast from the nest as unfit to live, unworthy of its parents.

(5) And so, an object may be invisible to one being and quite clearly seen by another without any prejudice to the corporeality of the object itself which is seen by one and not by the other. The sun in a bodily substance, being made of fire; the eagle gazes at it steadily but it is invisible to the owl, but the owl does not deny the object seen by the eagle. In such fashion, the bodily substance of the soul may generally be invisible to the eye of flesh, but it is clearly perceived by the

---

[1] From this chapter it is clear that Tertullian is trying to describe a corporeal soul that is different from ordinary material things.

spirit. Thus St. John 'in the spirit'[2] saw 'the souls of them that were slain for the word of God.'[3]

Chapter 9

(1) Now, when we assert that the soul is a body of a unique and peculiar kind, this fact will give us a hint as to the other normal accidents of bodies which will be found in the soul. If they are present in the soul they will be there after the fashion of its specific corporeality; if they are not, that also will be due to the soul's peculiar corporeality, that it does not possess all the conventional accidents that we normally find in bodies. And yet, I have no hesitation in asserting that the soul possesses the cardinal attributes of bodies such as external form and definite boundaries; these boundaries we express in terms of triple extension of length, breadth and height by which the philosophers measure all bodies.

(2) Suppose we thus say that the soul has a definite shape. Plato refused to admit this lest he endanger the immortality of the soul. His argument goes like this: Everything that has a definite shape is made up of parts fitted together. Now anything made of parts can be broken down into its component parts. But the soul is immortal: therefore it is indestructible because it is immortal; it is without a definite shape because it is indestructible; but it would be made up of parts fitted together, if it possessed a definite shape. Therefore, the only shape Plato would predicate of the soul is that impressed upon it by the intellectual forms which can mold it to beauty by the presence therein of justice and the principles of philosophy, while the soul can become 'deformed or misshapen' by the contrary vices.

(3) Contrary to Plato, we attribute corporeal extension

---
2 Apoc. 1.10.
3 Apoc. 6.9.

to the soul not merely because of the influence of our reasoning as to its corporeal nature but also because of the conviction we have from Revelation. For, since we acknowledge the existence of spiritual *Charismata*, we have deserved to enjoy the gift of prophecy after the death of St. John.

(4) There is among us [Montanists] a sister who has been favored with wonderful gifts of revelation which she experiences in an ecstasy of the spirit during the sacred ceremonies on the Lord's day.[1] She converses with the angels and, sometimes, with the Lord Himself. She perceives hidden mysteries and has the power of reading the hearts of men and of prescribing remedies for such as need them. In the course of the services, she finds the matter of her visions in the Scripture lessons, the psalms, the sermon, or the prayers. One time I happened to be preaching about the soul when she became rapt in ecstasy. After the services were over and the laity had left, we asked her as is our custom, what visions she had had. (All her visions are carefully written down for purposes of examination.) 'Among other things,' she reported, 'I have seen a soul in bodily shape and a spirit appeared to me, not an empty and filmy thing, but an object which could be taken in the hands, soft and light and of an ethereal color, and in shape altogether like a human being. That was my vision.' And God is witness to its truth and St. Paul assured us that there would be visions and revelations in the Church. Can you still refuse to believe when the fact proclaims its truth?

---

[1] This is the *locus classicus* for Montanist prophecy in Tertullian's works. At the time of writing this treatise, Tertullian was definitely of Montanist persuasion, though perhaps the formal break with the Church had not yet been made. He finally became persuaded that the revelations made during such 'ecstasy' were supplementary to, and at times, corrective of the teachings of Christ and the Apostles. In thus wandering from the apostolic rule of faith, he went into heresy. This incident may well have taken place at a Catholic service.

(5) If then the soul is a body it must possess the qualities that she mentioned, especially that of color, which is found in every body. What color would you expect the soul to be but ethereally bright? Not in the sense that the substance of the soul is air as Aenesidemus and Anaximenes believed, and according to some, Heraclitus, also. Nor is the soul composed of light as Heraclides of Pontus thought.

(6) For even though meteors gleam with a reddish glow they are not altogether made of fire; nor are beryls composed of water because they have a pure wavy lustre. There are indeed many things alike in color but very different in nature. Because anything thin and transparent is thought to be like air, the soul is so considered, especially since it is generated as air or breath. Hence it is that the tenuousness and subtlety of its structure militates against the belief in its corporeality.

(7) Likewise if you imagine a soul, you cannot picture it as being anything but human in shape. In fact, it must be exactly the shape of the body which it animates. A glance at the soul's original creation will persuade us of this. For, if you recall, when God breathed the breath of life into the face of man, and man became a living soul, the breath must have passed at once through the face into the interior of the body and diffused itself throughout all the space of the body. By the divine breath it was condensed and took on the lineaments of the body that it filled and, as it were, it was frozen into the exact shape of the body.

(8) Thus the corporeal form of the soul was fixed by this condensation and its shape was 'hardened in the mold' of the body. This is the interior man; the other is the outer but together they form one being. The soul has its own eyes and ears with which people must have seen and heard the Lord; it has also other members which it uses in thought and moves in its dreams. Thus, Dives in Hell has a tongue; Lazarus, a

finger; and Abraham, a bosom. By these features also, the souls of the martyrs are recognized under the altar. The soul that in the beginning took the form of the body of Adam became the germ not only of the substance of every human soul but also of the shape that each one was to bear.

Chapter 10

(1) It is one of the fundamentals of our faith to hold, with Plato, that the soul is essentially simple, which means at least uncompounded in its substance. (Let them say what they will about the influence of the arts and learning on the formation of the soul.)

(2) Some say that there is within the soul some substance, the breath,[1] distinct from the soul, as if to live (the effect of the soul) were one thing and to breathe (by means of the breath) were another! Not all animals possess both of these functions. There are many that are alive, but do not breathe since they have no lungs or windpipes, the instruments of breathing.

(3) But in an examination of the soul of man, what is the use of searching for arguments from the body of a gnat or an ant? Since God the Creator has assigned to each animal organs that are proper for the fulfillment of its function, such comparisons are useless. We do not have to say that man breathes by one process and lives by another, merely because he has lungs and a windpipe. No more should we say that an ant lives but does not breathe in the assumption that he lacks these organs.

---

1 Because of his belief that the soul was the 'breath of God' (relying on Gen. 2.7) and the concomitance of life and breathing, Tertullian assumed that the soul was breath, i.e., some tenuous form of airy substance.

(4) Who knows so much about the works of God that he would dare to say what any animal has or lacks? There was Herophilus, the famous surgeon, or rather, butcher, who cut up any number of bodies to investigate their nature. In the interests of knowledge, he showed his hatred of man. I doubt very much that he got a clear idea of the internal organs since death changes the vital functions and, apart from mere death, the process of dissection would further disturb the organs.

(5) Philosophers hold it certain that gnats, ants, and moths have no lungs or windpipes. Tell me, then, you lynx-eyed searchers, have they any eyes for seeing? They certainly go where they wish and they go after and avoid things they know by sight. Show me, then, their eyes; point out the pupils. Moths certainly can eat, but where are their jaws and their teeth? Gnats can buzz, and even in the dark they can find their way to our ears. Show me the tube which emits the sound and the opening of their mouths. Even the tiniest of animals has to be fed by some food or other. Can you point out to me their organs for the consumption, digestion, and disposal of their food? There is only one conclusion. If these are the means of sustaining life, then all living things must have them, even though they are too small to be perceived by our eyes or minds. This will be easier to believe if we recall that God the Creator is as wonderful in all His works both great and small.

(6) If, however, you choose to believe that the power of God cannot form such tiny bodies, still you must admire His wonderful power in that He can make the smallest animals live without providing them with the ordinary organs. Thus, they can see without eyes, eat without teeth, and digest their food without stomachs. Some animals can move without feet, as snakes who move by extending or stretching themselves;

worms, by lifting themselves forward; and snails, by a slimy crawl.

(7) Why, then, can't they breathe without bellows of the lungs and the tube of the windpipe? Then you would have a fine argument for the connection of the soul and breath because there are beings which don't breathe and they don't because they don't have organs of respiration. If you admit that a thing can live without breathing, then why can't something breathe without lungs? What do you mean by breathing? I suppose it means to exhale some air. What do you mean by death? Not being able to exhale air. This is the only answer I can give you if breathing and living are not the same thing. A dead man does not breathe; hence, breathing must be a sign of life. To have respiration is to breathe; hence, respiration is a sign of life. Now, if both living and breathing could be accomplished without a soul, breathing would not be a function of the soul but only of life. But, living is breathing and breathing is living. Therefore, the whole process of breathing and living belongs to that which makes us live, namely, the soul.

(8) If you insist on separating the breath and the soul, then separate their operations. Let each do something totally independent of the other. Let the soul live without breathing and the spirit breathe without the soul. Suppose one to have left the body, the other remaining, and you would have a union of life and death. If soul and breath are distinct, they can be separated so that one departs and the other remains. Again, you have a union of life and death. But, such a union could never happen. Two things are not distinct if they cannot be divided, but they surely could have been divided were they really separate things.

(9) Perhaps it would be possible for them to grow together into unity? No, this could not be unless living and

breathing are considered to be the same thing. The nature of a being is betrayed by its normal operations. Thus, it is clear that you have greater reason for believing the breath and the soul to be one, since you assign no real difference between them; hence, the soul and breath are one, both life and respiration being functions of the soul. Why make a distinction between day and the light which pertains to day, when day is, really, only light? To be sure, there are various kinds of light as there are various kinds of fires. And there will be different kinds of spirits, some from God and some from the Devil. Whenever question arises as to soul and breath, be sure that the soul *is* the breath just as day is the light [of day] itself. For, there is no difference between a being and that by which it is a being.

Chapter 11

(1) The nature of our present discussion compels me to say the soul is spirit *or* breath because the power of breathing is attributed to a substance other than the soul. It is true we claim breathing to be a function of the soul which we believe to be simple and uncompounded, and we also say that the soul is a spirit, but in a technical sense; not that it is *by nature* a spirit, but in its operation; not in substance, but merely in act. The soul is a spirit because it respires and not because it is actually a 'spirit.' Breathing and respiration are the same thing. Since one of the properties of the soul is respiration, we are forced to call the soul a spirit.[1]

(2) We have to insist on calling the soul 'breath' in

---

1 Tertullian is here hampered by his own terminology. The equivocal meaning of *spiritus* forces him to insist that the soul is not a 'spiritual substance,' because that, in his mind, would undermine its reality. Yet, he must use the word somehow to describe the process of breathing.

opposition to Hermogenes, who claims the soul arises from matter and not from 'the breath of God.' Against the obvious meaning of Scripture he changes breath to spirit, since he cannot believe that the spirit (which God breathed into man) could fall into sin and come to judgment.[2] Therefore, he believes the soul arose from matter and not from the spirit of God. Therefore, even from that passage, we hold the soul to be breath and not a spirit; and this in the Scriptural sense and keeping in mind the ambiguity of the word. Hence, it is with regret that I use the word spirit at all of the soul because of the equivocal sense of breath or respiration. Hence, we are discussing the substance of the soul and breathing is a natural function of the substance.

(3) Now, I should never delay so long on this topic were it not for some of the heretics who introduce into the soul some mysterious spiritual seed. This, they say, was put into it in secret, by the generosity of Mother Wisdom, without the knowledge of the Creator. Now, Holy Scripture, which surely has better knowledge of God, the Creator of the soul, tells us nothing more than that God breathed into the face of man the breath of life and man became a living soul through which he lives and breathes. In many books of Scripture, God has made a sufficiently clear distinction between spirit and soul. Thus, He has said: 'The spirit went forth from Me and I made all breathing.'[3] The soul is a breath made from the spirit. Again, He said: 'I have given breath to the people on the earth and spirit to them that tread thereon.'[4] Now, this means that first God gives the soul, that is, breath, to the people upon the earth; that is, those living live in the body according to the flesh. After that, He gives the spirit

---
2 Gen. 2.7.
3 Isa. 57.16.
4 Isa. 42.5.

to those who tread upon the earth; that is, those who control the tendencies of the flesh. This agrees with what St. Paul says: 'That was not first which is spiritual, but that which is natural; afterwards that which is spiritual.'[5]

(4) For, when Adam, at the very beginning prophesied: 'The great mystery in Christ and in the Church,' saying: 'This now is bone of my bones and flesh of my flesh... Wherefore a man shall leave father and mother and shall stick [*adglutinabit*] to his wife and they two shall be in one flesh,' he was speaking under the influence of the spirit. For, there descended upon him that ecstasy, the power of the Holy Spirit which produces prophecy.[6]

(5) It is possible for an evil spirit to influence a man. The spirit of God later turned Saul into another man, that is, into a prophet, when people said: 'What is this that has happened to the son of Cis? Is Saul also among the prophets?'[7] But the Evil Spirit also turned him into another man, in other words, into a renegade. For some time Judas was numbered among the chosen [Apostles], even becoming the keeper of the purse. He was then not yet a traitor, but he was dishonest. Later, the Devil entered into his soul.

(6) Therefore, if neither the spirit of God nor the Devil enters into the soul of man at the birth of the soul, then the soul must exist separately before the accession of either spirit. If it exists alone, then it is simple and uncompounded in substance and it breathes simply as a result of the substance which it received from God.

---

[5] 1 Cor. 15.46.
[6] Eph. 5.31-2; Gen. 2.23-24. This prophecy of Adam was for Tertullian a kind of model of Montanist revelations uttered in ecstasy.
[7] 1 Kings 10.11.

Chapter 12

(1) The next point is with regard to the *animus,* the mind, which the Greeks call *nous.* By 'mind' I mean merely that faculty which is inherent and implanted in the soul and proper to it by birth and by which the soul acts and gains knowledge. The possession of this faculty makes it possible for the soul to act upon itself, the soul being moved by the mind as if they were distinct substances. This is the opinion of those who hold that the soul is the moving principle of the universe, what Socrates calls 'God' or Valentinus 'the only-begotten of his father Bythus and Sige, his mother.'

(2) On this matter, Anaxagoras is very confused. He asserts the mind to be the beginning of all things; he says that it supports the motion of the universe,[1] while at the same time it is pure, simple, and incapable of admixture. Hence, it cannot be compounded with the soul. Elsewhere, he actually joins mind and soul.

(3) Aristotle[2] noted this inconsistency, probably not so much for the sake of supporting his own view as merely to weaken that of Anaxagoras. For, while he postpones his definition of the mind, he does discuss a second constituent principle of the mind, a divine principle which he understands as impassible and thereby devoid of any union with the soul. Since it is clear that the soul is subject to those emotions which it happens to undergo, it must feel them through the mind or at least in conjunction with the mind. If mind and soul are joined, the mind cannot be impervious to emotion. If, on the other hand, the soul feels nothing through or with the mind, it enjoys no union with that which is moved neither with the soul nor by itself. And, what is more, if the soul

---
1 Cf. *Phaedo* 97B-C.
2 Aristotle, *De anima* 404B 1.

suffers no emotion through or with the mind, then the soul neither feels, nor knows, nor is moved by the mind, as they would hold.

(4) Aristotle makes all sensations to be passions, and in this he is right.[3] To have sensation is to be acted upon and to be acted upon is to feel. Besides, to know is to feel, and to be moved is to feel, and the whole is a process of being acted upon. But, we see that the soul experiences none of these things unless the mind is also affected, for it is the mind which really effects all these things.

(5) Therefore, we hold against Anaxagoras that the mind is capable of admixture and against Aristotle that it undergoes emotions. Besides, if we postulate a complete distinction into mind and soul so that they are two different substances, then one of them must produce all emotion, sensation, and every sort of perception, action and motion, while the other is completely passive and unmovable. There is no other alternative: either the mind or the soul is completely useless.

(6) If, on the other hand, we predicate all these activities of both mind and soul, then they are really one, and Democritus will be proved correct in denying all distinction between them. The only question remaining, then, will be as to the nature of their union: whether one is swallowed up by the other or each has a separate function. We hold that the soul is so united to the mind that they are not distinct substances, but that the mind is a faculty of the soul.

---

[3] *Ibid.* 416B 33-35.

Chapter 13

(1) The next topic is, naturally, which of the two is superior to the other. In other words, which of the two holds primacy over the other in such a way that the one that appears to be superior may be the primary substance of which the other is merely a function or instrument. Now, as a matter of fact, everyone will admit that the soul is the greater since in common terminology 'soul' is a synonym for 'man.'

(2) The rich man asks: 'How many *souls* do I support?' He does not say: 'How many *minds?*' To the pilot of a ship are entrusted 'so many souls,' not minds. Thus, the laborer, at his toil; and the soldier in battle lays down his life, by which he means his soul, not his mind. Which are more familiar to us: the dangers and desires of the soul, or of the mind? When a man dies, we say his soul departs, and not his mind. In fact, when the philosophers and physicians write a treatise on the mind, the title of their books and the material itself are always concerned with the soul.

(3) That you may have God's testimony of the matter, He always speaks to the soul; it is the soul He stirs in order that the mind may turn to Him. Christ came to bring salvation to souls;[1] and it is souls that He threatens to bury in Hell.[2] He warns us not to be more solicitous for our souls than for Him,[3] and as the Good Shepherd He lays down His life, that is, His Soul for His sheep.[4] Therefore, we may conclude that the soul is superior, and to it the mind is united, with the mind as servant and not as master.

---

1 Luke 9.56.
2 Matt. 10.28.
3 Matt. 10.39.
4 John 10.15.

Chapter 14

(1) The soul, then, is a single substance, simple, and can no more be said to be made up of parts than that it can be divided into parts, since it is indivisible. For, if it were composite and divisible, it would not be immortal. Since it is not mortal, obviously it is not composite or divisible. For, to be divided is to be dissolved and to be dissolved is to die.

(2) Various philosophers have divided the soul into parts; Plato into two, Zeno into three, Aristotle into five, Panaetius into six, Soranus into seven, Chrysippus into eight, Apollophanes into nine, while some Stoics name twelve parts. Thus, Posidonius adds two more; he begins with two notions—the *leading,* which he calls *'hegemonikon,'* and the *rational* or *'logikon'*—and he goes on to make seventeen divisions in all. Thus, each school divides the soul into varying numbers of parts.

(3) Not that we are to declare that all these are strictly 'parts' of the soul; rather, we should say with Aristotle that some of them are powers or capabilities or operations of the soul.[1] They are not really organic parts of a living being, but, rather, functions it is capable of performing—as that of motion, action, or thought, or of any other activity which they wish to specify. The same should be said of the traditional five senses—sight, hearing, taste, touch, and smell. Now, although each of these senses has a definite part of the body assigned to it, there is no need to say that there is a similar division of parts in the soul itself. As a matter of fact, the various functions of the body are not so completely divided as they would divide the soul.

(4) One body is made up of various parts, so that the

---

1 Aristotle, *De Anima* 411B 5-10.

result is a union and not a division. Look at that marvelous instrument of Archimedes, his hydraulic organ, I mean, with its multiple sections, parts, bands, and passages. It has many variations of sound, various combinations of harmonies, and batteries of pipes. Yet, the whole makes up one unit. Likewise, the wind which is forced through the pipes by hydraulic pressure is not divided into separate 'winds' from the fact of its dispersion through the instrument. It is united in its substance, though divided in its efficacy.

(5) This example fits very well the theories of Strato, Aenesidemus and Heraclitus. They maintain the unity of the soul as diffused throughout the body but present in all parts of the body. Just as the wind is distributed through the pipes within the organ, the soul displays its various functions not by being separated but merely distributed in some natural order. Philosophers and physicians can tell us what to call these faculties, how they are to be distinctly classified, and in what portions of the body they are to be exercised. These few remarks will suffice for our purpose.

Chapter 15

(1) At the beginning, we must decide whether there is in the soul some supreme principle of life and intelligence, the so-called *hegemonikon* or directing principle. Otherwise, the very existence of the soul is called in question. For, the people who deny such a directing faculty do so on the assumption that there is no such thing as a soul.

(2) Dicaearchus from Messene and, among the medical men, Andreas and Asclepiades, dispense with this guiding faculty in that they declare the senses are in the soul and they hold the senses to be supreme. Asclepiades depends wholly on the following argument: Many animals will continue to

have a certain amount of life and sensation even after those parts of the body in which the soul is generally considered to reside have been amputated. Thus, flies, wasps, and locusts will live after their heads have been removed, and you can cut out the hearts of she-goats, tortoises, and eels and they will still move. Obviously, then, there is no supreme principle, because, if there were one, life could not continue in the soul after the seat of that principle had been removed.

(3) However, Dicaearchus has considerable opposition to his view among the philosophers, such as Plato, Strato, Epicurus, Democritus, Empedocles, Socrates, and Aristotle. The doctors, such as Herophilus, Erasistratus, Diocles, Hippocrates, and Soranus himself, disagree with Andreas and Asclepiades. Of course, as Christians, we oppose both schools, since we know from Revelation that there is a directive faculty in the soul which itself resides in a special place in the body.

(4) We read that God is the searcher and examiner of hearts.[1] The Prophet to whom God has revealed the secrets of the heart[2] is approved when God shows that He knows the workings of men's hearts: 'Why do you think evil in your hearts?'[3] David prayed: 'Create a clean heart in me, O God.'[4] St. Paul says that with the heart we believe unto justice;[5] St. John, that a man's heart will reprehend him.[6] Finally, Christ Himself said: 'Whosoever shall look upon a woman to lust after her, hath already committed adultery with her in his heart.'[7] From all these texts, two points become clear. First,

---

1 Wisd. 1.6.
2 Prov. 24.12.
3 Matt. 9.4.
4 Ps. 50.12.
5 Rom. 10.10.
6 John 3.20.
7 Matt. 5.28.

there is a directive faculty in the soul according to the divine charge, that is, a principle of life and intelligence (obviously, what can know, must be alive); secondly, the soul resides in that most precious part of the body into which God looks.

(5) Hence, one cannot agree with Heraclitus that the principal part of the soul can be stirred from without, nor with Moschion that it is somehow diffused throughout the whole body. Plato[8] also is wrong when he says the soul is in the head, as well as Xenocrates, who thought it was in the crown of the head. It does not repose in the brain, as Hippocrates taught, nor around the base of the brain, according to Herophilus. Strato and Erasistratus erred in saying it was in the outer membranes of the brain. Strato, the physician, wrongly placed it in between the eyebrows. Epicurus says the soul lies within the structure of the breast. The truth is rather to be found among the Egyptians, especially in the writings of those among them who knew Holy Scripture. There is a verse of Orpheus or Empedocles which reads: 'The seat of sensation lies in the blood around the heart.'

(6) We find that Protagoras, Apollodorus, and Chrysippus believe this; so, let Asclepiades go searching for his goats who are bleating without hearts and his flies flitting around without heads. And, as for the rest of them who try to argue to the nature of the soul from their experiments on animals, you can tell them that they are the ones who are 'living' without hearts or heads.

---

8 *Timaeus* 69D.

Chapter 16

(1) The view of Plato, that the soul has a rational and an irrational element, is in consonance with Revelation.[1] The only exception we take to this statement is that we would not say that each of these elements was equally based in the nature of the soul. To be sure, it is altogether natural to the soul to be rational, since it takes its origin from its Creator, who is rational. It is impossible that that be irrational which came from the will of God; in fact, resulted from His very breath. The irrational element, however, must be thought to have come later, resulting from the suggestion of the serpent and producing the very act of the first transgression. From then on, this irrational element became imbedded in the soul, developed with the soul, and, as it happened at the very beginning of the soul's existence, gave every appearance of being an essential element of the soul.

(2) However, as Plato says, since the rational element derives from the rational soul of God, we are in danger of attributing irrationality to God, also, the soul's Author, if we say that irrationality is natural to the soul. Now, the impulse to sin proceeds from the Devil and, since all sin is irrational, the irrational therefore proceeds from the Devil whence comes sin. Sin is alien to the nature of God, as is also anything irrational. The distinction, then, between these two elements of the soul arises from the difference of their authors.

---

[1] While apparently agreeing with Plato's triple division of the soul into *rational, spirited* and *concupiscible,* in which the latter two are considered irrational, Tertullian carefully points out that the effect of irrationality, i.e., sin, is in no sense a work of God or a part of the soul, but the result of the temptation of the serpent. Thus, original sin, contracted by Adam, is transmitted to all his progeny, a conception which fitted neatly into Tertullian's Traducianism. By the very fact of being born of Christian parents, however (and thus destined for baptism), children are said to be born 'holy'; Cf. 1 Cor. 7.14.

(3) Since Plato reserves complete rationality to God and in human souls divides the irrational into two parts,² the irascible *thumikon* and concupiscible *epithumetikon* (the first of which we have in common with lions, the second with flies, while the rational we share with God), I realize that we will have to treat this point more fully because of what we know of the nature of Christ.

(4) For, in Him we perceive the rational, by which He taught, preached, and pointed out the way of salvation. The irascible also was in Him whereby He inveighed against the Scribes and Pharisees,³ and the concupiscible by which He desired to eat the Pasch with His disciples.⁴

(5) Therefore, the irascible and concupiscible impulses in our souls are not always to be ascribed to the irrational element, which certainly, in our Lord, flowed from the rational element of His soul. God becomes angry in accordance with reason, with such as deserve His anger; and, equally reasonably, He desires such things as are worthy of Him. For, He will be angry with the evil man and for the good man He will desire salvation.

(6) St. Paul attributes the concupiscible quality to human nature: 'If a man desire the office of a bishop, he desireth a good work.'⁵ From the fact that he says 'a good work,' it is clear that the desire is a reasonable one. The irascible quality is also allowed to us, since he experiences it himself: 'I would that they were cut off, who trouble you.'⁶ Such anger, which arose from his desire for good order, was undoubtedly rational.

(7) However, when St. Paul says: 'We were one time

---

2 *Republic* 438D; 548C; 580D.
3 Matt. 12.34.
4 Luke 22.15.
5 1 Tim. 3.1.
6 Gal. 5.12.

children of wrath,'⁷ he is reproving an irrational anger which does not flow from the nature that was created by God, but from that which takes its origin from the Devil, who is said to be the master of his subjects. 'You cannot serve two masters.'⁸ He is also said to be a father: 'You are of the devil, your father.'⁹ Therefore, you need have no hesitation in ascribing to him the origin of that secondary element, the later and depraved part, since he is said to be the 'sower of cockle' and the enemy who spoils the crop of wheat by night.¹⁰

Chapter 17

(1) There also arises the question of the veracity of our five senses, of which we learn from earliest childhood, since the heretics seek to support their teaching on this score. They are the familiar five: sight, hearing, smell, taste, and touch.

(2) The Platonists seriously attack their validity, and Heraclitus, Diocles, and Empedocles are said to agree with them. It is certain that Plato in the *Timaeus*[1] declares sense knowledge to be irrational and capable of arriving at opinion, but not true knowledge. Our eyes deceive us, he says, in showing us oars under water as bent or broken in spite of our assurance that they are straight; thus, again, from a distance a square tower appears to be circular and on looking down a long corridor we seem to see the walls meeting at a point. Besides, we normally see on the horizon the meeting of the sea and the sky which is really high above it.

(3) Likewise, our ears deceive us; we mistake thunder for the rumble of a cart or *vice versa*. The senses of smell

---

7 Eph. 2.3.
8 Matt. 6.24.
9 John 8.44.
10 Matt. 13.25.

1 *Timaeus* 28C, 51A.

and taste are also faulty in that we become so accustomed to perfumes and wines that we no longer advert to their specific bouquet. Touch also fails us in that the same pavement which scratches our hands is smooth to our feet; and at the first touch our bath water may seem to be scalding, yet shortly it seems quite comfortable.

(4) Thus, they tell us, we are deceived by our senses and must continually revise our opinions. The Stoics are somewhat more moderate in that they do not always impugn the validity of all the senses. The Epicureans with complete consistency maintain that the senses always report the truth, but they explain the illusions in a way different from the Stoics. In their opinion, the senses report the truth, but our minds lead us astray. The function of the senses is to receive an impression, not to think; that is the function of the soul. They deny to the senses the power of thinking and to the soul all power of sensation.

(5) But, what is the basis of thought, if not the senses? Whence does the mind get the idea the tower is really round, unless from the senses? Whence comes the act of sensation, if not from the soul? On the other hand, a soul without a body would experience no sensation. Therefore, sensation takes place in the soul and thought begins in the senses, but the soul is the root of it all. It is a fact that there is something which causes the senses to report things otherwise than they really are. If the senses can report things which do not correspond to reality, isn't it possible that such things are caused not by the senses at all, but by something that takes place between sensation and thought?

(6) This fact ought surely be recognized. The water is the cause of making the oar appear bent or broken, because out of the water it is perfectly straight. Water is so delicate a medium that, when under the light of day it be-

comes a mirror, the slightest motion of the water will distort the image and appear to bend a straight line. We mistake the true shape of a tower because of the nature of the medium that lies between it and ourselves, for the uniform density of the surrounding air blurs the angles and dulls its sharp outlines. The equal sides of a corridor appear to come to a point in the distance because our vision is contracted within the enclosed space, thins out, and so seems to extend indefinitely. So, sea and sky meet when the power of our vision has been exhausted, for, as long as it could, the eye kept the two apart.

(7) Naturally, the ear will be deceived by similarity of sounds. And, if the perfume smells dull, the wine tastes flat, and the water no longer hot, still they are actually very much the same as they ever were. And, of course, tender hands and calloused feet will disagree as to the roughness of the pavement.

(8) So, you see, there is always a cause when our senses are mistaken. Now, if this cause deceives the senses and they in turn our opinions, then the error should not be imputed either to the senses which follow the cause or our opinions which are dependent on the data of our senses.

(9) Madmen think they see other people than they really do: Orestes looks at his sister and thinks she is his mother; Ajax sees Ulysses in the slaughtered cattle; Athamas and Agave see wild beasts in their children. Would you attribute these errors to defective vision or to insanity? When a man has an excess of bile or jaundice, everything tastes bitter. Which are you going to blame—his taste or the disease? All of the senses, then, may be occasionally disordered, but when functioning normally they are free of any error.

(10) Further still, the blame for these errors is not to be imputed to these 'causes' either. For, although these things happen for specific reasons, reason should not be blamed for

the mistake. The normal event should never be construed as a lie. Now, if we can absolve the 'causes' from blame, then surely we must acquit the senses which merely follow the 'causes.' The senses, then, can claim that they faithfully report the truth, since they never render any other account of their impressions save that which they receive from the often-mentioned causes; this latter it is which produces the discrepancy between sensation and reality.

(11) O Academics! What impudence you are showing! Don't you see that your assertions would destroy the normal conduct of human life and the very order of nature? Are you not claiming that Divine Providence was blind? The senses of man have been given the mastery over all God's creation that by them we might understand, inhabit, dispose of, and enjoy His goodness—and these you accuse of deliberate falsity! Is not all life dependent upon the senses? Are not our senses the second source of knowledge with which we are endowed? Whence, do you think, come the various arts, the ingenious developments in business, politics, commerce, medicine? Whence the technique of prudent advice and consolation, the resources that have made progress in all phases of human life and culture? Without his senses, man's life would be deprived of all joy and satisfaction, the only rational being in creation would thus be incapable of intelligence or learning, or even of founding an Academy!

(12) Plato in the *Phaedrus*[2] goes so far in disparaging the senses that he makes Socrates deny that he can know himself, which the Delphic Oracle had commanded him to do; in the *Theatetus*[3] he abdicates his power of thought and feeling; and in the *Phaedrus*[4] he denies that he can know truth till

---
2 *Phaedrus* 229E.
3 *Theatetus* 150C.
4 *Phaedrus* 247D,E.

after death; yet in spite of that, still alive, he continues the search for wisdom.

(13) We cannot, I insist, impugn the validity of the senses, for thus we will be denying that Christ really saw Satan cast down from heaven;[5] that He ever heard His Father's voice testifying to Him;[6] that He only *thought* He touched Peter's mother-in-law;[7] that He never smelled the fragrance of the ointment given Him in preparation for His burial[8] or of the wine He consecrated in memory of His Blood.[9]

(14) On this pernicious principle, Marcion denied that Christ had a real body and was but a phantom or a ghost. No, His Apostles really and truly perceived Him with their senses. They saw and heard Him at the Transfiguration;[10] they tasted the wine changed from water at Cana in Galilee.[11] Thomas believed when he touched the wound in His side.[12] Finally, listen to the word of St. John: 'What we have seen, and heard, perceived with our eyes, what our hands have handled of the word of life.[13] The witness of St. John is false if we cannot believe the testimony of our eyes, our ears, and our hands.

Chapter 18

(1) Now I turn to the consideration of our intellectual faculties which Plato holds to be completely independent of the body; this is part of his legacy to the heretics. This is a

---

5 Luke 10.18.
6 Matt. 3.17.
7 Matt. 8.15.
8 Matt. 26.12.
9 Luke 22.20.
10 Matt. 17.3.
11 John 2.1.
12 John 20.27.
13 1 John 1.1.

piece of knowledge which he seems to have acquired before death. In the *Phaedo*,[1] he asks: 'What is your opinion as to the possession of knowledge? Is the body a hindrance to it or not, if we admit at all that the body shares in the pursuit of knowledge? And, likewise, does truth come to man through sight and hearing? Are not the poets always mumbling something about the fallibility of your eyes and ears?' Here he was recalling the verse of the comic poet, Epicharmus: 'The mind sees, the mind hears; all else are deaf and blind.'

(2) Further, Plato holds that man to know most clearly who knows with his mind alone and never calls on the help of sight or any other sense; in solitary contemplation the mind, serene and isolated, surveys reality, cut off from the disturbing and distracting influence of the eyes and ears, in a word, of the whole body which might hinder it in the quest for truth and wisdom.

(3) Therefore, we see here another and more useful faculty offered in opposition to the bodily senses, namely, the powers of the soul, by which the intellect grasps such truths as do not fall within the purview of the bodily senses, but lie hidden far away from common knowledge in some lofty region or in the very bosom of God Himself. Plato believes in the existence of certain substances which are invisible, incorporeal, celestial, even divine and eternal, which he calls *ideas*, that is, forms. These, he says, are the patterns and models of all the objects that we see around us; these forms alone are truly real, visible things being but shadowy likenesses of the originals.

(4) Can't you catch a gleam there of the heretical teaching of the Gnostics and the Valentinians? This is where they get their distinction between the bodily senses and the intellect which they use in their interpretation of the parable of

---

[1] *Phaedo* 65A-E.

the wise and foolish virgins.[2] Thus, the five foolish virgins are said to be the senses, who are foolish because so easily deceived, while the wise virgins typify the intellect which can perceive the secret and supernal truth hidden in the fullness of God. Here, then, is the source of all their heretical ideas and their aeons and genealogies.

(5) Thus they divide sensation from intelligence, separating it from its spiritual source, and, again, they separate sense knowledge from the animal source, since *that* cannot in any way perceive what is spiritual. The objects perceived by the intellect are invisible, while the others are visible, mean and temporal, and, as contained in images, fitted to be perception of the senses. This is the reason why, at the outset, we said that the mind is merely an instrument and faculty of the soul; that the breath is not something distinct, but is the soul insofar as it exercises respiration. Whatever God or the Devil imparts to it subsequent to its origin must be considered an adventitious element.

(6) We now come to the matter of the distinction between the sensitive and the intellectual powers, which is seen to be based on the nature of the objects perceived. While corporeal, visible, and tangible things belong to the province of sense, the spiritual, visible, and secret things are under the dominion of the mind. Yet, both classes come under the soul for the purpose of being at its service; thus, the soul perceives corporeal things with the help of the body and spiritual things by means of the mind, since the soul is really exercising sensation when it is thinking.

(7) Isn't it true that to feel is to understand and to think is to have sensation? For, what else is sensation than the perception of the thing felt? Or what else is understanding than the perception of the thing known? Why, then, all this

---

2 Matt. 25.1-13.

torturing of simple truth into obscurity? Can you show me a sensation which does not understand what it feels or an intellect which does not perceive what it knows, so as to prove to me that one can get along without the other?

(8) If we must say that corporeal things are 'sensed' and spiritual things are 'understood,' it is the nature *of those objects* which causes the distinction and not the abode of sensation and understanding, that is, the soul and the mind. By what faculty do we perceive corporeal things? If the mind does it, then the mind is a sensual as well as an intellectual faculty, because, when it understands, it feels, and, if it doesn't feel, it has no understanding. If, however, corporeal things are perceived by the soul, then the power of the soul is intellectual as well as sensual, because, when it feels something, it understands it; because, if there is no understanding, there is no sensation. Likewise, by which faculty are incorporeal things perceived? If by the mind, where does the soul fit in, and, if by the soul, the mind? Things that are distinct should be separate from each other in the exercise of their specific functions.

(9) You would have to say that soul and mind are separated if it were possible to see and hear without knowing it, because, at the time, the mind was elsewhere. In that supposition we should have to say that the soul did not see or hear, since it was then deprived of its active agent, the mind. When a man is insane, the soul is mad and the mind, far from being separated from it, is the fellow sufferer of the soul. In fact, the soul is the principal sufferer in such a contingency.

(10) This is confirmed by the fact that, when the soul leaves a man, his mind goes, too; so closely does the mind follow the soul that it cannot remain in the man after death. Since it follows the soul, and is attached to the soul, so the

understanding must be attached to the soul which the mind follows, understanding being attached to the mind. Suppose we admit that the intellect is superior to the senses and has a deeper understanding of mysteries, what difference does that make as long as both intellect and sense are powers of the soul? My argument stands as long as the superiority of intellect over sense is not predicated on the assertion of a separation of one from the other. Now that I have refuted the assertion of the distinction of soul and mind, I must deal with this alleged superiority before I come to the belief in a better god.[3]

(11) On this matter we shall have to fight the heretics on their own ground. This work is concerned with the soul and we have to be careful lest the intellect should usurp the prerogative of superiority over the soul. Now, even though the object of the intellect, being spiritual, is superior to the object of sense—namely, material things—it is still merely a superiority in object—the exalted as against the humble—and not a superiority of intellect over sense. How can there be a real superiority of intellect over sense when the former depends on the latter for its guidance to the truth?

(12) We know that truth is apprehended by means of visible images, that is, the invisible through the visible. For, St. Paul tells us: 'The invisible attributes of God from the creation of the world are understood from the things that are made.'[4] Plato would tell the heretics: 'The things we see are merely the image of the hidden realities.'[5] Hence, this

---

[3] The heretic Marcion held that there were two gods, one having dominion over visible things and the other (*Deus Potior*) over invisible things. Tertullian barely alludes to this point here which he dealt with in his treatise *Against Marcion*. If a distinction is made between the realms of sense and intellect, he fears he may be forced to agree with Marcion, postulating this 'better god' as the guardian of the invisible things which the intellect alone can preceive. Cf. Waszink, *op. cit.* 265-266.
[4] Rom. 1.20.
[5] This quotation is not found in the works of Plato.

world must be a representation of some other world, else why would the intellect use the senses as its guide, authority, and support, if without them it could attain to truth? How, then, can it be superior to that through which it exists, which it needs for its operation, and to which it owes all that it gains?

(13) Two conclusions follow, therefore, from this discussion: (1) Intellect is not superior to sense on the argument that the instrument through which a thing exists is inferior to the thing itself. (2) Intellect must not be considered to be separate from the senses, since that by which a thing exists is united to that thing.

Chapter 19

(1) Mention must also be made of those philosophers who would deprive the soul of the intellect for even a short period of time, thus preparing a basis for the view that the intellect and the mind are introduced into man during childhood.

(2) Thus, they believe that the soul alone sustains the child, giving life without intelligence, since not all living things can think. Aristotle holds that trees have vegetative without intellectual life and others attribute some kind of soul to all beings. This we believe to be the exclusive prerogative of man, not merely as a creature of God, common with all things else, but rather as the breath of God which the human soul alone is, and which we say comes to man at birth with all its faculties.

(3) Let us take up their example of the trees:[1] it is a

---

1 The Stoics held that intelligence was not possessed by children, but reason came only when they reached maturity. Thus, they compared them to trees that possessed vegetative life but were devoid of reason. Tertullian goes far beyond what he had to, to combat their argument about the human soul, by making the extraordinary statement that even trees possess reason from the first moment of their growth.

fact of experience that even the smallest plants, not even yet young trees but mere shoots and twigs, have from the first moment they appear above ground the full potentiality of life. As time goes on, they grow and develop into a woody trunk until they reach the full maturity that is proper to the species. Otherwise, trees would not be capable of receiving grafts, of developing leaves, seeds, and flowers, or of a full flow of sap, unless [from the beginning] the full potency of their nature were present so as to grow and develop in all their parts.

(4) These, then, have intelligence from the same source as they have life, that is, the same [soul] gives life and intelligence from the beginning of their existence. I have often seen a young and tender vine, obviously knowing its function and striving to cling to something in union with which it intertwines itself and thus finds support. Without any instruction in horticulture, without hook or prop, it clings to whatever it touches and that with greater tenacity from instinct than you could by volition.

(5) I have seen ivy, no matter how young, striving upward, and faster than any other plant, obviously choosing to spread its lacy web over a wall rather than, by hugging the ground, run the chance of being trampled under foot. Have you ever noticed certain trees that are injured by contact with buildings drawing away from walls as they develop? You can tell that the branches are meant to go in the opposite direction and from so deliberate an avoidance you may judge the nature of the tree. Quite content with in significance, it follows the instinct which it manifested from the beginning of its growth and it even fears a crumbling wall.

(6) Why, then, cannot I stress these signs of wisdom and knowledge in plant life? To be sure, they have vegetative life as the philosophers say, but they also have intelligence which

they will not allow. If a baby tree has intelligence, there is all the more reason why a human infant must have it, too. The soul of a child, like a tender shoot, derives from Adam as its stem, comes into life from the womb of its mother, and begins to grow with its full complement of faculties of both sensation and intelligence.

(7) I am certain, then, that an infant, when first it cries at birth, by that act makes first use of the possession of intellect and sensation, proving it has all the senses: sight, by seeing; hearing, by perceiving sounds; taste, by savoring its milk; smell, by taking in air; and touch, by feeling the ground. That first voice of infancy undoubtedly springs from the earliest effort of the senses and from the initial impulse of intelligence.

(8) There are, indeed, those who would believe this first pitiful cry to be a sign of realization of the sorrows that lie before the child in life; as a result, we must say that the soul from the moment of birth is endowed not only with intelligence, but even with foreknowledge. By this same intuition the baby knows its mother, recognizes its nurse, distinguishes its servants; the child will refuse the breast of another and the bed that is unfamiliar, choosing only those things to which he is accustomed.

(9) How else but through intelligence should he be able to judge what is unusual or normal? How else would he be capable of being soothed or annoyed? Strange indeed it would be if an infant were without mind, since he is so lively; or so naturally affectionate, without intellect. Christ has told us that He has 'received praise out of the mouths of babes and sucklings'[2] and, hence, that infancy and childhood are not dull and stupid. While He was on earth, children, on meeting Him, testified to His divinity; and the innocents who were slaughtered for His sake surely must have known Him.

---

2 Ps. 8.3.

Chapter 20

(1) Here, then, we may offer our conclusion that all the properties that are natural to the soul are inherent in it as parts of its substance and they are born and develop with it from the moment it comes into existence. Seneca here as so often agrees, when he says: 'The seeds of all arts and ages are implanted in us and God, our Master, secretly produces the qualities of our mind,'[1] that is, through the seeds planted within us in infancy; mainly, our intellect. From this our mental qualities develop.

(2) There is a specific form for each seed of each plant, and each plant has its own mode of growth. Some come easily to full maturity, while others wither or thrive according to the conditions of sun and soil, the amount of care they receive, the variations of the weather, and the vicissitudes of chance. Thus, while souls may all come from one kind of seed, individuality manifests itself as soon as growth begins. For here, too, we also find environment among other relevant factors.

(3) They say all Thebans are born dull and stupid, while Athenians are clever in speech and understanding, and, around Colyttus, the children are so precocious that they talk before they are a month old. Plato in the *Timaeus*[2] tells us that Minerva, when building her beloved city, paid most attention to this quality of the climate which would favor mental development. Hence, in the *Laws*,[3] he commands Megillus and Clinias to take pains as to the site of their city. On the other hand, Empedocles felt that the source of genius or stupidity lay in the character of the blood, and that any progress or perfection was due to learning and training. National characteristics of this type, however, have become proverbial.

---

1 *De beneficiis* 4. 6.6.
2 *Timaeus* 24C-D.
3 *Laws* 704B.

The comic poets always joke about the cowardice of the Phrygians; Sallust reproaches the Moors as fickle and the Dalmatians as cruel; and even St. Paul brands all Cretans as liars.[4]

(4) It is likely, too, that bodily health has something to do with intellectual development. Obesity is not conducive to wisdom which thrives in the thin man; the mind wastes away in paralysis, while consumption sharpens it. Besides, there are many extrinsic conditions besides obesity and strength which in the arts, experimental knowledge, business, and sustained study have a way of developing the mind, while it loses its sharpness if allowed to wallow in ignorance, laziness, lust, idleness, and vice. To all of which may be added the influence of higher powers.

(5) For, according to our teaching, such higher powers are: the Lord God and His enemy, the Devil. In the view of ordinary men they are: providence, fate, necessity, fortune, and free will. The philosophers use all these terms; for my part, I have already written a special treatise on fate in the light of our faith.

(6) From all this it will be clear how important are these various influences which affect the soul, since they are commonly regarded as separate natures. Not that they are distinct species, but accidental qualities of that one nature which God bestowed on Adam and made the stem from which all other souls have developed. There will alway be such accidental qualities and never distinct species, nor was the variety of personality, so noticeable nowadays, to be found in the father of our race, Adam. If this variety were due to the nature of the soul, then, surely, all those divergent characteristics would have to have been existent in him and thus descended to us as from their source.

---

4 Tit. 1.12.

Chapter 21

(1) Now if [as shown above] the nature of the soul in Adam was simple before the development [in subsequent men] of disparate mental characters, then it does not become multiform, since it is evenly divided among so many men; nor is it triple in structure (to keep in view the heresy of Valentinus), since there is no sign of this division in the soul of Adam.

(2) What was there of the 'spiritual' inherent in Adam? If you adduce the power of prophecy by which he foretold the great mystery in Christ and in the Church, saying: 'This is bone of my bone and flesh of my flesh and she shall be called woman; wherefore let a man leave his father and mother and cling to his wife and these two shall be in one flesh,'[1] then I must remind you that this power only came to him later when God took him out of himself and infused into him the spiritual quality in which prophecy consists.

(3) If, further, the evil of deliberate sin is manifest in Adam, this must not be considered as something *natural* to him, which really took place because of the instigation of the serpent. It was no more *natural* than it was *material*, and the material we have already excluded from belief. Now, if neither the *spiritual* nor what heretics call the *material* was inherent in Adam, even if the seed of evil should have proceeded from matter, it still follows that the only natural element in him was the psychic, which we maintain to have been simple and uniform.

(4) On this we must ask whether, being natural, it has to be subject to change. The Valentinians deny that any change is possible, that they may bolster their view of a 'trinity' of divergent natures. The good tree does not bear

---
1 Gen. 2.23-24.

bad fruit, nor the bad tree good fruit,[2] and no man gathers figs from thorns or grapes from brambles. If that were possible, then God could not raise sons to Abraham from stones nor could a generation of vipers bring forth fruits of repentance.[3] St. Paul would be wrong when he said: 'You were heretofore darkness,'[4] and: 'we were once by nature children of wrath,'[5] and: 'in this were you also but you have been washed.'[6]

(5) Holy Scripture, however, is never contradictory. The evil tree will never bear good fruit unless the good branch be grafted onto it, and the good tree will not bear evil fruit unless it be cultivated. And stones will become sons to Abraham if they are formed in the faith of Abraham; a generation of vipers will bring forth fruits of repentance if they will but spit out the poison of their wickedness.

(6) Such is the power of Divine Grace, stronger than nature itself, that it can even make subject to itself the faculty of free will which is generally said to be master of itself. Now, since this faculty is naturally changeable, it varies; and so does nature. That we do possess this faculty which is master of itself has been proven in my works against Marcion and Hermogenes.

(7) Finally, therefore, if we must enunciate a definition of the natural state of the soul, it must be said to be twofold —there being the categories of the born and the unborn, of the made and the not made. Now, the nature of that which is born and made is capable of changes, but that which is unborn and not made is eternally immutable. Since this latter

---
2 Luke 6.43-44.
3 Matt. 3.7-9.
4 Eph. 5.8.
5 Eph. 2.3.
6 1 Cor. 6.11.

can be said only of God, who is alone unborn and not made, immortal and unchangeable, it is certain that the nature of all other beings that are born and made is variable and changeable. Hence, if a threefold composition is to be attributed to the soul, the cause must lie in extrinsic circumstances and not in the ordination of nature.

Chapter 22

(1) The other faculties of the soul have been explained to Hermogenes with their justification and proof and it was seen that they spring from God rather than from matter. I shall merely mention them here lest they should seem to be neglected. We have granted that the soul is endowed with free will, as we just mentioned, a certain power over things, and occasionally the gift of foresight—which is different from that capability of prophecy which comes from the grace of God. But, let us drop this subject of the character of the soul that I may list briefly its various attributes.

(2) The soul, therefore, we declare to be born of the breath of God, immortal, corporeal, possessed of a definite form, simple in substance, conscious of itself, developing in various ways, free in its choices, liable to accidental change, variable in disposition, rational, supreme, gifted with foresight, developed out of the one original soul. Now, we must discuss this last point, how it develops out of one soul; in other words, where the soul comes from when it joins the body and how it is produced.

Chapter 23

(1) The assurance with which certain heretics affirm that souls come down from Heaven is only equaled by their certainty that they are destined to return thither after death. Saturninus, a disciple of Menander, held this view, saying that man was made by angels. The first such product was ridiculously weak and unable to stand upright, but had to crawl on the ground like a worm. Later, by the mercy of God after whose image, though poorly understood, he had been clumsily made, a spark of life was infused, which roused man, stood him up on his feet and, granting him a higher grade of vitality, provided for his return to his source after death.

(2) Carpocrates, in fact, claims for himself such a degree of supernatural qualities that his disciples consider their souls equal to Christ—not to mention the Apostles—and at times even superior to them, believing that they partake of that sublime virtue which lords it over powers and principalities that govern the world.

(3) Apelles holds that our souls were enticed from Heaven in their desire of earthly delicacies by a fiery angel—Israel's God and ours—and, once here, were then imprisoned in this sinful flesh.

(4) The followers of Valentinus introduce into the soul the seed of Wisdom, and by means of this seed they recognize, in the images of visible objects, the stories and Milesian tales[1] about their own Aeons.

---

1 'Milesian tales,' the *Decameron* of antiquity, a collection of erotic novels, written by an otherwise unknown author, Aristides, toward the end of the second, or at the beginning of the first century, B.C. The scene of the tales is Miletus, hence the name. The novels of Aristides enjoyed great popularity; they were also translated into Latin.

(5) And I am sorry to say that Plato is the merchant who supplies them with such wares. In the *Phaedo*[2] he says that souls travel back and forth between this world and the other, while in the *Timaeus*[3] he imagines that God had delegated to his offspring the production of men. Thus they clothed the mortal body around the immortal soul, thereby indicating that this world is the image of some other.

(6) In order to win credence for this theory—that the soul formerly came from dwelling with God, where it shared in the contemplation of the ideas, thence to return here, and while here recollects the eternal exemplars once known—he concocted his notion of 'learning by reminiscence.'[4] He tells us that souls on their arrival in this world have forgotten what they learned in heaven, but gradually, under the stimulus of visible things, they recall what once they had known. Since, therefore, the ideas of the heretics are borrowed from this notion of Plato, I can take care of them by demolishing him.

Chapter 24

(1) On Plato's principles, I cannot admit that the soul could possibly forget anything, since he puts it on a par with God. He says the soul is unborn, and that for me is sufficient proof of its divinity. He goes on to say it is immortal, incorruptible, incorporeal—since he believes God to be so—invisible, without form, simple, supreme, rational, and

---

2 *Phaedo* 70C.
3 *Timaeus* 69C.
4 *Meno* 81C-D. Here, Socrates, by asking the proper questions of a young boy, elicits from him the proper solution of a problem in geometry. Since the boy had never studied the subject, Socrates argues that his questions had merely caused the boy to remember what he had forgotten from a previous existence.

intellectual. What more could he say of the soul unless he would call it God?

(2) We, however, do not attach the soul to God, but say that by the very fact of being born it is therefore a pale and shadowy replica of the divine happiness, being the breath of God but not His spirit. If it is immortal—a characteristic of divine beings—yet still is it passible, as a result of its birth, and so from the first moment of its appearance capable of and allied to forgetting.

(3) This matter has been sufficiently discussed with Hermogenes, but I may add that, if the soul is in all its properties to be equated with God, then it cannot be subject to any passion and, hence, to forgetting. For, the disgrace of forgetting is in proportion to the glory of memory possessed by the soul, since Plato[1] calls memory the warden of all knowledge and Cicero[2] says that it is the treasure house of all learning. The real question is not whether so divine a being as the soul is capable of forgetting, but, rather, whether it can ever get back what it has thus lost. I wonder if a faculty which has forgotten what it should never have lost could be capable of recalling it again? My soul can forget and remember, but Plato's can't!

(4) The second question I would ask Plato is this: 'Do you admit that souls can naturally understand *ideas* or not?' 'Surely, I do' will be his answer. In that supposition, then, no one will agree with you that a natural knowledge of the natural sciences can be deficient. But we do forget the facts of science, the train of ideas, and things we have learned. Perhaps we also can forget our ideas and emotions, which are not from nature, although they appear to be. For, as we said above, they are conditioned by circumstances of place,

---
1 *Philebus* 34A.
2 *De oratore* 1.18.

education, bodily health, the influence of higher powers, and by man's own free will.

(5) No, the instinctive knowledge of natural things never fails, not even in animals. Do you think a lion, under the influence of kindly training, will forget his instinctive ferocity? To be sure, he may, with his flowing mane, become the pet of some Queen Berenice and lick her checks with his tongue. But, though he may change some of his habits, his fundamental instincts will remain the same. Always will he look for his proper food and his natural remedies, and experience his instinctive fears. Suppose the queen offers him some fish and cakes? He will look for flesh. If he becomes sick and is offered some medicine, he will still want an ape. If no hunting spear will stop him, yet will he fear the rooster.

(6) Even man, perhaps the most forgetful of all creatures, will always retain consciousness of the things that are natural to him, precisely because they belong to his nature. Thus, when hungry, he will always desire to eat; when thirsty, to drink. Always will he use his eyes for seeing, his ears for hearing, his nose and mouth for smell and taste, and his hands for feeling. These are merely sense faculties, which philosophers, out of regard for intellectual powers, are wont to undervalue.

(7) But, if the natural knowledge of our senses is so lasting, is it likely that the power of the intellect, which is supposed to be stronger, will fail? What is the source of this forgetfulness which is said to precede remembrance? We are told it is caused by the lapse of time, which seems to me a foolish answer. What effect can time have on something which we are told is unborn and, by that very fact, must be considered eternal. Now, that which is eternal because it is unborn, having neither beginning nor end, has no relation whatever to time. But, what bears no relation to time obviously

can suffer no change because of time, nor can the lapse of time have any effect on it.

(8) If time is supposed to be the cause of forgetfulness, why does the memory fail as soon as soul and body are united? Are we to believe that the soul is, from that point, somehow dependent on time? Insofar as the soul is prior to the body, you can say that it bears that much of a relation to time. But, when does the soul forget? As soon as it joins the body, or shortly after? If immediately, where is the length of time which in an infant is still too short for consideration? If shortly after, will not the soul remember in that short interval before forgetfulness sets in? How do you explain the fact that the soul forgets, and then, later, remembers? How long does this period of oblivion last, during which time it affected the soul? I don't think the whole course of life would be long enough to erase a memory of a period before the soul came to the body.

(9) Plato would say that the body is the cause, as if we could believe that an unborn substance could be destroyed by something born. Since bodies differ a great deal because of race, size, character, age, and health, are there therefore to be different degrees of forgetfulness? No. Forgetfulness is said to be the same for all. Obviously, then, various bodily peculiarities cannot be the cause of an invariable effect.

(10) As I have already mentioned to Hermogenes, Plato[3] offers a number of proofs that the soul has the power of foresight. Now it is the common experience of all of us that our souls occasionally manifest some flash of foreknowledge in a case of future danger or advantage. If, then, the body is no obstacle to such experiences, why should it be a hindrance to memory? The supposition is that the soul, while remaining in the same body, both forgets and remembers.

---
3 *Timaeus* 71D.

If the body be the cause of forgetfulness, how can it permit the contrary—remembrance? Do you mean that memory revives after forgetting? But, if the body was a hindrance in the first case, why isn't it hostile in the second?

(11) As a matter of fact, children with young and vigorous souls have better memories. Since they have not yet become immersed in the cares of domestic and public life, they devote themselves exclusively to those studies whose very acquirement is a process of remembrance. Why don't we all remember to the same degree, since are all equal in forgetting? This, however, is true only of the philosophers—and only of some of them. It is curious that Plato is the only one, out of so great a number of races and so great a crowd of wise men, who can remember all the things that he had forgotten.[4]

(12) Therefore, since this, his fundamental argument, is seen to be weak, the whole structure of his theory it was intended to support must collapse: namely, that souls are unborn, dwell in the heavenly regions where they know divine mysteries, and, coming down to this earth, call to mind that previous existence—all of this, indeed, merely to give to heretics the basic idea of their systems.

Chapter 25

(1) To return, then, from this disgression on Plato, I shall explain how all souls are derived from one, and when, where, and in what manner souls join the body. The answers to

---

[4] It is here in the treatment of Plato's doctrine of 'Reminiscence' that Tertullian's unfair tactics appear most clearly. All too frequently he distorts the true meaning of an adversary's argument in order to hold it up to ridicule. Tertullian must have known the Myth of Er which explained that forgetfulness of the experiences of the soul in the other life was caused by the drinking from the river Lethe, the river of forgetfulness. Cf. Waszink, *op. cit.* 305-306.

these questions will be the same whether they are asked by a philosopher, a heretic, or an ordinary man.

(2) Those who profess the truth do not take seriously the theories of its opponents, especially those who say that the soul is not conceived in the womb, nor formed and produced along with the flesh, but is inserted into the body which comes from the womb in a lifeless state. This is how they describe the process. The seed is through intercourse deposited in the womb and, quickened by its natural motility, develops into the solid substance of flesh alone. In time, the body is born, still warm from the furnace of the womb, and it loses its heat just as a hot iron does when dipped into cold water; on feeling the cold air, the body is shocked into life and utters its first cry. This view is held by Aenesidemus and Stoics in general, and occasionally by Plato, as when he tells us that the soul is an alien thing and originates apart from the womb, since it is received at the first breath of air, just as it departs when a man draws his last breath. Let us see whether this really represents Plato's own view in this matter. Even among physicians there is Hicesius, a traitor to nature and his own profession.

(3) I suppose it was their modesty which forbade them to give the explanation which women would tell them was the true one. The result is that they have to blush even more when, far from agreeing with them, the women prove them wrong. In this matter the best teacher, judge, and witness is the sex that is concerned with birth. I call on you, mothers, whether you are now pregnant or have already borne children; let women who are barren and men keep silence! We are looking for the truth about the nature of woman; we are examining the reality of your pains. Tell us: Do you feel any stirring of life within you in the fetus? Does your groin tremble, your sides shake, your whole stomach throb as the

burden you carry changes its position? Are not these movements a source of joy and an assurance to you that the child within you is alive and playful? Should his restlessness subside, would you not be immediately concerned for him? In fact, would he not be aware of your worry, stirred by this new sound? Would you not go looking for special foods or, perhaps, lose your appetite? Would you not share your ailments even to the extent that, if you suffer a bruise, the child within you would be marked in the same part of the body as you are; as if he were claiming as his own the injuries to his mother?

(4) Now, if these bruises on the child's body are the result of the presence of blood, then without a soul there will be no blood, just as, if health be an attribute of the soul, without a soul there will be no health. If nourishment and fasting, growth and decay, fear and motion involve activities of the soul, the being who performs them must be alive. When he no longer experiences them, he dies. How can we speak of children being born dead unless they were once alive? Who can die unless he once lived? Sometimes, unfortunately, a child is killed while still in the womb, because he is in such a position that delivery is impossible without causing the death of his mother.

(5) Hence, among their instruments, physicians have one, curved in structure, which is used to hold the womb wide open; to this is fitted a kind of circular knife by which the limbs are all too carefully amputated; finally, there is a blunt hook, which is used to extract the victim in a violent delivery. Another deadly instrument is a brazen needle which performs the murder within the womb and is fittingly called the 'child-killer.' Such instruments were used by Hippocrates, Asclepiades and Erasistratus; Herophilus, who practiced dissection of adults, also had them, as did even the kindly Soranus. And

all of them were convinced that a living thing had been conceived, since they all feel pity for the poor child who must be killed in the womb to escape torture outside of it.

(6) I imagine that Hicesius was convinced of the necessity of such harsh measures even though he held the soul was inserted after birth, by means of a blast of cold air; and this, because the root meaning of the Greek word for soul implies some process of cooling. We might well ask him if barbarians and Romans received their souls by some other process, since they happen to call a soul something other than *psyche*. And, further, how many nations can we count who live under a sun so hot that their skins are darkened by its rays? How do they get their souls with no frosty air around them? Need I mention the warmth of delivery rooms and all the precautions to keep women warm at childbirth, to whom the slightest draught is considered dangerous? Why, the fetus is clearly alive in his first [warm] bath, because he immediately cries.

(7) And, if brisk, cold air is such an important item, no one could be born except in the territory of the Germanic and Scythian tribes, or high in the Alps or the Argae. As a matter of fact, the people who dwell in the temperate zones are more prolific and far more intelligent, and it is well known that the Sarmatians are all dull-witted. The minds of men, too, would become sharper because of the cold if their souls arose from cold air, because any substance must resemble its generative power.

(8) Next, we might consider the case of those who were cut out of their mothers' womb living and breathing, as were Bacchus and Scipio. If there be any who think, with Plato, that two souls cannot coexist in the same being any more than two bodies could, I can show him the case of two such souls and even two such bodies and of many other things

joined to the soul. Take the case of possession by the Devil; and not merely of one spirit, as in the case of Socrates' *daimon,* but of the seven devils driven out of Magdalen[1] and of the devils in the Gadarene swine whose number was legion.[2] Surely, a soul could more easily be united to another soul of the same nature than to a devil, who has a very different nature.

(9) I cannot decide which of his two opinions Plato is contradicting when he warns us (in Book 6 of the *Laws*)[3] to be careful lest we stain the soul and the body by the vitiation of the seed in some debased and illicit union. In thus warning us of a danger to the soul he is clearly teaching that it derived from the seed and not (as he said before) from the first breath of the new-born child. If we are not produced from the seed of the soul, how could we account for the fact that, because of resemblance of soul, we are like to our parents in disposition, as Cleanthes said? Why, indeed, did the ancient astrologers cast a man's horoscope from the time of his conception, if the soul does not exist from that moment? The inbreathing of the soul, however we explain it, pertains likewise to this moment of conception.

Chapter 26

(1) The vagaries of human opinion cease to matter as soon as we come to the words of Holy Scripture. Hence, I shall withdraw within our boundaries and there make a stand so that I may prove to the Christian the answer I have given to the philosophers and physicians. Build your faith, my brother, on the foundation that is yours! You know of the

---

1 Mark 16.9.
2 Mark 5.1.
3 *Laws* 775B-C.

living wombs of those holy women whose children not only breathed before being born but uttered prophecies.

(2) The very vitals of Rebecca[1] are stirred, though the child is a long way from birth and there is no breath of air. Behold, the twin offspring struggles in the womb of their mother, though there yet is no sign of the two nations. We might regard as prophetic this struggle of the two infants, who are at enmity before they are born, who show animosity before animation, if their restlessness merely disturbed their mother. When, however, the womb is opened, their number known, and the symbolic implications of their condition made manifest, we see clearly not only the separate souls of those children but, even then, the beginning of their rivalry.

(3) For, before the first of the twins was full born, he was almost detained in the womb by the second one, whose hand alone had emerged. If we hold the Platonic theory or the Stoic doctrine of the coming of life on exposure to the air, how are you going to explain this action of the second child, who, while still within the womb, tried to hold on to his brother who was already outside? I suppose he took hold of his brother's foot before he breathed and, so, earnestly desired to be born first, while still feeling the warmth of his mother's body. Surely, he was a remarkably vigorous child and even then asserting his rivalry—perhaps he was so because he was even then alive!

(4) You will also recall the accounts of those women who conceived under extraordinary circumstances—those of barren women and of the Virgin Mary. They could only have conceived imperfect children against the course of nature, because one was too old and the other knew not man. You might expect those children, if any, to be without souls, since they had been conceived in an extraordinary fashion.

---

1 Gen. 25.22.

But, they were both alive while still in the womb. Elizabeth rejoiced as the infant leaped in her womb; Mary glorifies the Lord because Christ within inspired her.[2] Each mother recognizes her child and each is known by her child who is alive, being not merely souls but also spirits.

(5) Thus, you read the word of God, spoken to Jeremias: 'Before I formed thee in the womb, I knew thee.'[3] If God forms us in the womb, He also breathes on us as He did in the beginning: 'And God formed man and breathed into him the breath of life.'[4] Nor could God have known man in the womb unless he were a whole man. 'And before thou camest forth from the womb, I sanctified thee.' Was it, then, a dead body at that stage? Surely it was not, for 'God is the God of the living and not of the dead.'[5]

Chapter 27[1]

(1) How is a human being really conceived? Is the substance of both body and soul formed at the same time, or

---

2 Luke 1.41,46.
3 Jer. 1.5.
4 Gen. 2.7.
5 Matt. 22.32.

---

1 In this (and the preceding) chapter, Tertullian's doctrine of Traducianism is implicit in his discussion of the origin of the body and soul. Just as the body was generated from the body of the parents, so the soul of the child is derived from the soul of the father and mother at the moment of conception. He was unable to envisage the doctrine of Creationism (the human soul is the result of a direct act of creation), since he felt that act would have to take place either before or after the existence of the body; if before, some approval of the doctrine (Platonic) of transmigration of souls might be taken; if after, then there is some period of time in which the embryo is not an animate being. He could accept neither possibility and he taught the simultaneous origin of body and soul. For St. Augustine and St. Jerome, Creationism seemed to weaken the doctrine of the transmission of Original Sin. Their difficulties were resolved when later theologians clarified the nature of Original Sin as a *privation* of Sanctifying Grace.

has one of them a priority over the other? My view is that both are conceived, formed, and perfected at the same time, just as they are born together, and there is not a moment's interval in their conception by which any priority might be assigned to either one of them.

(2) Now, from man's last moment of life we may get some idea of his first. If death is nothing else that the dissolution of body and soul, life, then, should be defined as the union of soul and body. If this separation occurs simultaneously to both through death, the law of their union must demand that life means the simultaneous joining of soul and body.

(3) Now we believe that life begins at conception, since we hold that the soul begins to exist at that time; for where life is, there must be a soul. Hence, they create life by their union, whose dissolution always means death. If we insist that one comes before the other, then we assign the precise times of semination according to the rank of each. What time can you assign to the bodily seed and what moment can you designate for the conception of the seed of the soul?

(4) If you insist on different times of conception then this difference of time is going to result in totally unrelated substances. Even though we admit that there are two kinds of seed, the one for the body and the other for the soul, we still insist they are unseparated and as such altogether contemporaneous in origin. There is no need to be ashamed of an explanation that is demanded by the truth. Nature should, for us, be an object of reverence and not the occasion of blushes. It is lust that has befouled the intercourse of the sexes, not the natural use of this function. It is the excess and not the normal activity which is unclean. Thus has natural intercourse been blessed by God: 'Increase and multiply.'[2]

---

[2] Gen. 1.28.

On the other hand, He has cursed excess as adultery, debauchery and lewdness.

(5) This natural union of the sexes, therefore, which brings man and woman together in common intercourse, is performed by both soul and body. The soul supplies desire and the body its gratification; the soul furnishes the impulse, the body affords its realization. By the united impulse of both substances, the whole man is stirred and the seminal substance is discharged as a products of both; the body supplying fluidity, the soul, warmth. Now, if the Greek word for soul implies cold, how does it happen that the body becomes cold as soon as the soul departs?

(6) Finally, if I may endanger modesty in the interests of accurate proof, is it not a fact that in the moment of orgasm, when the generative fluid is ejected, do we not feel that we have parted with a portion of our soul? As a result, do we not feel weak and faint, along with a blurring of our sight? This, then, must be the seed of the soul which proceeds from the dripping of the soul, just as the fluid which carries the bodily seed is a species of droppings from the body.

(7) Here, the account of the first creation is helpful to our understanding of this matter. The flesh of Adam was formed from the slime of the earth. Now, what is slime except a slightly solidified [or thickened] liquid? There you have the generative fluid. The soul came from the breath of God. Now, what is the breath of God except the exhalation of the spirit, and there you have what we lose in the seminal fluid [of the soul].

(8) In that first creation, therefore, there were two different and distinct elements, slime and breath, which produced man. Thus, by the mixture of the seeds of their two substances, they gave the human race its normal mode of propagation. So, even now, two different seeds flow forth

together, and together they are implanted in the furrow of their seed-plot, and from both there develops a man. In this man, in turn, is a seed contained according to his own species, just as the process of generation has been ordained for all creatures.

(9) And so from one man, Adam, flows this whole stream of souls, while nature obeys the command of God: 'Increase and multiply.' For, in God's declaration at the creation of the first man: 'Let us make man,' the whole human race was proclaimed: 'And let *them* have dominion over the fishes of the sea.'[3] And this is quite natural, for the promise of the future harvest lies in the seed.

Chapter 28

(1) What is the source of this ancient doctrine mentioned by Plato as to the successive migrations of souls? He says that they leave this world and go to the other, then come back here again, live their lives and depart once more, and once again from death return to life. Some people say it was invented by Pythagoras, and Albinus holds it to be a divine pronouncement, perhaps of the Egyptian Mercury. But there is no divine oracle save that of the one God which the Prophets, the Apostles and Christ Himself proclaimed. Moses is older than Saturn or even his great-grand children by some nine hundred years, and surely more divine is he in his writings. For he has traced out the history of the human race from the every beginning of the world, indicating according to names and ages the generations of great men, and his prophetic voice sufficiently establishes the divine character of his story.

---

3 Gen. 1.26. The Vulgate Text here reads *'praesit'* in the singular, but the Greek of the Septuagint is plural.

(2) Now, if the wise man of Samos is Plato's authority for this continuous transmigration of souls from life to death and death to life, then Pythagoras, however noble in other matters, in this at least surely did resort to a disgraceful and deceitful lie in order to establish this theory.[1] Here is his story, in case you never heard it, and you may take my word for it. Pretending to be dead, he condemned himself to hiding in a dungeon for seven years. The only one who knew of his hiding place, his mother, took care of him and kept him informed of those who had died in the interval about whom he was to tell on his return. When he felt that his appearance had changed so that he looked like a dead old man, he came out of his dungeon of deceit and pretended he had returned from the dead.

(3) Since he had been thought dead, anyone would have believed he really had come back to life, especially when he began to tell stories about men who had died in the preceding seven years, which he could only have learned in Hades. Stories were told in ancient time of men coming back from the grave. Why couldn't it happen now also? A story doesn't have to be old to be true, and many a tale of yesterday is false. Even though this theory of Pythagoras is from antiquity, I believe it is completely untrue. How could it be other than false when the evidence for it is founded on a lie? How can I help believing Pythagoras to be a liar (when he teaches transmigration), since he lies to make me believe that he came back from the dead? Why should I believe that in previous incarnations he had been Aethalides, Euphorbus, Pyrrhus the fisherman, and Hermotimus, when as Pythagoras he lies to bolster his doctrine? I might have believed that he had

---

[1] The method of argumentation used here is common throughout the treatise—that of attacking the general credibility of an opponent, without specifically refuting the details of his doctrine.

come back to life once, though not perhaps these many times, if only he had not deceived me in difficult matters and even in things that might easily have won credence.

(4) He pretended to recognize as his own the shield of Euphorbus that was consecrated at Delphi, and in proof he adduced evidence not generally known. Well, look at that underground dungeon of his and see if you can believe this story. Here is the man who concocted this trick: he buries himself in the earth for seven years, ruins his health, wasting his life on a fraud amidst hunger, idleness and darkness, refusing to look on the light of day. Why, he would descend to any deceit and manufacture any magic trick to pretend to have discovered that famous shield.

(5) It is possible that he might have discovered some recondite documents; he might well have chanced upon some tradition of ancient times; perhaps he bribed some caretaker to let him see them secretly. We all know that magic has great power for exploring secret things: through katabolic, paredral, and pythonic spirits. It is likely enough that Pherecydes, the master of Pythagoras, indulged in, or perhaps better, dreamed of such practices. Might he not have been possessed of the same demon which in Euphorbus did such bloody deeds? Finally, however, why is it that this man, who tried by means of the shield to prove he was Euphorbus, did not recognize any of his Trojan fellow soldiers? Surely, they, too, must have come to life again, since apparently the dead were rising from their graves.

Chapter 29

(1) There is surely no doubt that dead men come from living men, but there is no evidence of a reversal of the process.[1]

---
[1] *Phaedo* 72A.

From the beginning of time living men came first and, afterwards, dead men. There was only one source from which the dead could have come—the living. But, the living need by no means have come from the dead.

(2) Therefore, if the original process was that the living did not come from the dead, why should they afterwards? Perhaps because the original fountain of life had dried up? Perhaps because the law of human origin was found unsatisfactory? Why, then, did it hold in the case of the dead? Isn't it clear that, because the dead came from the living in the beginning, therefore they should always come from the same source? The law established in the beginning should have continued in both cases or changed in both cases, and, if it was later decided that living should come from dead men, then the parallel case should also have been changed.

(3) If the established order were not to be maintained, then opposites ought not to be formed alternately from opposites. There are many cases of opposites which do not come from another: born and unborn, sight and blindness, youth and age, wisdom and folly. The unborn does not issue from the born because of a supposed law of contraries, nor does youth come again to bloom from old age because it is normal for youth to deteriorate into senility, and, finally, wisdom does not become stupidity because folly may sometimes develop into wisdom.

(4) Albinus is here at pains to distinguish various kinds of opposites, solicitous for the reputation of his master, Plato. He would claim that these examples are not the same as that of life and death, which he had endeavored to explain in accordance with his teacher's principle. Finally, life does not return from death just because death follows upon the completion of life.

Chapter 30

(1) What answer can we give to the rest of their arguments? If, just as death follows life, life should follow death, the number of men in the human race must always remain the same, and that would be merely the number who first inaugurated human life. First, there were the living, and they died; from these dead came the living, and again the living from these dead men. Now, since this process was continually going on among the same group of people, no more came into the world than the original number. For, the men who died could not be more or less than those who had previously returned from death.[1]

(2) In the ancient records of the human race, however, we learn that the number of men has gradually increased; either as aborigines, as nomads, as exiles, or as conquerors, men have occupied new lands. The Scythians overran Parthia; the Temenidae, the Peloponnesus; the Athenians, in Asia; the Phrygians, in Italy: and the Phoenicians, Africa. Besides, many races have swarmed over unpopulated lands in large-scale migrations, in order to relieve the crowding of their cities. Native populations have remained in their original home or have loaned vast numbers of people to other lands.

(3) A glance at the face of the earth shows us that it is becoming daily better cultivated and more fully peopled than in olden times. There are few places now that are not accessible; few, unknown; few, unopened to commerce. Beautiful farms now cover what once were trackless wastes, the

---

[1] Tertullian is here altering the doctrine of his adversaries to make them appear ridiculous. Transmigrationists held that 'the number of souls in existence' was constant, but not that the population of the earth was always stable. Since there was an interval of a thousand years between death and reincarnation, it would appear that the majority of souls at any given time would not be on earth.

forests have given way before the plough, cattle have driven off the beasts of the jungle, the sands of the desert bear fruit and crops, the rocks have been ploughed under, the marshes have been drained of their water, and, where once there was but a settler's cabin, great cities are now to be seen. No longer do lonely islands frighten away the sailor nor does he fear their rocky coasts. Everywhere we see houses, people, stable governments, and the orderly conduct of life.

(4) The strongest witness is the vast population of the earth to which we are a burden and she scarcely can provide for our needs; as our demands grow greater, our complaints against nature's inadequacy are heard by all. The scourges of pestilence, famine, wars, and earthquakes have come to be regarded as a blessing to overcrowded nations, since they serve to prune away the luxuriant growth of the human race. Yet, when the sword of destruction has slaughtered vast hordes of men, the world has never yet been alarmed at the return from the dead of the masses that had died in that catastrophe of a thousand years before. Surely, the equalizing force of loss and gain would have long since become evident if men really returned to life from the grave.

(5) Why is it necessary to wait a thousand years for this return? Why does it not happen in a moment? There is a danger that the demand might exceed the supply if the deficiency is not made up in time. This brief period of our human life, compared to that one thousand years, seems to be very short; too short, in fact, when we consider that the spark of life is far more easily quenched than kindled. Finally, since the human race has not yet lived long enough to test the truth of this theory of transmigration of souls, we cannot agree that men come back to life from death.

Chapter 31

(1) Now if this recovery of life really takes place, personal individuality must be maintained. Hence, each of the souls which once inhabited a body must have returned each into a single body. Now, if two, three, or five souls all unite in the one womb, you will have no true return to life, because they will not return as separate individuals. Yet, in this supposition, the original plan of creation would be followed out, since you would have several souls coming from one.[1]

(2) Besides, since souls would have departed from this life at different ages, why do they all come back at the same age? At their birth, all men are imbued with the souls of infants; but, how comes it that a man who dies in old age returns to life as an infant? Far from slipping back in age during its exile of a thousand years, wouldn't it be more likely that is should return to life the richer for its millennial experience in the other world? At least, the soul ought to come back at the age it had when it departed, so as to resume life where it left off.

(3) If they did return as precisely the same souls, even though they might acquire different bodies and totally different fates in life, they ought to bring back with them the same characters, desires, and emotions they had before, since we should hardly have the right to pronounce them the same if they were lacking in precisely the characteristics which might prove their identity. You may ask me: 'How can you be sure all this doesn't happen by some secret process? After all, why should *you* recognize those who come back, strangers to you, after a thousand years?' Ah, but when you tell me Pythagoras was once Euphorbus, I know that it doesn't!

---

[1] Tertullian is guilty of a sophism here: even though twins were born of one mother, still, at birth, a single soul is found in a single body.

(4) Take Euphorbus. It is clear that his was a military and warlike soul, if we can judge by the renown of his sacred shields. Compare him with the timorous and unwarlike Pythagoras who preferred to pass the time in Italy at geometry, astronomy, and music at a time when Greece was teeming with wars — the very opposite of Euphorbus in character and temperament. Pyrrhus spent his time in catching fish, and Pythagoras wouldn't eat a fish or any animal food. Beans were doubtless part of the ordinary fare of Aethalides and Hermotimus, but Pythogoras wouldn't even allow his disciples to walk through a bean-patch!

(5) Tell me, then, if you please, how can you say they can recover their own souls, if you can show no proof of identity of personality, habits, or way of living? And, out of all of Greece, only four souls are claimed to have returned. But, why should we restrict ourselves to Greece, as if there wouldn't have been transmigration of souls and even of bodies in every country, among all ages, conditions, and sexes, and that, every day, too? And why does Pythagoras alone experience these changes from one personality to another? Why hasn't this happened to me?

(6) However, if it is an exclusive privilege of philosophers, and Greek ones at that (as if there were no philosophers among the Scythians and Indians!), why didn't Epicurus recognize he had once been another person? Why didn't Chrysippus, or Zeno, or, in fact, Plato himself, whom we might well believe to have been Nestor, because of his honeyed eloquence?

Chapter 32

(1) Empedocles, who had once dreamed that he was a god, disdained for that reason, I suppose, to declare that he

had been a mere hero in a previous incarnation, and so asserted: 'I was a shrub and a fish.' Why didn't he say he'd been a pumpkin, since he was such an empty-head? Or a chameleon, so puffed up was he with his own importance? Perhaps he chose a fish so as to avoid rotting in some obscure grave, and he preferred being roasted in the fires of Etna into which he jumped. That probably took care of any subsequent metensomatoses (or transmigrations of bodies), as he could hardly provide more than a light repast, after being so well cooked.

(2) Now we must deal with the horrible theory that some have imagined—that, in the process of transmigration, men become beasts and beasts are turned into men. So, enough for Empedocles and his shrubs and bushes; a passing mention of them will do, lest our amusement prevent us from teaching the truth. Our position may be stated in this way. It is impossible for the human soul to pass into beasts, even though the philosophers may hold that both are made up of the same substantial elements.

(3) Whether for the moment we assume that the soul is made of fire, water, blood, air, or light, we must remember that certain animals possess characteristics that are contrary to some of these elements. For instance, there are cold-blooded animals that are opposed to fire, such as snakes, lizards, and salamanders; and such others as are predominantly composed of water, the enemy of fire. Again, there are dried-up animals that seem to thrive on dryness, like locusts, butterflies, and chameleons. Then there are bloodless animals, like snails, worms, and most fish. As opposed to breath, we find such as have no lungs or windpipes, and hence cannot breathe—gnats, ants, moths, and other tiny insects. Opposed to air, there are countless creatures who live underground or under water; you've seen them, even though you can't give them

names. Finally, we know of many animals that are totally blind or see only in the dark, such as moles, bats and owls; it is clear that these have nothing to do with light. All these examples have been chosen so as to illustrate the point with clarity.

(4) But, apart from these, if I could get a handful of Epicurean 'atoms,' or get a glimpse of the 'numbers' of Pythagoras, if it were possible to trip over the 'ideals' of Plato or capture some of the 'entelechies' of Aristotle, I am sure I could find even in these some characteristics that would be opposed to some animals. No matter what elements may make up the human soul, I maintain that it could never be reborn into animals so contrary to its original nature. This transfer could never produce a new being; in fact, everything would lead us to expect that there would be violent opposition to such a union because of the inherent contrariety of those elements. A body so composed would be in a state of continual civil war, and, as each animal developed naturally, the strife would only grow fiercer.

(5) The human soul has obviously been destined to dwell in a certain type of abode; it has its proper food and care, feelings and emotions, its own process of reproduction and birth. In an individual body it has its own disposition, its proper functions—joys and sorrows, faults and desires, pleasures and pains, its specific remedies—finally, its own mode of life and its own end, in death.

(6) Now, will you tell me how a soul so afraid of great height and depth, which is exhausted from climbing stairs, which drowns if it falls into a fish pond, is ever in some future like to soar to the heavens as an eagle or dive to the depths of the sea as an eel? How is one who has been brought up on exotic and delicate foods to feed as a goat or a quail on straw, thorns, or the bitter leaves of wild plants, or root in

dunghills for worms and other poisonous vermin? Suppose it becomes a bear, or a lion, how can it stoop to devouring carrion or, remembering what it once was, even human flesh? We need not waste time on any more such absurdities. Now, since a human soul must be of a certain definite size and extent, how will it manage in very large or very small animals? Whatever its size, every body must be completely filled by its soul and, in turn, cover the soul entirely. How is a human soul going to fill the body of an elephant? How can it be squeezed into a gnat? Surely, it can't be so contracted or extended without serious danger.

(7) This naturally leads to another question. Since the soul is clearly incapable of adapting itself to the bodies of animals and their natural characteristics, is it going to shed all human qualities and, by this transfer, take on the characteristics of various species of animals? If, indeed, through this transmigration it loses what it had, it will cease to be what it was; if it becomes something altogether different, then this so-called metensomatosis is nonsense and there is no reason for assigning the change to the soul which will be so changed that it has practically ceased to exist. Only when the soul comes out just as it was in the beginning can there be said to be metensomatosis.

(8) Now, if the soul cannot change so as to lose its identity nor stay as it is, if it is to become so radically modified, I am still looking for some good reason for this alleged transformation. Even though we do call some men beasts because of their habits, characters, and desires—even God said: 'Man is made like to the senseless beasts'[1]—a rapacious man does not really become a hawk, nor the impure man a dog; vicious men are not panthers, good men, lambs, chatterers, swallows; nor do the pure become doves,

---
[1] Ps. 48.21.

as if the same substance of the soul would repeat its natural disposition everywhere in the properties of certain animals. There is a difference between a substance and the nature of that substance, since the substance is an exclusive property of one thing though the nature may be common to many individuals.

(9) For example, a stone or a piece of iron is a substance, but hardness is the nature of both of them. Because of hardness they are alike, but they differ in their respective substances. You'll find softness in wool and in a feather; their natures make them alike, but they are different in substance. So, though we may call a man a wild beast or a harmless one, we don't mean that he has the soul of a beast. Similarity of nature is clearest when there is the greatest dissimilarity of substance. By the very fact that you consider a man to be like a beast you admit that the souls are different; note that you say 'similar' and not 'identical.'

(10) This is what is meant by the word of the psalmist, quoted above—man is like the senseless beast in nature, but not in substance. Besides, God would not have said that of man, if He knew him to be a beast in his substance.

Chapter 33

(1) This doctrine is advanced as a means of assuring proper judicial retribution, on the supposition that human souls in accordance with their deserts are assigned (in a subsequent incarnation) to the bodies of animals. Some of them, in beasts destined for slaughter, are to be executed; some, in animals that slave and toil, are to be subjugated and worn out with labor; those in unclean animals are to suffer debasement.

(2) On this same principle, the souls placed in ani-

mals that are most beautiful, noble, useful, and attractive are to be honored, loved, cared for, and sought after. To this I say: If they are changed, then they won't get the punishment they deserve. The whole idea of punishment will be frustrated if they have no consciousness of what they truly deserve. This realization will be missing if the state of the soul is changed, and it is changed unless they remain the same personalities they were before. They should surely retain their individuality until the judgment, as was noted by Mercurius the Egyptian when he said that a soul on departing from the body was not dissolved into the world-soul, but maintained its individuality, so that it might be able to render an account to the Father for its sins during life. It would be well for us here to recall the awesome dignity and magnificence of Divine Justice, for I fear that we are likely to assign too high a place to human judgment. To it we allow too much freedom, and often it is too severe in visiting punishment and again too generous in dispensing its favors.

(3) Now, what do you suppose will be the fate of the soul of a murderer if merely human justice is to dictate the punishment? Perhaps it will inhabit some cow destined for the butcher's knife, that it may be killed just as he had murdered another, to be skinned as he had flayed a man, to be served up as food since he had thrown his victims to the beasts of the forest glens.

(4) If that is to be his punishment, it would seem that this soul would find more comfort than pain in such a fate. He would be cooked by expert chefs, served swimming in sauces that would do honor to Apicius or Lurco, served at the tables of gourmets like Cicero, on gleaming silver platters worthy of Sulla—in a word, his obsequies would be the *pièce de résistance* of a sumptuous banquet. He would finally be devoured by people like himself, instead of by buzzards

and wolves, and find his tomb in a human body. At last he would rise again, return to his own form, and, if in the end he had any realization of human judgments, what else would he do but laugh at their futility?

(5) Even while still alive, then, the murderer is to be delivered to various kinds of beasts, some of them trained to a ferocity that is not natural to them. His death is prolonged as much as possible so as to inflict the last possible stroke of punishment. If by chance the soul escape the final blow of the sword by dying, then the body is further tormented. The full price of its crime is exacted by stabbing of the throat and sides. The mangled body is then thrown into the fire, so that even burial may be a form of torture. The bodies must be burned, but the funeral pyre is not so carefully tended that the animals do not have a chance to tear the remains. Not a shred of mercy is to be shown even to the bare bones and his ashes.

(6) The punishment that men would assign for the murderer is thus as great (if not greater) than that which nature demands. Indeed, anyone would prefer the justice of the world, which, as the Apostle testifies: 'beareth not the sword in vain,'[1] and is, in fact, an instrument of Divine Justice in punishing murderers. Think of the torments attached to other crimes, such as the crosses, the bonfires, the sacks, the hooks, and the precipices—who wouldn't prefer the condemnations of Empedocles and Pythagoras to those?

(7) They would condemn a soul to dwell in the bodies of asses and mules, to be punished by drudgery and slavery turning a mill-stone of a water-wheel. But these tasks they would find easy compared to the horror of the metal mines, the workhouses, road-building, and the jails where men rot away in boredom. Those who surrender life to the judge

---
1 Rom. 13.4.

after lives of nobility might well look for rewards, but actually they, too, are punished. It must indeed be a handsome reward for a good man to be turned into an animal, however good or beautiful!

(8) Ennius once dreamed that Homer had lived in the body of a peacock. Now, I wouldn't believe a poet even when he was awake, though I do admit that a peacock is a beautiful bird and none has more beautiful tail feathers. But, since a poet's joy is in singing his songs, what good is a handsome tail when he has a raucous voice? So, it was no favor at all to Homer to imprison him in a peacock. Homer would get much more satisfaction out of the world's acclaim which heralds him as the father of the liberal arts; the laurels of his fame would be far more pleasing than the decorations of his tail.

(9) But, let the poets migrate into peacocks and swans! At any rate, a swan has a pleasing voice. Tell me, what animal you would choose for the good man Aeacus? In what beast would you clothe the chaste Dido? With what bird would you reward patience, what animal would become the abode of holiness, and what fish would cover innocence? All of these are the servants of man, his menials, or dependents. Is that to be the reward of the man whose virtues merited pictures, statues, titles of honor, distinguished public privileges, and even sacrifices from the Senate and the people?

(10) What kind of reward would that be for the gods to pronounce as man's recompense after death? Far more fallible are they than human judgments; contemptible they are as punishments, and, as rewards, disgusting. The vilest of men would have no fear of them and the best would scarcely be expected to look forward to them. They would provide more incentive to criminals than to saints, since the former would thus escape more quickly the world's judgment,

and the latter would be, by them, held up from their reward. Fine teachers you are, you philosophers who try to persuade us that punishments and rewards that come after death rest lightly upon our souls! Whatever sentence awaits us after death will surely hurt the more at the conclusion of life than while we are carrying out our duties. For, nothing is so complete as that which comes at the very end of life, and that which comes in our last days is the more divine.

(11) God's judgment will be for us the more complete since it will come after death, a sentence to eternal punishment or reward for souls which will not undergo transmigration into beasts but a resurrection in their own bodies. And this will happen once and for all and on that day which is known to the Father alone,[2] so that the soul continually solicitous for the reward she hopes for by faith may ever celebrate that day, never knowing when it will come, ever fearing the arrival of that for which she longs.

Chapter 34

(1) Although no foolish sect of heretics has up to the present espoused the doctrine of transmigration of souls, nevertheless I have felt it advisable to attack and refute it, since it is allied to other heresies. Thus, in getting rid of Homer and the peacock we can also dispose of Pythagoras and Euphorbus, and, once metempsychosis or, if you wish, metensomatosis is demolished, we will destroy another notion which has been of great help to the heretics.

(2) There was Simon of Samaria, who in the Acts of the Apostles[1] tried to buy the Holy Spirit. When he and his

---

2 Matt. 24.36.

---

1 Acts. 8.18.

money were condemned by the Holy Spirit, he feigned a kind of repentance, but then devoted himself to the destruction of truth, to console himself for his punishment. With the help of his magic arts and tricks, he bought out of a brothel some Tyrian woman named Helen with the same money with which he would have bought the Holy Spirit—a deal worthy of this miserable man.

(3) Then he pretended that he was the Supreme Father, and this woman his first conception, through whom he intended to create angels and archangels. When she became aware of this design, she deserted the father and, going down to the lower areas, in anticipation of his plan she produced the angelic powers who who were totally ignorant of the father, and they in turn created this world. These angels then took her prisoner, fearing, just as she had, that when she was gone they might appear to be the offspring of another. Hence, they exposed her to every abuse, and, that she might never escape from her degradation, she was imprisoned in the flesh, forced to take human form.

(4) So, for many centuries she flitted from one female form to another and became the notorious Helen who brought ruin to Priam, and later to Stesichorus, whom she blinded because of his abusive poems and whose sight she later restored when he had sung her praises. Finally, after passing through numerous other bodies, she further defiled the name of Helen as a prostitute. This was the lost sheep for whom the supreme father, Simon, went in search and, when he had found her, brought back on his shoulders or his loins. Then he turned his attention to the salvation of mankind, and out of revenge tried to free them from the angelic powers. To deceive them he took on a visible shape and in Judea he posed as the Son, as a man among men; but in Samaria, as the Father.

(5) Poor Helen! You have a hard time of it between the poets and the heretics who branded you as an adulteress and a prostitute. Perhaps her rescue from Troy was a more noble exploit than her liberation from the brothel! It took a thousand ships to get her out of Troy, but it woudn't need more than a thousand pence to free her from the brothel! Simon, you ought to be ashamed of yourself—it took you so long to find her, and you were so careless in holding on to her! You could learn gallantry from Menelaus; as soon as he missed her, he began to search, he follows when she was found to have been stolen, he rescues her after ten years of war. No deceit or trickery or delay for him! I am afraid that Menelaus looks like a much better 'father' who struggled so long and valiantly for the recovery of his Helen!

Chapter 35

(1) However, it was not for you alone, Simon, that they invented this theory of transmigration of souls. Carpocrates naturally made good use of it, too, and he is just like you, a magician and a fornicator, except that he had no Helen. He believed that souls continued to take new bodies in order to accomplish the complete overthrow of all human and divine truth. He held that no man's life was utterly complete until he had befouled himself with every iniquity that is considered vile. You see, he held that nothing was really bad but thinking makes it so. Hence, transmigration was demanded if any man in the first stage of life had not indulged in all that is forbidden. For, obviously, sin is the natural product of life! So, the soul had to be called back to life if it were found below the quota of sin, 'until it has paid the last farthing,'[1] and cast into the prison of the body.

---
[1] Matt. 5.26.

(2) Thus he distorts the meaning of that remark of our Lord which is perfectly clear and straightforward and should be understood in its obvious meaning. The 'adversary' whom Christ mentions is the heathen who, along with us, walks the road of this life. We would have to leave the world altogether[2] if we are to have no contact at all with him. Therefore, He bids us be kind to such a man: 'Love your enemies and pray for those who say evil of you,'[3] lest any man irritated by your injustice in some business transaction 'deliver you to his own judge'[4] who will throw you into jail until you have paid the whole debt that you owe him.

(3) Now, if you choose to interpret 'adversary' as the Devil, then you are bid by Christ to make even with him a compact which will be in accordance with your faith. The compact you have already made with him is to renounce him, his pomps, and his angels. There is agreement between you on that point. Your friendship with the Devil will arise from your adherence to your renunciation. Never will you try to get back from him anything that you have renounced, anything that you have handed over to him, lest he might hale you before God your judge as a cheat and as a violator of your agreement. For, we do read of the Devil as an accuser of the saints and as the prosecutor.[5] The Judge may then hand you over to the angel of retribution and he will cast you into the prison of Hell, whence there is no release until every sin has been expiated in the period before the Resurrection. No interpretation could be better or more true than this one.

(4) To come back to Carpocrates, who would be the enemy and adversary in his opinion, since the soul must pay

---
2 1 Cor. 5.10.
3 Matt. 5.44.
4 Matt. 5.25-26.
5 Apoc. 12.10.

its debt by committing all kinds of sins? I suppose it would have to be some wiser mind which would force the soul into some act of virtue and drive it from body to body until it should be found free of all debt to the virtuous life in any body. This is judging a tree to be good by its bad fruit and from the worst possible teachings to derive the doctrine of truth.

(5) I fully expect these heretics to seize upon the example of Elias as reincarnated in John the Baptist, and thus they would have our Lord espousing the doctrine of metempsychosis. 'Elias indeed has come and they knew him not.'[6] And again: 'And if you are willing to receive it, here is Elias who was to come.'[7] Was the question of the Jews to John, 'Art thou Elias,'[8] to be understood in a Pythagorean sense, and not in reference to the divine pronouncement: 'Behold I send you Elias, the Thesbite'?[9]

(6) But their theory of transmigration refers to the recall of a soul that had died long before and to its insertion in some other body. Elias, however, is to return not after leaving this life by death, not to be returned to his body, since he never left it, but he will come back to the world from which he has been removed. He will return not to take up a life he had left off, but for the fulfillment of a prophecy. He will come back as Elias, with the same name. How, then, could John be Elias? The voice of the angel tells us: 'And he shall go before the people in the spirit and power of Elias,'[10] and not in the soul or body of Elias. These substances are the specific property of each man, while 'spirit and power' are

---

6 Matt. 17.12.
7 Matt. 11.14.
8 John 1.21.
9 Mal. 4.5.
10 Luke 1.17.

extrinsic gifts conferred by the grace of God, and so they may be transferred to another according to the will of God as happened long ago with respect to the spirit of Moses.

Chapter 36

(1) Let us now go back to the matter we interrupted to take up this question of transmigration. In the discussion of the conflicting opinions of philosophers and heretics and of that old saying of Plato's, we established that the soul is a seed placed in man and transmitted by him, that from the beginning there was one seed of the soul, as there was one seed of the flesh, for the whole human race. Now we will take up the points which follow from these.

(2) Since the soul is implanted in the womb along with the body, and along with the body receives its sex, so neither one of them can be regarded as the cause of the sex. Now, if there were any interval of time between their conception, so that either soul or flesh were first implanted, one might ascribe a specific sex to one of them, owing to the difference of time of their impregnation, so that either soul or flesh would be the cause of the sex of the human being.

(3) Even so Apelles (I mean the heretic, not the painter) speaks of male and female souls before bodies are formed, as he learned from Philumena, and so holds that the flesh receives its sex from the soul. Those, however, who believe that the soul is placed after birth in the body which had previously been formed, naturally take the sex of the soul from the male or female body.

(4) As a matter of fact, the two seeds together are infused; hence, they share the same sex in accordance with this mysterious power of nature. Surely, the formation of our first parents attests to the truth of this view. The male was molded first

and the female somewhat later. So, for a certain length of time, her flesh was without specific form, such as she had when taken from Adam's side; but she was then herself, a living being, since I would then consider her soul as a part of Adam. Besides, God's breath would have given her life, if she had not received both soul and body from Adam.

Chapter 37

(1) There is undoubtedly some power, some servant of God's will, which controls the whole process by which the human embryo is implanted in the womb, and there developed and brought to its final form. All these stages were noticed by the Romans, who in their superstition designated the goddess, Alemona, to nourish the fetus in the womb; they appointed Nona and Decima to watch over the critical months, Partula was supposed to care for the actual birth, and Lucina brought the child to the light of day.

(2) The embryo, therefore, becomes a human being from the moment when its formation is completed. For, Moses imposed punishment in kind for the man who was guilty of causing an abortion on the ground that the embryo was rudimentary 'man,' exposed to the chances of life and death, since it has already been entered in the book of fate. And this, although it still dwells within the mother and shares with her their mutual life.

(3) Now, so as to cover the whole process of birth, I ought to say something of the different stages of pregnancy. A normal birth takes place at the beginning of the tenth month and those who are interested in numbers regard the number ten as the parent of all numbers and, so, as the master of human birth.

(4) I should rather attribute the choice of ten to God,

as if these ten months were man's introduction to the Ten Commandments, so that the ten months of our physical birth would be parallel to the means of our spiritual rebirth in God. Since a child born in the seventh month has a better chance of living than one born in the eighth, I think this is out of respect for the Sabbath. Thus, the image of God in a child would sometimes coincide with the number of the day on which God's creation was completed. So, even though a birth be premature, it may coincide with the number seven, a symbol of the Resurrection, of rest, and of the Kingdom. The number eight, however, is not concerned with birth, since in eternity, which it represents, there will be no marrying.

(5) We have already discussed the close union of soul and body from the moment of the joining of their seeds to the complete formation of the fetus. Now, we maintain their intimate conjunction even after they have been born; together, soul and body grow, each in accordance with its nature; as the body grows in size and external form, the soul develops in intelligence and perception. Not that the substance of the soul increases, lest we should imagine that it therefore could decrease; this would imply the possibility of its complete destruction. But, that power of the soul which contains all its native potentialities gradually develops along with the body, without any change in the initial substance which it received by being breathed into the man in the beginning.

(6) For instance, take a rough chunk of silver or gold: its mass is gathered together into a solid nugget which is all silver or gold. But, when it has been beaten out into a sheet of gold, it becomes larger than it was in its original form, but larger only by being extended into a flat surface—it has not increased its original bulk; it is broader, but no heavier.

So, though its extent may have increased, there is no more metal than before.

(7) Greater also is the gleam of the metal after beating, but that, too, was surely there before, even though not apparent. Later, various other changes may be made in it, in proportion to its malleability, but these are no more than variations of shape. In this fashion, the growth of the soul takes place. Age does not add bulk, but merely develops latent potentialities.

Chapter 38

(1) We established, above, the principle that all the natural potentialities of the soul with regard to sensation and intelligence are inherent in its very substance, as a result of the intrinsic nature of the soul. As the various stages of life pass, these powers develop, each in its own way, under the influence of circumstances, whether of education, environment, or of the supreme powers. At this point in our discussion of the union of soul and body, we now wish to affirm that the puberty of the soul coincides with that of the body; at about the age of fourteen years, puberty comes to the soul through the development of the senses and to the body by the growth of its organs. We choose this age, not because Asclepiades sets that as the age of reason, nor because civil law then considers a boy as competent to conduct business, but because this was determined from the beginning.

(2) If Adam and Eve felt it necessary to clothe themselves once they had come to the knowledge of good and evil, then we claim to have the same knowledge once we first experience shame. From this age when the genitals cause blushing and must be covered, concupiscence is fostered by the eyes, which in turn communicate desire to the

mind, until a full knowledge has been attained. Then, man covers himself with the fig leaves which themselves excite passion and he is driven out of the paradise of his innocence. From there he falls into unnatural vices, which are the perversion of nature's laws.

(3) There is only one strictly natural desire—that of food. This God conferred on man from the beginning: 'Of every tree of paradise thou shalt eat,'[1] and after the flood He said to Noe and his sons: 'Behold I have given you all things as food, even as the green herbs,'[2] and here He was looking to the good of the body primarily, even though food is also good for the soul. We have to cut the ground from beneath the argument of the quibbler who would argue to the mortality of the soul because the soul apparently desires food, is sustained by it, grows weak when it is withheld, and finally appears to die of starvation.

(4) At this point we should ask, not *which faculty* desires food but *for whose advantage* is it desired, and, if it be for its own advantage, why and when and how long? Besides, we must distinguish desires that are natural from those which are necessary, accidental from essential. The soul will desire food for itself because of an external circumstance, but for the body because the latter needs it for itself. For, the body is the dwelling place of the soul; the soul, merely its tenant for a time.

(5) The temporary lodger, then, will have desires for the good of the house for as long as he is to live in it; he will not become part of the foundations, of the plaster on the walls, or of the beams that support the house. He simply wants to live inside, and he can't live except in a soundly built structure.

---

1 Gen. 2.16.
2 Gen. 9.3.

(6) And so (to apply this to the soul), if the body collapses owing to the lack of the sustenance it once enjoyed, the soul may depart in full possession of all the attributes of its nature: immortality, reason, sensation, intelligence, and free will.

Chapter 39

(1) All the endowments which the soul received at birth are obscured and corrupted by the Devil, who from the very beginning cast an envious eye on them, so that they are not properly cared for nor perform their functions as they ought. For, the Devil lies in wait to trap every human soul from the moment of its birth, to which he is invited to assist by all the superstitious practices which surround childbirth.

(2) All men are born surrounded by the idolatry of the midwife: the wombs from which they are born are still wrapped in the ribbons which were hung on the idols, and thus the child is consecrated to the demons; in labor, they chant prayers to Lucina and Diana; for a whole week a table is set in honor of Juno; on the final day, the 'Writing Fates' are invoked; and the child's first step is sacred to Statina.

(3) After that, everyone dedicates the child's head to sin by cutting a lock of his hair, shaving the whole head with a razor, binding it up as for sacrifice, or sealing it for some sacred use—and all this for the sake of some devotion to the clan or the ancestors, either in public or in private. Thus it was that Socrates was found by the demonic spirit in his boyhood; and so to each person is assigned a genius, which is another name for a demon. As a result, there is hardly a birth that is free from impurity, at least among the pagans.

(4) This is the reason why St. Paul said that, when

either of the parents was sanctified, the children could be born holy, as much from the privilege of Christian birth as from the conferring of Christian baptism. For, he says: 'Otherwise they would have been born unclean,'[1] as if the children of believers were in some sense destined for holiness and salvation, and in the pledge of this hope he supported those marriages which he wished to continue. In general, of course, he was mindful of the words of Christ: 'Unless a man be born of water and the Spirit, he will not enter into the Kingdom of God';[2] in other words, he cannot be holy.

Chapter 40

(1) Every soul is considered as having been born in Adam until it has been reborn in Christ. Moreover, it is unclean until it has been thus regenerated.[1] It is sinful, too, because it is unclean, and its shame is shared by the body because of their union.

(2) Now, although the flesh is sinful and we are forbidden to walk in accordance with it, and since its works are condemned for lusting against the spirit,[2] and men therefore marked as carnal, still the body does not merit this disgrace in its own right. For, it is not of itself that it thinks or feels anything toward urging or commanding something sinful. How could it, when it is only an instrument? And, an instrument not as a servant or a friend—they are human

---

1 1 Cor. 7.14.
2 John 3-5. In his solicitude to make no exceptions to the inheritance of Original Sin, Tertullian here adds the general law, as contained in Christ's words to Nicodemus. The children of believing parents must be baptized even though they may be called (by anticipation of their Baptism) *sancti*. Cf. d'Alès, *op. cit.* 265-6.

---

1 Rom. 5.14; 6.4; 1 Cor. 15.22.
2 Rom. 6.12-14.

beings—but rather as a cup or something like that; it is body, and not soul. Now, a cup may serve the need of a thirsty man, but, unless he lifts the cup to his lips, the cup is no servant of his.

(3) Now, the specific characteristic of man is not that he is formed of clay nor is his flesh the human person as if a faculty of the soul and separate person, but it is a thing of altogether different substance and state, joined to the soul, however, as a possession, an instrument for the conduct of life. Hence, the flesh is blamed in the Scriptures because, without the flesh, the soul is unable to accomplish anything in the pursuit of passion, such as gluttony, drunkenness, cruelty, idolatry, and other works of the flesh, operations which are not merely internal sensations but result in external actions.

(4) Finally, sins of thought that do not result in action are imputed to the soul: 'Whosoever shall look on a woman to lust after her, hath already committed adultery with her in his heart.'[3] Besides, what has the flesh ever done independently of the soul in deeds of virtue, justice, suffering, and chastity? In fact, what kind of thing is that to which no praise is ever offered for good actions, but only blame for evil things? The one who assists in the commission of a crime is brought to trial for complicity and is accused along with the principal criminal. Greater is the disgrace of the master when his servants are punished because of him; the one who gives the orders is punished more severely, but the one who obeys them is not acquitted.

---

3 Matt. 5.28.

Chapter 41

(1) Besides the evil that mars the soul as a result of the machinations of the Devil, still another evil has previously affected it, and this is in a certain sense natural to it, since it flows from its origin. As we have said, the corruption of nature is a second nature, one which has its own god and father, namely, the author of all corruption. Nevertheless, there is some good in the soul, the remains of that original, divine, and genuine good which is its proper nature.

(2) That which comes from God is overshadowed, but not wholly extinguished. It can be obscured, since it is not God; but it cannot be completely extinguished, since it is of God. For, just as a light is not seen if it is obstructed by some opaque body, yet it is still there, so the good in the soul is still there even though blocked by evil and perhaps totally obscured or only a faint glimmer of its presence seen.

(3) Thus, some men are good, others, bad, yet their souls all belong to the same class. There is some good in the worst of us, and the best of us harbor some evil within us. God alone is without sin, and the only sinless man is Christ, since He is God. Hence, the soul, conscious of its divine origin and native goodness, renders prophetic testimony to God in such expressions as 'Good God,' 'God will provide,' and 'God bless you.' So, just as no soul is wholly without sin, so no soul is entirely bereft of some seeds of good.

(4) Therefore, when the soul embraces the faith, it is regenerated by this new birth in water and virtue celestial; the veil of its former corruption is removed and it at last perceives the full glory of the light. Then is it welcomed by the Holy Spirit as, at its physical birth, it was met by

the evil spirit. The flesh naturally follows the soul which is now wedded to the Spirit and, as part of the wedding dowry, it is no longer the slave of the soul but the servant of the Spirit. A blessed marriage, indeed; but, would that no infidelity were to follow![1]

Chapter 42

(1) It remains for us to speak of death, so that our discussion of the soul may end with that with which the soul concludes this life. Epicurus, according to his well-known doctrine, believed that death did not pertain to us. He says: 'Whatever is dissolved is without sensation, and what is without sensation is nothing to us.'[1] But it is not death (but man) who experiences dissolution and the loss of sensation. And even Epicurus admits that the man who dies suffers something. Besides, it is ridiculous to say that so great a force as death means nothing to the man for whom it means the separation of soul and body and the end of sense knowledge.

(2) Seneca is more to the point: 'After death, all things are at an end, even death itself.'[2] In that supposition, death certainly pertains to itself, since it, too, comes to an end; and much more to man, who himself comes to an end among all

---

[1] We must not look to Tertullian for the exact formulation of the doctrine of the nature of Original Sin which later resulted from the profound analyses of the scholastic theologians. Most prominently before his mind were the manifold revolts against the Good—the concrete effects of Original Sin as inherited from Adam. While not clearly distinguishing Original Sin (the privation of Divine Grace) from the effects that remain (even after baptism), he was perfectly clear as to the fact of our regeneration in Christ by baptism and on the indewilling of the Holy Spirit in a soul so sanctified. Cf. d'Alès *op. cit.* 267; 324-333.

[1] Epicurus, *Sententiae* #2.
[2] Seneca,*Troad.* 397.

the things that are finished. If death means nothing to us, then neither does life. For, if death by which we are dissolved is nothing, then life which unites us into one being is equally nothing. Thus, the loss or the acquistion of sensation also are unimportant.

(3) The fact is that, if you destroy the soul, you also destroy death. We, however, have to speak of death as a second life and another existence of the soul, for, even if death means nothing to us, we pertain to death. Hence, sleep, the image of death, is pertinent to our subject.

Chapter 43

(1) First, then, we will speak of sleep, and afterwards of the manner in which the soul meets death. Sleep is not something unnatural, as many philosophers held when they said that it came from causes that are beyond nature.

(2) The Stoics define sleep as a suspension of the activity of the senses: Epicurus, as the weakening of the animal spirit; Anaxagoras and Xenophanes describe it as a weariness of the soul; Empedocles and Parmenides say it is a cooling of the soul; Strato holds it to be a separation of the spirit from the body; Democritus, as the indigence of the soul; while Aristotle sees sleep as a result of the dispersal of heat around the heart. I must confess that I have slept a good deal and never experienced any of those conditions. I don't believe that sleep is some kind of weariness, either; in fact, it seems to be quite the opposite and removes weariness, and a man is refreshed rather than fatigued when he wakes up. Besides, sleep is not always the result of fatigue, but, when it is, the fatigue disappears in sleep.

(3) Nor can we admit that sleep is a process of cooling or dispersal of heat. In fact, our bodies become warm in

sleep and, on those theories, our food could not be properly distributed throughout the body during sleep if the process were hurried by heat or delayed by cold. Further proof is found in the fact that perspiration is a sign of an overheated digestion. In fact, the very word for 'digestion' [*concoquere*] implies heat and not cold.

(4) The immortality of the soul is sufficient proof of the falsity of the theories which say that sleep is a weakening of the animal spirit, the indigence of the soul, or the separation of the soul from the body, because, if the soul could decrease in any way, it could perish altogether.

(5) Nothing remains but to agree with the Stoics and to define sleep as the suspension of sense activity, since it brings quiet to the body but not to the soul. The soul is always in motion, always active, and it never succumbs to rest, because that would be contrary to immortality. Nothing that is immortal will permit a cessation of its activity, and that is just what sleep is. Sleep generously bestows the favor of quiet on the *body,* which is mortal.

(6) Anyone, therefore, who doubts the naturalness of sleep will run into the dialecticians in their controversies as to the distinction between natural and unnatural, so that he will begin to believe natural, things which he thought unnatural. For, nature has so arranged some things that they appear to be beyond its powers. As a result, anything can be natural or unnatural, as occasion requires. For us, as Christians, the matter must be settled by what we learn from God, the Author of all the things we are discussing.

(7) We believe that nature is a rational work of God. Now, reason presides over sleep, since it is so fitting for man; in fact, it is useful and even necessary. Without sleep, the soul could never find means of restoring the weary body, or rebuilding its energy, assuring its health, providing surcease

from toil and a remedy for overwork. Day departs that we may enjoy sleep; night makes sleep obligatory by stealing the color from all things. Since, then, sleep is indispensable for our life, and health, there is nothing irrational about it and, consequently, nothing unnatural.

(8) Thus, physicians consider as unnatural anything which is contrary to our complete good health, such as those diseases which prevent sleep—pains in the head and the stomach. By this they have implicitly declared sleep to be natural. Further, when they declare that lethargy is not natural, they are predicating their belief on the fact that the normal use of sleep is a natural thing. Every natural thing is impaired by excess or defect, but is maintained by the proper amount. The thing, therefore, that is rendered unnatural by defect or excess becomes natural in the proper measure.

(9) Suppose we were to declare eating and drinking to be functions unnatural to man. Yet, these are certainly an important preparation for sleep and the instinct for sleep was impressed upon man from the very beginning. If you look to God for instruction, you will see that Adam enjoyed sleep before rest; he slept before he had ever labored, or even before he had eaten or spoken.[1] Thus, men may learn that sleep is a natural function and one that takes precedence over all other natural powers.

(10) From this, then, we are led to trace even the image of death in sleep. If Adam is a type of Christ, then Adam's sleep is a symbol of the death of Christ,[2] and by the wound in the side of Christ was typified the Church, the true Mother of all the living. Hence, sleep is so salutary and rational and has become the model of that which is common to the whole race of man.

---
1 Gen. 2.21.
2 1 Cor. 15.22.

(11) By means of such types God has foreshadowed everything in the dispensation of His providence and so He has willed to set before us each day, with greater clarity than Plato ever did, the outlines of the beginning and end of human life. He uses for this all sorts of types and parables in both words and deeds, thus stretching out His hand to aid our faith. Thus He presents to your view the human body touched by the friendly gift of repose, stretched out by the kindly need of rest, immovably still in sleep as it was before life began and will be after life has closed, in proof of man's condition when he first was formed and after he has been buried—as if sleep awaited the soul before it was first bestowed on man and after it has been taken away.

(12) In sleep, the soul acts as if it were present elsewhere and the imitation of absence *which is sleep* is a preparation for its future departure in death (we will see this later in the story of Hermotimus.) Meantime, the soul dreams. Whence come its dreams? The soul does not altogether give in to rest and idleness nor surrender its immortality to the power of sleep. It continues to show itself in constant motion; it wanders over land and sea, engages in trade, is excited, labors, plays, sorrows and rejoices, pursues the lawful and the unlawful, and clearly shows that it can accomplish much without the body, that it is supplied with members of its own, although showing the need it has of exercising its activity in the body once again. Thus, when the body awakens, it portrays before your eyes the resurrection of the dead by returning to its natural functions. There you have the natural explanation and the rational nature of sleep. Thus, by the image of death, you are introduced to faith, you nourish hope, you learn both how to live and die, you learn watchfulness even when you are asleep.

Chapter 44

(1) They tell the story about Hermotimus that he used to be deprived of his soul during sleep as if the soul went off from the body, on the pretext that his human existence would be temporarily abolished. His wife let out the secret and some of his enemies, coming upon him asleep, burned his body as if it were a corpse. When his soul returned; too late, I suppose, it accepted the fact that it had been murdered. His fellow citizens of Clazomene paid him the honor of erecting a temple to him, which women are forbidden to enter because of the perfidy of his wife.

(2) Why do I tell this story? So that superstition may not be increased by the tale of Hermotimus among the common people who believe that sleep is the temporary departure of the soul. It must have been some kind of heavy sleep such as is caused by a nightmare or perhaps some special disease which Soranus suggests, rejecting the idea of a nightmare, or some such malady as took hold of Epimenides when he slept for almost fifty years. Suetonius reports that Nero never had dreams unless, perhaps, near the end of his life after some great fright. Theopompus says the same of Thrasymedes.

(3) Suppose it were believed that the soul of Hermotimus actually went into such complete idleness and repose in sleep that it was separated from his body? You can imagine anything you like so long as it does not entail freedom for the soul to escape from time to time from the body without death. If such a thing were declared to have happened to his soul once (like a total eclipse of the sun or moon), I should imagine it happened through divine intervention. It would not be unlikely that a man might be warned or frightened by God, as by a bolt of lightning or a sudden stroke of death,

but it would be much more natural to think that such a warning would come in a drean. But, if this were not a dream, then it ought to have happened to Hermotimus when he was awake.

Chapter 45

(1) Here we are obliged to discuss the Christian explanation of dreams as accidents of sleep and rather serious disturbances of the soul. The soul we hold to be perennially active because of its continual movement which is a sign both of its divinity and its immortality. So, then, when that special comfort of bodies, rest, comes, the soul disdains an idleness which is alien to its nature and, deprived of the faculties of the body, makes use of its own.

(2) Just imagine a gladiator without his weapons or a charioteer without his team, but still going through the motions of their respective employments. They fight and struggle, but nothing happens. They appear to go through the whole performance, but they accomplish nothing at all. You have action, but no result.

(3) This power we call 'ecstasy,' a deprivation of the activity of the senses which is an image of insanity. Thus, in the beginning, sleep was preceded by ecstasy, as we read: 'And God sent an ecstasy upon Adam and he slept.'[1] Sleep brought rest to the body, but ecstasy came over the soul and prevented it from resting, and from that time this combination constitutes the natural and normal form of the dream.

(4) Of course you have observed how anxiously and with what feeling we rejoice, mourn, and are frightened in dreams. If we were fully masters of ourselves, we should not be

---

[1] Gen. 2.21. Tertullian is here following the Septuagint; the Vulgate reads *'soporem,'* and the Douai, 'a deep sleep.'

affected at all by such emotions, which would be only empty fantasies. In our dreams, any good actions we perform are without merit and our crimes are blameless. We will no more be condemned for a rape committed in a dream than we will be crowned for dreaming we were martyrs.

(5) But, you may object, how can the soul remember its dreams if during them we are presumably without control of the actions of the soul? This must be a peculiarity of this form of insanity which does not result from the failure of a healthy state, but from some natural process. It does not destroy the mental functions, but only withdraws them temporarily. There is a difference between shaking a thing and really moving it; it is one thing to destroy something, another to stir it.

(6) The fact that we remember dreams is proof of the fundamental soundness of the mind, but the dulling of a sound mind while memory continues to function is a species of madness. In that state, therefore, we are not considered insane, but only dreaming, and hence to be in full possession of our faculties, the same as at any other time. Although the power of exercising these faculties is dimmed, it is not completely extinguished and, while control seems to be lacking just at the time when ecstasy is affecting us in a special manner, still it then brings before us images of wisdom as well as those of error.

Chapter 46

(1) Next, we have to express still further the Christian view about the subject of those very dreams which move the soul so strongly. But, when are we going to get around to the topic of death? To this I answer: 'When God permits it; for nothing is really delayed which ultimately gets done.'

(2) Epicurus, when trying to prove that the gods are not interested in men and that there is, hence, no intelligent governance of the world, but that everything happens by blind chance, claims that all dreams are vain and meaningless. On that basis, however, some dreams should sometimes turn out to be true, since it is unreasonable to suppose that dreams alone should be outside the laws of chance. Homer says there are two gates from which all dreams issue: the gate of horn, for true dreams; the gate of ivory, for false ones—and this because horn is transparent while ivory is opaque.

(3) When Aristotle says that most dreams are false, he implicitly admits that some of them are true. The people of Telmessus admit that all dreams have some meaning and blame their own intelligence when they can't explain them. Now, any normal human being has sometimes had a dream that made sense. To shame Epicurus, I'll tell you some stories of really prophetic dreams.

(4) Astyages, King of the Medes, as we read in Herodotus, saw in a dream a flood which issued from the womb of his virgin daughter, Mandana, and inundated all Asia. In the years following her marriage, he dreamed that a vine grew out of her womb and covered all Asia. The same story is told by Charon of Lampsacus, before Herodotus. The men who interpreted these dreams were not mistaken, because Cyrus actually inundated and overspread Asia.

(5) Ephorus tells us that, before Philip of Macedon became a father, he dreamed that a ring with a lion as a signet was imprinted upon the body of his wife, Olympias. When he had thence concluded that she would have no children (in the belief, I suppose, that a lion becomes a father only once), Aristodemus and Aristophon assured him that the portent had great promise of an illustrious son. Anyone who knows

anything of Alexander the Great will see in him the lion of the ring.

(6) According to Heraclides, a woman of Himera foresaw in a dream the tyrannical rule of Dionysius over Sicily. Euphorion testified that Laodice, the mother of Seleucus, knew before his birth that he was to be master of Asia. From Strabo I learn that it was through a dream that Mithridates took Pontus, and from Callisthenes that Baraliris the Illyrian by the same means extended his control from the Molossi to Macedonia.

(7) The Romans, too, believed in the truth of such dreams. Cicero learned from a dream that one Julius Octavius, then but a boy and unknown to him or anybody else, was to be the reformer of the Empire, the suppressor of Rome's civil wars, the Emperor Augustus. This is related in the commentaries of Vitellius.

(8) Nor were dreams of this kind restricted to prophecies of supreme power; they also foretold dangers and catastrophes. It was through illness that Caesar missed the Battle of Philippi and, hence, destruction at the hands of Brutus and Cassius; though he expected to undergo greater dangers from the enemy, he escaped, being warned by a vision of Artorius. Also, the daughter of Polycrates of Samos foresaw his crucifixion from the anointing of the sun and the bath of Jupiter.

(9) Future honors and talents have also been foretold in sleep, remedies discovered, thefts revealed, and treasures indicated. Thus, Cicero's nurse foresaw his greatness when he was still a child. The swan that was supposed to come from the breast of Socrates for the comfort of mankind is clearly his pupil, Plato. Leonymus, the boxer, was cured by Achilles in his dreams and the tragedian, Sophocles, rediscovered the golden crown which had been lost from the citadel of Athens. Then there was the tragic actor, Neoptolemus, who through

intimations received in sleep saved from ruin the tomb of Ajax on the shores of Troy; when he removed the ancient stones he found a treasure of gold.

(10) The whole of world literature testifies to the truth of dreams, as for instance, Artemon, Antiphon, Strato, Philochorus, Epicharmus, Serapion, Cratippus, Dionysius of Rhodes, and Hermippus. I can't help laughing at the man who thought to persuade us that Saturn was the first one ever to dream, as if Saturn had lived before everybody else. You will pardon me for laughing, Aristotle!

(11) Among all the means of foretelling the future, dreams are awarded the first place by Epicharmus and by Philochorus the Athenian. You'll find oracles of this kind all over the world: there are the oracles of Amphiaraus at Oropus, of Amphilochus at Mallus, of Sarpedon in Troy, Trophonius in Boeotia, Mopus in Cilicia, Hermione in Macedonia, Pasiphae in Laconia, and many others with their rites, histories, and chroniclers. In fact, there is a whole literature of dreams of which you will find more than enough in the five volumes of Hermippus of Berytus. It is a favorite doctrine of the Stoics that God in His providence over human affairs gave us dreams; among the many other helps to the preservation of the arts and techniques of divination, He especially intended dreams to be of particular assistance to natural foresight.

(12) This will be sufficient for those dreams which we must believe, even though we have a different interpretation of their nature. As for other oracles, where no dreams are involved, they must be the results of diabolical possession of the person in question, or else they try to fool us by using the tombs of the dead to perfect the deceit staged by their malignity, even counterfeiting some divine power in the form of a man. And through their deceitful endeavors they grant us the favors of cures, warnings and prophecies. Thus

they hope to harm us when seeming to help us, and by their good deeds to distract us from the investigation of the true God by suggesting a false one to our minds.

(13) This vicious power is not restricted to the precincts of their shrines, but it roams all over with complete freedom. There is no doubt that the doors of our homes are open to such spirits and they impose on us in our bedrooms as well as in their own temples.

Chapter 47

(1) The first type of dreams we have declared to emanate from the Devil, even though they are sometimes true and favorable to us. But, when they deliberately set out to delude us with favors, as mentioned above, they betray themselves as vain, deceitful, vague, licentious, and impure. This is not surprising, since images generally resemble the realities they reflect.

(2) The second class of dreams must be considered to come from God, since He has promised to pour out the grace of the Holy Spirit upon all flesh and has ordained that His sons and handmaidens shall utter prophecies and dream dreams.[1] Such dreams may be compared to the grace of God as being honest, holy, prophetic, inspired, edifying, and inducing to virtue. Their bountiful nature causes them to overflow even to the infidels since God with divine impartiality causes the rain to fall and the sun to shine upon just and unjust alike.[2] Surely, it was under the inspiration of God that Nabuchodonosor[3] had his famous dream, and the majority of mankind get their knowledge of God from dreams.[4] There-

---

1 Joel. 2.28-29.
2 Matt. 5.45.
3 Dan. 2.1.
4 Placing so great an importance on special revelations, in this case, while asleep, is another hint of Tertullian's Montanist tendencies.

fore, just as the mercy of God abounds for the pagans, so the temptations of the Devil attack the saints; he never relaxes his vigor, trying to trap them while they are asleep, if he is unsuccessful while they are awake.

(3) The third kind of dreams are those which the soul somehow seems to induce of itself by the attentive contemplation of the things surrounding it. Yet, since the soul is not capable of dreaming when it wants to (even Epicharmus agrees with this), how can it be itself the cause of any vision? Is it not the best solution to refer this class to the natural form of dreams, allowing the soul to endure even in ecstasy whatever happens to it?

(4) Finally, those dreams which cannot be attributed to God, or the Devil, or the soul itself, since they are beyond expectation, or any ordinary explanation, or even of being intelligibly related, will have to be placed in a special category as arising from ecstasy and its attendant circumstances.

Chapter 48

(1) It is generally believed that the clearest and purest dreams occur toward morning, when the soul is restored by rest and sleep is light. Dreams are generally calmer in the springtime, since spring relaxes and winter hardens the soul. Autumn is generally hard on health, particularly because of the heady juice of its fruits which enervate the soul.

(2) We are told that we should not lie flat on our back while sleeping, nor on the right side, nor twisted so as to wrench the cavities of the intestines; a tremor of the heart then ensues and the pressure on the liver may effect the mind. I believe these to be more ingenious conjectures than demonstrable facts; even though Plato is their source,[1] they may all

---

1 *Timaeus* 70D-72D.

result from chance. Otherwise, dreams would have to be under control of man if they can in any way be directed.

(3) The next point to be examined is what superstition and prejudice have dictated in the matter of selecting and restricting foods for the control of dreams. Thus, superstition demands that a fast be imposed on those consulting an incubation-oracle, so as to achieve the proper degree of ritual purity. On the other hand, the Pythagoreans for the same end proscribe beans as tending to heaviness and flatulence. But Daniel and his three companions ate only vegetables, lest they be contaminated by the royal food, and as a reward received from God not only the gift of wisdom but a special power of experiencing dreams and of explaining their meaning.

(4) In my own experience, I can but say that fasting made me dream so profoundly that I could not remember whether or not I dreamed. But, you may ask: 'Hasn't sobriety got anything to do with dreams?' Certainly, and as much to do with dreams as with our whole subject; and, if it is any help to superstition, it is more to religion. Even the demons require their dreaming subjects to fast in order to give themselves the [deceptive] appearance of true divinity. For they know its power of making man a friend of God. Daniel ate dry food for a period of three weeks, but he did this in order to win God's favor by acts of humiliation and not that he might augment the perception and mental vision of his soul as a preparation for a dream, as though the soul were meant to act without being in the state of ecstasy. Sobriety, then, will have no effect of neutralizing the ecstasy, but of recommending the ecstasy to God so that it might take place in Him.

Chapter 49

(1) Those who believe that infants do not dream, on the basis that all functions of the soul are accomplished according to age, ought to observe how they toss in their sleep, wag their heads, and sometimes smile. From such facts they will understand that these are the emotions of their souls, generated by dreams breaking through the barrier of their tender flesh.

(2) Then there is the story of the African tribe, the Atlantes, who are reputed to pass the whole night in dreamless sleep, the implication being that they are mentally defective. Now, either Herodotus was taken in by a rumor which was unfavorable to these barbarians, or else a large band of devils is in control of that region. Aristotle tells us that there was a demigod in Sardinia who had the power of inhibiting dreams for those who slept at his shrine; from this we may infer that it lies within the discretion of the demons to take away as well as give the power to dream. This also may be the explanation of the cases of Nero and Thrasymedes, who only dreamed late in life.

(3) But, we believe dreams come from God. Why couldn't God make the Atlanteans dream? There is now no race of men completely ignorant of Him, since the light of the Gospel now gleams in every land and to all the ends of the earth. Perhaps Aristotle was deceived by a rumor; it may be that this is the practice of the devils; in any case, no soul is naturally free of all dreams.

Chapter 50

(1) Let that much suffice for sleep, which is only the mirror of death, and for dreams, the business of sleep. We

will now discuss the cause of our departure, in all its aspects; it presents a number of questions, although it is itself the end of all questioning.

(2) It is the acknowledged opinion of the whole human race that death is 'the debt we owe to nature.' This has been established by the voice of God, and everything that is born must sign this contract. This should be enough to refute the foolish opinion of Epicurus, who refused to acknowledge such a debt. It demolishes the mad doctrine of Menander, the Samaritan heretic, who thinks not only that death is no concern of his disciples but that it will never touch them. He pretends to have received from the Supreme Power on high the privilege that all whom he baptizes become immortal, incorruptible, and immediately ready for the resurrection.

(3) The remarkable properties of certain waters are well known. Thus, the water of the Lyncestris River tasted like wine and men became intoxicated from drinking it; at Colophon the waters of a fountain, through diabolical influence, make men mad; and it is known that Alexander was poisoned by the water from Mt. Nonacris in Arcadia. Even before the time of Christ there was a medicinal pool in Judea, and the poet claims that the marshy Styx made men immune to death, although Thetis still wept for the loss of her son. As a matter of fact, even if Menander washed in the Styx, he would die; you have to be dead to get there, since it flows through the lower regions.

(4) But, what is this marvelous virtue of water and where can it be found if even John the Baptist could not use it, and Christ himself never mentioned it to His disciples? What is this wonderful bath of Menander? Why, *he* seems to be a comedian, too. How does it happen that so few people know about it or use it? This leads me to suspect the existence of this sacrament which has the power of making us so wonder-

fully secure and immune from death. Why, this would even dispense us from the law of dying for God, when, on the contrary, all nations have 'to ascend the mount of the Lord and to the house of the God of Jacob,'[1] who demands death by martyrdom from His own and exacted it even from Christ. No one will attribute such power to magic that it could free man from death or so renew the vine that it enjoys a renewal of life. Not even Medea had this power over man, although she could do it to a silly sheep.

(5) Enoch and Elias were transported hence without suffering death, which was only postponed.[2] The day will come when they will actually die that they may extinguish Anti-Christ with their blood. There was a legend that St. John the Evangelist was to live till the Second Coming, but he died.[3] Heresies generally crop up out of statements made by ourselves and they borrow their armor from the doctrines they attack. The whole case comes down to this question: Where are these men Menander has baptized and plunged into his Styx? Let me see some of these immortal apostles. If this doubting Thomas can see them, hear them, and touch them, then he will believe.[4]

Chapter 51

(1) The function of death is obvious to all—the separation of body and soul. There are some people, however, who do not hold very firmly to the immortality of the soul, since they have learned it not from God, but only from very feeble arguments, and they think that souls sometimes remain united to bodies after death.

---
1 Gen. 28.12.
2 Gen. 5.24; Heb. 11.5; 4 Kings 2.11.
3 John 21.23.
4 Cf. John 20.24-29.

(2) Now, although Plato generally holds that souls go to heaven immediately after death, he tells us in the *Republic*[1] of an unburied corpse which lasted a long time without corruption because of the inseparability of body and soul. Democritus mentions the growth of the hair and nails for some time after burial. Now, it is possible that the nature of the atmosphere prevented the body of Er from decaying.

(3) This could happen if the air were very dry and the earth saline, or if the body itself were unusually dry. It is possible that the manner of death had already caused the elimination of all corruptive matter. Since the nails are the ends of the nerves, they may appear to be lengthened and to project further than usual, because of the decay of the flesh which would cause it to contract. The hair draws its nourishment from the brain, which would cause it to last longer as a kind of protection. In fact, physicians will tell you there is a relation in living people between the amount of hair and the size of the brain.

(4) But, not a particle of the soul can remain after death in the body, which itself is destined for destruction when time has finally dismantled the stage on which the body has played its part. Still, this idea of a partial survival makes an impression on some men; therefore, out of pity for this small part, they will not allow bodies to be cremated. There is, however, still another explanation of this kindliness, not so much out of respect for the soul but in order to spare the body this cruel treatment, since the body is human and does not deserve a murderer's end.

(5) The soul, being immortal, is necessarily indivisible; therefore, we must believe death to be an indivisible process which happens to the soul not because *that* is immortal but because death comes, as one act, to an indivisible soul.

---

[1] *Republic* 614B-621D.

Death also would have to be divided into stages if the soul could be divided into parts, with a part of the soul dying later; thus, a portion of death would have to wait behind for the part of the soul that remained.

(6) My own experience has shown me that some vestiges of this opinion still remain. There was a woman born of Christian parents who died in her maturity and beauty after a brief but happy marriage. Before the burial the priest came to pray over her, and, as soon as he uttered the first word of the prayer, she lifted her hands and joined them together in a suppliant attitude; at the end, she put her hands back at her sides.

(7) There is another story current among our own people of the body that moved over in the grave to make room for another. If you hear any stories like these among the heathen, you can conclude that God everywhere manifests His power for the consolation of His own and in testimony of His might to the heathen. I should much rather believe that such things happen by divine intervention than because of any particles of the soul; if any such were left in the body, they ought to move the other limbs as well, and, if only the hands, not for the sake of prayer. And that body not only made room for its new neighbor by moving, but it also made itself more comfortable as a result.

(8) But, whatever cause you assign to these events, you cannot say they are the normal practices of nature, but they must be put down as signs and portents. If death is not complete, it is not death; if any of the soul is still there, there you have life. Death will no more unite with life than night with day.

Chapter 52

(1) This, then, is the function of death—the complete separation of body and soul. Apart from the consideration of fate and fortuitous circumstances, men have distinguished two forms of death—the ordinary and the extraordinary. An ordinary death is a calm and peaceful end and it is ascribed to nature; any violent death is considered extraordinary and contrary to nature.

(2) Well acquainted as we are with man's origin, we know that death results from sin, and that neither death nor sin is a natural result of man's nature. It is true that things which are attached to man from birth easily appear to flow from his nature. And, likewise, had man been created with death as his destiny, then death would be imputed to his human nature. Now, that death was not appointed for him by nature is made clear by the law which made his fate dependent on God's warning and death itself the result of man's voluntary choice. Had he not sinned, he would not have died. Therefore, that cannot be the result of nature which depends on the free choice of an alternative and is not at all imposed by absolute necessity.

(3) Hence, though death may come in various ways (and there are many), no death is so easy as not to be in some sense violent. The very law which produces death, though simple in itself, is still violent. How can it be otherwise, when it causes the rupture and division of two substances which have been as closely united from birth as have the soul and body? Although a man may expire with joy as did Chilon while embracing his son after an Olympic victory; or from

glory, as did the Athenian Clidemus while receiving the golden crown for the excellence of his historical writings; or in a dream, like Plato, or in a burst of laughter like P. Crassus—yet death is always much too violent, coming as it does by means alien to man's nature, in its own time, and snatching man from life just when he could pass his days in joy, happiness, honor, peace, and pleasure.

(4) It is still a violent end for a ship when, owing to some internal shock, it founders far from the Caphaerean rocks, wracked by no storms, buffeted by no waves, lulled by a calm breeze, gliding on its course with a cheerful crew. The coming of a peaceful death is no less a shipwreck than this. It makes no difference if the ship of life goes to the bottom with its timbers intact or shattered by a gale, so long as its power of navigation is destroyed.

Chapter 53

(1) But, where is the soul going to find lodging when it is expelled naked from the body? There must we follow it in our discussion. First, however, we must state what is germane to the topic before us, lest people should expect from us a description of each of the types of death we mention—these are really the business of the physicians, who are competent to judge the incidents which cause death and of the various states of the human body.

(2) In order to safeguard the immortality of the soul, I shall have to insert some remarks about the passing of the soul, when talking of death, according to which it might seem that the soul leaves the body bit by bit and gradually. Its departure looks like a decline, and it seems to suffer dissolution, and it gives the impression of being annihilated by the slow process of its departure. But, this is all explained by

the nature of the body. For, whatever be the cause of death, it produces destruction of either the vital matter or the organs or the passages of the body—matter, such as gall and blood; organs, like the heart and the liver; or passages, such as the veins and arteries.

(3) Now, as each one of these parts of the body is destroyed by the proper agent until there is a complete disintegration and collapse of the vital powers, that is, of the natural parts and functions of the body, it necessarily happens that the soul, because of the gradual decay of its instruments, spaces, and situations, is gradually forced to abandon various parts and seems to fade away to nothing. Thus, the charioteer is considered to have weakened when his horses, worn out by fatigue, can no longer run. This is no actual failure of the wearied man, but of the circumstances in which he finds himself. Likewise, the charioteer of the body—the vital spirit of man—fails because of the collapse of the vehicle, not through its own weakness. It gives up its task, but not its inherent strength; its action is impeded, but its state is not changed; with no alteration of its substance, it no longer appears as strong as it was.

(4) When death comes suddenly, as from decapitation, it opens at once a large outlet for the soul; when it comes from some sudden ruin, like that internal disintegration, apoplexy, which crushes every vital function, the departure of the soul is not delayed nor is death a long-drawn-out process. But, in a lingering death, the soul withdraws in much the same way as it is being deserted. In this process, however, it is not broken off piecemeal, but is it drawn from the body, and, while being gradually drawn off, the last portion appears to be an isolated part. Yet, no portion can be considered to be actually detached because it is the last, nor, because it is small, is it destined for immediate destruction. The last sec-

tion to leave is in accord with the process whereby the middle portion is drawn by the extremes; the remnants are attached to the whole and are awaited but never abandoned. I should go so far as to say that the last part of the whole is the whole, for, although it is smaller and the last, it still belongs to the whole.

(5) Thus, it sometimes happens that the soul in the moment of its departure will be more violently stirred, will show a piercing gaze, and talk a great deal. Because of its loftier and freer position, it enunciates, by means of its last remnant clinging to the flesh, the things which it sees and hears and is now beginning to know. In the Platonic view, the body is a prison; in that of St. Paul, it is the temple of God because it is in Christ.[1] But it is a fact that the body by enclosing the soul obstructs, obscures, and sullies it by the union with the flesh, and its vision is obscured as if it were looking through a window of horn.

(6) Without a doubt, the soul is purified when by the power of death it is released from the bondage to the flesh; it is further certain that is escapes from the veil of the flesh into its own pure and clear light; then it finds itself enjoying its liberation from matter, and in this new-found liberty it regains its divinity as a man awaking from sleep and passing from shadows to realities. Then does it speak out what it sees; then it rejoices or trembles according to which lodging it sees in store for it, as soon as it sees the face of the angel, the one who issues the final call to souls, the Mercury of the poets.

Chapter 54

(1) We must now give an answer to the question of where the soul goes after death. Practically all the philosophers

---
[1] 1 Cor. 6.19.

who believe in the immortality of the soul, however much they differ in their understanding of it, still claim the soul has some abode after death. This Pythagoras, Empedocles, and Plato will admit, even though they envisage some temorary abode between death and the end of the world. The Stoics make this reservation, that only the souls of the Wise Men, that is, Stoics, find a place in the heavenly mansions.

(2) To be sure, Plato does not destine the souls of all philosophers for heaven indiscriminately,[1] but only of those who have enhanced the philosophic life by the love of boys. Such, indeed, is the great privilege accorded to impurity among the philosophers. According to his system, then, the souls of the wise are raised into the ether; according to Arius, into the air; and in the teaching of the Stoics, to the moon.

(3) (I find it surprising that they restrict the souls of the unwise to the earth, especially since they declare that they are to be instructed by the wise who are thus so far above them. Where can they find a school in which this may be done, with so much distance between their habitations? How can teachers and pupils get together when they are so far apart? Finally, what good will they get out of their posthumous education, since they are all destined soon for the eternal fire?)

(4) All other souls they thrust down into Hades, which Plato in the *Phaedo*[2] places in the bosom of the earth, to which all the filth of the world settles and accumulates and evaporates. There, every particular draught of air only serves to render more noxious the impurities of the seething mass.

---

[1] *Symposium* 203; *Phaedrus* 248.
[2] *Phaedo* 112.

Chapter 55

(1) We Christians do not consider Hell to be an empty cavern or some subterranean sewer of the world, but a profound and vast space hidden away in the deepest interior of the world. For, we read that Christ spent three days in the heart of the earth,[1] that is, in the hidden recess in the inner part of the earth, totally enclosed by the earth and built over the abyss which lies still lower down.[2]

(2) Now, Christ, being God and man, according to the Scriptures, died and was buried. Thus, He chose to submit to the law of death which belongs to human nature, going down to Hell in the form of a dead man; nor did He ascend[3] to the heights of heaven before He descended into the lower regions of the earth, that there He might acquaint the Patriarchs and Prophets with His [redeeming] mission.[4] There you have proof that Hell is a subterranean region, with which to confute those who, in their pride, think that the souls of the just are too good for Hell. Such people would place the servants above their Lord, disciples above their Master,[5] and, if offered the privilege, would no doubt loftily disdain the solace of awaiting the resurrection in the bosom of Abraham.[6]

(3) 'But,' they will tell us, 'that is just the reason why Christ went down into Hell—so that we should not have to go. Besides, what difference is there between pagan and Christian, if the same prison is open for both after death?' But, how can a soul rise up to Heaven, where Christ is

---

1 Matt. 12.40.
2 Ps. 85.13.
3 Eph. 4.9; John 3.13.
4 1 Pet. 3.19.
5 Matt. 10.24.
6 Luke 16.22.

sitting at the right hand of the Father, when the command of God has not been promulgated by the trumpet of the Archangel? How, indeed, when those whom the Lord at His Coming is to find on the earth have not been caught up into the air to meet Him, in company with the dead in Christ who will be the first to rise?[7] As long as the earth remains, Heaven is not open; in fact, the gates are barred. When the world shall have passed away, the portals of Paradise will be opened.

(4) In the meantime, then, will our resting place be in the ether with those lovers of boys of Plato, or in the air with Arius, or around the moon with the Endymions of the Stoics? 'Oh, no,' you say, 'but in Paradise whither the Patriarchs and the Prophets have traveled as a result of the Lord's Resurrection.' If that is so, how is it that the region of Paradise which was revealed in the spirit of St. John as being 'under the altar'[8] contains no other souls but those of the martyrs? How is it that St. Perpetua, that bravest martyr of Christ, on the day of her death saw only the souls of the martyrs in Paradise, unless it be that the sword which guarded the entrance allowed none to pass save those that had died in Christ and not in Adam?[9]

(5) Those who die this new death for God, and violently as Christ did, are welcomed into a special abode. Here, then, is the difference between pagan and Christian in death: If you lay down your life for God as the Paraclete recommends,[10] then it will not be of some gentle fever in a soft bed, but in the torture of martyrdom. You must take up your cross and

---

7 1 Thess. 4.15-16.
8 Apoc. 6.9.
9 The privileged position here accorded to martyrs was common in early Christian literature, but, in Tertullian, it is perhaps enhanced by the Montanist predilection for martyrdom.
10 Cf. Introduction, p. 171, and d'Alès *op. cit.* 448-454.

follow Him, according to the precept of Christ. The only key that unlocks the gates of Paradise is your own blood. Look at my treatise on Paradise where I showed that all [other] souls are kept in Hell until the Second Coming of the Lord.

Chapter 56

(1) Here, there arise several questions which must be answered. Are souls assigned to the temporary abode immediately after death? Are some souls detained for a time here on earth? And, finally, is it possible for them to leave their place either of their own free will or at the bidding of authority?

(2) Cogent reasons are advanced for these opinions. It has been widely believed that souls could not go to Hades until their bodies had been properly buried. Homer relates how Patroclus asks in a dream for burial by Achilles because otherwise his soul could not enter Hades, being thrust away by the souls of those whose bodies had been buried. Now, we know that Homer is here espousing the rights of the dead and not merely indulging in poetic fancy. His desire that the dead receive the due honors of burial is proportional to the harm the soul suffers because of the delay in burial. He was also influenced by the fact that by keeping the body too long at home, he may expose both the survivors and the deceased to increased trouble by excessively prolonging the period of mourning. Therefore, his portrayal of the complaint of the unburied soul has two purposes: that honor be paid to the dead by a prompt funeral and that the grief of the bereaved be curtailed.

(3) But, isn't it a foolish idea to suppose that the soul awaits the burial rites, as if it could carry some of them off

to Hades? It is much more ridiculous to imagine that the soul would consider the lack of burial as an injury, when really it is in the nature of a favor. Surely, the soul that didn't want to die would be pleased at anything that would postpone its entry into Hades. The careless heir will be beloved through whose neglect the soul still enjoys the light. But, if some harm is really done to the soul by the neglect of burial (and it is the *delay* that is alleged to be bad), how unfair it is to blame this on the soul of the dead man, when any fault should really be imputed to his relatives!

(4) A second idea that has been handed down is that those who die prematurely roam about the earth until the completion of the time they would have lived had they not been cut off before their time. To that I reply: Either the number of a man's days are determined beforehand, and then I do not believe they can be shortened; or else, having been determined, they can be changed by the will of God or by some other power. Then, I say, this change is useless, since in any case they have to await their completion; or they are not predetermined at all, and then there is no period that has to be filled out.

(5) And, further, let us suppose the case of an infant who dies while still being nursed at his mother's breast, or of an immature boy, or a youth, all of whom were supposed to live to be eighty years old. How will it be possible for them to pass those years after death on earth without a body? They can't grow older without a body because the body is the thing that ages.[1] Here let me remind our people that we will at the Resurrection be restored to the bodies in which we died.

(6) Therefore, we must expect our bodies to return under

---

1 In Chap. 38, Tertullian implied that the soul underwent a process of development, in that it reached an age of 'puberty of the soul.'

the same conditions and in the same state as when we died, for such particulars make the body to be a certain age. How then can the soul of an infant a month old spend all those years here after death, so as to be able to be an octogenarian at the Resurrection? Or, if the soul has to fill out the appointed years here on earth, will it have to pass through all the trials and experiences it would have had had it lived? Will a certain period be assigned to childhood and its years at school? Will it then pass on to the excitement of a young man in the army? Between youth and old age will he have to apply himself to serious responsibilities? Must he work at business, plough as a farmer, go to sea, engage in lawsuits, get married, struggle, suffer illness and, in a word, undergo all the experiences of joy and sadness of the destined length of years?

(7) But, how is he going to do all this without a body? Will he live without being alive? 'But,' you say, 'the time is merely to pass without incident.' What is to prevent his fulfilling all these things in Hades, where there is no use for any one of them? Therefore, it is my opinion that any soul, no matter what its age at death, stays at that age until the time arrives when the promised perfect age will be realized in accordance with the measure of angelic fullness.

(8) The third class, those who die by violence, are also believed to be kept from Hades, especially those who die by cruel tortures, the cross, the axe, the sword, and wild beasts. But, death that comes from the hands of justice, the avenger of violence, should not be accounted as violent. 'But,' you will say, 'only the souls of the wicked are excluded from Hades.' You must make clear which of the two regions of Hades you mean: that of the good or that of the bad. If you mean the bad, then that is where evil souls are consigned; if the good, why do you hold the souls of infants and virgins

and those who by their age were necessarily pure and innocent to be unworthy of such a resting place?²

Chapter 57

(1) So, either it is a good thing to be detained here on earth with the *Aoroi* or an evil thing with the *Biaiothanatoi*, if I may now at last be permitted to use the terminology with which the magic arts resound, the words of their inventors, Ostanes, Typhon, Dardanus, Damigeron, Nectabis, and Berenice.

(2) There is a great deal of literature which attempts to call back from Hades the souls of those who are sleeping out their destined time, those who died through violence and those deprived of burial. What are we to say, then, of these pretensions of magic, except what everyone says—that it is a fraud. Christians are the only ones to see through this fraud, since we have come to know the evil spirits, not, of course, by consorting with them, but by the knowledge that unmasks them; not by trying to solicit their assistance, but by a power which subjugates them. Thus do we deal with that universal pollution of the human mind, the inventor of all falsehood, that plunderer of the soul's salvation. By magic, a second form of idolatry, the demons pretend to be dead men [come to life], just as in ordinary idolatry they pass themselves off as gods. And that is reasonable, since the gods are dead.

(3) Hence, the *Aoroi* and the *Biaiothanatoi* are actually

---

2 Although Tertullian has here mingled some Montanist ideas of a millenium to be passed by all but the souls of martyrs before their resurrection, he is definite as to the fact that the just will spend a period of purification before they are eligible for Paradise. Even though they will have to wait during what remains of the millenium for their final glory, the period of purification is substantially the doctrine of Purgatory. Cf. d'Alès, *op. cit.* 133-134 n.

invoked in prayer on the supposition that they should be most capable of committing harm [to enemies] who themselves were by unjust violence snatched away to a premature death, as if in revenge for their own fate.

(4) The demons inhabit those souls especially in whom they used to dwell when they were alive and whom they drove to this kind of untimely end. We have already suggested that every man is attended by a demon and many are aware that sudden and horrible deaths, which usually pass for accidents, are really work of demons.

(5) And, I think we can prove that the evil spirit tries to deceive us by hiding in the persons of dead men, from the facts that come to light in exorcisms. We know that the demon tries to pose as a relative of the person possessed, or sometimes as a gladiator or as a fighter of the beasts, or even as a god. And, in this, his object is always to disprove what we are here affirming, namely, that all souls go down to Hell at their death, and to weaken our faith in the Judgment and Resurrection. Yet, the Devil, after trying to deceive the bystanders, is overcome by the power of Divine Grace, and at last, much against his will, admits that he is an evil spirit.

(6) Then there is another form of magic in which this same trickery is attempted, where the Devil brings back the souls of the dead and exhibits them to view. This is clearly more effective, since it provides a visual image—the body of which the Devil has taken possession. And, of course, it is easy to deceive the eyes of a man whose mind is so easily taken in.

(7) The serpents which emerged from the magician's rods certainly were seen as material substances by Pharaoh and the Egyptians, and only Moses with the truth could prove them false.[1] Simon Magus and Elymas made many

---
1 Exod. 7.12.

attempts against the Apostles, but the blindness that afflicted them was no magician's trick.² What is new about a devil trying to counterfeit the truth? Why, even now the followers of Simon are so confident of their art that they undertake to bring back the souls of the Prophets from Hell.

(8) And this, I believe, because their power lies in their ability to deceive. This power was actually granted to the witch of Endor, who brought back the soul of Samuel after Saul had consulted God in vain.³ Apart from that case, God forbid we should believe that any soul, much less a Prophet, could be called forth by a demon. We are told that 'Satan himself is transformed into an angel of light,'⁴—and more easily into a man of light—and that at the end he will work marvelous signs and show himself as God, so much so that, 'if possible, he will deceive even the elect.'⁵ He hardly hesitated to declare to Saul that he was the Prophet [Samuel] in whom the Devil was then dwelling.

(9) So, you must not think that the spirit which created the apparition was different from the one who made Saul believe in it; but, the same spirit was in the witch of Endor and in the Apostate [Saul], and so it was easy for him to suggest the lie that he had already made Saul believe. Saul's treasure, indeed, was then where his heart was,⁶ where God most certainly was not. Thus, he saw only the Devil, through whom he believed he would see Samuel, for he believed in the spirit who showed him the apparition.

(10) The objection is offered that visions of the dead seen in dreams must be real. For instance, the Nasamones con-

---

2 Acts. 8.9; 13.8.
3 1 Kings 28.6.
4 2 Thess. 11.14.
5 Matt. 24.24.
6 Matt. 6.21.

sult their own oracles by lengthy visits to the tombs of their ancestors, as we are told in Heraclides, Nymphodorus, and Herodotus. Nicander also reports that the Celts keep watch all night at the tombs of their heroes for the same purpose. But, I will not admit that the apparitions of dead persons (any more than those of living persons) seen in dreams are real, but the same explanation holds for all, living, dead, or anything else that is seen. These things are not real because they are seen, but because they are fulfilled. A dream is true because it works out, and not because a vision is seen.

(11) Now, the fact that the gates of Hell are not opened for any soul is sufficiently proven by the Lord in His story of Abraham, about the poor man at peace and the rich man in torment. It is not possible that any messenger be sent to this world to tell us about Hell, which would have been allowed then, if ever, for the purpose of making men believe in Moses and the Prophets.[7]

(12) Although God has on occasion called back the souls of men to their bodies as proof of His power, there is no reason to believe that He gives this power to the credulous magicians with their fallacious dreams and poetic fancies. In all cases of true resurrection, whether done by the power of God, the Prophets, Christ Himself or the Apostles, we have certain truth in the solidity, mass, and reality of the revived body, so that we can be sure that any incorporeal apparitions of the dead are due to the trickery of magicians.

---

[7] Luke 16.30f. Tertullian is apparently quoting from memory, as he implies that the rich man asked Abraham to send a messenger to his brethren so that *then* they would believe in Moses and the Prophets. Actually, Abraham says: 'If they hear not Moses and the Prophets, neither will they believe, if one rise again from the dead.'

Chapter 58

(1) All souls, therefore, are consigned to Hell. Whether you believe it or not, there they suffer either punishment or reward, according to the story of Lazarus and Dives. Now, since I have delayed the treatment of some questions which pertain to this matter, I can now treat of them in concluding my remarks.

(2) Why don't you want to believe that souls are punished or rewarded in the meantime while awaiting the judgment to glory or damnation? There they remain in hopeful confidence while anticipating their fate. You feel that God's judgment ought to be definitive, and that no inkling of His sentence should be betrayed beforehand, and that punishment or reward must await the restoration of the flesh which should share the retribution of the deeds performed when they were together.

(3) How do they spend that time? Asleep? But, souls never sleep even in living men and sleep is a property of bodies, along with its image, death, Would you hold that nothing at all happens there whither all humanity yearns and the hopes of all mankind are centered? Is it a foretaste of the fate to come or its actual beginning? Is it a complete condemnation or only a sample of what is to come? But, wouldn't it be the rankest injustice if the wicked were at peace and the good still held in suspense? Would you add this further torture to death, that afterwards we should not know what was going to happen to us or that we should be trembling before the possibility of an accounting of our life and a subsequent decree of condemnation?

(4) Does the soul always have to await the body that it may feel sorrow or joy? Can't the soul of itself experience these emotions? Often, in fact, with no pain of body the soul

alone is tortured by indignation, anger, or boredom, sometimes without being conscious of it. And again, when the body ails, the soul seeks out some haven of joy all its own and scorns the irritating company of the body.

(5) If I mistake not, the soul even rejoices and glories in the sufferings of the body. Take the case of Mucius Scaevola, when the fire was melting his right hand, or of Zeno when the torments of Dionysius passed over him. The bites of wild animals are the pride of youth, as Cyrus who gloried in the scars left by the bear. So the soul can easily manage to rejoice or be sad without the body in Hell; during life it can weep when it pleases, though the body is unhurt, and likewise it can rejoice even in the midst of bodily suffering. Now, if it can do this by its own power in life, much more so after death can it by divine decree.

(6) But, during life, the soul does not share all its operations with the flesh, for in God's judgment even secret thoughts and unfulfilled volitions can be accounted sinful. 'Whosoever shall look on a woman to lust after her, hath already committed adultery with her in his heart.'[1] For this reason it is most fitting that the soul, without waiting for the restoration of the flesh, should be punished for the sins it committed without help from the body. Likewise, it will be rewarded before the flesh is restored for the pious and kindly thought elicited independently of the body.

(7) Besides, even in actions which need the assistance of the body, it is the soul which first conceives, plans, orders, and carries out the acts in question. And, although sometimes it is unwilling to act, the soul always deals first with the matter which the body is going to accomplish and it never happens that an act is performed without previous consciousness. So, on this basis it is fitting that that part of man

---

[1] Matt. 5.28.

should have its reward which has the prior right to its enjoyment.

(8) In conclusion, if we understand the 'prison,' of which the Gospel speaks, as Hell, and 'the last farthing'[2] as the smallest defect that has to be atoned for there before the resurrection, there will be no doubt that the soul suffers in Hell some retributory penalty, without denying the complete resurrection, when the body also will pay or be paid in full. This fact has often been stressed by the Paraclete, if one is willing to admit His words on the basis of His promised spiritual disclosures.

(9) Now, at last, I believe I have dealt satisfactorily with all the human views as to the soul which arise from the teaching of our faith and from any normal curiosity. As for foolish and idle speculations—there will always be more of those than a wise man could ever answer.

---

2 Matt. 5.25-26.

MINUCIUS FELIX
OCTAVIUS

Translated

by

RUDOLPH ARBESMANN, O.S.A., Ph.D.

Fordham University

INTRODUCTION

THE OCTAVIUS of Marcus[1] Minucius Felix is called after the Christian interlocutor in the first Christian dialogue in Latin. We know very little about the life of its author, but we are able to draw a general picture by linking up the few facts which he himself mentions in his work.[2] According to these statements, he probably came from North Africa and was a pagan by birth. In his youth, he had received an excellent education, especially in rhetoric, and had accumulated a vast store of knowledge through extensive readings in literature, particularly Latin. During his years of study, he had formed a lasting friendship with Octavius Januarius,[3] who, like himself, was a lawyer. Their profession had given them ample opportunity to take part in trials against Christians. During these trials, they saw the absurdity of the accusations, the lack of evidence offered to prove the guilt of the defendants, the complete dishonesty of court procedure, and, above all, the heroic behavior of so many Christians more enduring in suffering and death than were their enemies in torturing and killing. All this made a deep impression on the two friends and set them thinking. As a result, after mature consideration, Octavius embraced the new faith and Minucius followed his example.

While Octavius had remained in his native country and,

---

1 This is the name under which Minucius Felix appears in the dialogue.
2 The information about the author, furnished by Lactantius (*Divinae Institutiones* 1.11.55; 5.1.21f.) and St. Jerome (*De viris illustribus* 58; *Ep.* 70.5) are drawn from the *Octavius*, and do not add anything new to the meagre indications in the dialogue itself.
3 This is the surname given to Octavius in the dialogue.

at the same time the dialogue took place, was in Rome only on a visit, Minucius had established himself as a lawyer in the capital of the Empire. Apparently, however, he held no public office at that time, since such a position might have compelled him to take part in trials against his co-religionists. The dialogue acquaints us with a friend of both men, Caecilius Natalis, the pagan interlocutor in the dialogue, also a North African, and perhaps from the city of Cirta (modern Constantine). He also had taken up his residence in Rome, for, in the dialogue, he is said to associate freely with Minucius. At the time the dialogue was written, Octavius, and probably Caecilius as well, were no longer alive. Thus, the dialogue also represents a touching and lasting memorial of his two friends. The treatise *On Fate*, promised in Chapter 36.2, if it was written at all, has not come down to us.

The *Octavius* is written in the literary form of a dialogue, which is, however, *sui generis*. The usual form of literary dialogue, especially as practiced and brought to perfection by Plato, and imitated by Cicero in his *De natura deorum*, presents several interlocutors who carry on a dialogue in the form of a conversation, enlivened by questions and answers, difficulties raised and solutions given, in the manner of a serious conversation. The *Octavius* begins in the manner of a Platonic dialogue, with the introductory narrative of the one who is recounting the whole. The loss of Octavius, the intimate friend of his youth, brings back to Minucius' mind the vivid discussion Octavius and a pagan friend, Caecilius, had concerning the truth of the Christian religion. The discussion took place during a pleasure trip the three friends made from Rome to Ostia to enjoy the invigorating sea breezes and salt baths.

The author gives a beautiful description of nature, in some instances reminiscent of Theocritean naturalism: the mild

autumn weather, the gentle breeze blowing from the sea, the
beach where the sand yields to the footsteps, the play of the
waves, the boats drawn up on their baulks, the breakwater
of piled rocks running out into the sea, the merry scene of
boys eagerly engaged in the sport of throwing flat stones and
making them skim over the water. The setting possesses such
a graceful charm that it can hardly be surpassed by any other
piece of its kind in Latin literature.

Yet, while the setting follows the Platonic, or Ciceronian,
pattern, the main body of the work, the dialogue itself,
touched off by Caecilius paying homage to an image of the
god Serapis, is not in the form of a conversational dialogue,
but resembles much more a forensic debate: the plea of the
public prosecutor, and the answer of the defending attorney,
both addressed to the presiding arbiter. This form is quite in
keeping with what Minucius tells of himself: that he was a
lawyer by profession.

In the field of literature there is a definite resemblance to
the form of *controversia* as exemplified by the elder Seneca.
In the rhetorical schools of the day the students were trained
by having to compose and deliver *declamationes,* a term
which, in those days, did not have the derogatory notion
which the modern 'declamation' imparts. The *declamationes*
would take the form of *suasoriae* and *controversiae.* The *suasoria* was a monologue in which some legendary or historical
person ponders the course of action he should take in a certain set of circumstances: for instance, Agamemnon, whether
he should obey the directions of the seer Calchas and sacrifice his daughter Iphigenia or not; Cicero, whether he should
ask mercy of Antony or not. The *controversia,* which was an
exercise for more advanced students, was in the nature of a
forensic debate which consisted in imaginary indictment and
defense. Thus, there was occasion for two speeches, one for

each side of the question, and a third person could be assigned as arbiter.

While the introduction, the setting of the scene (Chapters 1-4), is modeled on the Platonic dialogue, the main body of the work, the two speeches of Caecilius and Octavius, is similar to the form of the *controversia*. This opens with the speech (*actio*) of the pagan Caecilius, who presents the case against the Christians (Chapters 5-13). According to him, the claims of the ignorant Christians to have arrived at the truth cannot be maintained, since this truth has eluded philosophers for ages. He advises a recourse to skepticism, therefore, especially since Fate rules all and no such thing as Divine Providence exists. The safest procedure is thus to put one's trust in the traditional cult of the gods who have made Rome great. The second part of the speech of Caecilius contains a catalogue of the accusations against the Christians current in his day.

A short interlude (Chapters 14-15) follows, in which Minucius, the presiding arbiter, speaks of the allurements of fine oratory as a dangerous way of obscuring the evidence and, hence, the truth, a suggestion to which Caecilius objects as betraying prejudice on the part of a judge who ought to be impartial.

The reply of the Christian Octavius easily constitutes the major part of the work (Chapters 16-38) both in length and content. Since he closely follows the order of points raised by his opponent, his speech is also divisible into two parts: in the first, he launches a condemnation of the ancient religion just proposed; in the second, he makes answer to the accusations against the Christians.

In the epilogue (Chapters 39-40), Caecilius admits his defeat and becomes a Christian.

The style of Minucius Felix has been greatly admired ever since Franciscus Balduinus (1520-1573) discovered the *Octa-*

vius in the disguise of the *liber octavus* (eighth book) of Arnobius' *Adversus Nationes.* In antiquity, Lactantius and Jerome also speak highly of its literary excellence. Minucius' style should properly be termed neither as Ciceronian nor as Senecan, but is really a harmonious mixture of the two, resulting in a new style that is the author's very own. The first chapter of the dialogue and the calmer, philosophical passages show us the old style, characterized by the long, involved, flowing periodic sentences reminiscent of Cicero. On the other hand, the passages expressing the heated emotions of the two interlocutors reveal the influence of the *elocutio novella,* the new style, characterized by short, terse, crisp sentences and a special liking for certain rhetorical figures, especially antithesis, parallel sentence structure, and *homoioteleuton,* or the use of the same or similar endings near one another, as in neighboring clauses. The younger Seneca's prose had established him as representative of these modern tendencies. Minucius Felix's own personal style is, then, a blending of the two: it combines the long climactic sentences of Cicero with the terseness and pointedness of the new style, its rapid sequence of clauses within the sentence, its piling up of verbs, often two or three in succession with asyndeton, that is, omission of connectives.

In content, the *Octavius* presents the current pagan beliefs: skepticism, reliance on the traditional Roman religion, the calumnious reports spread concerning Christianity; and, on the other hand, an eloquent apology for Christianity, refuting the pagan accusations and defending the fundamental beliefs of Christianity. It is remarkable in this last respect that the *Octavius* presents so little of positive Christian doctrine: there is no Christology; nothing is said of Christ's work of Redemption and mystical union with the believer, of the Holy Spirit, of the well-established orders of ministry and the sacraments; belief in resurrection is not grounded on the Resurrection of Christ.

Yet, as pointed out in the general introduction to this volume,[4] if the Christian teaching of the dialogue is surprisingly meagre, one of the reasons is that Felix does not wish to discourage the prospective convert with a lengthy theological treatise which might confuse him, leaving, we are led to believe,[5] further elucidation to a later date. In order the better to attract the pagan, he aims to present Christianity through pagan eyes, as it were, in a form which the pagan would readily comprehend. It is a highly polished production, freely employing the learning of ancient literature, using the arms of the ancient philosophers so as to represent his own faith simply as the true philosophy on which to form one's life.

In its philosophical content, the *Octavius* relies heavily on Cicero's *De natura deorum*; in its strictly apologetical content it resembles strongly the *Apologeticum* of Tertullian, although scholars are still arguing whether Minucius Felix drew on Tertullian, or vice versa.

The Latin text of the *Octavius* is based on a single ninth-century manuscript of the Bibliothèque Nationale of Paris, the *Codex Parisinus* 1661. The MS 10847 of the Bibliothèque Royale of Brussels is only a copy of the *Parisinus*. The text followed in the present translation is that of J. P. Waltzing (Editio Stereotypa. Bibl. Teubneriana Leipzig 1931), the edition by J. Martin (Florilegium Patristicum fasc. 8, Bonn 1930) was consulted throughout. The English version by G. H. Rendall in *The Loeb Classical Library,* and the German version by A. Müller in the *Bibliothek der Kirchenväter,* have proved helpful.

---

4 Cf. above, p. xv.
5 Cf. 40.2.

SELECT BIBLIOGRAPHY

Texts:

C. Halm, *CSEL* 2 (Vienna 1867) 1ff.

J. Martin, *M. Minucii Felicis Octavius* (Florilegium Patristicum fasc. 8, Bonn 1930).

Adelaide Douglas Simpson, *M. Minucci Felicis Octavius. Prolegomena, Text and Critical Notes* (New York 1938).

J. P. Waltzing, *M. Minucius Felix. Octavius* (Editio Stereotypa. Bibl. Teubneriana, Leipzig 1931); *Octavius de M. Minucius Felix* (with commentary, Bruges 1909).

Translations:

J. H. Freese, *The Octavius of Minucius Felix* (London 1920).

A. Müller, *Des Minucius Felix Dialog Oktavius*, in *Frühchristliche Apologeten und Märtyrerakten* II (Bibl. d. Kirchenväter 14, Kempten and Munich 1913) 123 ff.

G. H. Rendall, *Minucius Felix*, in *The Loeb Classical Library* (London and New York 1931).

R. E. Wallis, *The Ante-Nicene Fathers* IV (American reprint of the Edinburgh edition, New York 1890) 167ff.

Other Sources:

H. J. Baylis, *Minucius Felix and His Place among the Early Fathers of the Latin Church* (London 1928).

R. Bentler, *Philosophie und Apologetik bei Minucius Felix.* (Königsberg 1936).

S. Colombo, 'Osservazioni sulla composizione letteraria e sulle fonti di M. Minucio Felice,' *Didaskaleion* 3 (1914) 312ff.; 4 (1915) 215ff.

H. Jordan, *Geschichte der altchristlichen Literatur* (Leipzig 1911) 254ff.

P. De Labriolle, *History and Literature of Christianity from Tertullian to Boethius*, tr. by H. Wilson (New York 1925) 109-130.

P. Monceaux, *Histoire littéraire de l'Afrique chrétienne* I (Paris 1901) 463-508.

M. Schanz, C. Hosius, and G. Krüger, *Geschichte der römischen Litteratur, Handbuch der Altertumswissenschaft* VIII 3 (3rd ed., Munich 1922) 262-272.

J. P. Waltzing, *Lexicon Minucianum* (Liége and Paris 1909).

OCTAVIUS

Chapter 1

AS I WAS CONTEMPLATING and refreshing in my mind the memory of my good and most faithful companion, Octavius, such a sweet affection for the man remained with me that I myself seemed in some way to return to the past and not merely to recall things which were passed and gone. 2 So deeply did his image, though removed from my eyes, remain engraved in my breast and, so to speak, in my innermost senses. 3 And, not without good reason, did this distinguished and saintly man leave with us on his departure an immense feeling of longing for him, since he himself always burned with such affection for us that both in our amusements and serious occupations we were in perfect accord with regard to our likes and dislikes, so that you would think that one mind had been divided between two men. 4 Thus, he who alone shared my tastes was also the companion of my errors, and, when the mist had been dispelled and I came forth from the very depths of darkness into the light of true wisdom,[1] he did not reject my accompanying him, but, the more to his honor, led the way.

5 Therefore, when my thoughts were roving over the entire period of our intimate association, my attention settled particularly on that remarkable discourse in which, by sheer weight of his reasoning, he converted to the true religion Caecilius, who was still clinging to the folly of superstitions.

---
1 Cf. 1 Peter 2.9.

Chapter 2

1 He had come to Rome on business and to see me, leaving his home, wife, and children. The children were still at the age of innocence when they are most lovable, trying to utter half-words, a language more sweet because of the broken sounds of a stumbling tongue. 2 I cannot express in words how great and boundless my joy was at his arrival, since my happiness was increased beyond measure by the fact that this visit of my dearest friend was unexpected.

3 So, after a day or two, when constant companionship had satisfied the eagerness of our longing, and when, by exchanging our experiences, we had learned what we did not know about each other because of our mutual separation, we decided to visit Ostia,[1] a most charming town. The sea baths would be a pleasant and appropriate cure for drying the humors from my body. Besides, the vintage holidays had just relieved me from the duties of the law court. It was the time when, after the heat of the summer, the autumn weather was turning into a season of mildness.

4 So, we started out at daybreak for the sea, to take a walk along the shore, so that the breeze as it gently blew might invigorate our limbs and the sand as it yielded to our soft footsteps might give us delightful pleasure. It was then that Caecilius[2] noticed an image of Serapis,[3] and, as is the super-

---

1 Ostia ('river mouth'), the ancient seaport of Rome at the mouth of the Tiber, for some eight centuries lived the same life as Rome and shared in the good and ill fortunes of the Republic and the Empire, forming, as it were, part of the Eternal City. Like Baiae in the Gulf of Naples, it was a favorite resort of the wealthy Romans.
2 Caecilius had joined Minucius and Octavius on this excursion.
3 Ostia offers a good example of the religious syncretism of the Roman Empire. There have been found there the Oriental cults of Cybele of Asia Minor, the Egyptian divinities Isis, Serapis, Bubastis, the Syrian Jupiter Heliopolitanus and Dolichenus, Maiumas, and the cult of Mithras. Because of their mysterious melancholy, the cults of Isis and Serapis were widespread among the upper classes of Rome.

stitious custom of the vulgar, raised his hand to his mouth and blew a kiss from his lips.

Chapter 3

1 Then Octavius said: 'Brother Marcus,[1] it is not becoming for a good man to forsake so far in this blind stupidity of vulgar ignorance a friend who does not budge from your side in private or in public as to allow him in broad daylight to dash himself on stones, however well carved, anointed and crowned with garlands they may be. Surely, you know that this disreputable error is laid to your door no less than to his.'

2 While he was speaking thus, we had walked the stretch between the town and the sea and were now reaching the open shore. 3 There, gentle waves, rippling over the farthermost edge of the sand, were levelling it as if to prepare it for a promenade. The sea is always restless, even when the winds are still. Although it did not come up to the land in white and foaming waves, we were exceedingly delighted by its curling, twisting, and ever-changing movements when we wet our feet at the very edge of the water. It alternately sent its waves to play about our feet as it was driven upon the shore, or sucked them back into itself as it slipped away again and receded. 4 Progressing leisurely and serenely along the shore of the gently curving coast, we made our way, shortening it with stories. These stories came from Octavius, who was telling about his sea voyage. 5 When, after conversing thus, we had gone a reasonable distance, we retraced our steps and went back the same way. When we came to that place where

---

[1] First name (*praenomen*) of Minucius Felix. 'Brother' is used in the wider sense, meaning friend. Moreover, the Christians addressed each other in this way as children of the same heavenly Father (cf. Matt. 23.8f.).

boats had been drawn up on oak supports and were resting, raised up to preserve them from the destructive rot of the soil, we saw boys eagerly vying with one another in a game of throwing stones into the sea. 6 The game consists in picking up from the shore a flat stone worn smooth by the beating of the waves, holding that stone with the fingers in a horizontal position, bending low, and making it skip as far as possible over the waves. That missile then either would skim the surface of the sea and swim along, gliding with a gentle impulse, or, cutting the tops of the waves, would be carried along with a hop and a skip in continuous leaps. He considered himself the winner among the boys whose stone went the farthest and made the most leaps.[2]

Chapter 4

1 While all of us were captivated by this merry scene, Caecilius neither paid attention nor laughed at the game. Silent, uneasy, and distracted, he betrayed by the expression on his face that he was troubled by something. 2 I said to him: 'What is the matter, Caecilius? How is it I fail to see your usual liveliness and miss that cheerfulness in your eyes which is characteristic of you even in serious matters?'

3 He rejoined: 'For a long time I have been greatly annoyed, and actually cut to the quick, by the remarks of our friend Octavius who attacked and scolded you for disloyalty, so that, under this guise, he might bring against me the more serious charge of ignorance. 4 Therefore, I would go further. I would have an exhaustive and comprehensive discussion

---

[2] The Greeks had a special word for this game, which is still played today (*epostrakizein*, to send potsherds skimming over the water, to play at ducks and drakes).

with Octavius on this matter. If he is willing that I, a follower of this philosophy of life, should dispute with him, he will indeed soon experience that it is easier to have a discussion among friends than to engage in a formal contest over philosophy. 5 Let us just sit down on those piles of rocks which are heaped up for the protection of the baths and run out into the sea, so that we can both rest from our walk and debate with more concentration.'

6 At his suggestion, we sat down. The two opponents taking their place on either side flanked me as the middle of the three. This was done not through courtesy or because of rank or honor—since friendship always presupposes equals or creates them—but that I, as arbiter, sitting close to both, might give heed to them, and, being in the middle, might separate the two contestants.

Chapter 5

1 Caecilius then began as follows: 'Brother Marcus, for you personally there are no doubts concerning the subject of the present discussion. Because you have been a careful student of both ways of life, you have repudiated the one and embraced the other. Yet, in the present case, you must guide your mind by this intention, that you hold the scales of justice most impartially and do not tend by inclination toward either side, lest the verdict seem not the result of our argumentation, but, rather, the product of your personal feelings. 2 If, then, you will please take your seat as though you were some judge unknown to both parties and unacquainted with either side of the case, there will be no difficulty in showing that in human affairs everything is doubtful, uncertain and unsettled; that everything is a matter of probability rather

than truth.¹ 3 So much the more strange is it that some people, because they are weary of thoroughly investigating the truth, rashly yield to any sort of opinion rather than persevere in the search with untiring diligence. 4 Since this is the case, everyone must feel a righteous indignation and be annoyed that certain persons—persons, in addition, innocent of learning, untouched by letters, unskilled even in manual arts²—boldly utter categorical statements concerning the majesty of the universe: a problem over which countless schools of philosophy have pondered through so many centuries and are continuing to do so up to this day. 5 And not without good reason. For, man, because of the limitation of his intellectual power, is so incapable of exploring things divine that neither is he privileged to know, nor does religious awe allow him to examine thoroughly, things which are suspended high above us in heaven or lie deeply submerged within the womb of the earth; and we may rightly esteem ourselves sufficiently happy and sufficiently experienced if, according to that ancient oracle of the sage, we know ourselves more intimately.³ 6 But, since, in devoting ourselves

---

1 This is the skepticism or, rather, probabilism of the New Academy (cf. Ch. 13, n.3). Carneades (213-129 B.C.), the founder of this school, considering knowledge impossible, substituted probability. Though skepticism subsided for a while after his death, it revived again with Cicero's contemporary, Aenesidemus, and again under the Antonine Emperors (2nd century A.D.). St. Augustine followed this school of philosophy for a while in his youth and his farewell to it is found in his three books *Contra Academicos*, in which he endeavored to raise up an unbreakable dam against the destructive flood of skepticism.

2 Cf. Acts. 4.13, where the Jews marvel, 'seeing the boldness of Peter and John, and finding that they were uneducated and ordinary men.' It was principally among the lower classes that the new religion spread at first though we do find that some individuals of high social standing embraced Christianity and were very ardent in promoting it.

3 The famous motto, 'Know thyself,' which, according to tradition, was inscribed upon the temple of Apollo at Delphi. It is the basic doctrine of Socrates: man must first seek to know himself, his own end and duty; to know what is right and then to do it. With regard to the movements of the heavenly bodies, or to the number of primitive elements, man may console himself with the thought that such knowledge would be of no use to him if he possessed it.

to an absurd and fruitless task, we stray beyond the bounds of our limited intellect, and, though banished to the dust of earth, we seek with daring ambition to rise above heaven itself and the stellar world, let us at least avoid making our error more complex by adding vain and frightening reveries.

7 'Supposing that, in the beginning, the seeds of all things were assembled by spontaneous generation of nature—what god was the creator here? Or, let us suppose that by their fortuitous concurrence the elements of the whole cosmos were joined together, organized, and fashioned[4]—what god was the artificer? Fire may have lit the stars; the very nature of their substance may have raised high the aerial region and firmly planted the earth by its weight; the sea may have flowed together from the liquid element—what reason, then, is there for religious awe, for terror and excessive dread of the divine? 8 Man, and every living creature that comes into existence, receives life and grows up; is, so to speak, a spontaneous aggregation of elements. Into these elements man and every living creature is again divided, resolved, and scattered. Thus, all things flow back to their source and, in a circular course, return unto themselves. There is no need for any artificer, or judge, or creator. 9 Thus, by the concentration of atoms of fire, new suns shine forth over and over again; thus, by the exhalation of vapors from the earth, mists grow without cessation, and by condensation and conglobation

---

[4] This is the atomic theory of Leucippus of Miletus (5th century B.C.), which was further developed by his pupil Democritus of Abdera. It was adopted by Epicurus (341-270 B.C.) as the easiest way to free man from his fear of the gods and death and found a poetical expression in Lucretius' (1st century B.C.) poem, *The Nature of Things*. The only realities were the atoms, which are of the same essence, but may vary in size, shape and weight. The phenomena of the sensible world are the result of the various combinations and disunions of the many but limited atoms, which are brought about by sheer necessity and not by Divine Mind. The atomic theory was the first materialistic and purely mechanical philosophy.

rise on high as clouds. When the latter begin to fall, showers pour down, winds blow, hail-storms clatter; or, when banks of clouds collide, thunders roar, lightning gleams, thunderbolts flash through the air and, what is more, fall at random, crash upon mountains, strike trees, hit indiscriminately places sacred or profane, smite men who are guilty or, often enough, those who are godfearing. 10 Why should I even mention the capriciousness and uncertainty of catastrophes by which all things are upset without plan or distinction? In shipwrecks, are not the good and the wicked overtaken by their fate in the same manner, without consideration of their deserts? In fires, do not the innocent and the guilty meet their doom together? When some region of the air is tainted with a deadly plague, do not all perish without discrimination? Finally, in the heat and fury of battle, is it not chiefly the good men who fall? 11 In peace, too, the wicked are not only put on a level with the good, but even esteemed, so that, in the case of many, one does not know whether to detest their depravity or hope for their good fortune. 12 If the world were ruled by divine providence and the direction of some deity, never would Phalaris[5] and Dionysius[6] have deserved a kingdom, or Rutilius[7] and Camillus[8] exile, or Socrates[9] the hemlock.

---

5 Phalaris, Tyrant of Acragas (570-554 B.C.), became notorious for his cruel method of wreaking vengeance upon his enemies by roasting them in a brazen bull

6 Dionysius I (died 367 B.C.), Tyrant of Syracuse, was frequently quoted by orators and writers as the prototype of the cruel, unscrupulous, and treacherous tyrant.

7 P. Rutilius Rufus, famous for the integrity with which he administered the province of Asia, protected the provincials against the rapacious publicans. Hated by the latter, he had to go into exile in 92 B.C.

8 M. Furius Camillus, the legendary hero and savior of Rome from the Gauls. Having incurred the people's enmity, he also had to go into exile.

9 The well-known Athenian philosopher (469-399 B.C.). The examples of Phalaris, Dionysius, Rufus and Socrates occur also in Cicero and Seneca.

13 Behold the trees laden with fruit, the fields already white for the harvest, the grapes in the vineyards heavy with juice—how they are rotted by rain, beaten down by hail! So much is this true that either the uncertain truth is hidden and kept back from our eyes or—what is more credible—chance, unrestrained by laws, rules supreme by capricious and hazardous whims.

Chapter 6

1 'Since, then, either fortune is certain or the principle of nature uncertain, how much more reverent and better it is to accept the teaching of our forefathers as a guide to truth, to cherish the religious practices handed down to us, to adore the gods whom your parents taught you to fear rather than to know more familiarly![1] How much better it is not to give your own opinion about divinities, but to believe our ancestors, who, in a primeval age, on the very birthday of this world, were so fortunate as to possess gods either as friends or as kings.[2] And this is precisely the reason why, throughout whole empires, provinces, and towns, we see each people having its own religious customs and worshipping its local gods: for example, the Eleusinians, Ceres;[3] the Phrygians,

---

[1] Note how the same skeptic, who has just denied the existence of the gods, suddenly becomes an ardent defender of the old Roman religion. In his reply (cf. 16.2) Octavius reminds Caecilius of this inconsistency.

[2] Cf. 21.5, where Saturn is mentioned as coming to Italy and teaching its inhabitants many useful arts.

[3] The Roman Ceres was identified with the Greek corn goddess Demeter, whose shrine at Eleusis near Athens became the object of an annual pilgrimage from that city. On this occasion, a great number of devotees of the goddess were initiated into her sacred rites.

the Great Mother;[4] the Epidaurians, Aesculapius;[5] the Chaldeans, Bel;[6] the Syrians, Astarte;[7] the Taurians, Diana;[8] the Gauls, Mercury;[9] the Romans, each and all of them. 2 If the power and authority of the Romans thus have encompassed the circuit of the whole world, and their rule has been extended beyond the paths of the sun and the bounds of the ocean itself, it is because in battle they combine valor with fear of the gods; they protect their city with sacred rites, chaste virgins, and many priesthoods distinguished with dignity and titles. Their city besieged and captured by the enemy, with the single exception of the Capitoline citadel, they still worship the gods whom others would have spurned long ago as impropitious, and proceed, armed not with weapons but with reverential regard for religious custom, through the ranks of Gauls amazed at such intrepid and scrupulous practice of religion.[10] Within the captured ramparts of the enemy, while

---

4 The Great Mother of the Phrygians is Cybele, the mother goddess of Asia Minor; like Demeter, she was a goddess of vegetation. These mystery cults have in common the worship of that mysterious force in nature which is the source of all life and growth, in plants and animals as well as in men.
5 Aesculapius, the Greek Asclepius, the god of medicine. He had a famous shrine about eight miles west of Argolic Epidaurus in Greece.
6 Bel, or Baal ('Lord') was the generic name for the local deities of the Chaldeans and other peoples of Semitic stock; the national divinity of Oriental peoples.
7 Astarte, Lucian's 'Syrian goddess,' a Syro-Phoenician divinity, and chief goddess of Tyre.
8 The Taurians were the people of the Tauric Chersonese, the Crimea, where, according to a legend, Iphigenia became priestess of the local goddess to whom human sacrifices were offered (cf. 30.4). Later, the goddess was identified with Artemis or Diana.
9 The chief god of the Gauls was Teutates, god of commerce (whom the Romans identified with their Mercury) and god of war, to whom human sacrifices were offered (cf. 30.4).
10 This refers to a story told by the Roman historian, Livy. During the sack of Rome by the Gauls (ca. 390 B.C.), the pontiff Fabius went through the ranks of the Gauls who were besieging the Capitoline citadel, performed a sacrifice on the Quirinal hill, and returned to the citadel.

still flushed with victory, they venerate the deities they have conquered; from every part of the world they hospitably receive these gods and make them their own;[11] they build altars even to the unknown deities[12] and to the spirits of the dead.[13] 3 Thus, in taking over the religious institutions of all nations, they have also deserved their dominions. Since then, this godfearing disposition, which, by length of time is not impaired but strengthened, has steadily maintained itself. Indeed, the ancients were wont to attribute to ceremonies and temples as much of sanctity as they possessed of age.

Chapter 7

1 'It was not by mere chance (for, I myself might venture for a moment both to make a concession and thus commit an error, more excusable though than yours) that our ancestors applied themselves to observing auguries, or consulting entrails,[1] or instituting sacrifices, or dedicating temples. 2 Ex-

---

11 People whom the Romans conquered usually were allowed to retain their religious cults, and their deities were even admitted into the circle of the Roman gods. This toleration was based on the belief that religion was a kind of sacred covenant between a god and his worshippers which both parties were bound to respect. Whenever the Romans were about to assault a city, they always first called upon its gods to come out and go to Rome where they were promised new temples.
12 In fear lest they should omit any god from among their divinities. Cf. St. Paul's discourse on the Areopagus at Athens (Acts 17.23): 'For as I was going about and observing objects of your worship, I found also an altar with this inscription: "To the unknown God."' In his *Description of Greece* (1.1.4), the Greek antiquarian and traveler Pausanias mentions that 'there are altars of gods named Unknown' at the Athenian harbor of Phalerum.
13 The Romans observed a ritual for the worship of the dead from February 13 to February 21 or 22.

---

1 In the auguries, the will of the gods was interpreted from the singing, chattering, flight, and feeding of birds, whereas in the haruspication, the Etruscan kind of divination, it was done by inspecting the entrails of sacrificial victims.

amine the written records. You will presently discover that they have introduced the sacred rites of all religions either to return thanks to gods for favors granted, or to avert their impending anger, or to appease their wrath which had begun to swell and increase in fury. 3 Witness the Idaean Mother, who at her arrival both vindicated a matron's chastity and freed the city from the fear of the enemy;[2] witness the statues of the twin horsemen, erected in their honor in the lake basin and representing them just as they appeared when, breathless on their foaming and steaming steeds, they announced the victory over Perseus on the same day on which they brought it about;[3] witness the resumption of the games in honor of offended Jupiter, prompted by the dream of a commoner;[4] witness, also, the acceptance by heaven of the self-sacrificing vow of the Decii;[5] witness, finally, Curtius, who by the bulk of horse and rider or by the gifts given in his honor closed

---

2 The Idaean Mother is again Cybele, worshipped on Mount Ida in Phrygia. In 205 B.C., toward the end of the Second Punic War, the Sibylline Books predicted that Hannibal could be driven from Italy if the Idaean Mother were brought from Pessinus in Phrygia to Rome. Accordingly, the sacred stone, representing the mother goddess, was brought by sea to Ostia. There, the ship ran aground, but was at once refloated by the noble lady Quinta Claudia, who had only to use her girdle as a rope. Her chastity had been suspected, but she thus proved her innocence. The goddess found a temporary home in the Temple of Victory until she was given one of her own in 191 B.C.

3 The twin horsemen are Castor and Pollux. The lake basin is the 'Lake' (pool) of the nymph Juturna in the Roman Forum. In the middle of the basin stood a marble altar, with figures in relief of several deities, among them Castor and Pollux. Perseus was the last king of Macedonia and was defeated at Pydna in 168 B.C.

4 According to a story told by Livy and others, Jupiter appeared in a dream to the plebeian Titus Latinus, saying that the leading dancer at the games had not been to his liking, and that unless there were a repetition of the festival, Rome would be in danger.

5 In the critical moment of a battle, the Roman general promised by a vow to the infernal gods his own life or that of a certain Roman soldier, together with the lives of all the enemy. P. Decius Mus is said to have sacrificed himself in a battle against the Latins; his son, of the same name, made the vow in the battle against the Samnites at Sentinum in 295 B.C.

the deep and yawning gap.⁶ 4 More frequently even than we wanted has the spurning of the auspices attested to the presence of the gods. Thus, Allia⁷ has become a name that bodes no good; so, too, the names of Claudius and Junius⁸ bring to mind not a combat with the Carthaginians, but a fatal shipwreck. Did not Flaminius spurn the auguries, only to make Trasimene rise and change its color from Roman blood?⁹ Did not Crassus deserve to have fulfilled the imprecations of the Dread Goddess mocked by him, only to make us reclaim our standards from the Parthians?¹⁰ 5 I omit the instances of old, though they are many. I pass over in silence the songs of the poets celebrating the births of the gods and their gifts and benefits. I also omit the prophecies uttered by the oracles, lest you would deem antiquity too much a world of fable. Look at the temples and shrines of the gods by which the city of Rome is protected and adorned; they are more venerable from the presence of the divinities who dwell and have made their abode there than they are rich from their

---

6 Cf. Tertullian, *The Testimony of the Soul* 4, n. 3.
7 A small tributary of the Tiber, where the Roman army was defeated by the invading Gauls about 390 B.C.
8 Minucius Felix is inaccurate here. P. Claudius Pulcher and L. Junius Pullus were the consuls of the year 249 B.C. The former was defeated when the Carthaginian fleet fell upon him in the harbor of Drapanum in western Sicily; the latter lost his fleet in rounding the promontory of Pachynum in southern Sicily. Minucius Felix, however, speaks as if both had suffered shipwreck. When told that the sacred chickens would not eat, Claudius ordered them thrown into the sea, exclaiming: 'Then let them drink.' In augury it was a good omen if the chickens rushed eagerly out of their cages at their food and dropped a bit out of their beaks; it was unfavorable if they were unwilling or refused altogether.
9 The consul Caius Flaminius was defeated by Hannibal at Trasimene, a lake in Etruria, between Clusum (Chiusi) and Perusia (Perugia) in 217 B.C. He had ordered the army to battle, in spite of unfavorable omens.
10 M. Licinius Crassus, who, with Caesar and Pompey, formed the first triumvirate, was defeated by the Parthians at Carrhae in 53 B.C., and treacherously slain a few days later. The Roman standards lost in the battle were restored to Augustus in 20 B.C.

external appearance, ornaments, and votive gifts. 6 This is precisely why prophets filled and permeated with the deity lay hold of the future beforehand, giving warning in times of danger, healing in distress, hope to the afflicted, succor to the wretched, comfort in disasters, relief in hardships. Even in the quiet of the night we see, hear, and recognize the gods whom during the day we blasphemously deny, refuse, and perjure.

Chapter 8

1 'Among all nations, then, unanimous belief in the existence of the immortal gods is firmly established, however uncertain man's notion of them and their origin may be. Since this is so, I cannot approve of anyone who is so puffed up with insolence and impious, sham enlightenment as to attempt to abolish and undermine this religion which is so ancient, so useful, and so beneficial. 2 No doubt, one could cite the famous instance of Theodorus of Cyrene,[1] or, going back further, that of Diagoras of Melos,[2] surnamed atheist by the ancients, who both alike, by denying the existence of the gods, utterly destroyed all religious fear and reverence by which mankind is governed: yet, never will they gain fame and influence on the basis of a sham philosophy.

3 'Moreover, when Protagoras of Abdera, in a circumspect rather than frivolous manner, expressed his opinion concerning the godhead, the men of Athens expelled him from their country and burned his writings in the market place.[3] Is it not deplorable, then, that fellows (you will excuse me for the

---

[1] Theodorus of Cyrene (4th-3rd century B.C.) preached atheism so openly in Athens that the Assembly indicted him for impiety. Banished from Athens, he went to Alexandria.
[2] Diagoras of Melos, lyric poet, contemporary of Socrates, was likewise banished from Athens for ridiculing the mysteries of Eleusis.

vehement and unrestrained expression of my thoughts on the score of the case I have taken on)—fellows, I say, belonging to an incorrigible, outlawed, and desperate gang, riot against the gods? 4 Fellows who gather together ignoramuses from the lowest dregs of society, and credulous women, an easy prey because of the instability of their sex, and thus organize an unholy mob of conspirators who become leagued together in nocturnal gatherings, by solemn fasts and atrocious repasts, not by any rite, but by an inexpiable crime—a furtive race which shuns the light, mute in the open but garrulous in the corners. They despise the temples as no better than sepulchres, abominate the gods, sneer at our sacred rites. Pitiable themselves, they pity (if this is possible at all) the priests; half-naked themselves, they spurn positions of honor and purple robes. 5 What strange folly! What incredible insolence! They do not care about present tortures, but dread those of an uncertain future; while they fear death after death, they are not afraid of death here on earth. Thus, deceptive hope soothes their fear with the comforting idea of a future life.

Chapter 9

1 'And now—for the evil grows apace—the corruption of morals gains ground from day to day, and throughout the entire world those abominable shrines[1] of this evil confederacy

---

3 Protagoras, celebrated sophist, born at Abdera in Thrace about 480 B.C., was accused of impiety. His impeachment was based on his book on the gods, which began, 'Respecting the gods, I am unable to know whether they exist or do not exist.' The impeachment was followed by his being expelled and the burning of his book.

1 These shrines were not churches in the strict sense of the word, but suitable private houses which had come into the possession of the Church by will or donation. They were fitted up as community centers or places of assembly for the Christian community and residences for the bishop and a staff of clerics. It was not until after the final victory of Christianity that magnificent basilicas replaced the 'church houses.'

increase in number. This conspiracy must be radically rooted out and execrated. 2 They recognize each other by secret marks and signs[2] and fall in love before they scarcely know each other. Everywhere they practice among themselves, a kind of cult of lust, so to speak, and indiscriminately call each other brothers and sisters, so that even ordinary fornication, under the cloak of a hallowed name, becomes incest. Thus, their vain and insane superstition actually boasts of its crimes.

3 'Concerning the latter, if there were no truth at their base, keen-sighted public opinion would not mention such terribly abominable acts which need to be prefaced by an apology. I am told that, because of I know not what foolish belief, they consecrate and worship the head of an ass,[3] the meanest of all animals—a religion worthy of and sprung from such morals. 4 Others tell that they reverence even the genital organs of their bishop and priest,[4] and adore, as it were, the creative power of their parent. This suspicion may be false, but, at any rate, it has been attached to their secret and nocturnal rites. And anyone who says that the objects of their worship are a man who suffered the death penalty for his crime, and the deadly wood of the cross, assigns them altars appropriate for incorrigibly wicked men, so that they actually worship what they deserve.

---

2 By 'secret marks and signs' Caecilius means 'distinguishing marks on the body' (cf. 31.8). They do not refer, therefore, to the Sign of the Cross or other Christian symbols found in the Catacombs, such as the fish, the monogram of Christ, the anchor, or the dove.

3 In his *Apology* (Ch. 16), Tertullian refutes this accusation in detail. The same charge had been made against the Jews. In 1856, there was found the famous Caricature of the Crucifixion scratched on a wall of the so-called Paedagogium on the Palatine Hill: a man with the head of an ass, affixed to a cross, with a praying figure at one side, and the words, 'Alexamenos worshipping his god.' It is usually explained as the work of an imperial page ridiculing some Christian companion.

4 For this slanderous accusation Minucius Felix is the only witness. It probably must be attributed to the custom whereby the penitent knelt before the priest and embraced his knees.

5 'And, now, the stories told about the initiation of their novices: they are as detestable as they are notorious. An infant covered with a dough crust to deceive the unsuspecting is placed beside the person to be initiated into their sacred rites. This infant is killed at the hands of the novice by wounds inflicted unintentionally and hidden from his eyes, since he has been urged on as if to harmless blows upon the surface of the dough. The infant's blood—oh, horrible—they sip up eagerly; its limbs they tear to pieces, trying to outdo each other; by this victim they are leagued together; by being privy to this crime they pledge themselves to mutual silence.[5] These sacred rites are more shocking than any sacrilege.

6 'Their form of banqueting is notorious;[6] far and wide everyone speaks of it, as our fellow citizen of Cirta[7] witnesses in his speech. On the appointed day, they assemble for their banquets with all their children, sisters, and mothers—people of both sexes and every age. After many sumptuous dishes, when the company at table has grown warm and the passion of incestuous lust has been fired by drunkenness, a dog which has been tied to a lamp stand is tempted by throwing a morsel beyond the length of the leash by which it is bound. It makes a dash, and jumps for the catch. 7 Thus, when the witnessing light has been overturned and extinguished, in the ensuing darkness which favors shamelessness, they unite

---

5 The ceremonies of the Christians while celebrating the Holy Eucharist were distorted by gruesome rumors to be akin to cannibalism. Christian phraseology about eating Christ's flesh and drinking His blood led to the notion that Christians observed cannibalistic rites.
6 The following is a distortion of the Christian *agápe* ('love feast'), a common meal, to which each of the guests contributed his share. There were prayers and singing of psalms and improvised hymns; during the meal they talked on pious subjects. Cf. Tertullian, *Apology* 7.1; 8.7; 39.16-21.
7 This is M. Cornelius Fronto, from Numidian Cirta, rhetor and teacher of Emperor Marcus Aurelius. In an oration against the Christians, which has been lost, he repeated the vulgar accusations of Thyestian feasts and Oedipean intercourse.

in whatever revoltingly lustful embraces the hazard of chance will permit. Thus, they are all equally guilty of incest, if not in deed, yet by privity, since whatever can happen in the actions of individuals is sought for by the general desire of all.

Chapter 10

1 'Many things I pass over purposely, for even those I mentioned are more than enough; that either all or most of them are true is evident from the mysterious conduct of this perverted religion. 2 Why do they strive with so much effort to keep secret and conceal whatever the object of their worship is?[1] Is it not because honorable deeds rejoice in publicity, while evil deeds keep in hiding? Why do they have no altars,[2] no temples,[3] none of the usual images of the gods? Why do they never speak in public, never assemble in open? Is it not because the very object of their worship and secretiveness is something shameful or liable to punishment?

3 'Moreover, whence or who or where is this unparalleled, solitary, and forsaken god, of whom no free nation, no kingdom—not even the Romans with their scrupulous fear of the gods—have knowledge? 4 The forlorn and wretched Jewish

---

1 This may refer to the so-called *Disciplina Arcani* (the Discipline of the Secret), a theological term expressing the custom of the early Church of keeping the knowledge of its most intimate Mysteries (especially that of the Holy Eucharist) from the heathen and even from the catechumens. The latter were allowed to attend the first part of the Mass, consisting of prayers, readings from Holy Scripture, and instruction, but were formally asked to leave before the solemn part of the Mass, the sacrifice in the strict sense of the word. The reason was not only to provide gradual instruction to candidates, but also to prevent the gaining of entrance by informers. There is no relation between the Discipline of the Secret in early Christianity and the customs of the pagan mysteries. The similarities are of a purely external nature.
2 Altars like those of the heathen, on which they offered sacrifices to their gods.
3 Cf. Ch. 9, n. 1.

nation also worshipped one god, but openly in temples, at altars, with victims and sacred rites; however, his strength and power is so negligible that he and his nation are captives of the Romans who are but men.[4] 5 Yet, now considering the Christians, what preposterous monstrosities they produce out of sheer imagination! This God of theirs can neither be shown nor seen by them. Yet they say that He inquires diligently into the moral conduct and actions of all men, even into their words and secret thoughts. He must, then, rush now here, now there, and be ubiquitous. Thus, they make Him a mischievous and restless spirit who, moreover, is shamelessly inquisitive—if He actually is present at all deeds and roams about everywhere. For, He can neither devote Himself to particulars because He is busy with the whole, nor can He attend satisfactorily to the whole because He is occupied with particulars.

Chapter 11

1 'What is even more: they threaten the whole world, the universe itself and its stars, with conflagration. They meditate on their downfall as if either the eternal order of nature, founded on divine laws, could be thrown into confusion, or the bonds tying all the elements together, once severed and the celestial frame broken up into pieces, that gigantic structure by which it is kept together and girded could collapse. 2 Further, not content with this lunatic idea, they build up and intertwine it with old wives' tales: they say that they will be born again after death, when they will have become ashes

---

[4] During the reign of Vespasian, his son Titus captured and destroyed Jerusalem with frightful massacres of the Jews in A.D. 70. Many thousands were made prisoners and sold as slaves; Judea became a Roman province. In A.D. 135, the temple of Jehovah was replaced by that of Jupiter Capitolinus.

and cinders, and, with a confidence which is difficult to grasp, they believe in each other's lies: you would think that they had already come to life a second time. 3 It is, indeed, a twofold perversion and a folly on the one hand to herald destruction for heaven and the stars which we leave in the same condition as we find them; on the other hand to hold out a prospect of eternal life to themselves after death, when we perish just as we are born. 4 For this same reason, evidently, they denounce funeral pyres and condemn cremation, just as though each body, even if it were spared the flames, would not be resolved into dust in the course of years and by the length of time; and just as though it made any difference whether it be torn to pieces by wild beasts, or swallowed up in the sea, or covered over by the earth, or devoured by flames. For, if corpses have sensation, they must find any kind of interment afflictive; while, if sensation has become extinct, the best way of treating them consists in having them disintegrate as quickly as possible. 5 Under the spell of this delusion they promise themselves, as morally good, a life of everlasting bliss after death; to all the rest, as evildoers, eternal punishment.

'I have much more in store on this subject, but I must hasten to come to an end with my speech. That they themselves are evildoers I have already shown and need not labor to prove once again. Even if I were to admit that they were righteous, I know that in the opinion of most people guilt or innocence are attributed to fate. 6 And with this opinion you concur; for, as others make fate, you make God responsible for every human act: thus, men become followers of your religion not by their own free will, but because they are elected. Therefore, you invent an unjust judge who punishes men for their fate, not for their use of free will.

7 'Here I should like to raise the question of how the resur-

rection will take place. With bodies or without bodies? And, if with bodies, with what bodies? Will it be with the same or with renewed bodies? Without a body? That, according to my knowledge, is neither mind nor soul nor life. With the same body? But, that has already disintegrated a long time ago. With another body? In that case, a new man comes into existence and the former man is not restored. 8 Moreover, so much time has elapsed, generations without number have passed away. Yet, what single individual has ever returned from the infernal regions, even if it were only after the fashion of fortunate Protesilaus,[1] with a leave of absence for a few hours, and for the sole purpose that through his example we might believe? 9 All those fables of a morbid imagination and silly motives for consolation, invented deceitfully by poets to give more charm to their poetry, have been raked up by you, overcredulous people, and applied to your God in a shameful manner.

Chapter 12

1 'Not even from your present life do you learn by experience how fallacious the promises and vain the desires are which deceive you. You wretched fools, judge from your present life what awaits you after death. 2 Look here. A part of you, and that the greater part, and even in your opinion the better part, is in want, endures cold, and suffers toil and hunger—and your God allows it and acts as if He does not see it. Either He is unwilling to help His own, or else He cannot. He is, then, either weak or wicked. 3 You yourself

---

[1] Protesilaus was the first hero who leaped ashore when the Greeks landed before Troy, but he was slain. He received a short leave of absence from the nether world to see his inconsolable wife Laodamia, who died with him when the period expired.

dream about a never-ending life after death. When you are shaken by a serious illness and are burning with fever and wracked with pain, do you not even then realize how matters stand with you? Do you not even then recognize your frailty? Whether you like it or not, O wretched fool, you have a proof of your own weakness, and yet you do not admit it.

4 'I pass over, however, what is common to all men. But, look, is not your own lot one of menacing edicts, capital punishment, and tortures; crosses no longer to be adored, but endured; even fires which you predict and dread?[1] Where is this God of yours who can come to your rescue in the future life but cannot in this? 5 Do not the Romans rule and reign without your God and enjoy the world as their possession; and are they not also your masters? In the meantime, troubled and worried, you refrain from proper pleasures: you do not frequent the theatres; you do not take part in the processions; the public banquets are held without you; you shun the sacred games, the viands set apart for the altars and the drinks poured in libation upon them.[2] Thus, you are afraid of the very gods you deny. 6 You do not crown your heads with flowers[3] and you begrudge your bodies perfume; you keep the ointments for the corpses and you even hold back the garlands from the tombs—you quaking palefaces, deserving

---

[1] Caecilius alludes to the tortures and punishments to which the Christians were exposed during persecutions. The fire which the Christians 'predict and dread' is that of hell.
[2] Not only the Roman processions, but such social events as theatrical performances, public banquets, and games, had their origin in religion. Moreover, they were frequently celebrated with immorality, and for these reasons the Christians refused to participate in them. In the sacrifice, only a small portion of the flesh was offered on the altar to the god; the rest was consumed by the worshippers. The same was done with the libations. Cf. Acts 15.29, where the Christians are instructed to 'abstain from things sacrificed to idols.'
[3] This was the pagan custom at sacrifices and banquets.

pity: but that of our gods. Thus, in your wretched folly, you will neither rise for another life nor live this one.

7 'Well, then, if there is still left in you any brains or shame, stop searching the regions of the sky and the destiny and mysteries of the world. Let this be enough: to look at the things at your feet—especially for people without learning and refinement, without education and good breeding, to whom it is not given to understand civic affairs, and who are still less capable of discussing things divine.

Chapter 13

1 'However, if an urge to philosophize does exist, let anyone who feels capable of it imitate, if he can, Socrates, the prince of wisdom. His answer, when asked about things in heaven, is famous: "What is above us is no concern of ours."[1] 2 Justly, therefore, he merited from the oracle the testimony of his unusual wisdom.[2] Like the oracle, he also had this realization, namely, that he had been placed before all others, not because he had acquired a knowledge of everything, but because he had learned that he knew nothing; thus, the highest wisdom consists in the avowal of one's own ignorance. 3 From this source flowed the circumspect skepticism of Arcesilas, and, in much later times, that of Carneades and the majority of the Academicians on all fundamental questions.[3]

---

[1] Cf. Ch. 5, n. 3.
[2] Chaerephon, a student of Socrates, inquired of the oracle at Delphi whether any man was wiser than Socrates. The answer was: 'Sophocles is wise, Euripides is wiser, but Socrates is wisest of all.'
[3] This statement of Caecilius should be qualified. To Socrates and his pupil, Plato (the founder of a philosophical school called the 'Old' Academy because of its location in the grove of the hero Academus), doubt was only the beginning and not the end of philosophy. It was the great contribution of Socrates to Occidental thought that he answered the sophistic doctrine of the relativity of judgment by asserting

This is a course in philosophizing which can be pursued both by the unlearned, without danger, and the learned, with distinction. 4 Moreover, why should not the delaying attitude of Simonides,[4] the lyric poet, be admired and followed by all? When this Simonides was questioned by Hiero, the tyrant, about the essence and the attributes of the gods, he at first begged leave for a day's reflection; the next day, he asked for a two-day extension; then, upon a reminder, he added still another to his request. Finally, when the tyrant inquired the reasons for so much delay, he replied that the more slowly he proceeded in his investigation, the more obscure the truth became. 5 This is my opinion, also. Things which are doubtful should be left as they are, and, while so many of the greatest minds are undecided, one should not rashly and recklessly pass judgment in favor of either side. Otherwise, a religious belief fit for old women takes root or all piety is destroyed.'

Chapter 14

1 Thus Caecilius came to an end and said with a triumphant smile (for the impetuous flow of his discourse had relieved the swelling of his indignation): 'And, now, is there anything that Octavius ventures to answer to these things, Octavius, a

---

the existence of an absolute and eternal truth. He also held that the individual has the duty of arriving at this truth by a process of hard thinking. Arcesilas (316-241 B.C.), head of the 'Middle' Academy, departed from the traditions of Socrates and Plato by transforming the latter's rejection of sense knowledge into complete skepticism: 'Nothing is certain, and not even that.' Carneades (213-129 B.C.), who took charge of the 'New' Academy, introduced the doctrine of probability: 'A thing may not be capable of proof, but it still may be more probable than its opposite' (cf. Ch. 5, n. 1).

4 Simonides of Ceos (*ca.* 556-468 B.C.) lived during old age at the court of Hiero I, Tyrant of Syracuse.

man of the progeny of Plautus: the best of bakers, but the poorest of philosophers?"[1]

2 'Stop your self-praise by sneering at him,' I said, 'for it is contrary to the rules of a well-arranged discussion to triumph before both sides have finished arguing the case more fully, especially since your debate strives not for praise, but for truth. 3 And, however much I have been delighted by the subtle variety of your speech, yet—not so much with regard to the present question at issue as to discussions of every kind—I am more deeply moved by the fact that, very often, even self-evident truth appears in a totally different light according to the talents of the disputants and the power of their eloquence. 4 The reason for this phenomenon lies, as everybody knows, in the complaisance of the audience. Their attention to facts diverted by the captivating charm of words, they assent without discrimination to everything which is said; they do not distinguish the false from the true, unaware of the fact that there can be elements of truth in that which is incredible and elements of falsehood in that which sounds probable. 5 Accordingly, the more often they give credence to assertions, the more frequently their errors are brought home to them by people of greater experience. Thus, constantly deceived by their own rashness, they complain about the uncertainty of things, instead of finding fault with their own judgment. The result is a wholesale condemnation and an inclination to leave everything in suspense, rather than to pass judgment about things which may prove deceptive. 6 We must therefore take care lest, harassed by a persistent

---

[1] Caecilius seems to refer sarcastically to the poverty and insignificance of the Christians. Plautus, the great Latin comedy writer (d. 184 B.C.), is said to have worked for a miller in his youth. Bakers and millers belonged to the lowest class of Roman society.

dislike of all discussion, we cause a great number of simple-minded people to be swept into execration and hatred of their fellow men. For, incautiously credulous, they become the dupes of those whom they thought good: soon, repeating their mistake, they come to suspect all alike and to shun as wicked even those whose moral integrity they could have known by experience.

7 'Let us be on our guard, then, because in every question there are arguments on both sides. While on the one hand, truth is very often obscure; on the other hand, ingenious cunning, by a rich flow of words, sometimes puts on the semblance of an irrefutable demonstration entitled to credence. We should, therefore, evaluate each point as diligently as possible, so that, while acknowledging the elegance of presentation, we are able to choose, approve, and accept what is correct.'

Chapter 15

1 'You are departing,' Caecilius said, 'from the duty of a conscientious judge. It is a flagrant injustice on your part to weaken the strength of my pleading by bringing such a weighty argument into the debate: it is Octavius who has to refute each charge in turn, whole and unabridged—if he can.'

2 'Those words of mine to which you object,' I replied, 'were meant for the common interest, if I am not mistaken. In a scrupulous examination, we wish to weigh our judgment, not according to rhetorical bombast, but according to the solid value of the things themselves. But, the distraction about which you are complaining ought not to keep us any longer from listening in attentive and absolute silence to the reply our friend Januarius[1] is eagerly desirous of making.'

---

[1] The surname of Octavius.

Chapter 16

1 Octavius then began: 'I will reply, indeed, to the best of my ability, and it is your duty to combine your efforts with mine in order to remove the stains of scathing slanders by the cleansing stream of truthful statements.

'To begin with, I do not wish to leave it unnoticed that our good friend Natalis[1] has been so wavering and shifting, so unsteady and uncertain in his views that we are free to be in doubt as to whether the confusion was brought about by an ingenious device, or his wavering was due to a misapprehension. 2 For, he varied his opinion from belief in the gods at one time to being skeptical about their existence at another time;[2] thus, the course of my reply, based on an equivocal proposition, might become even more equivocal. But, to my friend Natalis I will not, and do not, attribute craftiness; scheming trickery is alien to his candid character. 3 What, then, is the state of the case? Natalis is like a man who does not know the right way when, as it happens, the road branches out into several; not knowing the way, the man is at a loss and uneasy, and does not dare either to choose any one road or approve all of them. In like manner, the fluctuating views of a man who has no fixed criterion of truth move now this way, now that, according as unsafe hypotheses pop up. 4 It is, then, no wonder that Caecilius is constantly tossed about in an ebb and flow of contradictions and inconsistencies. To make this impossible henceforth, I will thoroughly disprove his statements, however much they diverge from each other, by means of the one well-established and tested truth. Thus, he will be freed from further doubt and hesitation.

5 'Our good brother has disclosed feelings of displeasure,

---
[1] The surname of Caecilius.
[2] Cf. Ch. 6, n. 1.

annoyance, indignation, and grief that unlearned, poor, and ignorant people should discuss heavenly things. Yet, he should know that all human beings, without respect to age, sex, or rank, are born capable of and fit for reasoning and understanding; they do not acquire wisdom by good fortune, but receive it as an innate gift from nature. Why, the very philosophers or other discoverers of arts whose names have passed into the pages of history, were they not considered common and ignorant beggars before their brilliance of mind brought fame to their names? What is more, while the rich, ensnared by their wealth, were wont to have their minds fixed more on gold than on heaven, poor people of our class have discovered the true wisdom and handed on its teaching. Hence, it follows that talents are not furnished by wealth or obtained through studies, but are begotten with the very fashioning of the mind. 6 There is, then, no reason for indignation or grief if a common man makes inquiries into things divine and holds and pronounces his views on the subject, since it is not the authority in the discussing person, but the truth in his discussion, that matters. Further, the more unskilled the speech, the clearer is the reasoning, because it is not vitiated by a display of eloquence and graceful style, but sustained in its true character by the rule of right.

Chapter 17

1 'I do not object to what Caecilius has endeavored to lay down as one of his principles—namely, that man ought to know himself and to ponder upon his nature, his origin, and his destiny: whether he is an aggregation of elements or an appropriate arrangement of atoms, or whether he is created, formed, and endowed with a soul by God. 2 But, this is just the thing we cannot thoroughly investigate without inquiring

into the universe. For, both problems are so intimately linked together and concatenated that, without a careful inquiry into the nature of deity, you cannot know that of man, just as you are unable to administer affairs of state successfully without a knowledge of that state which is common to all men—the world. This argument holds good all the more because we differ from the beasts in this, that they, ever prone and bending toward the ground, have no other goal in life than that of looking for food, while we, endowed with uplifted countenance and gaze directed toward heaven, gifted with speech and reason, enabling us to recognize, perceive and imitate God, neither ought to nor are able to ignore the heavenly majesty which thrusts itself upon our eyes and senses; for, it approaches sacrilege, and very much so, if you look on the ground for that which you ought to find on high.

3 'Hence, I feel the more convinced that people who hold this universe of consummate artistic beauty to be not the work of divine planning, but a conglomeration of some kind of fragments clinging together by chance, are themselves devoid of reason and perception—even of the very power of seeing. 4 For, what is so manifest, so acknowledged, and so evident, when you lift your eyes to heaven and examine all the things which are below and around you, than that there exists some divine Being of unequaled mental power by whom all nature is inspired, moved, nourished, and governed?

5 'Look at the sky itself: how widely it extends, how rapidly it revolves; at night it is resplendent with the lustre of the stars, by day it is made bright by the light of the sun. From this you will at once understand in what marvellous and divine balance it is kept by the supreme Ruler. Consider, furthermore, how the course of the sun makes the year, and how the moon, by its waxing, waning, and disappearance, determines the month. 6 I only mention the ever-recurring changes

of darkness and light, providing us with the alternate renewal of work and rest. A more exhaustive discussion of the stars, however—how they regulate the course of navigation or usher in the proper seasons for ploughing and reaping—must be left to the astronomers. Not only did the creation, fashioning, and disposal of each of these things require a supreme Artificer and utmost Intelligence, but, in addition, they cannot be perceived, examined, and understood without a supreme effort of skill and reasoning.

7 'Again, the seasons of the year and its crops succeed one another in regular variety. Do not all alike—spring with its flowers, summer with its harvests, autumn with its mature and delicious fruits, and winter with its needed olive crop—bear testimony to their Originator and Founder? This order, if it were not based on a supreme Intelligence, could easily be disturbed. 8 What depth of thoughtful wisdom manifests itself in the insertion of the moderate temperature of autumn and spring, lest nature be pinched with the icy cold of a perpetual winter or scorched by the burning heat of a perpetual summer; in this way the gentle change from one season to the other within the circular course of the year is hardly perceptible and causes no harm.

9 'Look at the sea: it is checked by the bounds of its shore. Observe the different trees: how each receives life from the bowels of the earth. Behold the ocean: it is kept flowing back and forth by alternate tides. Notice the springs: they gush forth from inexhaustible veins. Gaze on the rivers: they roll on in a continuous, never-ceasing flow.

10 'Why speak about the right apportionment of the steep mountains, winding hills, and outstreched plains? Why, about the various means of defense animals possess against each other? Some are armed with horns, some fenced with teeth, shod with hoofs, and spiked with stings, while others enjoy

their freedom because of the swiftness of their feet or soaring wings. 11 Above all, the very beauty of the human form proclaims the creative genius of God: our carriage erect, our countenance uplifted, our eyes fixed on the very heights as though in a watchtower, and all the other organs of sense arranged as though in a citadel.

Chapter 18

1 'A detailed account would lead me too far. No limb of man exists which is not there either for the discharge of a necessary task or as an ornament. And, what is even more wonderful, all men have the same figure, yet in each man there are certain traits which are different; thus, all of us seem to be similar, while as individuals we are found to differ from each other.

2 'And the way in which we are born? What does it prove? Has not the procreative instinct been given by God? Does not God bring it about that, while the embryo matures, the mother's breasts fill with milk and the tender new-born child grows stronger through the copious flow of this milky moisture?

3 'Nor is it to the whole only that God attends, but in similar manner to each of its parts. Britain, for instance, lacks sunshine, but gets a milder temperature by the gentle warmth of the surrounding sea;[1] in Egypt, the river Nile usually tempers the drought;[2] the Euphrates compensates Mesopotamia for the want of rain;[3] the river Indus is said both to plant and

---
[1] This refers to the Gulf Stream, issuing from the Gulf of Mexico and flowing northeastward across the Atlantic.
[2] The fertility of Egypt is brought about by the annual inundation of the Nile. The long soaking moistens the soil and, as the water recedes, a rich loam dressing is left.
[3] The luxuriant vegetation of the stretch of land extending northwest from the Persian Gulf is the work of the Tigris and Euphrates Rivers.

water the East.⁴ 4 If, upon entering some house, you found there everything kept in neatness, perfect order, and in accordance with good taste, you would no doubt assume that some master was in charge of it, one far superior to those fine possessions of his: so, in this house of the world, when you see providence, order, and law prevailing in heaven and on earth, you may rest assured that there is a Master and Author of the universe, one more beautiful than the stars themselves and the single parts of the whole world.

5 'Perhaps, since there cannot be any doubt about the existence of Providence, you think that we must investigate whether the heavenly kingdom is governed by the authority of One or by the will of many. The solution of this problem does not offer any great difficulty to a man reflecting upon earthly dominions, which surely have their patterns in heaven. 6 When has a partnership in royal power ever begun in good faith and come to an end without bloodshed? I say nothing of the Persians, who chose their rulers according to omens based on the neighing of horses,⁵ and I pass over the long-forgotten tale of the two Theban brothers.⁶ Everyone knows the story of the twins who quarreled because of a kingship over shepherds and a hut.⁷ The conflict between son-in-law and

---

4 The naturally arid lands of the Indus Delta largely depend for their fertility on the waters of the Indus.

5 According to the Greek historian Herodotus, the noble Persians had agreed that they would ride out the next morning into the suburbs of the city, and he whose steed first neighed after the sun was up should have the kingdom. A sharp-witted groom of Darius brought a mare, the favorite of the horse which his master rode, to the suburb the night before. When the nobles neared the spot where the mare was, Darius' stallion sprang forward and neighed. The nobles recognized Darius as their king.

6 Eteocles and Polyneices, the sons of Oedipus, who, in fighting for the throne of Thebes, fell each by the other's hand.

7 Romulus and Remus.

father-in-law[8] involved the whole world, and the fortunes of so great an empire had no room for two.

7 'Mark these additional instances: bees have but one queen, flocks but one bellwether, herds but one leader. How can you assume that in heaven the supreme power is divided, the absolute sovereignty of that true and divine Authority is split, when it is as clear as daylight that God, the Author of all, has neither a beginning nor an end? While giving birth to all things, He has given to Himself eternal life; before creating this world, He has been a world unto Himself; by His word He calls into existence all things that are, disposes them according to His wisdom, and perfects them by His goodness.

8 'God is invisible, because too bright for our sight; intangible, because too fine for our sense of touch; immeasurable, because He is beyond the grasp of our senses; infinite, limitless, His real magnitude being known to Himself alone. Our intelligence is too limited to comprehend Him, therefore we can only measure Him fittingly when we call Him immeasurable. 9 Here is my candid opinion: a man who thinks to know God's magnitude diminishes it; he who does not wish to diminish it knows it not.

10 'Nor should one search for a name for God: "God" is His name. There is a need for names when, among a crowd, individuals have to be distinguished by giving them their specific appellations. To God, who is the only One, the

---

8 Caesar and Pompey. The latter had married the former's daughter, Julia, in 59 B.C., after the two men, with Crassus, had formed the first triumvirate. Though the issue between Caesar and Pompey was decided by the battle of Pharsalus in 48 B.C., the Pompeians held out for years in Spain, Africa, and Sicily. The campaigns caused untold loss and misery in the western Mediterranean.

name "God" belongs in an exclusive and total manner. If I should call Him "Father," you would think Him made of flesh; if "King," you would infer that He is of this world; if "Lord," you surely would understand Him to be a mortal. Away with these added names, and you will behold Him in His splendor.

11 'Besides, do not all men share my opinion about this point? Hearken to the common people: when they stretch forth their hands to heaven, they say nothing else but "God" or "God is great" or "God is true" or "If God grant it." Is that the natural language of the common crowd or is it the prayerful profession of faith made by a Christian?[9] Even those who acknowledge Jupiter to be supreme err, to be sure, concerning the name, but are in agreement about the one indivisible power.

Chapter 19

1 'I hear poets, too, proclaiming one "Father of gods and men,"[1] and declaring that "Such are the minds of men, as is the daylight which the Father of all made shine forth."[2] 2 What about Mantuan Maro? Are not his words even more clear, more exact, and more truthful when he says that "from the beginning heaven and earth" and the other parts of the universe "are sustained by an indwelling spirit and moved by an infused mind; thence comes the race of men and of the flocks"[3] and of all the other living creatures. The same poet elsewhere calls the mind and spirit God; his words are these:

---

9 Cf. Tertullian, *Apology* 17.6: 'O testimony of the soul, which is by natural instinct Christian!'

1 Cf. Homer, *Odyssey* 18.137; Vergil, *Aeneid* 10.2.
2 Cf. Homer, *Odyssey* 18.136f.
3 Cf. P. Vergilius Maro (born at Andes, a small village near Mantua in Cisalpine Gaul in 70 B.C.), *Aeneid* 6.724-729.

"For God pervades the whole,
All lands, and tracts of the sea, and the farthest reach of heaven,
Whence come the race of men and the flocks, whence rain and fire."[4]

What else is the God whom we proclaim but mind and reason and spirit?

3 'Next, with your leave, let us review the teaching of the philosophers. You will discover that, although their phraseology differs, in the main they are in complete agreement on this one point. 4 I pass over those unsophisticated men of old who earned the name of Wise Men from their sayings.[5] Let Milesian Thales[6] be mentioned first, because he was the earliest to discuss heavenly matters. This Thales of Miletus asserted that water was the first principle, and that God was the mind which formed everything from it (a theory of water and spirit much too lofty and sublime to be of human origin, and therefore based on divine revelation). So, you see that the teaching of the earliest of philosophers is in complete agreement

---

[4] The first two lines are from Vergil's *Georgics* 4.221f.; the third line from his *Aeneid* 1.743.
[5] According to Hermippus, a Greek comic poet of the 5th century B.C., the 'Seven Wise Men' were seventeen, for different Greeks made different lists of them. Their sayings became proverbial among the Greeks.
[6] Philosophy was a creation of the sixth-century Ionian Greeks. Previously, the Greeks, like the Orientals, explained natural phenomena as actions of the gods. Then, men in Ionia recognized the regularity of nature and, for the first time, sought for the laws which govern the universe. In their naive self-confidence, they did not reason inductively, but rather relied upon speculative thought and sought for the first principle, the origin of all things. They came to contradictory conclusions. Hence, the first principle for Thales of Miletus was water; for Anaximander, the infinite, with no specific qualities; for Anaximenes, air. Yet, they deserve great praise for recognizing the existence of this problem and for being the first to consider knowledge a striving for truth, utterly divorced from practical application.

with ours. 5 Next comes Anaximenes, and after him Diogenes of Apollonia,[7] who affirm the air to be God, infinite and immeasurable; these two philosophers, then, also similarly agree as to the nature of the Deity. 6 By Anaxagoras[8] God is called the infinite intelligence, disposing and moving, and for Pythagoras[9] God is mind, permeating and commensurate with the entire nature of creation, from which also springs the life of all living things. 7 That Xenophanes[10] taught the infinite All, endowed with intelligence, to be God is well known; so is the assertion of Antisthenes[11] that there were many gods in popular religion, but only One supreme in nature; and that Speusippus[12] recognized as God that vital force by which all things are governed. 8 Why, even Democritus,[13] though he was the first to advance the atomic theory, frequently speaks of nature, the font of imagination, and of intelligence, as God. Strato[14] also speaks of nature as God. The well-known Epicurus[15] also, who conceives of the gods either as having no

---

7 Diogenes of Apollonia (5th century B.C.) went beyond Anaximenes in that he not only considered air the first principle, but he also attributed to it mental qualities, reason, and knowledge.
8 Anaxagoras of Clazomenae (500-428 B.C.), the father of the philosophical concept of God, declared that, besides the elements, there exists one basic force. He called this force Mind, the moving and ordering principle of the universe.
9 Pythagoras (ca. 580-500 B.C.) found the most characteristic quality of the world to be the purposeful order and regularity which he saw everywhere. As a mathematician, he expressed this order and regularity by number and called the universe *kosmos,* a well-ordered structure.
10 Xenophanes of Colophon (ca. 580-485 B.C.) was the founder of the Eleatic School, called after Elea in South Italy, where these philosophers resided. They asserted that the first principle must not only be eternal, but also of an unchanging unity, from which results the flux and variety of forms.
11 Antisthenes of Cyrene (444-365 B.C.) was the founder of the Cynic School.
12 Speusippus was the successor of Plato in the Academy; cf. Ch. 13, n. 3.
13 Cf. Ch. 5, n. 4.
14 Strato of Lampsacus succeeded (in 288 B.C.) Theophrastus as head of the Peripatetic School.
15 Cf. Ch. 5, n. 4.

active interest or as non-existent, places nature above them.
9 Aristotle[16] is not consistent, yet he also accepts a single
power: for sometimes he says that intelligence is God, at
another time the universe, and then at another he sets God
above the universe. Theophrastus[17] likewise is inconsistent,
sometimes making the universe supreme and sometimes divine
intelligence. Similarly, Heracleides of Pontus,[18] though he uses
varying terms, attributes to the universe divine intelligence.
10 As to Zeno, Chrysippus and Cleanthes,[19] though their
opinions are expressed in varied forms, they all boil down to
the idea of one and the same Providence. Cleanthes in one
instance speaks of God as intelligence, in another as the soul
of nature, in another as aether, and in most instances as reason. Zeno, his teacher, considers natural law, which is also
divine, the first principle of all things, though occasionally he
gives that prerogative to the aether, and sometimes to reason;
by identifying Juno with air, Jupiter with heaven, Neptune
with the sea, and Vulcan with fire, and pointing out that all
other gods of popular belief are similarly elements, the same
philosopher vigorously attacks and refutes a common error.
11 Chrysippus expresses almost the same opinion: he believes
that a divine force, endowed with reason, that nature, the
universe, and sometimes a fate-ordained necessity, are God,
and he follows Zeno in the latter's physiological interpreta-

---

16 Aristotle (382-322 B.C.), the most illustrious pupil of Plato, was the founder of the Peripatetic School. In reality, Aristotle conceived God, the mover of the universe and absolute Spirit, as distinct from the world.
17 Theophrastus (372-283 B.C.), Aristotle's most famous pupil, who wrote a classic treatise, *The History of Plants*.
18 Heracleides of Pontus (4th century B.C.) was a pupil of Plato.
19 Zeno of Citium in Cyprus (*ca.* 336-264 B.C.) was the founder of the Stoic School. He was succeeded first by Cleanthes of Assos and then by Chrysippus of Soli, who laid down the tenets of the school in many books. His pupil, Panaetius (*ca.* 185-110 B.C.), brought Stoicism to Rome.

tion of the poems of Hesiod, Homer, and Orpheus. 12 This is also the method of Diogenes of Babylonia[20] in his exposition and discussion of the birth of Jupiter, the origin of Minerva, and the like, that they are terms denoting cosmic occurrences, not gods. 13 Xenophon, the follower of Socrates, asserts that the form of the true God cannot be seen, and therefore ought not to be inquired into; according to Aristo,[21] the Stoic, it cannot be comprehended at all: both, then, grasped the majesty of God, while despairing of ever understanding Him. 14 Plato's discussion of God is clearer, both in subject matter and terminology, and would be altogether heavenly were it not at times adulterated by the admixture of political prejudices. In Plato's mind, as we see from his *Timaeus*,[22] God is by His very name the Begetter of the universe, the Artificer of the soul, the Builder of all that is in heaven and on earth. Moreover, it is difficult to discover Him, as Plato says in the Introduction, because of His extraordinary and unparalleled power, which is beyond measure and without parallel; and, once discovered, it is quite impossible to describe Him to the man in the street.

15 'Plato's position, then, is almost the same as ours; for we, too, recognize God and call Him the Father of all, but we never speak of Him in public, unless questioned by a judge on that account.

---

20 Diogenes of Seleucia (the Babylonian) was one of Chrysippus' successors in the 2nd century B.C.
21 Aristo of Chios was a pupil of Zeno.
22 In his dialogue, *Timaeus,* Plato develops his ideas concerning the origin of the world and God, the author and fashioner of the world. Cicero translated this dialogue into Latin and a part of this translation has come down to us.

Chapter 20

1 'I have now reported on the opinions of almost all the philosophers of great reputation, showing that they described God as one, though under many names. Indeed, one might think that either the Christians of today are philosophers or that the philosophers of old were already Christians.

2 'But, if the universe is governed by Providence and guided by the will of one God, our unsophisticated forefathers, delighted, or rather ensnared by their pet fables, ought not to rush us into agreeing with them. For, they are refuted by the teachings of their own philosophers, bolstered by the authority of reason and tradition. 3 Our ancestors were so ready to believe in any product of imagination that, without critical judgment, they accepted even such monstrous and marvellous wonders as Scylla[1] with many bodies, Chimaera[2] of many shapes, Hydra[3] being reborn from its life-giving wounds, and the Centaurs,[4] beings with the dual nature of horse and man.

---

1 Scylla was a monster which barked like a young dog, had six mouths and twelve front legs, and lived in a dark sea cave under a rock from which it snatched at its victims. On the opposite side was another rock, from under which Charybdis sucked in and spit out the sea water three times a day, thus causing a dangerous whirlpool. Odysseus was the sole survivor of a shipwreck at this place, probably the straits of Messina.
2 Chimaera was a fire-breathing female monster, resembling a lion in the fore part, a goat in the middle, and a dragon at the rear. In later antiquity, the legend was interpreted as a mythological explanation of the volcanic activity in the mountainous region of Lycia in Asia Minor.
3 Hydra, a gigantic, many-headed monster. Each head cut off brought forth two new ones. The monster haunted the marshes of Lerna by Argos. Its destruction, interpreted as the draining of the marshes, was one of the twelve 'labors' of Heracles.
4 A race of beings part horse, part man, dwelling in the mountains about Pelion. Greek art never tired of representing the struggle between the Centaurs and the Lapiths, a mountain tribe of Thessaly. The story probably symbolized the victory of man over untamed woodland nature. The most famous representation was on the western gable of the Doric temple of Zeus at Olympia.'

In short, whatever popular imagination could invent they were eager to hear. 4 What about those old women's tales of human beings turned into birds and wild beasts, and of people transformed into trees and flowers? If such things had ever happened, they would still happen today; but, since they cannot happen today, they never happened at all. 5 In a similar way, our ancestors were mistaken about their gods; uncritical, credulous, they formed their faith with naive simplicity. While religiously reverencing their kings, while longing to behold them in the form of images after their death, while eager to preserve their memory in statues, they made things which had begun as comforts in their grief into objects of their worship. 6 Finally, before the world lay open to commerce, and nations interchanged their rites and customs, each people venerated its founder, or some renowned leader, or virtuous queen of more than womanly strength, or the originator of some social institution or art, as a citizen deserving of the tribute of commemoration. Thus, a distinction was given to the dead and, at the same time, an example was set for future generations.

Chapter 21

1 'Read the works of the historians, or the writings of the philosophers, and you will come to the same conclusion as I.

'Euhemerus[1] gives a list of persons who were accepted as gods because of their merits as courageous leaders or benefactors; he enumerates the days on which they were born

---

1 According to Euhemerus of Messana in Sicily (*ca.* 300 B.C.), the gods were either personified powers of nature, or, more often, human heroes deified by popular imagination and gratitude for the benefits they had bestowed on mankind; religious ceremonies were originally exercises in commemoration of the dead. After its founder, this rationalistic school of thought is called Euhemerism.

and the places of their birth and burial, and points out, province by province, the local character of their cults, as of Dictaean Jupiter,² Delphic Apollo,³ Pharian Isis,⁴ and Eleusinian Ceres.⁵ 2 Prodicus⁶ declares that men were received among the gods who, in their wanderings, bestowed great blessings upon mankind by the discovery of new crops.⁷ The same line of argument is followed also by Persaeus⁸ who brings together under the same names the new crops and their discoverers, just as the comic poet says: "Venus pines away without Liber and Ceres."⁹ 3 The famous Alexander the Great, of Macedon,¹⁰ in a remarkable letter to his mother, wrote that his power had awed a priest into unfolding to him the secret concerning deified men: in it, he makes Vulcan first of the line,

---

2 According to a myth, which shows Minoan peculiarities, Zeus was nursed in a cave of Mount Dicte.
3 The most famous shrine of Apollo was at Delphi.
4 Pharos, a small island opposite Alexandria in Egypt, with a lighthouse for the safety of mariners. The adjective 'Pharian' is used metonymically for Egyptian. The cult of the Egyptian goddess found wide acceptance among the Greeks and Romans.
5 Cf. Ch. 6, n. 3.
6 Prodicus of Ceos was a sophist and contemporary of Socrates.
7 In a beautiful hymn to Demeter, we are told that the goddess came to Eleusis in search of her daughter Kore, whom Pluto, the god of the nether world, had abducted. In her grief, Demeter did not suffer the seed to grow in the earth, and men nearly died of hunger. After Zeus had compelled Pluto to send Kore back to the upper world for two thirds of the year, Demeter, the corn goddess, made the corn sprout. Isis is credited with the discovery of wheat and barley. Wine and the fig were the gifts of Dionysus.
8 Persaeus (3rd century B.C.) was a pupil of the Stoic philosopher Zeno.
9 The passage is quoted as a proverb by the Roman poet Terence (d. 159 B.C.) in his comedy, *The Eunuch* (733). The Roman god Liber was identified with Dionysus, the Greek god of wine.
10 After the conquest of Egypt in 331 B.C., Alexander the Great made a pilgrimage to the shrine of Zeus Ammon, a famous oracle of the ancient world. A priest there declared him the son of the god. The letter mentioned above is spurious. It is quoted also by Athenagoras (*Supplication for the Christians* 28), St. Cyprian (*The Idols are not Gods 3*), and St. Augustine (*City of God* 8.5.27).

followed by the family of Jupiter. 4 As a matter of fact, according to all Greek and Roman writers of antiquities, Saturn, the fountainhead of this clan and host, was a mortal. Nepos[11] and Cassius[12] give testimony to this tradition in their annals, and Thallus[13] and Diodorus[14] say the same. 5 As the story goes, this Saturn was a fugitive from Crete, who, out of fear of his son's raging cruelty, had come to Italy where he was hospitably received by Janus. Since he was a refined and highly cultured Greek, he taught the unpolished and rustic people of that country many arts, such as writing, minting coins, and manufacturing implements. 6 For his hiding place, because he had kept in safe hiding there, he chose the name of Latium,[15] while the Saturnian city,[16] called by his own name, and the Janiculum,[17] named after Janus, have perpetuated the memory of both men among later generations. 7 At any rate, a fugitive and one who remained in hiding, he was a man, and a father of a man as well as a son of a man. For, he was considered a son of Earth and Heaven merely because his parents were unknown to the people of Italy, just as to this day we speak of those whom we come across quite un-

---

11 The biographer Cornelius Nepos (1st century B.C.) also wrote a world chronicle in three books, with special emphasis on Roman history.
12 L. Cassius Hemina (2nd century B.C.) wrote four books of *Annals*, comprising all of Roman history up to his time.
13 Thallus (1st century A.D.) is the author of a chronography in three books, from the Assyrian king Belus to his own time.
14 The *Historical Library* of Diodorus of Sicily, a contemporary of Caesar and Augustus, is a universal history.
15 The false popular etymology of Latium, which is probably taken from Vergil (*Aeneid* 8.322f.): *Latebrae* (hiding place), *latere* (to hide) = *Latium*, cannot be rendered in English. It is also found in Ovid, *Fasti* 1.238.
16 According to the Roman antiquarian Varro, the Capitol was also called the Saturnian hill, and the settlement on it, the Saturnian city. Cf. also Vergil, *Aeneid* 8.357f.
17 The Janiculum is one of the hills of Rome, on the right bank of the Tiber.

expectedly as having dropped right out of the sky, and of people of lowly and obscure social status as sons of earth.[18]
8 His son Jupiter, after his father's expulsion, ruled over Crete; there, he died and had sons. The cave of Jupiter still attracts visitors to whom his tomb is also pointed out,[19] and the cult paid to him suffices to prove his human nature.

9 'It is superfluous to examine the gods one by one, and to set forth the entire genealogy of that race, since the mortal nature, established in the case of the first parents, has been transmitted to the rest of them by the very order of succession. But, perhaps you think that they have become gods after death, as Romulus was made a god by the false oath of Proculus,[20] Juba deified by the will of the Mauretanians,[21] and the other kings placed among the gods.[22] Yet they were apotheosized, not for the sake of testifying to their divinity, but in order to honor the memory of their reign deserving of

---

18 The idea of the origin of the human race from Earth, the All-Mother, was very familiar to ancient man. In his *Metamorphoses*, Ovid tells the story of Deucalion and Pyrrha, who consulted the oracle of Themis at Delphi after the flood and were told to repopulate the earth with men by throwing the bones of their great mother behind them. The meaning was that the great mother was the earth, and the stones in the body of the earth were the bones. The expression 'son of earth' became proverbial.
19 The isolated peak of Mt. Iouktas, almost due south of Candia, the largest city of Crete, was regarded as the burial place of Zeus.
20 According to a story preserved in Livy and Cicero's *Republic*, Romulus appeared to Julius Proculus in a form of more than mortal majesty and bade him convey to the Romans his wish for divine worship.
21 Juba II, son of King Juba I of Numidia, was transferred by Augustus to Mauretania. He won the hearts of his subjects, and a reputation for wisdom and learning. An inscription, discovered in Morocco, mentions Juba, beside Jupiter and a local Genius.
22 Divine worship paid to a ruler was common in ancient Egypt, Babylonia, and Assyria. It was embodied in a western ruler in the person of Alexander the Great, and survived in the different realms of his successors. It was this type of Graeco-Oriental monarchy that influenced Roman Caesarism and made the Roman Emperor an object of worship.

reward. 10 In short, this appellation is forced upon them against their will: they would like to remain men; they dread becoming gods;[23] in spite of old age, they do not want it.

11 'Consequently, men who have died cannot become gods, because a god cannot die; neither can men who have been born, because everything that is born dies: that alone is divine which has neither beginning nor end. Why, I pray, are gods not born today, if such have ever been born? Is it, perhaps, because Jupiter has become old, Juno barren, and Minerva gray before she came to motherhood? Or has that procreation ceased, because fables of this sort have been universally discredited?

12 'Besides, if gods were able to propagate their race, but could not die, we would see the number of gods far exceed that of all mankind combined, so that by now neither heaven could receive them, nor the air hold them, nor the earth support them. Hence, it is evident that those gods were men whom we read were born and whom we know died.

Chapter 22

1 'Who can doubt that it is to the consecrated images of such men that the common folk pray and pay public worship, while the imagination and judgment of their undiscriminating minds is led astray by the artistic beauty of style, blinded by the glitter of gold, dulled by the lustre of silver and the whiteness of ivory? 2 But, if anyone would turn over in his mind by what instruments of torture and by what devices the image of a god is shaped, he would blush at the thought of being afraid of raw material which the playful fancy of an artist has metamorphosed into a god. 3 A god of wood, a piece

---

[23] According to Suetonius, Emperor Vespasian said, when he felt himself dying: 'Bad luck! I think I am turning into a god.'

taken perhaps from a funeral pile or a gibbet, is hung up, rough-hewed, chiselled, and smoothed. 4 A god of bronze or silver, very often made of a dirty vessel, as happened at the command of an Egyptian king,[1] is melted down, pounded with hammers, and forged into shape on anvils. A god of stone, cut, carved, and polished by some vile fellow, feels the disgrace of his birth no more than he afterwards feels the honor conferred on him by your worship.

5 'Perhaps you reply that the stone, or wood, or silver is not yet a god. When, then, does he come into existence? Behold! here he is cast, carved, sculptured; he is not yet a god. Lo! here he is soldered, put together, set up; he is not yet a god. See! here he is adorned, consecrated, supplicated; now at last he is a god, that is, when man has designated and dedicated him as such.

6 'How much more accurately do the dumb animals in their natural instinct size up these gods of yours! Mice, swallows, kites know that they have no feeling: they gnaw them, trample and perch on them, and, if you do not chase them away, build their nests in the very mouth of your god; spiders spin their webs across his face and attach their threads to his head. 7 You wipe these images clean, and scrape them; you both protect and dread your own creations; while none of you realizes that he ought to know a god before he worships him; while you, in cheerful yet thoughtless obedience to your parents, prefer to join others in their error rather than to trust yourselves; while you know nothing of the things of which you are afraid. Thus, avarice is consecrated in gold

---

[1] At first, the subjects of King Amasis of Egypt (569-525 B.C.) looked down on him because he came from an undistinguished house. The king caused a golden foot pan to be broken into pieces and made into an image of a god. This image was worshipped by the Egyptians with the utmost reverence. Amasis pointed this out to his subjects and asked them to draw a lesson therefrom. In this way, we are told by Herodotus, he won over the Egyptians.

and silver; thus, prestige is given to the form of empty statues; thus, superstition came into existence among the Romans.

8 'If you examine their rites, how much will you find that is ridiculous, how much that is even pitiable! Some run about naked in the bitter cold of winter;[2] others march in procession with felt caps on their heads and carry around old shields;[3] others beat their drums and lead their gods around from street to street, while begging alms.[4] In some shrines, visitors are allowed but once a year; some cannot lawfully be entered at all.[5] There are places from which men are barred[6] and sacred rites to which no women are admitted;[7] even the presence of a slave at certain ceremonies is an evil act which requires expiation.[8] Some sacred objects are crowned with garlands by a woman who has been married but once; others by a woman who has been married several times; and, with great religious scrupulosity, search is made for the champion

---

2 On the festival of the Lupercalia (February 15th), the priests of the god Faunus, clad only in the fleece of a goat, ran around the Palatine hill, drawing a magic circle which nothing evil could pass.
3 The Salii, or dancing priests of Mars, wearing high conical caps, marched through the city for many days in the month of March, singing their ancient hymns and clashing their spears against their shields.
4 The priests of Atargatis, whom the Romans called the Syrian goddess, held processions through the streets of the city, performing frenzied dances, inflicting wounds on their own bodies, and collecting coins from the spectators. Similar ceremonies occurred in the cults of Cybele and Bellona.
5 According to Pausanias, men could enter the shrine of Kore at Megalopolis in Arcadia only once a year; the temple of Poseidon at Mantinea was always closed.
6 There was a temple and grove of Demeter, near Megalopolis in Arcadia, which only women were allowed to enter. Men were excluded from the Thesmophoria and some other festivals of Demeter, and they were not allowed to be present at the sacred rites of the Bona Dea (the Good Goddess).
7 Women were excluded from sacrifices to Silvanus.
8 Female slaves were excluded from the Matralia (June 11th), the festival of the Roman matrons in honor of the Mater Matuta. Foreign slaves, especially, were not allowed to take part in certain rites.

woman in adultery.⁹ 9 Do you not agree that a man who pours libations from his own blood and worships God by self-inflicted wounds[10] would better be godless than god-fearing in this fashion? Or, take a man who allows himself to be emasculated[11] — with what insolence does he treat God, whom he hopes to appease in this manner! If God wanted eunuchs, could He not create them without resorting to artificial production?

10 'Is there anyone who cannot see that only deranged minds lacking common sense and reality, could fall into such absurdities, and that the very numbers of those going astray affords them mutual protection? In this case the defense of general insanity rests in the great number of the insane.

Chapter 23

1 'Finally, consider the sacred rites and mysteries themselves: you will find that the stories of those pitiable gods consist of tragic ends, dooms and burials, mourning and wailing.[1]

---

9 It may be that Minucius Felix here holds the same rigorous opinion concerning second and third nuptials as Tertullian, and calls them adulterous. Tertullian always merely tolerated marriage. In his treatise, *To My Wife (Ad uxorem)*, he exhorted his wife not to marry again after his death, or at least not to marry a pagan. In a second treatise, *Exhortation to Chastity*, he repeated this advice to a widowed friend in a much sharper tone. Finally, he made a last step toward error in his treatise, *On Monogamy*, by maintaining the absolute illicitness of second marriages.
10 The Bellonarii, priests of the goddess Bellona, who was identified with the goddess Mâ of Comana in Cappadocia, held wild processions through the city, inflicting wounds on their own arms and thighs, offering their blood as a sacrifice and sipping it, and prophesying in a frenzy of religious excitement.
11 Cybele and the Ephesian Artemis were served by eunuch priests. The ministers of Cybele were called Galli; those of Artemis, Megabyzi. At the great festival of the Syrian goddess, Atagartis, at Hierapolis on the Euphrates, the devotees of the goddess voluntarily sacrificed their virility.

Isis, with her dog-headed companion[2] and shaven priests, bemoans, bewails, and seeks her lost son;[3] her miserable followers beat their breasts and imitate the grief of the hapless mother. Soon, when the child is found, Isis rejoices, the priests exult, and the dog-headed finder boasts of his feat, and so, year in and year out, they do not cease losing what they find or finding what they lose. Is it not ridiculous either to mourn for what you worship or to worship for what you mourn? Yet, these rites, once strictly Egyptian, are now at home also in Rome,[4] so that you may make a fool of yourself with the swallow and rattle of Isis or before the empty tomb of your Serapis or Osiris, whose limbs are strewn about.

---

1 The myths of Isis, Demeter (Ceres), and Cybele, sketched in this chapter, are explanatory tales deriving the practices of original agrarian cults from exciting experiences of the goddesses, and suggesting a motive for, and an interpretation of, the rites commemorated in semi-dramatic form for the candidates at initiation. The essential point of these mysteries is that each of these three deities of vegetation is connected with a young god or goddess, whose annual loss and restoration to life, symbolizing the annual decay and revival of vegetation, was celebrated. We know very little about the central rites, since the silence imposed upon the initiated was well kept and the testimony given by Christian authors is not only fragmentary but subject to doubts.

2 The dog-headed companion of Isis is Anubis, who is depicted with a human body and the head of a jackal.

3 This is a mistake. It is not her son whom Isis seeks, but her husband Osiris, also known as Serapis.

4 The cult of Isis invaded Rome during the 1st century B.C. Unlike the cult of Cybele, which had been introduced by the state in 203 B.C., it spread by individual conversions. The emperors regarded it with suspicion until the Flavian period. Domitian, himself a devotee of Isis, favored it, and in the second and third centuries it enjoyed special vogue in aristocratic circles. The Latin text of the following lines, to the end of the sentence, has come down to us in such a corrupt form that it can hardly be reconstructed. The rattle (*sistrum*) is a musical instrument, formed of a loop of bronze ribbon fastened to a handle, crossed by three or four metal bars passing through holes in each side of the loop. It was used in the rites of Isis. Apuleius (2nd century A.D.), who, in his *Metamorphoses*, depicts the mysteries of the Egyptian goddess, also gives an exact description of the rattle.

2 'Ceres, anxious and careworn, with lighted torches and with a snake girt about her, traces in her wanderings her daughter Libera,[5] victim of abduction and violence: these are the Eleusinian mysteries. 3 And what are the rites of Jupiter? His nurse is a nanny-goat; as a babe he is snatched from his greedy father, lest he be eaten, and the Corybants' cymbals are clashed together with ringing sound, lest the father hear his crying.[6] 4 Modesty is loath to speak of the Dindymaean mysteries of Cybele.[7] When she could not entice to shame her unlawful lover, who unfortunately pleased her—for she was both old and ugly, being the mother of many gods—she mutilated him so as to make of him an unmanned god. Because of this tale, her Galli priests and unmanly followers worship her by the same physical disablement. Such things are not religious practices, they are tortures.

5 'Moreover, do not the very forms and appearances of your gods expose them to ridicule and contempt?—Vulcan,[8] a lame and crippled god; Apollo, still beardless after all the years; Aesculapius, with a bushy beard, although he is the son of the ever-youthful Apollo; Neptune, with sea-green eyes; Minerva, cat-eyed; Juno, ox-eyed; Mercury,[9] with

---
[5] Libera is the Greek Kore. Cf. Ch. 21, n. 7.
[6] According to the common myth, which is probably of Minoan origin, Rhea, the mother of Zeus, hid the infant in a cave away from Cronus, who devoured his new-born children. There, the infant was suckled by the goat Amalthea. The task of watching it was entrusted to the Curetes, who drowned the cries of the infant by the noise they made with their bronze weapons. The Curetes were later identified with the Corybantes, the priests of Cybele; hence, also, the cymbals, the musical instruments used on the festivals of that goddess. The basis of this cult of Zeus was likewise agrarian. The infant was born annually; it was the year god, the spirit of fertility, the new life of spring.
[7] On Mount Dindymus in Phrygia stood the earliest sanctuary of the goddess.
[8] Vulcan, identified with the Greek Hephaestus, was said to have been crippled when he was thrown from Olympus by the angry Zeus.
[9] Mercury, identified with the Greek Hermes, was the messenger of the gods and, hence, represented with wings on his feet.

winged feet; Pan,[10] with hoofs; Saturn,[11] with shackled feet. Yes, and Janus[12] sports two faces as if he meant to walk backward, also; Diana[13] is sometimes short-skirted like a huntress, while at Ephesus[14] she is represented with many breasts and paps, and, as goddess of the crossroads,[15] she is horrible to behold, with three heads and many hands. 6 Why, your Jupiter himself is at one time shown beardless and at another is displayed with a beard. When he is called Hammon,[16] he has horns; when the Capitoline, he wields thunderbolts; when Latiaris,[17] he is drenched in blood; and as Feretrius,[18] he wears a wreath. And, not to linger too long over multitudinous Jupiters, there are as many strange forms for him as there are names. 7 Erigone[19] hanged herself that she

---

10 Pan was the Arcadian god of the hills and woods, flocks, and herdsmen. He was represented with a pug nose, a beard, shaggy hair, and goat's feet.
11 Saturn, originally a seed spirit, was identified with the Greek Cronus. According to the myth, Cronus and the Titans were condemned to the Tartarus by Zeus.
12 Janus was the guardian spirit of entrances. His double-headed figure, placed in gateways (called *jani*), signified that he was concerned with entrance and exit.
13 Diana was identified with the Greek Artemis, the goddess of the hunt and of wild nature who haunts the mountains and forests.
14 The great goddess of motherhood and fertility in Asia Minor—for instance, the Ephesian goddess—came to be identified with Artemis.
15 From the time of Ennius (239-169 B.C.), the Greek goddess Hecate was called Diana by Roman poets. She could not only avert magical evils, but was the goddess of witchcraft who walked at crossroads on moonless nights, accompanied by ghosts. Hence, images of Hecate were set up at crossroads. Her image was triple because she had to look in three directions (crossroads, Lat. *trivia*, where three roads meet).
16 Hammon, the Egyptian god Ammon, was identified with Zeus-Jupiter. He was represented in the shape of a ram with curving horns.
17 The Feriae Latinae, the great Latin festival, was held on the Alban Mount, the religious center of all the Latin stock. Here, a pure white heifer was sacrificed to Jupiter and its flesh divided among the deputies of all the Latin communities, to signify their common kinship of blood.
18 The meaning of this cult title is disputed.
19 With the help of her faithful dog, Maera, Erigone searched for the body of her slain father, Icarius. When she had found it, she hanged herself on a tree over the tomb. Zeus or Dionysus placed all three among the stars, Erigone as Virgo.

might shine as Virgo among the stars; Castor and his twin brother [20] take turns in dying in order to live; Aesculapius[21] is struck by lightning that he may rise a god; and Hercules,[22] to shake off this mortal coil, is consumed by fire on Mount Oeta.

Chapter 24

1 'These fables and absurdities we learn from our unenlightened parents. What is worse, we improve them with great care by our own studies and subjects of instruction, especially in the works of the poets who have done the greatest possible harm to the truth because of the high esteem in which they are held. 2 Rightly, therefore, did Plato[1] exclude the renowned poet Homer, praised and crowned with laurel though he was, from the ideal state which he contrived in his dialogue. 3 For he, above all others, in his story of the Trojan War, entangled your gods in the affairs and deeds of men, even though he does it in a playful manner. He arranged them in pairs;[2] he wounded Venus;[3] he chained Mars, and hurt him,

---

20 The twin brothers were born of the same mother, Leda, but by different fathers: Pollux was begotten by Zeus, and hence immortal; Castor was begotten by Leda's human husband, Tyndareus, and hence mortal. After Castor had been killed in combat, Zeus allowed them to spend half their time together beneath the earth and half in heaven.
21 Aesculapius was so good a physician that Hades, the god of the nether world, complained to Zeus that the rate of mortality was being lowered every day. Thereupon, Zeus killed the too skillful physician with a thunderbolt, but raised him to the rank of a god.
22 Deianira, wife of Hercules, sent her husband a robe stained with the poisoned blood of the centaur Nessus thus unwittingly causing her husband's death. A funeral pile was built for him on the top of Mount Oeta. When the flames started to burn, a cloud descended from the sky with thunder and lightning and carried Hercules to heaven.

---

1 In his *Republic* 3.9 (p. 398A).
2 *Iliad* 20.67ff.
3 Venus (Aphrodite) was wounded by Diomedes (*ibid.* 5.330ff.).

and put him to flight.⁴ 4 He tells us that Jupiter was freed by Briareus, lest he be tied up by the other gods;⁵ that he wept showers of bloody tears for his son Sarpedon, because he could not snatch him from death;⁶ and that, enchanted by the girdle of Venus, he had more eager intercourse with his wife Juno than he was wont to have with others.⁷ 5 Elsewhere, Hercules clears stables of dung⁸ and Apollo tends the sheep of Admetus.⁹ Neptune built walls for Laomedon,¹⁰ and the luckless builder did not even get paid for his toil. 6 In another poet, Jupiter's thunderbolt is forged on the anvil with the arms of Aeneas,¹¹ though sky and thunder and lightning existed long before Jupiter was born in Crete, and no Cyclops could have imitated the flames of a real thunderbolt nor could Jupiter have failed to fear them. 7 Why should I mention Mars and Venus caught in adultery, and Jupiter's shameful infatuation for Ganymede,¹² sanctioned by heaven? All these stories have been brought forth with no other end in view than to furnish a certain justification for the vices of men.

8 'By these and such like inventions and charming fictions, the minds of boys are corrupted; with the same stories sticking

---

4 Mars (Ares) was bound in chains by Otus and Ephialtes (*ibid.* 5.385f.); wounded and put to flight by Diomedes (*ibid.* 5.855ff.).
5 When the gods intended to chain Zeus, Thetis summoned the hundred-handed Briareus to Olympus (*ibid.* 1.396ff.).
6 Sarpedon was killed by Patroclus (*ibid.* 16.459ff.).
7 *Ibid.* 14.312ff.
8 One of the twelve famous 'labors' of Heracles. In one day he cleaned all the stables of Augias, king of Elis, by diverting the rivers Alpheus and Peneus into the stables.
9 Zeus forced Apollo, who had killed the Cyclopes for having forged the thunderbolt, to tend the flocks of Admetus, king of Thessalian Pherae.
10 King of Troy.
11 Vergil, *Aeneid* 8.423ff.
12 Zeus had the handsome Ganymede kidnapped by an eagle in order to make him his cupbearer at Olympus.

in their memories, they grow to the full strength of their mature years; and, in the same opinions, the poor fellows grow old, though the truth is plain to see if they would only look for it.

Chapter 25

1 'But, you claim, it was that very superstition which gave the Romans their empire, enlarged it, and laid its solid foundation, since they became powerful not so much by valor as by reverence for and dutiful conduct toward the gods. Most certainly! The glorious and celebrated Roman justice made an auspicious beginning while the infant empire still lay in its cradle! 2 Is it not true that their history began with a partnership in crime, and that they owed their growth in power to the immunity resulting from the terror of their savagery? For it was to an asylum[1] that the first *plebs* was gathered; into it poured a stream of scamps, criminals, lewd fellows, assassins, and traitors; and Romulus himself, their commander and leader, in order to outstrip his people in crime, slew his own brother. Such were the first auspices of our god-fearing commonwealth. 3 Shortly afterward, ignoring time-honored custom, they seized the maidens of another people[2]—some of them betrothed, some promised, and some of them already married women—outraged them, and made sport of them. Then, they went to war with their parents, in other words, with their own fathers-in-law, shedding kindred blood. What deed could be more irreligious, more audacious, or show more

---
1 In order to promote the growth of the first settlement on the Palatine hill, Romulus, according to Livy, declared it a place of refuge (*asylum*) into which men of all sorts were received.
2 Since this settlement was a community of men only, and they could not get women in a peaceful way, they took them by force from neighboring settlements. This was the famous rape of the Sabine girls.

impudent confidence in the success of crime? 4 Thenceforward, they drive out their neighbors from their lands, they overthrow neighboring states along with their temples and altars, enslave their peoples, and thus grow strong by other men's losses and their own evil deeds. This is the policy the succeeding kings and later Roman generals have in common with Romulus.

5 'Thus, whatever the Romans hold, inhabit and possess is the booty of their audacity. Their temples are built with plunder; I mean with the ruins of cities, the loot of gods, the slaughter of priests.

6 'It is an insult and a farce to pay homage to vanquished gods, to take them captive, and then, after the conquest, to worship them. For, to worship what you have carried off as booty is to consecrate sacrilege, not deities. Therefore, as often as Rome has triumphed, so often has she committed sacrilege, and her spoliations of gods are numbered as many as her trophies of victories over nations. 7 Consequently, the Romans owe their greatness not to their reverence for the gods, but to sacrileges committed with impunity. They could not reckon on the help of the gods, against whom they were taking up arms in these very wars. Yet, when they had laid them low and become their absolute masters, then they began to worship them. But, what can such gods do for the Romans, if they lacked the power of doing anything for their own people against Roman arms?

8 'We know the indigenous gods of the Romans: Romulus,[3]

---

[3] Cf. Ch. 21, n. 20.
[4] The god Picus appears not only in Rome but also among the Aequi, the Umbrians of Iguvium (Gubbio), and the Picentes. Concerning the last mentioned, the inhabitants of Picenum in Central Italy on the Adriatic coast, the geographer Strabo (*ca.* 63 B.C.-24 A.D.) tells us: 'The Picentes proceeded originally from the land of the Sabines. A woodpecker led the way for their chieftains, and from this bird they have taken their name, it being called in their language *picus,* and it is regarded as sacred to Mars.' There was also the form Picumnus.

Picus,[4] Tiberinus,[5] Consus,[6] Pilumnus, and Volumnus.[7] Cloacina[8] was invented and her cult introduced by Tatius;[9] Pavor (*Panic*) and Pallor by Hostilius.[10] Soon after, someone or other made Febris (*Fever*) a goddess:[11] the cult of the latter—namely, of diseases and insanitary conditions—is the veritable foster mother of this noble city of yours. Yes, and I suppose Acca Larentia, too, and Flora,[12] harlots without shame, must be counted among the diseases of Rome—and her gods.

9 'These, of course, were the gods who made the sway of Rome prevail against the gods worshipped by other nations. Thracian Mars, or Cretan Jupiter, or Juno who is Argive,

---

Picumnus and Pilumnus, also mentioned in this list, were two brother deities and companions of Mars. The first was the personification of the woodpecker, the second a personification of the pestle (*pilum*). Both were tutelary spirits of married people and little children.

5 Rivers and springs were worshipped in Italy at a very early time. There was a shrine of 'Father Tiber' on the island of the Tiber at Rome.

6 Consus received his name from the hiding (*condere*) of the harvest. His altar, in the valley southwest of the Palatine, was under the ground and covered with earth, reminiscent of the early practice of hiding the fruits of the fields.

7 Volumnus (the 'well-wisher') was a tutelary spirit of new-born infants.

8 Cloacina was the goddess of drains at Rome.

9 Titus Tatius was a king of the Sabines, who afterwards reigned jointly with Romulus.

10 In Roman religion we meet a class of deities who are usually described as personifications of abstract ideas. Livy tells us that, in a war with the Veientes, Tullus Hostilius, one of the legendary kings of Rome, vowed shrines to Pavor and Pallor, personified gods of fear.

11 The Romans worshipped the mysterious power (*numen*), which they felt active in illnesses accompanied by fever (especially malaria), as *dea Febris* (goddess Fever). This deification of a hostile and malignant power was often attacked by such Christian writers as St. Cyprian, Lactantius, St. Jerome, St. Augustine, and Prudentius.

12 Both Acca Larentia and Flora were said by late writers to have been harlots. According to one story, Larentia, the foster-mother of Romulus and Remus, was a common prostitute; another burlesque tale made her a mistress of Hercules. Flora was the goddess of flowers. Her festival (April 28th) was often celebrated with unbridled license. The prostitutes of Rome hailed it as their feast day.

Samian and Carthaginian by turns, or Taurian Diana, or the Idaean Mother, or those Egyptian monsters—beware of calling them deities—have not rendered assistance to the Romans against their own people.

10 'Or do you claim, perhaps, that your virgins were more chaste and your priests more saintly men: when practically a majority of those virgins—those who were too indiscreet in their affairs with men (of course, without the knowledge of Vesta)—were punished for immorality while the rest were saved from punishment, not by a stricter observance of chastity, but by greater luck in keeping their unchasteness secret?[13] 11 And where, more than by priests among the altars and shrines, are lewd bargains made, the work of the pander carried on, and adulteries planned? In fine, flagrant lust is more frequently enjoyed in the small chambers of temple guardians than in the very houses of ill-fame.

12 'After all, before the Roman era, by the dispensation of God, Assyrians, Medes, Persians, Greeks, too, and Egyptians had long periods of imperial sway, though they had no Pontiffs, nor Arvals,[14] nor Salii,[15] nor Vestals, nor Augurs,[16] nor chickens kept safe in their coop, by whose appetite or lack of it state affairs of the highest importance were directed.[17]

---

13 The Vestal Virgins took care of the hearth fire of the state in the temple of Vesta on the Roman Forum. Both the temple and the house of the Vestals stood next to the *Regia,* the residence of the *pontifex maximus* under whose supervision the Vestals performed their duties. They lived a kind of monastic life and were bound to chastity. A Vestal violating this obligation was buried alive in an underground chamber close to the Colline Gate.
14 A college of twelve priests, who yearly made offerings to the tutelary deities of the fields for the growth of the crops.
15 Cf. Ch. 22, n. 3.
16 Cf. Ch. 7, n. 1.
17 Cf. Ch. 7, n. 8.

Chapter 26

1 'Next, I come to those famous Roman auspices and auguries which, collected with great labor, you have cited as showing that their neglect brought remorse; their observance, good fortune. 2 You claim that Clodius, Flaminius, and Junius[1] lost their armies because they did not think it necessary to wait for the most favorable omen from the chicken coop. 3 Well! Did Regulus[2] not observe the auguries, and was he not captured just the same? Mancinus[3] was most scrupulous in observing religious practices, yet he had to pass under the yoke, and was handed over to the enemy. Paulus[4] also had chickens which greedily ate their food, yet at Cannae he was crushed with the greater part of the Republic's forces. 4 Gaius Caesar, on the other hand, when auguries and auspices forbade his sending the fleet across to Africa before winter, spurned them; as a result, he made the crossing and won his victory all the more easily.[5]

5 'In continuing my discussion, what shall I say, and to what extent shall I treat, of oracles? After his death, Amphiaraus[6] answered queries about the future—that same Amphiaraus who did not know that he would be betrayed by his wife for a necklace. Tiresias,[7] the blind man, would look into the

---

1 Cf. Ch. 7, n. 8 and 9.
2 Cf. Tertullian, *The Testimony of the Soul* 4, n. 4.
3 C. Hostilius Mancinus was defeated by the Numantines in Spain in 136 B.C., and concluded a treaty of peace with them. The treaty was not ratified by Rome, and Mancinus was delivered up to the Numantines.
4 L. Aemilius Paulus, one of the consuls of 216 B.C., fell in the battle of Cannae.
5 This occurred in December, 46 B.C., in Caesar's campaign in Africa. Cf. Ch. 18, n. 8.
6 A famous Greek seer who foresaw that he would die if he participated in the war against Thebes, and went into hiding. However, his wife Eriphyle disclosed his hiding place for a golden necklace.
7 Tiresias was struck blind by Hera, but received from Zeus the gift of prophecy.

future, though he could not see the things that happened right in front of him. 6 Ennius manufactured the responses of Pythian Apollo about Pyrrhus,[8] though Apollo had already ceased to speak in verses; that cautious and ambiguous oracle of his lost its influence when men began to be both more educated and less credulous. And Demosthenes, because he knew that the oracular responses were forged, complained that the Pythian priestess was 'Philippizing.'[9]

7 'Yet, once in a while, auspices or oracles have hit upon the truth. To be sure, one could believe that, among the many falsehoods, mere chance may have given the impression of methodical planning. Yet, I will approach to the very source of error and depravity, whence all this darkness has flowed, and try to dig it out more thoroughly and expose it more clearly to view.

8 'There exist deceitful and wandering spirits who have lost their heavenly vigor from having been dragged down by earthly stains and lusts. These spirits, then, burdened with and steeped in vice, have forfeited the original simplicity of their nature; now damned themselves, they seek to bring others to damnation as a consolation for their own ruin; perverted, they seek to spread their perverting error; cast out by God, they seek, by introducing wicked cults, to win others away from Him. 9 These spirits were known as 'demons' to the poets, were discussed by the philosophers, and were recognized by Socrates,[10] who, according to the command and will

---

[8] The oracle, preserved in the fragments of the *Annals* of the Roman poet Ennius (239-169 B.C.), was so ambiguously worded that both the Romans and Pyrrhus could expect victory.

[9] In the struggle of Philip of Macedon (359-336 B.C.) for the leadership of the Greeks, Demosthenes accused the Delphic priesthood of espousing Philip's cause.

[10] Minucius Felix regarded the *daimonion* of Socrates as evil. To Socrates, however, the word had a very different meaning. Cicero rendered it correctly by translating it as 'something divine.' The promptings of Socrates' *daimonion* were the dictates of conscience.

of his attendant demon, would reject or pursue a certain line of action. 10 The Magi, also, not only know these demons, but it is by their help that they perform their queer hocus-pocus; by their inspirations and intimations they produce their conjuring acts of making visible what is really not there, or of making invisible what is really there. 11 The foremost of these Magi both in eloquence and art, Hostanes,[11] renders due homage to the true God; he also recognizes that angels, that is, ministers and messengers, surround the throne of God and stand there to worship Him, trembling in awe of their Lord's nod and expression. The same Hostanes also has told us of earthly demons, wandering spirits, the enemies of mankind. 12 And what about Plato, who considered it a difficult task to discover God? Does he not speak of both angels and demons, without experiencing the same difficulty? And in his *Symposium* does he not endeavor to explain the nature of demons? He holds that there is a substance in between mortal and immortal, that is to say, halfway between body and spirit, compounded of a mixture of earthly weight and heavenly lightness. From this, he informs us, love is fashioned, slips into the hearts of men, stirs their feelings, forms their affections, and kindles the fire of passion.

Chapter 27

1 'These unclean spirits or demons, as it has been shown by Magi and philosophers, have their lurking places under statues and consecrated images.[1] By their suggestive power they acquire the authority of a present divinity; while at one

---

[11] In ancient literature, Hostanes is considered the unequalled master and expert in medicinal magic. His name occurs, for instance, in the great magic papyrus of Paris.

---

[1] That demons and gods could be conjured up, and confined especially within statues and images, was taken for granted by many pagans as well as early Christian writers.

time they inspire prophets or linger around temples, at another they animate the fibres of a sacrificed animal's entrails, or direct the flights of birds, or manage the drawing of lots, or produce oracles cloaked in plenty of falsehoods. 2 They deceive themselves as well as others, since they do not know the absolute truth, and what they know of it they do not confess to their own destruction. Thus, they drag men down from heaven and divert their minds from the true God to material things; they disturb their lives and trouble their slumbers; they even creep into their bodies stealthily, as subtle spirits, cause diseases, terrify minds, distort the limbs. By such practices, they force people to their worship and make them believe that, gratified by the fumes from altars and sacrifices of animals, they have effected a cure, while they have released only what they themselves had bound. 3 From the same sources comes the insanity of the maniacs whom you see running out into the streets; they, too, are seers —though outside the temple—but their raving, revelling, and whirling around is just the same; the same demoniac influence works in them, though the frenzy manifests itself in a different way. 4 The demons are responsible, also, for those things which you have mentioned a short while ago, that by a dream Jupiter demanded the renewal of the games in his honor,[2] that Castor and Pollux appeared with their horses,[3] that the boat followed a matron's girdle.[4]

5 'All of this, as the greater part of you know, the demons themselves admit to be their work, as often as they are driven out by us from men's bodies through the torture of exorcism and the fervor of prayer. 6 Saturn himself, Serapis, Jupiter, and the entire host of demons you worship, collapsing under

---

2 Cf. Ch. 7, n. 4.
3 Cf. Ch. 7, n. 3.
4 Cf. Ch. 7, n. 2.

the strain of vexation, say plainly what they are, and they certainly do not lie to bring disgrace upon themselves, especially when some of you are standing around. 7 Believe, then, their own testimony and truthful confession concerning themselves, that they are demons; for, when adjured by the true and one God, against their will, they quake with pitiable fear in those bodies, and either jump out at once, or vanish gradually, according to the strength of faith in the possessed or the gift of grace in the healer. Thus, at close quarters, they used to run away from Christians whom they had tried to assail before in their gatherings from a safe distance. 8 For this reason, they infiltrate into the minds of the ignorant and there secretly sow hatred against us by means of fear; for, it is natural to hate whom you fear, and, if possible, to attack whom you dread. Thus, they seize the minds and block the hearts, so that people may begin to hate us before even knowing us; lest, when they come to know us, they may imitate us or be unable to condemn us.

Chapter 28

1 'Accept it from us, as from people who remember with sorrow their own attitude, how unfair it is to pass judgment, as you do, without knowledge and examination of the facts.[1] 2 We, too, were once not different from you; still blind and ignorant, we thought the same as you, fancying that Christians worshipped monsters, devoured infants, and joined in incestuous banquets. We were unaware that it was by the demons that such stories were continually spread about, without ever being investigated or proved; that in all that time there was not one who played the traitor in order to gain not only par-

---

[1] This and the following refer to the time when Octavius and Minucius, both of them lawyers, were still pagans.

don for his offense, but also reward for his denunciation; and that criminal action is so little involved that Christians, when accused, neither blushed nor were afraid, but regretted one thing only: not having been Christians sooner. 3 Yet we, while accustomed to undertake the defense and protection of men guilty of sacrilege, incest, and even murder of close relatives, thought the Christians not even entitled to a hearing. Sometimes, using pity as a pretext, we were even more ruthless and cruel. We tortured those who confessed, to make them recant, in order to save their lives. Thus, in their case, we applied an absurd trial procedure, calculated not to elicit the truth but to compel people to lie. 4 And, if anyone, weaker than his brethren, collapsed under the pressure of pain and denied that he was a Christian, then we used to be kindly disposed toward him, as if, after abjuring the Christian name, forthwith by this denial he had made amends for all the wrong done by him. 5 Do you recognize that we felt and acted in precisely the same way you feel and act now? Whereas, if reason were the judge, and not a goading demon, more pressure should be put on them, not for making them deny their Christian faith, but for making them confess their incestuous lewdness, impious rites, and child sacrifices. 6 For, it is with these and such like stories that the same demons stuff the ears of the ignorant in order to make us an object of detestation and execration. Nor should we think this strange, since common gossip, which always lives on the spreading of falsehoods and fades away in the clear light of truth, is likewise the work of the demons; it is by them that false rumor is sown and kept circulating about.

7 'This explains the story you have from hearsay, that an ass's head is the object of our worship. Who is so big a fool as to worship such a thing? And a bigger fool still, to believe in the existence of such a worship? Unless it would be such

among you, as those who consecrate whole asses in their stables together with your or their Epona,[2] or those who eat the same animals piously in company with Isis,[3] or those who sacrifice as well as worship the heads of oxen and wethers, and, finally, those who pay divine honors to gods half-goat and half-man,[4] or to lion- and dog-faced deities. 8 Do you not join with the Egyptians in adoring and feeding the bull Apis? And you do not disapprove of their cults of snakes and crocodiles and all the other beasts and birds and fish;[5] and whosoever kills even one of these animal gods suffers the death penalty. 9 The same Egyptians, like a great many of you, dread Isis no more than the pungent smell of onions,[6] and have no greater fear of Serapis than of the noises caused by certain parts of the body.

10 'In like manner, he who peddles slanderous stories about our adoring the genitals of a priest only tries to burden us with his own misdeeds. Such obscenities may be considered holy rites where people of either sex offer themselves to indiscriminate lewdness, where shamelessness of every kind is called good breeding, where harlots are envied because of their dissoluteness, . . . where people have wicked tongues even if they keep silent, and grow weary of their shamelessness before being ashamed of it. 11 O horrible! These offenses they commit against themselves are too shocking even

---

2 The Celtic goddess of stables, horses, mules, and asses.
3 Plutarch (ca. 46-120 A.D.) tells us that, on a certain feast of Isis, the Egyptians made cakes in the form of a chained ass. Sacrificial cakes in animal form were substituted for real victims. As was the custom in sacrifices, a small portion was reserved for the deity; the greater part was consumed by the worshippers.
4 The god Pan and his attendants, the fauns and satyrs.
5 The animal worship usually attributed to Egypt was a degeneration belonging to the last stage of the dying Egyptian religion. Originally, the animals were not gods, but only symbols of divine beings.
6 Minucius Felix refers to a special food taboo. We know from other ancient writers that the Egyptians were not allowed to eat onions.

for the tolerance of our liberal-minded age; nor could they be forced upon slaves who are more hardened in vice.

Chapter 29

1 'These and similar indecencies are taboo to our ears, and discussing them at greater length than necessary, even for the sake of self-defense, is considered immoral. People who live a chaste and virtuous life are falsely charged by you with acts which we would not consider possible, if you did not prove them by your own conduct.

2 'Moreover, when you ascribe to us the worship of a malefactor and his cross, you are traveling a long way from the truth, in assuming that an evil-doer deserved, or a mortal could bring it about, to be believed in as God. 3 That man is to be pitied indeed whose entire hope rests on a mortal man, at whose death all assistance coming from him is at an end. 4 I grant you that the Egyptians choose a man for their worship; they propitiate only him, they consult him on all matters, they slay sacrificial victims in his honor. Yet, though he is a god in the eyes of others, in his own he is certainly a man, whether he likes it or not, for he does not deceive his own consciousness, whatever he does to that of others. 5 The same applies to princes and kings, who are not hailed as great and outstanding men, as would be proper, but overwhelmed with flatteries falsely praising them as gods; whereas, honor would be the most fitting tribute to a man of distinction and affection the greatest comfort to a benefactor. But, it is in this way that people invoke the divinity of these men, pray to their statues, implore their genius, that is, their demon, and think it safer to swear a false oath by the genius of Jupiter than by that of their king.

6 'As to crosses, we do not adore them, nor do we wish for them. It is clearly you who, consecrating gods made of wood, in all likelihood adore wooden crosses as essential parts of your gods. 7 What else are your military standards and banners and ensigns but gilded and decorated crosses? Your trophies of victory represent not only the shape of a simple cross, but even that of a man fastened to it. 8 Indeed, we see the sign of the cross naturally formed by a ship when it carries a full press of sail, or when it glides over the sea with outspread oars. When a crossbeam is raised aloft, it forms the sign of a cross; so, too, when a man stretches out his hands to worship God with a pure heart. In this way, the sign of the cross either is the basis of the system of nature or it shapes the objects of your cult.

Chapter 30

1 'Next, I should like to challenge the man who says or believes that the rites of our initiation are concerned with the slaughter and blood of an infant. Do you think it possible that so tender and so tiny a body could be the object of fatal wounds? that anyone would murder a babe, hardly brought into the world, and shed and sip that infant blood? No one can believe this, except one who has the heart to do it. 2 In fact, it is among you that I see newly-begotten sons at times exposed to wild beasts and birds, or dispatched by the violent death of strangulation; and there are women who, by the use of medicinal potions, destroy the nascent life in their wombs, and murder the child before they bring it forth.

3 'These practices undoubtedly are derived from a custom established by your gods: Saturn, though he did not expose his sons, certainly devoured them. Accordingly, in some parts

of Africa, infants are sacrificed to him[1] by their parents, who stifle their squalling by caresses and kisses to prevent the sacrifice of a tearful victim. 4 Moreover, it was a custom among the Taurians on the Black Sea[2] and for the Egyptian king Busiris to sacrifice strangers,[3] as it was with the Gauls to slay human, or rather inhuman, victims.[4] It was a sacrifice peculiar to the Romans to bury alive a Greek man and woman, and a Gallic man and woman.[5] Even today, their worship of Jupiter Latiaris includes a human sacrifice,[6] and, as befits the son of Saturn, he gorges upon the blood of a scoundrel and evil-doer. 5 It was he, I believe, who taught Catiline to league his fellow conspirators by a covenant of blood,[7] and Bellona to initiate her devotees into her cult by the sipping of human blood,[8] and to cure epilepsy with the blood of a man,[9] that is, a grave ill with one graver. 6 They are not unlike those who feast on wild beasts from the arena, still smeared and tainted with human blood and stuffed with the

---

1 Saturn was identified with the Phoenician Ba'alchammân to whom, according to a number of ancient pagan and Christian writers, human sacrifices were offered. Cf., for instance, St. Augustine, *City of God* 7.19: 'Then he [Varro] says that boys were wont to be immolated to him [Saturn] by certain peoples, the Carthaginians for instance.'
2 Cf. Ch. 6, n. 8.
3 Busiris was a mythical king of Egypt, who sacrificed strangers who had landed in his country.
4 Cf. Ch. 6, n. 9.
5 Livy reports that twice toward the close of the third century B.C. the sacrifice of a pair of Gauls and Greeks was accomplished by burial alive, a practice which seems to have come from the Etruscans, human sacrifices being originally foreign to Rome.
6 The reports we have on human sacrifices in the cult of Jupiter Latiaris are of a late date. Cf. Ch. 23, n. 17.
7 The Roman historian Sallust tells of the rumor that Catiline bound his fellow conspirators by an oath, handing around, as was the custom in sacred rites, cups of human blood mixed with wine.
8 Cf. Ch. 22, n. 10.
9 According to Celsus, a contemporary of Augustus and Tiberius, epileptic patients tried to cure themselves by drinking the blood of a slain gladiator. A similar prescription is found in a collection of Scribonius Largus, physician of Emperor Claudius.

limbs and vitals of man. We, however, are not allowed either to witness or to hear of human slaughter, and the awe we have of human blood is so great that we do not even taste that of animals for food.[10]

Chapter 31

1 'The monstrous story of incestuous banqueting is a lie concocted against us by a horde of demons, in order to soil the honorable record of our innocent life by spreading odious and disreputable accusations, so that men might be turned away from us by the horror of our shocking reputation even before they have examined the truth. 2 On this point, your own Fronto, for instance, did not substantiate his testimony, but expatiated upon it in rhetorical invective.[1] As a matter of fact, such things are rather found among your own people. 3 Among the Persians it is lawful for sons to have intercourse with their mothers, and in Egypt and Athens the marriage of brother and sister is legal. Your tales and tragedies display cases of incest in boastful language, and you read and listen to them with pleasure. In like manner you worship gods joined in incestuous wedlock with a mother, a daughter, or a sister. 4 It is not to be wondered at, then, if among you cases of incest are often discovered and constantly being perpetrated. Even unbeknown to you, poor fellows, you may run into the danger of illicit relations. While going in search of promiscuous love adventures, begetting children here and there, and abandoning even those begotten under your own roof, you necessarily must come across your own stock again, and, be-

---

10 Cf. Acts 15.29, where the Christians are instructed to 'abstain from things sacrificed to idols and from blood and from that which is strangled.'

---

1 Cf. Ch. 9, n. 7.

cause of this erratic course, stumble upon your own offspring. Thus, you contrive a tragic plot of incest even when you are not aware of it.

5 'We, on the other hand, prove our modesty not by external appearance but by character; with a good heart we cling to the bond of one marriage; in our desire for offspring we have only one wife or none at all. The banquets we conduct are distinguished not only by their modesty, but also by their soberness. We do not indulge in sumptuous meals or produce good fellowship by drawn out wine bibbing, but hold in check our cheerful spirits by the sobriety of our manners. Chaste in conversation and even more chaste in body, very many enjoy the perpetual virginity of a body undefiled rather than boast of it. In short, the desire of incest is so far from our thoughts that some blush even at the idea of a chaste union.

6 'Moreover, from the fact that we decline your public offices and high dignities, it does not follow that we are made up of the dregs of the people. Nor are we led by any factious spirit, if, peaceable equally in our gatherings and as individuals, we feel inspired by one good only. Nor are we garrulous in corners, if you are either ashamed or afraid of listening to us in public.

7 'The further fact that our number is increasing daily does not furnish any proof of error, but testifies to a conduct deserving praise, for a beautiful mode of life makes old followers persevere and attracts new ones. 8 Lastly, we easily recognize one another, not as you imagine by some distinguishing mark on the body,[2] but by the sign of innocence and modesty. Thus, to your great mortification, we practice mutual love, because we do not know how to hate; and to your displeasure, we call ourselves brethren, as being human children of one

---

2 Cf. Ch. 9, n. 2.

divine Father, sharers in one faith, and joint heirs of the same hope.³ You, on the other hand, do not acknowledge each other, and a fit of bad temper leads you to mutual hatred; nor do you recognize each other as brothers unless for the purpose of fratricide.

Chapter 32

1 'Moreover, do you think that we hide the object of our worship because we have no shrines and altars? What image am I to contrive of God, since logical reasoning tells you that man himself is an image of God? What temple am I to build for Him, since this whole world, fashioned by His hand, cannot hold Him?¹ Am I to confine so vast and majestic a power to one little shrine, while I, a mere man, live in a larger place? 2 Are our mind and heart not better places to be dedicated and consecrated to Him? Am I to offer to God sacrificial victims, small or large, which He has produced for my use, and so disdain His gifts? This would be ungrateful, since the sacrifice pleasing to God is a good heart and a pure mind and a clear conscience. 3 He, then, who preserves his innocence, implores God's mercy; he who practices justice, offers libations to God; he who abstains from fraud, propitiates God; he who saves a man from danger, slays the best victim. These are our sacrifices, these our sacred rites. Thus, among us, the most just is considered the most pious.

4 'Truly, the God we worship we neither show nor see. It is for this very reason that we believe in His existence, because we can perceive Him though we cannot see Him.² In His works, and in all the motions of the universe, we behold

---
3 Cf. Rom. 8.17; Titus 3.7; 1 Peter 3.7; 2 Peter 1.1.

1 Cf. Acts 17.24.
2 Cf. 1 Tim. 6.16; Rom. 1.20f.

His ever-present power: in the thunder and the lightning, in the thunder bolt and the clear sky. 5 You need not be surprised that you cannot see God. Blasts of wind set all things moving, swinging, shaking, yet the eyes do not see the blasts of wind. Again, we cannot even look into the sun which is the means by which all of us are able to see; by its rays your sight is impaired, by gazing at it your vision is dimmed, and, if you look at it too long, your visual power is totally extinguished. 6 How could you endure the sight of the Maker of the sun Himself, the original Source of light, you who turn your eyes away from His lightnings and hide yourself from His thunderbolts? Do you expect to see God with the eyes of flesh, when you can neither behold nor take hold of your own soul by which you are endowed with life and speech?

7 'But, God, you say, cannot be aware of the doings and dealings of man; seated on His heavenly throne, He can neither call on everybody nor know each individual. There, O man, you are mistaken and deceived. For, where is the place from which God is remote, since all things in heaven and on earth and beyond the reach of this globe are full of Him? Everywhere He is not only near us, but within us. 8 Once more direct your attention to the sun: it is fixed in heaven, yet its light spreads into all lands; it is equally present everywhere, penetrates all things, and nowhere is its brightness dimmed. 9 How much more is God, the Creator and Searcher of all things, from whom nothing can remain hidden, present in the darkness, present in our thoughts, which are, so to speak, a darkness of another kind! Not only do we act under His eye, but—as I felt almost inclined to say—we live with Him.

Chapter 33

1 'Let us not compliment ourselves upon our numbers: to our own eyes we seem to be many, but in God's sight we are very few. We distinguish between nations and tribes; to God this whole world is but one household. Kings are well posted on all affairs of their kingdom through the official reports of their ministers. God has no need of information; we live not only under His eyes but in His bosom.

2 'But, you object, it did not yield any profit to the Jews that they, too, most scrupulously worshipped one God with altars and temples. There, you fall into error through ignorance, by either forgetting or not knowing their early history, and remembering only later events. 3 In the case of the Jews, as long as they, too, worshipped our God—for He is the God of all mankind—I say, as long as they worshipped Him with chastity, innocence, and reverence, as long as they walked in the way of His wholesome commandments, they, from being a few, grew to a people without number, from being poor to a people of wealth, from being slaves to a people of kings. Being but a handful of unarmed men, they have put to flight and routed strong and well-armed hosts, at the command of God and with the assistance of the elements. 4 Read their writings; or, passing over the early authors, search in Flavius Josephus;[1] or, if you prefer Romans, consult Antonius Julianus[2] for what they have written on the Jews. Then you will find that it was their own wickedness which brought about their doom; that nothing ever happened to them that had not been foretold would happen if they persisted in their

---

[1] A Jewish historian (1st century A.D.) who wrote two works: *The Jewish War* (ending with the destruction of Jerusalem in 70 A.D.), and *Jewish Antiquities*.
[2] He took part in the siege of Jerusalem, and, as a member of the war council, voted for the destruction of the city.

obstinacy. 5 Thus you will understand that they forsook God before they were forsaken by Him, and that they were not —as you impiously say—led captives along with their God, but were handed over by God as traitors to His Law.

Chapter 34

1 'Again, as to the conflagration of the world, it is an error typical of the common people to consider a sudden fall of fire from heaven, or a lack of moisture, as incredible. 2 Who among the philosophers doubts, or does not know, that all things born die; that all things created perish; that heaven and all things contained in it come to an end just as they had a beginning. That in this manner the universe, if sun, moon and the rest of the stars are no longer fed by the fresh water of the springs and the water of the seas, will vanish in a fiery ocean, the Stoics firmly maintain; that is to say, if the moisture is consumed, this whole world will catch fire. 3 And the Epicureans quite agree with this opinion about the conflagration of the elements and the destruction of the universe. 4 Plato speaks of alternating turns of flood and fire to which parts of the world are subject; although he declares that the world was created eternal and indestructible, he adds that it lies solely in the power of the divine Creator Himself to make it destructible and perishable. Thus, there is nothing to be wondered at, if this huge structure be destroyed by its builder.

5 'You notice that the philosophers maintain the same opinion as we; not that we have tread in their footsteps, but because from the divine instructions of the prophets they have taken over the mere shadow of a garbled truth.

6 'Thus it also came about that the most outstanding among the philosophers, first Pythagoras, but above all Plato,

have taught the established course of our resurrection in a way full of misrepresentation and half-truth; for, they hold that, after the dissolution of our bodies, our souls alone continue to exist eternally, and migrate again and again into other new bodies. 7 To distort the truth still more, they add that human souls seek abodes in the bodies of domesticated animals, birds, and wild beasts. This opinion certainly does not look like the product of a serious philosophical mind, but like a joke out of mimic play. 8 However, for our argument, it suffices to show that even in this point your philosophers are in agreement with us to a certain degree. 9 After all, who is so stupid and so devoid of reason as to venture to contradict the principle that as man could be originally created by God, so he can afterwards be reshaped by Him? that man is nothing after death, just as before birth he was nothing? that, as he could be born from nothing, so he can be remade from nothing? Besides, it is more difficult to give a beginning to what does not exist than to recall into existence what has once existed. 10 Do you believe that, if something is removed from our feeble eyes, it is lost also to God? The whole body, whether it withers away to dust, or dissolves into moisture, or crumbles away to ashes or passes off in vapor, is removed from our eyes, but it still exists for God, the Preserver of the elements. Nor are we, as you imagine, afraid of any damage resulting from the manner of burial, but we practice the time-honored and more dignified custom of consigning the dead body to the earth.

11 'Notice, also, how all nature hints at a future resurrection for our consolation. The sun sets and rises again; the stars sink below the horizon and return; the flowers die and come to life again; the shrubs spend themselves and then put forth buds; seeds must decompose in order to sprout forth new life. Thus, the body in the grave is like the tree in the winter, which conceals its live sap under an apparent dryness.

12 Why do you urge that in the depths of winter it should revive and return to life? We must also wait for the spring of the body.

'I know perfectly well, of course, that many, because of their guilty conscience, hope rather than believe that they are reduced to nothing after death. They prefer to be annihilated rather than to be restored for punishment. They swerve farther from the right path because of the liberty allowed to them in this life and because of God's infinite patience, whose judgment is the juster the later it comes.

Chapter 35

1 'Yet, outstanding men of learning in their writings, and poets[1] in their verses, warn mankind of that river of fire and the circles of glowing flood issuing from the Stygian morass; they recorded those means of eternal torture, as they found them disclosed in the statements of demons and the oracles of prophets. 2 Hence it is that, in their works, even King Jupiter himself swears in awe by the burning shores of Styx and its black abyss,[2] for he knows beforehand and dreads the punishment destined for him and his followers. 3 Nor is there set any limit or end to these torments. The fire there below, endowed with ingenuity, consumes and renews, wears away and sustains the limbs. As the fiery flashes of lightning strike the bodies without consuming them, as the fires of Etna, and Vesuvius, and volcanoes all the world over burn without being exhausted, so that avenging fire is not fed by destroying those who are exposed to the flames, but is sustained by the never ending mangling of their bodies.

4 'That those who do not know God are tortured for their

---
1 Minucius Felix refers to Vergil, *Aeneid* 6.313-439.
2 Cf. *ibid.* 9.104ff.

impiety and injustice according to their deserts, none but an atheist can doubt, since the crime of ignoring the Father and Lord of all is not less than that of offending Him. 5 And, although ignorance of God is sufficient reason for punishment, just as knowledge of Him helps to obtain His pardon, still, if we Christians are compared with you, although some fail to come up to the standard of our teaching, we shall be found far better than you. 6 For, you prohibit adultery, yet practice it, while we are found to be husbands for our wives alone. You punish crimes committed, while with us the mere thought of crime is sin. You are afraid of witnesses, while we even dread our mere conscience which always accompanies us. Finally, while the jails are crammed with people of your kind, they do not hold a single Christian, unless he be accused on account of his religion, or unless he be an apostate.

Chapter 36

1 'Let no one either seek solace or excuse the result of his actions by referring to fate. Suppose one's lot does depend on fortune—his mind is free, so that it is a man's manner of acting and not his social position which is judged. What else is destiny but what God has destined for each of us? 2 Since He is in a position to know beforehand our natural abilities, He also determines the destinies of individuals according to their deserts and qualities. Thus, in our case, it is not the condition of birth which is chastised, but our inner disposition which suffers the penalty. Let my few remarks on fate suffice for the moment; we shall discuss the subject more fully and more completely elsewhere.[1]

3 'Moreover, that most of us are considered poor is no

---

[1] Minucius Felix promises a work, *On Fate*, which either was not written or has been lost.

disgrace, but does us credit; for, as the mind is weakened by luxurious living, so it is strengthened by a frugal life. 4 Yet, who can be poor, who is free from want, who does not covet another's goods, who is rich in the sight of God? That man is rather poor who, though he has great possessions, craves for more. 5 I shall give you my honest opinion: no man can be so poor as he was on the day of his birth.[2] The birds live without ancestral inheritance, the herds feed day in and day out; yet, these creatures have been called into existence for our use, and we possess them all, if we do not covet them. 6 As the wayfarer's step is the jauntier the lighter he travels, so in this journey of life that man is happier who lightens his needs by poverty and does not groan under the burden of riches.

7 'Besides, if we considered wealth an asset, we would ask God for it; surely, the Owner of all could grant us a portion of it. But, we prefer to despise riches rather than to hoard them; we rather desire innocence and pray with fervor for patience; we would rather be honest than prodigal.

8 'The bodily weaknesses inherent in our human nature which we feel and suffer are not a punishment but a warfare. Fortitude is strengthened by infirmities and misfortune is frequently a training school for virtue; finally, both mental and physical powers become torpid without laborious exercise. Even all your heroes, whom you commend as models, gained their renown and fame through the hardships they endured. 9 Thus, God is neither unable to come to our aid nor does He neglect us, since He is the ruler of all and the lover of His own. But, in adversities He tests and tries every one of us, in situations fraught with peril He weighs each man's character, until man's fatal hour He puts his will to the proof,

---

2 Cf. Seneca, *On Providence* 6.5: 'No man lives so poor as he was born.'

never fearing lest something might escape Him. Thus, as gold is tested by fire, we are tried by tribulations.[3]

Chapter 37

1 'How beautiful a spectacle for God, when a Christian measures his strength with pain; when he is in the jaws of threats and punishments and tortures; when, with a scornful smile, he looks down upon the rattling instruments of death and the grim executioner; when, in the face of kings and princes, he esteems his liberty above all things; when he yields to God alone, whose he is; when he, triumphant victor, defies the very one who has pronounced sentence on him! That man has gained the victory who has obtained that for which he strove. 2 What soldier does not court danger more boldly under the eyes of his general? For, none receives the prize before standing the test. Yet, the general cannot give what he does not own; he cannot prolong life, though he can grant distinction for good service. 3 Besides, the soldier of God neither is forsaken when in pain nor is his life ended by death. Thus, the Christian, though he may seem wretched, cannot be found so. You yourselves extol to the sky men visited by great misfortunes, like Mucius Scaevola,[1] who, after his abortive attempt on the king's life, would have perished among the enemy, had he not sacrificed his right hand. 4 How many of our brethren, without a cry of pain, have allowed not only their right hand but their whole body to be

---

[3] Cf. Prov. 3.1; 17.3; Wisd. 3.6; 1 Peter 1.6f.; James 1.12

[1] A Roman general who wished to liberate his country by killing Porsenna, the Etruscan king of Clusium, but mistook Porsenna's secretary for the king. Taken prisoner, he proved his courage but lost his right hand by holding it in a sacrificial brazier. Porsenna, admiring the youth's fortitude, released him and gave up the siege of Rome. Mucius was thereafter called Scaevola, which means a left-handed person. The legend was later embellished by Roman writers.

scorched and burned to ashes, when it depended entirely on them to gain their release. 5 Am I comparing only men with Mucius or Aquilius[2] or Regulus?[3] Why, even our boys and tender women, fortified against pain by heaven, scoff at crosses and tortures, wild beasts, and all the terrors of punishment. 6 And you, miserable wretches, you do not see that, without reason, no one would undergo punishment of his own accord, or be able to endure the tortures without divine assistance. 7 But you may possibly be misled, seeing that people who do not know God are rolling in wealth, are distinguished by honors, and are placed in powerful positions. The poor wretches are raised the higher that their downfall may be greater. For, like sacrificial animals, they are fattened for offering; like victims they are crowned for slaughter. To no other end, in fact, are some lifted to stations of supreme and unrestricted authority except that, by a reckless use of power, they may freely market the character of their wicked minds. 8 To be sure, without the knowledge of God, what real happiness can there be, when death awaits us? Like a dream it slips away, before we lay hold of it. 9 Are you a king? You feel as much fear as you fill others with, and, however great the number of your bodyguard, in time of danger you are alone. Are you rich? Fortune is fickle and a great store of provisions does not facilitate the brief journey of life, but makes it more difficult. 10 Are you proud of your high offices and purple robes? It is a foolish mistake of man and an empty display of grandeur to shine in purple while the mind is vile. Are you of noble descent? Do you boast of your ancestors? We are all born equal and moral goodness alone gives us a mark of distinction.

---

2 Manius Aquilius was defeated by Mithridates on the river Sangarius in Bithynia, and fled to Pergamum and Mytilene; here, he was surrendered to Mithridates and tortured, allegedly by having melted gold poured down his throat.
3 Cf. Ch. 26, n. 2, and Tertullian, *The Testimony of the Soul* 4, n. 4.

11 'As a logical result, we, who judge ourselves by our conduct and purity of morals, keep aloof from your wicked amusements, processions, and public shows; we know that they have sprung from your sacred rites, and we condemn their obnoxious seductions. At the chariot races in the circus, who would not be horrified at the frenzy of the brawling populace, or at the fine art of manslaughter in the gladiatoral combats? 12 Nor does raving madness subside in the stage plays, where indecencies are even more luxuriant: at one, a mimic player describes and exhibits ways of adultery; at another, an effeminate actor arouses feelings of love while he is only playing a role: he vilifies your gods by mimicking their lewd love affairs, their sighs, their hates; feigning grief, he moves you to tears by senseless gestures and motions. Thus, you call for real murder and weep over fictitious ones on the stage.

Chapter 38

1 'The fact that we scorn the parts left over from your sacrifices and the cups of libation is not an admission of fear but an assertion of true liberty. For, although every naturally grown thing, as an inviolable gift of God, cannot be adulterated by any use, we abstain from these offerings, lest anyone think that either we acknowledge the demons to whom the libations are poured, or that we are ashamed of our religion.

2 'Who can doubt that we are fond of the flowers of spring, when we gather the spring rose and the lily and every kind of flower with charming color and delightful scent. We use them strewn about or untied, we wind them about our necks in soft garlands. Pray excuse us for not crowning our heads; we are accustomed to breathe in the sweet perfume of flowers with our noses, not to inhale it with the back of the head and the hair.

3 'Nor do we place wreaths on the dead. As to this custom, I am rather surprised at you: how you can apply a torch to the dead person if he is still capable of feeling, or present him with a wreath if he is devoid of it. If he is happy, he does not need flowers; if unhappy, he finds no delight in them. 4 Our funerals, on the other hand, are distinguished by the same peace of mind as our lives; we do not wind a fading crown, but expect from God an imperishable crown[1] wrought from everlasting flowers. In quietude and modesty, putting our trust in the kindness of our God, we raise our hope of future happiness by our belief in His ever-present majesty. Thus do we rise again to heavenly joy, while our present life is filled with bliss by the contemplation of the future.

5 'Hence, let Socrates see to it himself, 'the buffoon of Athens,'[2] who confessed that he knew nothing, though he boasted of the suggestion of his most deceitful demon! Arcesilas too, and Carneades, and Pyrrho,[3] and the whole host of Academics, let them doubt everything,[4] and Simonides postpone his reply to all eternity![5] We hold in contempt the supercilious airs of the philosophers, whom we know as corrupters of morals, adulterers, and tyrants, ever ready to declaim against vices which are their own. 6 As for us, our wisdom manifests itself not by what we wear, but by our inner disposition; our strength lies not in our words, but in our mode of life, we may boast to have obtained what they with the utmost exertion have sought, but could not find.

7 'Why are we ungrateful, why unjust to ourselves, if the true idea of the godhead has come to maturity in these our days? Let us enjoy our happiness and keep our sense of right

---

1 Cf. 1 Peter 5.4.
2 This epithet is taken from Cicero, who attributes it to Zeno.
3 Pyrrho of Elis (365-275 B.C.) was the first representative of skepticism.
4 Cf. Ch. 13, n. 3.
5 Cf. Ch. 13.4.

within due bounds. Superstition should be repressed, impiety done away with, and true religion kept untouched.'

Chapter 39

Octavius had ended his speech. Stunned into silence, we kept our eyes intently fixed upon him for a while. As for myself, I was transported with feelings of deep admiration for the brilliant manner in which he had furnished arguments, examples, and authoritative passages in favor of things which are more easily felt than expressed, and for the manner in which he had repelled those ill-disposed toward us by the very weapons, which they take from the arsenal of the philosophers, and had demonstrated that truth is not only easy to grasp but also to accept.

Chapter 40

1 While I was pondering over these thoughts in silence, Caecilius burst out, saying: 'I extend my heartiest congratulations to my friend Octavius and to myself, nor do I wait for a decision. As things turned out, we have both won. It may seem impudent, but I, too, claim a victory. As he gained a victory over me, so I gained a triumph over error.

2 'Accordingly, with regard to the main point of our inquiry, I acknowledge Providence, agree with you on the concept of God, and recognize the moral purity of the religion which has just become my own. But, even now, some points remain, not exactly obstacles to the truth, but necessary for complete instruction. However, since the sun is already sinking in the west, we shall discuss them more quickly tomorrow, considering that we agree on the issue as a whole.'

3 'But,' said I, 'my joy on behalf of all of us is the greater

as the victory of Octavius is also to my interest, because it relieves me from the most odious task of passing judgment. However, my words of praise cannot do justice to his merits. The testimony of man—in addition, that of one man alone—carries little weight. He possesses an extraordinary gift from God whose spirit inspired him in his speech and whose assistance gained him the victory.'

4 After this we left, rejoicing and in good spirits—Caecilius, because he had found the faith; Octavius, because he had won a victory; and I, because of the faith of the one and the victory of the other.

INDEX

INDEX

Abortion, 31, 32, 266, 385
Abraham, 199, 229, 306; bosom of, 194, 298
Academics, 217, 343, 400
Academy, 217
Acca Larentia, *see* Larentina
Achilles, 283, 300
Acts of Peter and Paul, apocryphal, 21 n.
Adam, 212 n., 225, 227, 228, 245, 266, 268, 271, 277, 299; prophesied, 204; type of Christ, 277
Admetus (King of Pherae), 46, 372
Aeacus, 259
Aemilius (M. Aemilius Scaurus), 20
Aeneas, 31, 45, 372
Aenesidemus, 198, 209, 237, 326 n.
Aeons, Gnostic, 220, 231
Aesculapius, 46, 72, 112, 135, 181, 330, 369, 371
Aethalides, 246, 252
Affections, of Christ, 213; of God, 213; of man, 212-214
agápe, xiv, 100-101, 337
Agave, 216
Agnes, St., 125 n.

Agobardus (Bishop of Lyons), xii
Ajax, 216, 284
Albinus (philosopher), 245, 248
Albinus, D. Clodius, 92, 152, 156 n.
Alburnus (god), 20
Alemona (Roman goddess), 266
Alexander the Great, 40, 114, 283, 289, 361
Allia, ill-boding name, 333
Amalthea, 79, 369 n.
Amasis (King of Egypt), 365
Ambrose, St., 125 n.
Amphiaraus, 284, 377
Amphilochus, oracle of, 284
Amphitheater, cruelty of, 48, 97; gods reviled in, 48
Amulets, used by pregnant women, 270
Anacharsis, 9
Anaphe (island), 102
Anatomists, early, 167
Anatomy, 200, 238-239
Anaxagoras, 113, 205, 206, 275, 356
Anaxarchus, 124
Anaximander, 355 n.

INDEX

Anaximenes (philosopher), 198, 355 n., 356
Ancharia (goddess), 77
Andreas (physician), 209, 210
Angel, fiery, 231; of retribution, 263
Angels, 197, 231; caring for unborn children, 266; guides of souls after death, 296
Animals, characteristics of certain, 253-254; estimation of minute, 200-201; habits of, 234; retention of life by, after removal of vital organs, 209-210
Animal worship, Egyptian, 76-77, 383
animus, 205
Antichrist, 290
Antinous (favorite of Hadrian), 45 n.
Antisthenes (Cynic), 356
Antiphon, on interpretation of dreams, 284
Antonius Julianus, 391
Anubis, 24, 47, 52, 368
Anytus, 180
Aoroi, 303
Apaturia, festival of, 100
Apelles (heretic), 231, 265
Apicius, 257
Apion, 59
Apis, 283
Apocryphal Books, 182 n.
Apollinaris (apologist), 131 n.
Apollo, 46, 70, 112, 326 n., 361, 369, 372, 378
Apollodorus (physician), 211

Apollophanes (philosopher), 208
Apologists, Christian, xii-xviii; attitude toward Greek philosophy and rhetoric, xv-xvi; chief aim, xv; early, 131 n.; methods, 129
Apuleius, 135 n., 368 n.
Aquilicium, sacrificed to for rain, 104
Aquilius, Manlius, 398
Arcesilas (of Middle Academy), 343, 344 n., 400
Archigallus (priest of Cybele), 78-79
Archimedes, 209
Argae (mountains), 239
Aristaeus (Aristeas), 55
Aristides (apologist), 131 n.
Aristides (Athenian statesman), 40
Aristides (erotic novelist), 231 n.
Aristippus (philosopher), 114
Aristo (Stoic philosopher), 358
Aristodemus, 282
Aristogiton (tyrannicide), 124 n.
Aristophon, 282
Aristotle, 114, 185 n., 186, 187, 191 n., 192, 210, 223, 275, 282, 284, 288, 357; *De anima* quoted, 205 n., 206 n., 208 n.
Arius, 297, 299
Arnobius, 41 n.
Arrius Antoninus (Roman governor), 160

Artemis, 330 n.; Ephesian, 370 n.; priests of Ephesian, 367 n.
Artemon (dream-interpreter), 284
Artorius, 283
Arvals (college of priests), 376
Asclepiades (physician), 209-211, 238, 268
Asclepiodotus, 72
Asclepius, 330 n.
Asper, C. Julius (proconsul), 157
Ass's head fable, 49-52, 336, 382
Astarte, 42 n., 72 n., 330; [Atargatis], 77, 366 n.
Astrologers, 93, 108, 155, 240
Astyages (King of the Medes), 282
Atheism, Christians charged with, xiv, 35
Athamas, 216
Athenagoras (apologist), 131 n., 361 n.
Athenians, described as clever, 226; as loquacious, 185-186
Atlantes (African tribe), 288
Atomic theory, of Leucippus of Miletus, 327-329
Attis, 47, 48, 78 n.
Augias (King of Elis), 372 n.
Auguries, 371, 333 n., 376; fallacy of, 377
Augurs, 376
Augustine, St., xi n., 23 n., 31 n., 42 n., 44 n., 170, 242 n., 326 n., 361 n., 375 n., 386 n.

Augustus (emperor), 98-90, 283, 333 n., 363 n.
Autumn, insalubrious, 286

Bacchanals, 107; prohibition of, 24; restoration of, 24-25
Bacchus, 24-25, 107, 239
Balduinus, Franciscus, 316-317
Banquets, pagan, condemned, 342
Baptism, 271, 273-274; of Menander, 289
Baraliris the Illyrian, 283
Barbarians, Greek and Tertullian's estimation of, 192
Bardenhewer, O., xix, 3 n.
Baths, Christian attitude toward the, 107
Baylis, H. J., 319
Beans, influence of, on dreams, 287; prohibition of, by Pythagoras, 252, 287
Bede, Venerable, 153 n.
Bel, 330
Belenus (deity of Norucum), 77
Bellona, 32, 136 n., 386; priests of, 366 n., 367 n.
Belus (King of Assyrians), 56, 362 n.
Bentler, R., 319
Berenice (magician), 303
Berenice (queen), 234
Berosus (Chaldean chronicler), 59
Biaiothanatoi, 303
Bindley, T. H., 148, 149, 156 n., 158 n.

Birth, in 7th or 8th month of pregnancy, 267
Birthplaces of gods, 36, 42, 361
Birth rites, 270
Blood, abstinence of Christians from, 33; cure for epilepsy, 32, 386; drunk at compacts, 32; in Bellona rites, 32; in Cybele rites, 78; of Christians, a seed, 125
Body, apparent increase in weight of, after death, 195; compared to cup, 272; dwelling place of soul, 269; instrument for conduct of life, 272; prison of soul, 262; relation of, and soul in sinning, 272-274, 307-309
Bono Dea cult, 366 n.
Bonnet, M., 21 n.
Book of fate, 266
Brahmans, 106
Briareus, 46 n., 372
Brother, as Christian title, 99, 336, 388-389
Brotherhood, of men, 99
Brutus, M. Junius, 283
Burial places of gods, 36, 42, 361, 363
Busiris (mythical Egyptian king), 386
Bythus (heretic conception), 205

Caecilius Capella (Roman governor), 155-156
Caecilius Natalis (interlocutor in dialogue), 314
Caelestis (goddess), 42, 72, 77

Caesar, C. Julius, vii, 333 n., 353 n., 377
Callinicus (rhetor), 126
Callisthenes, 283
Camillus, M. Furius, 328
Cannae, 103, 377
Cannibalism, Christians charged with, xiv, 11, 25, 28, 29, 337
Caphaerean rocks, 294
Capitol, 43, 53, 80, 81, 103, 104, 330
Caracalla, M. Aurelius Antoninus, 158
Carneades (head of New Academy), 326 n., 344 n., 400
Carpocrates (heretic), 231, 262-263
Carthage, 51, 154; Church in, viii; restoration by Caesar, vii
Cassius (C. Cassius Longinus), 283
Cassius, Avidius (Roman general), 92, 152
Cassius Hemina (Roman annalist), 36 n., 362
Cassius Severus (Roman orator), 36
Castor, 70, 332, 371, 380
Catiline, 32, 386
Cato, M. Porcius, the Elder, 40, 100
Cato, M. Porcius Uticensis, the Younger, 100 n.
Celsus (encyclopedist), 32 n., 386 n.
Celsus (Platonist), xiii

INDEX 409

Celts, expect oracles at tombs of heroes, 306
Centaurs, 359
Ceres, 39, 44, 135, 329; [Pharian=Isis] 50; [Eleusinian=Demeter] 361; [Demeter] 369; *sacrum anniversarium Cereris*, 135 n.
Chaerephon (student of Socrates), 343 n.
Chance, doctrine of Epicurus on blind, 282; pagan philosophers finding Truth by, 182
Charioteer, soul compared to, 295
Charismata, Montanist, 169, 197
Charity, Christian, 99, 107-108, 159
Charon of Lampsacus (logographer), 282
Charybdis, 359 n.
Cherry, intrdouced by Lucullus from Pontus, 39
Chilon, death of, 293
Chimaera, 52, 359
Chrestian, variant for Christian, 16
Christ, as Good Shepherd, 207; descent into Hell, 298; God and man, 273, 298; Incarnation, 64; Jews' unbelief in, 64-66; miracles of Death and Resurrection, 65-66; nature and divinity, 62-64; orginal first-born Logos, 65; reality of His body, 218
Christian, derivation of name, 16, 17, 61; name of, hated, 8-10, 15, 16; name only charged against, 10, 14-15, 17, 19-20
Christians, alleged secret signs of recognition, 336; blamed for public calamities, xiv-xv, 102-105; called conspirators, 335; called detractors of old religion, 335; called enemies of human race, 96; called public enemies, xiv, 90, 93; calumnies against, xiv-xv, 11, 25, 28, 29, 35, 75, 84-85, 87, 91-94, 96, 102-108, 335-338; chastity of, 34, 113, 159, 388; commanded to love enemies, 94, 151; condemned to banishment on islands, 42; to crosses and stakes, 41, 122, 342; to death by fire, 42, 122, 342; to mines, 42; to wild beasts, 42, 122; cries against, 13, 102; eagerness for martyrdom, 151, 160; funeral rites, 292; gratitude for sentences, 10, 113, 126, 151; innocence of, 15-17; 104, 108-110, 125, 152, 156, 159, 387, 388; loyal toward emperor, 88-89, 94, 153, 154; more loyal than heathen, 92-93, 152-153; mutual love, 99, 336, 388; not only low-born and ignorant, 8, 160; power over demons, 72-75, 83, 108, 153, 158, 303; protected by good

rulers, 21-22; regarded as coming from lowest ranks of society, 335, 344-345; as fools and madmen, 121-123, 125; as ignorant, 326, 335; as worthless in business, 106-108; value to state, 106-108; victory in death, 123

Christianity, attitude of Roman state toward, xiii-xviii; illegal, 18; not to be classed with philosophy, 116; novelty of, 61; origin of, 61-67; pagan ignorance concerning, 8-9, 15-17, 151; wide diffusion of, 8, 95, 154, 335-336, 391; *see* Christians

Chrysippus (physician), 211

Chrysippus (Stoic philosopher), 136, 189, 191 n., 192, 208, 252, 357

Cicero, 35 n., 38 n., 41, 63 n., 68 n., 70 n., 78 n., 86 n., 110 n., 112 n., 124 n., 125, 233, 257, 283, 314, 317, 318, 328 n., 363 n., 378 n., 400 n.

Cincius Severus (Roman governor), 157

Circumcision, 61

Circus, madness of, 97, 399

Claudia Quinta (Roman matron), 332

Claudius Lucius Herminianus (Roman proconsul), 155

Claudius (P. Claudius Pulcher), 333, 337

Cleanthes (Stoic philosopher), 63, 136 n., 188-189, 240, 357

Clement of Alexandria, xvi, xvii, 55 n., 131 n.

Clement of Rome, 85 n.

Clidemus, 294

Climate, influence on mind and character, 226, 239

Clinias, 226

Cloacina (Roman deity), 375

Cock, sacrificed by Socrates, 112, 181

Cohabitation, estimation of, 243

Colombo, S., 319

Colophon, water from fountain at, inducing madness, 289

Colyttus, precocious children of, 226

Commodus (M. Aurelius Commodus Antoninus, emperor), 92 n., 152 n:, 157 n., 158 n.

Common sense, 182

Conception, 242-245; in astrology, 240

Concupiscence, 268-269

Consus (Roman deity), 375

Contraries, classification of, 248

Corybantes, 79, 369

Cos (island), 102

Cosmopolitanism, 97

Crassus, 41, 294, 333, 353 n.

Cratippus, on dreams, 284

Creationism, 242 n.

Creator, omnipotence of, 194

Cremation of the dead, after execution, 258; forbidden to Christians, 291, 340

Cretans, regarded as mendacious, 227
Critias, 188
Critolaus, 187, 188
Croesus, 40, 57, 70, 112
Cronus, 369 n., 370 n.
Cross, as instrument of torture, 41; fanciful discovery of, everywhere, 50-51, 385
Crucifixion, caricature of, 51 n., 336 n.
Ctesias (historian), 34
Curetes, 369 n.
Curtius (Roman hero), 139, 332-333
Cybele, 42, 44 n., 47, 78-79, 330, 332, 376; mysteries of, 78, 330 n., 369; priests of, 44 n., 72 n., 78 n., 366 n., 367 n., 369
Cyclopes, 372
Cynopennae (fabulous monsters), 29
Cyprian, St., 10 n., 99 n., 361 n., 375 n.,; on Tertullian, xii
Cyrus (King of Persia), 57, 282
Cyrus the Younger, 308

daimon, of Socrates, 68, 112, 180, 181, 240, 270, 378 n.
daimonia, 88
daimonion, 68 n., 378 n.
D'Ales, A., xix, 173, 188 n., 271 n., 274 n., 299 n., 303 n.
Dalmatians, character of, 227
Damigeron (magician), 303
Danae, 62
Danaus, 56, 58
Daniel, his 'ecstacy,' 287
Dardanus (magician), 303
Darius I, 57, 352 n.
David, 210
Dead, honor paid to, 44, 137-138, 331
Death, always violent, according to Tertullian, 293-294; cause of, 288-290; function of, 290-292; kinds of, 293; nature of, 274-275; pagan idea of, 137-138; soul leaving body by degress, 294-295
Decima (Roman goddess), 266
Decil, vow of, 332
Deianira, 371 n.
de Labriolle, P., xi n., xix, 3 n., 4 n., 169, 173, 319
Delos, 102
Delphic oracle, 181, 217, 343 n., 378
de L. Shortt, C., xix
Deluge, 102-103, 154
Delventinus (local god of Casinum), 77
Demeter, 329 n., 330 n., 361 n.,; mysteries of, 368 n., 369; temple of, near Megalopolis, 366 n.
Demetrius of Phalerum, 55, 59
Democritus (philosopher), 113, 206, 210, 275, 291, 327 n., 356
Demons, activity of, 69-71, 204, 284-285, 304, 378-381; cause

epilepsy, 158; cause insanity, 380; consoled by corruption of man, 83; existence proved by Christians, 136; food of, 69, 74, 153; identical with pagan gods, 71-73; influence on human bodies, 69-70, 96, 379; influence oracles, 284-285, 380; nature of, 69-70; 378-379; offspring of fallen angels, 68; persecution due to, 13-15, 82-83, 381, 382, 387; subject to Christians, 72-75, 83, 136, 303, 304, 380-381

Demosthenes, 40, 378
de Rohden, P., 158 n.
Desire, natural, 213, 269
Dessau, H., 158 n.
Deucalion, 363 n.
Devil, adversary and prosecutor, 263; enemy of God, 227; father of falsehood, 181; inspirer of dreams, 285; invitation to, by superstitious practices at birth, 270
Diagoras of Melos (lyric poet), 334
Dialecticians, estimation of, 276
Diana, 44, 47, 270, 330, 375; [Artemis] 370; [Hecate] 370
Dicaearchus of Messene, 209, 210
Dido, 124, 259
dies sanguinis, in Cybele cult, 78 n.

Digests, vii
Dio Cassius, 24 n., 78 n.
Diocles (physician), 210, 214
Diodorus (historian), 36, 362
Diogenes (Cynic philosopher), 47, 100, 113, 126
Diogenes Laertius, 47 n., 55 n., 100 n., 123 n., 124 n.
Diogenes of Apollonia (natural philosopher), 356
Diogenes of Seleucia (Stoic philosopher), 358
Diognetus, Epistle to, xvii
Diomedes, 45, 372 n.
Dionysia, 100
Dionysius, 361 n., 370 n.
Dionysius (Tryant of Syracuse), 114, 124, 283, 308, 328
Dionysius of Rhodes, 284
Disasters, regarded as remedy against overpopulation, 250
Discipline of the Secret, 338
Dissection of foetus, 238-239
Divorce, unknown in early Rome, 24
Dog, alleged use of, to help incest, 25, 28, 29, 337
Domitian (emperor), 92 n., 368 n.,; persecution of, 21
Doorposts, decoration of, 91, 93
Dreams, activity of soul in dreams, 278, 280; classification of, 285-286; dream- interpreters, 284; dream- oracles, 284; famous, 282-284;

INDEX

gates of, 282; literature on, 284; occurring toward morning or in spring more trustworthy, 286; source of knowledge of God, 168, 285-286; whether children dream or not, 288
Dusares (deity in Arabia), 77

Eagle, in metempsychosis, 254; vigor of its eyes, 195
Earth, the all-mother, 363 n.
East, turning to, in prayer, 51
Eclipse, of the sun, 155
Ecstasy, as means of divine communication with soul, 280-281; example of Montanist, 166, 197; of Adam, 204; of Daniel, 287
Eight, symbolic number, 267
Eleusinian mysteries, 26, 100, 329 n., 334 n., 369
Elias, 264, 290
Elizabeth (mother of John the Baptist), 242
Eloquence, deceptive, 345, 348
Elymas (magician), 304-305
Elysinian Fields, 117
Embryo, 266
Empedocles (philosopher), 123, 186, 188, 194, 210, 211, 214, 226, 252 n., 258, 275, 297
Emperor, not divine, but subject to God, 89-90, 153; prayed for by Christians, xiv, 85-87, 98; rules by appointment of God, 98, 153; true and false loyalty to, 90-93
Emperor worship, xiv, 35, 44, 84, 88, 153 n., 363 n.
Empire, Roman, necessity of continued existence, 88, 153
Endymions, of the Stoics, 299
Ennius, 259, 370 n., 378
Enoch, 290
Ephialtes, 372 n.
Ephorus (historian), 282
Epicharmus, 219, 286; as authority on dreams, 284
Epicureans, 97, 115-116, 215, 392
Epicurus, 110, 115, 132, 186, 188, 210, 211, 252, 254, 274, 275, 282, 289, 327 n., 356 n.
Epimenides, his sheep, 279
epithumetikon, 213
Epona (Celtic goddess), 50, 383
Erasistratus (physician), 210, 211, 238
Erigone, 370-371
Eriphyle, 377 n.
Eschatology, 296-309, 394-395
Esser, G., xix, 5, 130, 149, 173, 188 n.
Eteocles, 352 n.
Eucharist, Holy, celebration of, distorted by rumors, 337
Eubulus, 187
Euhemerism, 360 n.
Euhemerus (Greek mythographer), 35 n., 360
Euphorbus, 246, 247, 251, 252, 260

Euphorion, 283
Euphrates, 351
Euripides, 343 n.
Eusebius of Caesarea, vii, x, xi, 44 n., 55 n., 169
Eve, 265-266, 268
Exposure, of children, 34, 385

Fabius (C. Fabius Dorsuo), 330 n.
Falsification, of Old Testament, 183
Fasting, 104, 159, 171; as means for control of dreams, 287
Fate, 395; treatise of Minucius Felix on, 395; of Tertullian on, 227; 'Writing Fates,' 270
Father of the country, as imperial title, 90
Faunus, 366 n.
Febris (Roman deity), 375
Felicitas, St., 154 n.
Feriae Latinae, 370 n.
Fides (Roman deity), 76
Fig leaves, symbol of concupiscence, 269
Flaminius, Caius, 333, 377
Flora, 375
Forcellini, E., 156 n.
Freese, J. H., 319
Free will, 229, 230, 234
Fronto, M. Cornelius (rhetor), xiii, 337, 387

Gabinius, A. (consul), 24
Games, public (Christian attitude toward, 107 342; to be repeated by order of Jupiter, 332
Ganymede, 372
Garlands, Christian attitude toward, 107, 342, 399-400
Gates of dreams, 282
Gauls, human sacrifice among, 31
Genealogies, heretic conception of, 220
Gellius, Aulus, 23 n.
genius, evil spirit, 88 270; of the emperor, 84, 88, 93, 152-153; tutelary deity of a person, 270
Gladiators, souls of, conjured up by necromancers, 304
Glory, pagan philosophers' thirst for, 180
Glover, T., 5
Gnostics, interpretation of Matthew, 219-220; systems compared to mythological stories, 231
God, acknowledged in various ways, 133-134, 398-399; attested to by poets and philosophers, 345-358; by unanimous consent of human race, 354; attributes of, 52, 352-353; Creator of the universe, 52, 153, 349-352; how revealed in Old Testament, 53-54; name of, 353-354; proved by His works and the order in the universe, 53, 349-352; true object of Christian worship, 52, 133,

151; 'true Prometheus,' 54; unity of, 352-353
Gods, pagan, absurdities of their worship, 43-45; depicted with human passions, 131; despised and ridiculed by own worshippers, 152; forms and appearances ridiculous, 369-371; human origin of, 35-41, 79, 360-364; identical with demons, 71-73, 152; in literature, 36, 45-47; local, 77; not true divinities, 35, 42; refusal of Christians to worship, 35; 'unknown,' 331; vile character of, 40; witness to Christianity, 74-75; worship of, a late invention, 79-80
Goodspeed, E. J., xix
Government, Roman, controlled by free citizens, 13
Grace, 229, 304
Graves, how honored by heathen, 137-138
Guignebert, C., xix
Guilloux, P., xix
Gulf stream, 351 n.
Gynaecological instruments, 238

Hades, 371 n.
Hadrian (emperor), 22, 45 n., 157
Hair, growth of in dead bodies, 291; offerings of, 270
Halm, C., 319

Hands, raised in prayer, 76, 86-87
Hannibal, 78 n., 103, 332 n.
Harmodius (tyrannicide), 124 n.
Harnack, A., xi n.
Harpocrates (Egyptian god), 24
Haruspication, 331
Head, covered in prayer, 86 n., uncovered, 86
Heart, animals existing after removal of, 210; directive faculty of soul situated in, 210-211
Hecate, 370 n.
hegemonikon, 208, 209
Helen, 261-262
Hell, 117, 121, 193, 263, 298, 300, 304, 307-309, 394-395
Hennecke, E., 21 n.
Hera, 377 n.
Heraclides of Pontus, 191 n., 198, 283, 357
Heraclitus (philosopher), 115, 185, 186, 188, 198, 209, 211, 214
Hercules, 45, 47, 48, 86 n., 100, 371, 372, 375 n.
Heretics, drawing on Greek philosophers, 185; on sense-perception, 214
Hermetic literature, 183, 211, 257
Hermias, 114
Hermione, oracle of, 284
Hermippus (comic poet), 355

416 INDEX

Hermippus of Berytus, 284 n.
Hermogenes (heretic), 165, 179, 186, 202-203, 229, 230, 233, 235
Hermotimus, 183, 246, 252, 278, 280
Herodotus, 32, 70 n., 282, 288, 306, 352 n., 365 n.
Herophylus (physician), 200, 210, 211, 238
Hesiod, 358
Hesychius (grammarian), 51 n.
Hicesius (physician), 237, 239
Hiera (island), 102
Hiero (Tyrant of Syracuse), 112 n., 344
Hieromus (King of Tyre), 59
Hilarian (Roman governor), 152
Hipparchus, 188
Hippo, 188
Hippocrates, 210, 211, 238
Homer, 45 n., 46 n., 58, 259, 260, 282, 300, 354 n., 358, 371, 372
Hoppe, H., xix, 4, 5
Horace, 51 n.
Hosius, C., xix, 319
Hostanes (magician), 303, 379
Hostia (local goddess of Sutrium), 77
Hostilius (writer of mimes), 47
Hostilius, Tullus (Roman king), 375
Hydra, 359

Hydraulic organ, 209

Ideas, of Plato, 219; thoughts of God, 278
Idolatry, at the root of sin and error, 303
Inachus, 58
Incense, cost of, 86-87; from Arabia, 87, 107; use of, 86-87, 107
Incest, 34; charge of, against Christians, xiv, 11, 25, 28, 29, 336-338
Incubation-oracles, 287
Indus, 351-352
Infanticide, 31-32, 385; charged against Christians, 11, 25, 28, 29, 337
Insanity, 216, 221
Iphigenia, 330 n.
Irenaeus, St., 44 n., 83 n., 131 n.
Isiac mysteries, at Rome, 368; banished, 24; origin and nature of, 368 n.; restored, 24-25
Isidore of Seville, St., 58 n.
Isis, 24, 135, 368, 383; festival of, 135 n.; Pharian, 361
Ivy, described as living being, 224

Janiculum, 362
Janus, 36, 362
Jerome, St., viii, xii n., 30 n., 32 n., 242 n., 313 n., 317, 375 n.; on Tertullian, ix, 169
Jerusalem, capture of, 339 n.

Jews, attitude of Roman state toward, xiii; attitude toward Christ, 61, 64-66; toward Christians, 26, 66; dispersion of, 62; food taboos of, 61; history of, 391-392; religion lawful, xiii, 61; ridiculed, 338-339; source of Christianity, 61, 141

John the Baptist, St., 197, 242, 289; regarded as reincarnation of Elias, 264

John, St. (evangelist), 196, 210, 218, 299; legend that he was to live until Second Coming, 290

Jordan, H., 319

Josephus Flavius, 55 n., 59, 391

Juba, 59, 363

Judaea, 82

Judas, 204

Judgment, after death, 256; Last, 54, 74, 105, 117, 118, 120-121, 137, 152, 193, 304, 307

Julian law, 19

Julian the Apostate, xiii

Junius (L. Junius Pullus), 333, 377

Juno, 44, 46, 47, 79, 136, 270, 357, 364, 369, 372, 375; Curitis (local goddess of Falerii), 77

Jupiter, 34, 37, 39, 44, 46, 47, 56, 62, 63, 76, 79, 92, 104, 105, 107, 133, 283, 332, 339 n., 354, 357, 358, 363, 364, 369, 372, 375, 380, 384; Capitolinus, 370; Dictaean, 361; Feretrius, 370; Hammon, 370; Latiaris, 370; human sacrifice to Jupiter Latiaris, 31, 386

Justinian (emperor), xii

Justin Martyr, St., xvi, xvii, 13 n., 44 n., 55 n., 83 n., 99 n., 117 n., 131 n.

Justinus, 124 n.

Juturna (nymph), 'Lake' of, 332 n.

Juvenal, 4, 76 n., 89 n., 91 n., 135 n., 138 n.

Kellner, K., 5, 130, 149

Klebs, E., 158 n.

Knopf, R., 13 n.

'Know thyself' (inscription at Delphic temple of Apollo), 326

Kore, 361 n.; in Eleusinian mysteries, 369; temple of, at Megapolis, 366 n.

Kruger, G., xix, 13 n., 319

Laberius (writer of mimes), 117

Lactantius, 16 n., 34 n., 58 n., 148, 153 n., 313 n., 317, 375 n.

Lais, 44

Lamps, for decoration in daytime, 91, 111

Laodamia, 341 n.

Laodice (mother of Seleucus), 283

Laomedon (King of Tyre), 46, 372
Larentina, 44, 78, 79, 375
Lares, 43
Latium, popular etymology of, 362
Laws, against luxury, 22-23; define age for legal capacity, 268; invoked against Christians, 18; Roman, 13-14, 19
Lazarus, interpretation of story of, 166, 193
Leaena, 124 n.
Lebreton, J., 173
Leda, 371 n.
Legion, 'Thundering,' 21-22, 159 n.
Lentulus (writer of mimes), 47
Leonymus, 283
Leucippus of Miletus (philosopher), 327 n.
Liber, 39, 42, 361
Libera [Kore], 369
Lightning, persons struck by, 121
Lion, always retains fundamental instincts, 234; in metempsychosis, 255; thought to have no more than one cub, 282
Lipsius, K. A., 21 n.
Liver, importance of, for dreams, 286
Livy, 66 n., 71 n., 123 n., 330 n., 332 n., 363 n., 373 n., 375 n., 386 n.
Lofstedt, E., xix

logikon, 208
Logos, 63, 65
Lord, as imperial title, 90
Lortz, J., xix
Lucania, 102
Lucian of Samosata, xiii, 330 n.
Lucina (goddess of childbirth; surname of Juno), 260, 270
Lucretius, 86 n., 189
Lucullus (L. Lincinius Lucullus Ponticus), 39
Lupercalia, 366 n.
Luperci, 81
Lurco, 257
Luxury, at Rome, 23-24; laws against, 22-23
Lycurgus, 19, 113
Lyncestris River, water of, intoxicating, 289

Macedonians, incestuous, 34
Macrobius, 23 n., 86 n.
Magdalen, 240
Magic, 'a second form of idolatry,' 303
Magicians, 71, 93, 108, 379
Man, born equal, 398; striving after truth, 348-349
Mancinus, C. Hostilius, 377
Mandana (daughter of Astyages), 282
Manetho (Egyptian historian), 59
Marcia (wife of Emperor Commodus), 158 n.
Marcion (heretic), 171, 218, 222 n., 229

INDEX

Marcus Aurelius Antoninus (emperor), 78-79, 92 n., 152 n., 158-159, 337 n.; attitude toward Christians, 21-22
Marriage. Christian, chaste, 99-100, 387; of soul and Holy Spirit at baptism, 274; Tertullian's condemnation of second, 170, 172, 367 n.
Mars, 45-46, 133, 366 n., 371-372, 374 n., 375
Martial, 138 n.
Martin, J., 5, 318, 319
Martyrdom, 123-126, 397-398; Christians' eagerness for, 151, 160; demanded by God, 290; qualified as baptism of blood, 299-300; regarded as superfluous by various heretics, 289-290
Martyrs, fortune of, in hereafter, 299-300
Mary, St., 241, 242
Mater Matuta (Roman goddess), 366 n.
Matralia, female slaves excluded from, 366 n.
Mavilus (martyr of Hadrumetum), 156
Maximilla, xi n., 169
Meat, abstinence from, 118
Medea, 290
Megillus, 226
Melampus (seer), 67
Melito (apologist), 131 n.
Melitus, 180
Memory, qualifications of, 233

Menander (heretic), 231, 289, 290
Menander of Ephesus (historian,) 59
Menedemus (philosopher), 55
Menelaus, 262
Mercury, 31, 48, 141, 296, 330; Egyptian, 183, 245, 257; [Hermes], 369-370
Metempsychosis, *see* Transmigration
Metennius, 24
Meyer, H., xix
Midas, 183
Milesian tales, 231
Military service, Origen on, xiv; Tertullian on, xiv, 106
Millenarianism, 168, 170
Miltiades (apologist), 131 n.
Minerva, 39, 43, 47, 133, 136, 226, 358, 364, 369
Minos, 74
Minucius Felix, conversion, 313, 321, 325; education, 313; from North Africa, 313; name, 313; Roman stay, 314; *Octavius:* its content, 317-318; literary form, 314-316; style, 316-317; text tradition, 318; *On Fate,* 314, 395; otherwise quoted, xiii n., xvii, xviii, 25 n., 29-32 nn., 34-37 nn., 41 n., 44 n., 49-53 nn., 63 n., 66 n., 89 n., 101 n., 109 n., 112 n., 113 n., 115 n., 117 n., 119 n., 121 n., 123 n.

Minucius Fundanus (Roman governor), 157 n.
Minucius Oppianus (Roman governor), 154 n.
Miodonski, A., 130
Mithridates, 283, 398 n.
Monceaux, P., xix, 319
Monotheism, attested to by unanimous consent of human race, 354; by poets and philosophers, 354-358; proofs for, 352-353
Montanism, viii; divine service of, 197; doctrine of, xi n., 169-172; ecstasy, 197, 204, 287; oracles, 170, 171; prophecy, 197; revelations in, 166, 197, 287; revelations obtained from God by fasting, 287
Montanus, xi n., 169, 183 n.
Moors, character of, 227
Mopsus, oracle of, 284
Moschion (physician), 211
Moses, 67, 110, 265, 266, 304, 306; date of, 56, 58, 245; first of Prophets, 56; gives chronology of world, 245
Mother Church, 277
Mucius (C. Mucius Scaevola), 123, 308, 397, 398
Müller, A., 318, 319
Musaeus, 67, 183
Mutunus (Roman deity), 78
Mysteries, origin and nature, 368 n., 369 n.; pagan, ridiculous, 367-369
Myths, impressed on children during education, 371-373; invented to interpret sacred rituals, 41, 368 n.

Nabuchodnosor, dream of, 285
Nails, growth of, in dead bodies, 291
Nasamones, expect oracles at tombs of ancestors, 305-306
Necromancy, 303-304
Nectabis (magician), 303
Neoptolemus (tragic actor), 283
Nepos, Cornelius, 36, 362
Neptune, 46, 357, 369, 372
Nero (emperor), 91 n., 279, 288; as persecutor of Christians, 21, 66
Nessus (centaur), 371 n.
Nestor, 252
Nicander, 306
Niger, C. Pescennius, 92, 152, 156 n.
Nile, 102, 351
Noe, 269
Nona (Roman goddess), 266
Nonacris, Mt., water from, poisonous, 289
Norden, E., xi n., xix, 4 n.
Nortia (local goddess of Volsinii), 77
Numa, 67, 80
Nymphodorus, 306

Oath, by the genius of Caesar, 88
Obesity, influence on mind of, 227

Octavius Januarius (interlocutor in *Octavius*), 313-314
Oehler, F., 51 n., 130, 136 n., 148, 149, 158 n.
Oenotria, 37
Olympias (wife of Philip of Macedon), 282
Onions, taboo in Egypt, 383
Oracles, 70, 284, 306; fallacy of, 377-378
Orestes, mentioned as instance of insanity, 216
Origen, ix, xiv, xvii, 170
Original sin, 167, 212 n., 242 n., 271, 273, 274 n.
Orpheus, 67, 183, 211, 358
Osiris, 368
Ostanes, *see* Hostanes
Ostia, good example of religious syncretism, 322 n.; scene of *Octavius*, 314-315, 322
Otus, 372 n.
Ovid, 51 n., 54 n., 78 n., 138 n., 362 n., 363 n.
Owl, cannot endure light of sun, 195

Pallas, 50
Pallor (Roman deity), 375
Pan, 52, 370, 383
Panaetius (philosopher), 208, 357 n.
Pantomimes, 47
Papian law, 19
Paraclete, 170-172, 299, 309
Paradise, 117
Parentalia, feast of, 138 n.
Parmenides (philosopher), on sleep, 275
Parthenius, Titus Claudius, 92
Partula (Roman goddess), 266
Pasiphae, oracle of, 284
Patroclus, 200, 272 n.
Paul, St., xvi-xvii, 170, 172, 185-186 197, 210, 213, 227, 229, 331 n.
Paulus, L. Aemilius, 377
Pausanias, 50 n., 124 n., 331 n., 366 n.
Pavor (Roman deity), 375
Peacock, in metempsychosis, 259, 260
Perfume, Christian attitude toward, 342
Peripatetics, 188
Perpetua, St., 154 n., 299
Persaeus (Stoic philosopher), 361
Perseus (King of Macedon), 332
Persians, incestuous, 34
Persius, 4
Peter, St., 218
Pertinax (emperor), 92 n.
Phaedo, 181
Phaethon, 47
Phalaris (Tyrant of Acragas), 328
Pharaoh, 304
Pharisees, 213
Pherecydes, regarded as magician, 247; teacher of Pythagoras, 183
Philip of Macedon, 282
Philo, 55 n.

INDEX

Philochorus, on dreams, 284

Philosophers, borrowed from Scripture, 114-118, 182, 183 n.; drawing upon apocryphal books, 182 n., 183; upon Orpheus, etc., 183; impunity of, 17, 111; love for glory, 113; put on a level with poets, 180; qualified as 'patriarchs of the heretics,' 165, 185; reproached with corrupting youth, 181; sometimes find truth by chance or through common sense, 182; sometimes knock at gates of truth, 131-132; vain speculation on things divine, 112

Philosophy, derivation of word, 57; failure in morals, 112-114; not a substitute for Christianity, 111-112, 116; relationship to medicine, 184

Philumena, 265

Phrygians, qualified as cowards, 227

Phryne, 44, 113

Picus [Picumnus] (Roman deity), 375

Pilate, Pontius, 65; supposed report of trail and death of Christ, 21 n., 66

Pilumnus (Roman deity), 375

Pindar, 46

Pisistratus, interest in libraries, 54

Piso (C. Calpurnius Piso Frugi), 24

Pius, T. Aelius Hadrianus Antoninus Augustus (emperor), 157 n.; attitude toward Christians, 22

Plagiarism, from Old Testament by pagan philosophers, 183

Plants, philosophers' view of, 223-225

Plato, 38, 68, 74, 76, 100 n., 102-103, 112 n., 113, 114, 166, 167, 179 n., 181 n., 183, 185 n., 186, 187, 189, 190, 191 n., 192, 196, 199, 208, 210-214, 217-219, 222, 226, 232, 233, 235-237, 239, 240, 245-246, 248, 252, 254, 265, 283, 286, 291, 294, 297, 299, 314, 343 n., 357 n., 358, 371, 379, 392

Platonists, 115-116, 190; on sense-perception, 214

Plautus, 23 n., 345 n.

Pliny the Elder, 29 n., 32 n., 39 n., 86 n., 121 n., 124 n.

Pliny the Younger, 126; letter to Trajan concerning Christians, 11

Plutarch, 9 n., 19 n., 121 n.

Pluto, 48, 361 n.

Poets, borrowed from Scripture, 114-118; depict gods with human passion, 131; put on level with philosophers, 180; responsible fables and absurdities in pagan

INDEX

religion, 371-372; said to change into swans, 259
Polemical writers, pagan, xiii
Pollux, 70, 332, 371, 380
Polycrates, 40, 283
Polyneices, 352 n.
Pompeii, 103
Pompey (Cn. Pompeius Magnus), 41, 49, 333 n., 353 n.
Pontiffs, 81, 376
Porphyry (Neo-Platonist), xiii
Porsenna (Etruscan king), 397 n.
Poseidon, temple of, at Mantinea, 366 n,
Posidonius, 208
Poverty, panegyric of, 396
Prayer, of Christians, for emperor, empire, xiv, 85-87, 98, 153; for enemies, persecutors, 87; for obtaining rain, 158-159; prayer leaders, 86; precise formula of, observed in Roman ritual, 86 n.
Preaching, in divine service, 197
Pregnancy, stages of, 266-267
Priam, 58, 261
Prisca (Priscilla), xi n., 169
Probabilism, of New Academy, 326 n., 344 n.
Processions, pagan, condemned by Christians, 342, 399
Proculus (Roman senator), 66, 363
Proculus (Torpacion), 158

Procidus of Ceos (sophist), 361
Prometheus, 54 n.
Prophecy, deathbed, 296; derivation of word, 57; examination and noting down of prophecies, 197; whether possible after St. John the Baptist, 197
Prophets, mission of, 54; Moses as first, 245; source for philosophers and poets, 115
Protagoras (philosopher), 211, 334
Protesilaus (Greek hero), 341
Providence, existence of divine, 349-352
Prudentius, 375 n.
Psalms, singing of, in divine service, 197
psyche, derivation of word, 239
Ptolemy I Soter, 55 n.
Ptolemy II Philadelphus, and Septuagint, 55; as founder of libraries, 54
Ptolemy of Mendes, 59
Puberty, 168, 268-269
Pudens, C. Valerius (proconsul), 157
Purgatory, 168, 303 n., 309
Pyriphlegethon, 117
Pyrrha, 363 n.
Pyrrho (philosopher), 126, 400
Pyrrhus (fisherman), 246, 252
Pyrrhus (King of Epirus), 70, 378

Pythagoras, 38, 113, 115, 117, 183, 245-247, 251-252, 254, 258, 260, 297, 356, 392
Pythagoreans, prohibition of beans, 252, 287; of fish and animal food, 252
Pythian priestess, 120; accused of 'Philippizing,' 378

Quadratus (apologist), 131
quindecimviri, 81
Quintilian, 100 n.
Quintuplets, 192

Rebecca, 241
Regulus, M. Atilius, 124, 139, 377
Reifferscheid, A., 130
Religion, freedom of, 76-77, 152; panegyric of old Roman, 329-334; Roman attitude toward, xiii
Reminiscence, Plato's theory of, 167, 232-236
Remus, 352 n., 373, 375 n.
Rendall, G. H., 318, 319
Resurrection, of the body, 54, 117-122, 137-140, 301-302, 393-394; moment of, known to God alone, 260; possibility of, denied by pagan interlocutor, 339-341; symbolized by awakening after sleep, 278; by number seven, 267
Revelation, divine, concerning soul, 185; contradicts opinions of philosophers, 210-211

Rhadamanthus, 74
Rhea, 369 n.
Rhodes, 102
Rites, of pagan religion, ridiculous, 366-367
Roberts, R. E., xix
Romans, attitude toward religion, xiii; credulity of, 359-360; piety of, challenged, 359-360; piety of, praised, 330-332, 338
Rome, beginnings of, as an asylum, 373; sack of, by Gauls, 330-331
Romulus, 24, 66, 352 n., 373, 374, 375 n.
Rutilius (P. Rutilius Rufus), 328

Sabbath, 56, 267
Sabine girls, rape of, 373
Sackcloth and ashes, 104-105
Sacrifice, human, 30-31, 386
Sacrifices, Christians do not use parts left over from, 399; only inferior portions set aside for gods in, 45; performance of pagan, refused by Christians, 35, 82, 342
Salii (college of priests), 36, 81, 100, 366 n., 376
Sallust, 32 n., 227, 386 n.
Samothrace, mysteries of, 26
Samuel, 305
Sarmatians, dull-witted, 239
Sarpedon, 46, 372; oracle of, 284

INDEX

Satan, corrupter of whole world, 136; leader of demons, 68
Saturn, 30, 31 n., 36-37, 39, 43, 56, 79, 86 n., 133, 135, 245, 284, 329 n., 362, 370, 380, 385, 386
Saturnalia, 107
Saturnia, 36-37, 39, 362
Saturnian Hill, 36, 362 n.
Saturninus (heretic), 231
Saturninus Vigellius (proconsul), 13 n., 155
Satyrs, 52, 383 n.
Saul, 204, 305
Schanz, M., xix, 319
Schmidt, J., 149
Scholte, W., 130
Sciapodes (fabulous monsters), 29
Scilli, martyrs of, 13 n., 155 n.
Scipio (P. Cornelius Scipio Africanus major), 239
Scipio (P. Cornelius Scipio Aemilianus Africanus minor,) 40-41
Scribonius Largus (physician), 386 n.
Scriptures, Holy, antiquity of, 56-59, 111, 114, 118; authority of, 53, 56-60, 111; distorted by philosophers, 116; heathen do not believe in, 129, 132; source of philosophers and poets, 114-118

Quotations from or references to Biblical writers or books:

Acts, xvi n., 33 n., 44 n., 156 n., 186 n., 260 n., 305 n., 326 n., 342 n., 387 n., 389 n.
Apocalypse, 196 n., 263 n., 299 n.
Colossians, 186 n.
1 Corinthians, 99 n., 172 n., 204 n., 212 n., 229 n., 263 n., 271 n., 277 n., 296 n.
2 Corinthians, 99 n.
Daniel, 285 n.
Ephesians, 70 n., 204 n., 214 n., 229 n., 298 n.,
Exodus, 304 n.
Galatians, 213 n.
Genesis, 68 n., 103 n., 166 n., 186 n., 199 n., 203 n., 204 n., 228 n., 241-243 nn., 245 n., 269 n., 277 n., 280 n., 290 n.,
Hebrews, 290 n.
Isaias, 64 n., 203 n.
James, 397 n.
Jeremias, 242 n.
Joel, 285 n.
John, 65 n., 207 n., 210 n., 214 n., 218 n., 264 n., 271 n., 290 n., 298 n.
1 John, 218 n.
1 Kings, 204 n., 305 n.
4 Kings, 290 n.
Luke, 151 n., 193 n., 207 n., 213 n., 218 n., 229 n., 242 n., 264 n., 298 n., 306 n.
Malachias, 264 n.
Mark, 240 n.
Matthew, 87 n., 105 n., 109 n., 110 n., 151 n., 207 n., 210

n., 213 n., 214 n., 218 n., 220 n., 229 n., 242 n., 260 n., 262-264 nn., 272 n., 285 n., 298 n., 305 n., 308 n., 309 n., 323 n.
1 Peter, 298 n., 331 n., 389 n., 397 n.
2 Peter, 389 n.
Proverbs, 210 n., 397 n.
Psalms, 210 n., 225 n., 255 n., 298 n.
Romans, 141 n., 151 n., 210 n., 222 n., 258 n., 271 n., 389 n.
1 Thessalonians, 299 n.
2 Thessalonians, 88 n., 305 n.
1 Timothy, 87 n., 213 n., 389 n.
Titus, 227 n., 389 n.
Wisdom, 210 n., 397 n.

Scylla, 359
Scythians, eat corpses of relatives, 32
Seleucus, 283
Semo Sancus (deity), 44 n.
Seneca (philosopher), 42, 63 n., 125-126, 226, 274, 317, 328 n., 396 n.
Seneca (rhetor), 315
Senones, 103
Sense-perception, 167, 214-218
Senses, illusion of, 214-217; necessary to human life, 217
Septuagint, 55
Serapeum, 55
Serapion (dream-interpreter), 284
Serapis, 24, 25, 101, 322, 368, 380, 383
Services, divine, order of, 197
Seven, symbolic number, 267
Severus, L. Septimius (emperor), 19, 147, 152 n., 156 n., 157 n., 158
Sibyl, 58
Sibylline books, 78 n., 332 n.
Sicily, 103
Sige (heretic conception), 205
Sigerius, 92
Silence, in mysteries, 26
Silenus, 183
Silvanus, women excluded from cult of, 366 n.
Simon (heretic), 44, 260-262, 304-305
Simonides, 112 n., 344, 400
Simpson, A. D., 319
Sin, 212 n., 270-274, 293, 307-309; distinction between original, and that caused by Devil, 271, 273; enumeration of, 272
Skepticism, 325-329, 343, 344 n.
Slaves, excluded from certain pagan rites, 366
Sleep, 168, 275-280; image of death, 275; panegyric of, 276-277
Socordices, 72
Socrates, 40, 46-47, 68, 100, 112, 113, 179-181, 192, 205, 210, 217, 232 n., 240, 270, 283, 326 n., 328, 343, 358, 361 n., 378, 400

Sodom, 102
Sol, 47
Solon, 57
Sons of Earth, 37, 363
Soothsayers, 93, 108
Sophocles, 283, 343 n.
Soranus (physician), 191-192, 195, 208, 210, 238, 279
Soul, against heathen living, 143; color of, 198; conscious witness to God, 53, 133-136, 140-142; to Christian truth, 141-142; treatise on, analyzed, 166-168
Spartans, hardness of, 124-125
Speusippus (philosopher), 113, 356
Statina (Roman goddess), 270
Statues of gods, introduced to Rome from Etruria and Greece, 80; lurking places of demons, 379; manufacture of, 42, 364-365; material used for, 41, 364-366
Sterculus (Roman deity), 78, 79
Stesichorus, 261
Stoics, 115-116, 166, 188, 192, 208, 215, 223 n., 237, 241, 275-276, 284, 297, 299, 392
Strabo (geographer), 283, 374 n.
Strato (philosopher), 209-211, 275, 284, 356
Styx, water of, makes immortal, 289
Suetonius, xiv, 16 n., 31 n., 71 n., 90 n., 279, 364 n.

Sulla, 41, 257
Sun, eclipse of, 155
Sunday, its observance not worship of sun, 51
Surgery, estimation of, 200, 238
Swan song, 259
Swans, poets thought to change into, 259

Tacitus, x, xiv, 4, 16 n., 21 n., 49, 91 n., 96 n.
Tatian (apologist), 131 n.
Tatius, Titus (Sabine king), 375
Taurians, human sacrifice among, 31
Tax, imposed on Jews by Vespasian, 56
Telmessus, divination at, 282
Temples, dues, 44, 107; prescriptions for entering, 366; used as places for unchastity, 48, 376
Ten, symbolic number, 266-267
Terence, 18 n., 26 n., 46 n., 112 n., 361 n.
Tertullian, apostasy to Montanism of, viii, xi n., 169-172, 197 n.; at Rome, vii-viii; attitude toward philosophy, ix-x; birth, vii; character, viii-ix; conversion, viii; 'creator of the Latin of the Church,' xi; death, viii; education, vii; family, vii-viii; importance in early

Christian literature, viii-ix; knowledge of jurisprudence, vii-viii; language and style, x-xi; name, vii; role in the Carthaginian church, viii; works: classification of, xii; fate of, xi; text tradition, xi-xii; *Ad Scapulam,* 147-148; *Apologeticum,* 3; *De anima,* 165-168; *De testimonio animae,* 129; lost works; *On Fate,* 227; *On the Origin of the Soul,* 165, 179 n., 185 n., 187, 190 n., 229, 230,.233, 235; *On Paradise,* 300; works quoted; *Ad nationes,* ix, xvii, xviii, 9 n., 20 n., 29 n., 51 n., 112 n.; *Ad Scapulam,* xii n., xiv n., xvii, xviii, 4, 22 n., 88 n.; *Ad uxorem,* 172, 367 n.; *Adversus Hermogenem,* 188 n.; *Adversus Judaeos,* xviii; *Adversus Marcionem,* 20 n., 32 n., 222 n., 229; *Adversus Praxean,* 64 n., *Apologeticum,* viii n., ix, x n., xii, xiii n., xvii, xviii, 3-4, 21 n., 129, 130, 141, 318, 336 n., 337 n., 354 n.; *De anima,* x n., xix, 124 n.; *De carne Christi,* 188 n.; *De cultu feminarum,* vii n., 23 n.; *De exhortatione castitatis,* 367 n.; *De fuga,* 171; *De monogamia,* 170, 172, 367 n.; *De pallio,* 135 n.; *De praescriptione haereticorum,* x n., 4; *De pudicitia,* 171; *De resurrectione Christi,* 119 n.; *De spectaculis.* 4, 23 n.; *De testimonio animae,* x, xviii, 4, 53 n., 118 n., 333 n.; 398 n., *De virginbus velandis,* 170

Tertullianists, viii, xi n.

Teutates (chief gods of the Gauls), 330 n.

Thales, 57, 112, 188, 192, 355

Thallus (historian), 36, 56, 59, 362

Thanatius, 72

Theater, condemned by Christians, 23, 97, 342, 399

Thebans, born dull, 226

Thelwall, S., 130, 149

Themis, oracle of, 363 n.

Themistocles, 40

Theodorus of Cyrene (philosopher), 334

Theophilus of Antioch (apologist), xvii, 131 n.

Theophrastus, 357

Theopompus, 279

Thesmophoria, men excluded from, 366 n.

Thetis, 289, 372 n.

Thomas, St. (Apostle), 218, 290

Thrasymedes, 279, 288

thumikon, 213

Tiberinus (Roman deity), 375

Tiberius (emperor), 20-21, 26, 30, 61, 66, 102

Tibullus, 138 n.

Timaeus (historian), 124 n.

Tiresias, 377-378

INDEX

Titus (emperor), 339 n.
Torture, applied to Christians, 12-14, 41-42
Traducianism, 212 n., 224-225, 242 n., 265-266
Trajan (emperor), answer to Pliny the Younger concerning Christians, 11; attitude toward Christians, 22
Transmigration of souls, 117, 137, 167, 242 n., 245-265, 393
Transmigrationists, 249 n.
Treason, charged against Christians, 75, 84-85, 87, 90-93
Treasury, of Christian Church, purpose of, 98-99
Trophies, how constructed, 50
Trophonius, 67; oracle of, 284
Tyndareus, 371 n.
Typhon (magician), 303

Ulpianus, Domitius (jurist), 147
Ulysses, 216
Universe, conflagration of, 339-340

Valentia (local goddess of Ocriculum), 77
Valentinus (heretic), 205, 228, 231
Valentinians, 219, 228, 231
Valerius Maximus, 23 n., 71 n.
Varro, M. Terentius, 47, 362 n.

Venus, 45, 47, 361, 371, 372
Vergil, 27, 46 n., 79 n. 81 n., 86 n. 354-355, 362 n., 372 n., 394 n.
Verus, L. Aurelius (emperor), attitude toward Christians, 22
Vespasian (emperor), 56 n., 339 n., 364 n.; attitude toward Christians, 22
Vespronius Candidus (proconsul), 157
Vesta, 376
Vestal Virgins, 81, 376
Victory (deity), 50, 332 n.
Vincent of Lerins, on Tertullian, ix, 169
Visidianus (local god of Narnia), 77
Vitellius, family chronicle of, 283
Volsinii, 103
Volumnus (Roman deity), 375
Vulcan, 357, 361; [Hephaestus], 369

Wallis, R. E., 319
Waltzing, J. P., 5, 318, 319
Waszink, J. H., 165 n., 179 n., 185 n., 222 n., 236 n.
Water, properties of, 289
Wise Men, sayings of, 355
Wissowa, G., 130
Wine, forbidden to women, 23-24
Wisdom (Sophia: heretical conception), 203, 231
Witch of Endor, 305

Wives, Christian, chaste, 16, 26
Women, position of, in Montanist sect, 197
Worship, Christian, 98; places of, 335

Xenocrates, 187, 211
Xenophanes, 275, 356
Xenophon, 358

Zacharias, 57
Zeiller, J., 173
Zeno (Eleatic philosopher), 124, 309
Zeno (Stoic philosopher), 63, 113, 136 n., 186, 188, 208, 252, 357, 361 n., 400 n.
Zeus, 361 n., 369 n., 370 n., 371 n., 377 n.; Zeus Ammon, 361 n.